Subject Women

Ann Oakley, currently Deputy Director of the Thomas Coram Research Unit, is a feminist, writer, researcher, sociologist and mother, and author of a number of books about women, including *Sex, Gender and Society*, *The Sociology of Housework*, *Becoming a Mother*, *Women Confined*, *Miscarriage* (with Ann McPherson and Helen Roberts; available in Fontana) and *The Captive Womb: a History of Medical Care for Pregnant Women*. Her autobiography *Taking it Like a Woman*, published in 1984, is available in Flamingo.

Ann Oakley

Subject Women

Fontana Press

First published in Great Britain
by Martin Robertson & Co. Ltd 1981

First issued in 1982 by Fontana Paperbacks,
8 Grafton Street, London W1X 3LA
Second impression, in Fontana Press, March 1985

Reproduced, printed and bound in Great Britain by
Hazell Watson & Viney Limited,
Member of the BPCC Group,
Aylesbury, Bucks

Contents

Acknowledgements

I gratefully acknowledge permission to reproduce extracts from the following works:

Woman's Consciousness, Man's World by Sheila Rowbotham (Pelican Books, 1973).

Perceiving Women by Shirley Ardener (Malaby Press, 1975).

Articles and extracts from *Spare Rib* (22, 53 & 59).

Letters Home edited by Aurelia Plath (Bantam Books, 1977).

Women and the Power to Change edited by F. Howe (McGraw-Hill Book Company, 1975).

Memoirs of a Dutiful Daughter by Simone de Beauvoir (Andre Deutsch, 1963).

Male Roles and Men's Lives by Robert Fein (unpublished paper).

'I once was a dull, narrow housewife', poem by Celia Fremlin.

For R, my friend

'Now, if you'll only attend, Kitty, and not talk so much, I'll tell you all my ideas about Looking-Glass House. First, there's the room you can see through the glass — that's just the same as our drawing-room, only the things go the other way . . . the books are something like our books, only the words go the wrong way . . . .

Oh, Kitty! how nice it would be if we could get through into Looking-Glass House! I'm sure it's got, oh! such beautiful things in it! Let's pretend there's a way of getting through into it somehow, Kitty. Let's pretend the glass has got soft like gauze, so that we can get through. Why, it's turning into a sort of mist now, I declare! It'll be easy enough to get through —' She was up on the chimney-piece while she said this, though she hardly knew how she had got here. And certainly the glass *was* beginning to melt away, just like a bright silvery mist.

[Lewis Carroll *Alice Through the Looking Glass*, pp.146 – 7]

If we conceive of feminism as more than a frivolous label, if we conceive of it as an ethics, a methodology, a more complex way of thinking about, thus more responsibly acting upon, the conditions of human life, we need a self-knowledge which can only develop through a steady, passionate attention to *all* female experience. I cannot imagine a feminist evolution leading to radical change in the private/political realm of gender that is not rooted in the conviction that all women's lives are important; that the lives of men cannot be understood by burying the lives of women; and that to make visible the full meaning of women's experience, to reinterpret knowledge in terms of that experience, is now the most important task of thinking.

[Adrienne Rich *On Lies, Secrets and Silence*, p.213]

Preface

In *Alice Through the Looking Glass*, Lewis Carroll asks Alice to describe the world on the other side of the looking glass — a world in which mirror images reflect a familiar, yet also oddly contradictory, reality. The metaphor is appropriate to women's studies, the subject of this book. To enquire how the situation of women is represented in what passes for academic 'knowledge' — and, more profoundly, what the situation of women is — we have, first of all, to alter the way in which we see the world. Feminism, as Adrienne Rich so eloquently observes, is more than a frivolous label: it is an ethics and a methodology, a serious enterprise not only for women but for men. The situations of the two sexes are intermingled, and the profit men make out of women's subordination can only be considered a blot on human dignity.

Neither the winter-afternoon fantasies of Alice nor the academic ethics of Rich, neither the moral urgency of change nor the oppression of men by women's oppression, can be fully grasped without an intensive charting of women's world and experiences. *Subject Women* maps this terrain. Although not strictly a textbook, it is intended to be of use on women's studies courses. I also hope it will be appreciated by a wider readership. Indeed, because women are half the human race, an important claim I would like to make for the book is that it is more than a sociology 'of' or 'for' women (though such a goal must, of course, be considered to be authentic in its own right); it is a history and a sociology of late twentieth-century industrialized society, albeit of a different kind. The difference is that the spotlight is on women, whose presence is rendered more than the mere shadow discernible in conventional histories and sociologies. This reverse of the usual practice cannot reasonably be considered an invalidation, though the temptation thus to dismiss it will no doubt prove too much for some reviewers and readers.

The book, in most places, takes Britain as a case-study, but draws heavily on material from the United States. In many respects (particularly those that concern us in this book) the two societies are really not all that different. Moreover, the conditions of late twentieth-century capitalism are forcing an international similarity in women's lives that transcends many of the idiosyncrasies of separate countries.

I would like to thank all those individuals (they will know who they are) who have helped me research and write this book. I have benefited enormously from their support and advice; even, indeed, from their criticism — since in giving it they have paid me the important compliment of taking my enterprise seriously. However, I must also apologize for not always acting on their suggestions. The faults in this book, as authors habitually say, are all mine.

Ann Oakley
August 1980

Citizenship
Are women people?

CHAPTER ONE

Emancipation

What does history disclose but marks of inferiority, and how few women have emancipated themselves from the galling yoke of sovereign man? [Wollstonecraft, 1929, p.39]

Any discussion of women's place in Western society today has to begin with the movement for their emancipation that emerged in Britain in the Victorian period — not because there is necessarily any direct connection between the two, but because most people think there is. It is part of our cultural mythology about women that since the mid-nineteenth century women's progress towards equality has been more or less unbroken, an achievement that must be credited chiefly to the suffragettes as the predecessors of today's feminists. How true is this? What were the characteristics of nineteenth-century feminism? And what was the condition that women had to be emancipated from — or to?

CLOUDED MOONS

In the late 1840s and early 1850s when women's rights organizations began to form in Europe and America, women's condition was that of a legally inferior caste. The 'Declaration of Sentiments' and 'Resolutions' adopted by the first American women's suffrage convention in 1848 summarized the outlines of women's position in many countries of the world at that time. It stated the feminist grievance in no uncertain terms:

The history of mankind is a history of repeated injuries and usurpations on the part of man toward woman, having in direct object the establishment of an absolute tyranny over her . . .

He has never permitted her to exercise her inalienable right to the elective franchise . . .

He has made her, if married, in the eye of the law, civilly dead.

He has taken from her all right in property, even to the wages she earns . . .

He has so framed the laws of divorce, as to what shall be the proper causes, and in cases of separation, to whom the guardianship of the children shall be given, as to be wholly regardless of the happiness of women — the law, in all cases, going upon a false supposition of the supremacy of man, and giving all power into his hands . . .

He has monopolized nearly all the profitable employments, and from those she is permitted to follow, she receives but a scanty remuneration. He closes against her all the avenues to wealth and distinction which he considers most honourable to himself. As a teacher of theology, medicine, or law, she is not known.

He has denied her the facilities for obtaining a thorough education, all colleges being closed against her . . .

He has endeavoured, in every way that he could, to destroy her confidence in her own powers, to lessen her self-respect, and to make her willing to lead a dependent and abject life . . .

[Cited in O'Neill, 1969, pp.109 – 10]

In Britain, for example, women in general did not exist as 'persons' under the law. Their personhood was 'merged' with or under the direction of their fathers or husbands. Although single women did have some rights, the non-existence of women in the eyes of the law was complete in the case of the married woman: her body, earnings, children and domestic services belonged to her husband. Married women could not be held responsible for certain classes of criminal action, they could not sue or be sued, be liable for their own debts, they could make wills only if permitted to do so by their husbands, and could own no personal property of any kind. Some men argued that they could sell, or at least 'lend' their wives, an opinion that was contrary to the letter, but not the spirit, of the law (Hollis, 1979, pp.174 – 5). Women were not allowed to vote, although technically they were not excluded until 1832 when the word 'male' was inserted before the word 'persons' in the Reform Act of that year; 'persons' included both sexes (Whittick, 1979, p.20).

These injustices were most remarked on by upper- and middle-class women who possessed both the personal property annexed to male control and the necessary time, energy and voice to complain about the situation. Caroline Norton, an upper-class socialite, was representative of this genre. In April 1836 she was discarded by her husband and not allowed to see her three sons. She conducted a battle for the recognition of mothers' rights over their children, and in 1839 an Infant Custody Act was passed barely acknowledging the point: mothers could petition the Lord Chancellor for access to their children, providing they could prove an unblemished character. Caroline Norton's own view could hardly be described as feminist:

The natural position of woman is inferiority to man. Amen! That is a thing of God's appointing, not of man's devising. I believe it sincerely, as a part of my religion: and I accept it as a matter proved to my reason. I never pretended to the wild and ridiculous doctrine of equality. I will even hold that (as one coming under the general rule that the wife must be inferior to the husband) . . . I am Mr Norton's inferior. I am the clouded moon of that sun. Put me then — (my ambition extends no further) — in the same position as all his other inferiors! In that of his housekeeper, whom he could not libel with impunity . . . of an apprentice whom he could not maltreat lawlessly . . .; of a scullion, whose wages he could not refuse . . . Put me under some law of protection.   [Cited in O'Faolain and Martines, 1973, p.329]

Victorian judges did their best to do just that. When considering whether, in the face of their new demands, women could be counted as 'persons', they persistently argued that the law did not impose disabilities based on inferiority, but, instead, granted exemptions based on respect. Thus women's exclusion from medical school was justified on the grounds that women would be upset if they consorted with male students and with male corpses, and especially if they were to be seen at work on male corpses by male students. (This led to the *reductio ad absurdum* of the judicial suggestion that a partition down the middle of the anatomy room, akin to the one segregating the sexes in the Pentonville Prison Chapel, might save the day.) In this view of women, their legal disabilities simply *proved* their favourable position, venerated as one of the 'glories of civilization' (Sachs, 1978, p.29) and separated from its cruder workings by restriction to a gentler, domestic sphere.

'A century after the courts had decided that it was unlawful in England to use force to keep a slave in the house, lawyers were still maintaining that it was permissible to use force to keep a wife in the house' (Sachs, 1978, p.35). Feminists argued that the ideology of male protectiveness not only actually debased women, it put the interests of men first. Male doctors objected to women doctors, and, later, to the practice of female midwifery, on economic grounds, perceiving women as a direct financial threat. Male academics deplored the fall in standards that would result from women's admission to university, concealing their own wish to be protected from the exercise of female intellect and from the breakdown in family relationships that they thought would be an inevitable sequel. Mary Wollstonecraft, whose life, despite her feminism, well illustrated the fate of women dependent on the uncertain fortune of sexual relationships, lamented

that women are systematically degraded by receiving the trivial attentions which men think it manly to pay to the sex, when in fact, they are insultingly supporting their own superiority . . . So ludicrous, in fact, do these ceremonies appear to me that I scarcely am able to govern my muscles when I see a man start with eager and serious solicitude to lift a handkerchief or shut a door, when the *lady* could have done it herself, had she only moved a pace or two. [Wollstonecraft, 1929, p.63]

Wollstonecraft's *Vindication of the Rights of Woman*, first published in 1792, is an attack on the tradition of 'sensibility', which to her was the mark of women's character in a male-governed society. Prevented from exercising their intellects and energies in the public world outside the home, women, says Wollstonecraft, are reared to place inordinate emphasis on their senses; confined 'in cages like the feathered race, they have nothing to do but to plume themselves, and stalk with mock majesty from perch to perch'. In exchange for their keep, they yield their liberty, health and virtue, 'treated like queens only to be deluded by hollow respect' (Wollstonecraft, 1929, p.62).

The *Vindication* was the first great feminist statement in English, and it is often said that all histories of feminism properly begin with it (see, for example, O'Neill, 1969, and Banks and Banks, 1965). Its author's insights grew out of the wave of radical — intellectual enthusiasm produced by the French and American revolutions; what Wollstonecraft was trying to do was to extend to women the bourgeois idea that all men should control their own fate. The most radical aspect of the *Vindication* is its central idea that femininity is an artificial construct, an imposition of patriarchal culture, yet is regarded as an immutably natural state. (This point is made by Walters, 1976.)

The notion that women's 'nature' is formed through their socialization was not widely accepted when Wollstonecraft wrote, and has only in the second half of the twentieth century had its credentials thoroughly established (see Chapters 3, 4 and 5). The tenor of her writing seems historically misplaced — ahead of, or at least outside, its time. Although, in Britain, women's groups in the early years of the nineteenth century supported the Chartists and the Anti-Corn Law League and participated in a moral questioning of the new economic order and in a vision of a truly democratic and cooperative society, they did not, by and large, argue their own case. In the United States feminism arose earlier than in Britain on the great tide of the anti-slavery movement, but shared a similar background of militant trade unionism which was not highly conscious of discrimination against women as a class.

It is also true that the debate about the relative positions of the sexes is an old one. According to Sheila Rowbotham, 'An impetus towards feminism came with the Renaissance cult of the woman of poise, grace, beauty, wit and erudition . . . it established the themes of education and emancipation which were to be crucial demands of feminism' (Rowbotham, 1972, p.20). Between the early seventeenth and the early nineteenth centuries a considerable decline in women's status occurred. Four factors were crucial: the destruction of the nunneries; the growth of Parliament and the replacement of hereditary office by appointed office; the development of the professions and the universities; and the removal of production from the home to the factory.

Although religious attitudes have been an important source of sexually inegalitarian ideology (see pp.70-1), it is also clear that women's religious orders considerably facilitated the participation of women in public life in the period up to the end of the sixteenth century. Abbesses and prioresses had a respected place in the councils of government, and since such women were regarded as being in direct communion with God, their voices were acknowledged to have a general authority. The substitution of Parliament for the Church and the monarchy as the governing body of the land may have abolished hereditary supremacy but it entrenched sexual supremacy instead. With the growth of the universities, the production of knowledge was separated from economic production, and the status of women was further weakened. Both the universities and the professions made the exclusion of women mandatory, if only because they demanded extensive residence away from home. Even married women's inheritance of their husband's work (a principle that gave women as a whole limited freedom of action and was extensive in the pre-industrial period) became impossible, since the professions were defined as requiring expertise in Latin and philosophy, subjects that were placed beyond women's reach.

But it was the removal of production from the home to the factory that was to have by far the most profound consequences for women. Not surprisingly, it is this change that is given most prominence in historical accounts of women's situation, although the fundamentals of its effects on women's status are often missed. In pre-capitalist society the family was the unit of economic production, which allowed there to be a firm division of labour by sex (and age) within the family, but prevented there being a division between the world of the family and the world of commodity production. Women's productive role was respected because it was a necessary part of domestic production as a whole. More importantly, as Eli Zaretsky puts it, women's 'sense of themselves as "outside" the larger society was fundamentally limited by the fact that "society" was overwhelmingly composed of family units, based upon widely dispersed, individually owned productive property' (Zaretsky, 1976, p.29).

When capitalism socialized production, two divisions took place: work was separated from the family, and also became an activity distinct from personal life. An ethic of personal fulfilment, which had hitherto characterized only the leisured classes, became possible for the masses, and the family became the major location of personal meaning for the individual. Because women were more obviously tied by reproduction to the home, it was on their shoulders that this new responsibility for personal relations was laid. It was a role that emerged not overnight, but gradually, as the solution engineered by male supremacy to the very substantial social dislocations of the early capitalist system (Zaretsky, 1976). Ivy Pinchbeck's *Women Workers and the Industrial Revolution* documents the salient stages: the agrarian enclosures and later agricultural depression, which lowered men's wages and led rural women to become wage-labourers (against 'expert' opinion, which denounced such work as physically and morally degrading for them); the transformation of cotton manufacture and the woollen industry as processes largely controlled by women to a series of differentiated and mechanical operations performed in factories increasingly by men and under the control of male capitalists; the accompanying reduction of women's wages, and later of their industrial employment, following the exclusion of children from the factory and the necessity for someone to take care of them at home.

Men's economic objections to women's employment are a relatively early theme, but the whole ideology of married women's employment as a domestically disruptive influence does not become prominent until the 1830s. It was during the discussion preceding the Factory Bill of 1833 that the question of putting legal limits on women's employment first cropped up, and in 1841 representatives of male operatives on the Short Time Committees demanded 'the gradual withdrawal of all females from the factories'. They said that the 'home, its cares and its employments, is woman's true sphere' and that women's industrial work was 'an inversion of the order of nature' (cited in Pinchbeck, 1969, p.200).

In the 1844 Factory Act women became 'protected persons', for reasons fundamentally the same as those favoured by judges determining their legally inferior position. In the succeeding half century, the ideology of women's natural and necessary restriction to the home blossomed, and the home itself came to be the apotheosis of retreat, salvation and restoration in the harsh competitiveness of the commercial and public world: 'the place of Peace; the shelter, not only from all injury, but from all terror, doubt and division . . . a sacred place, a vestal temple, a temple of the hearth . . .' as John Ruskin highmindedly put it (cited in Wohl, 1978, p.10). The family was felt to be part of nature, and since it was in the countryside that a natural deference between master and servant, between husband and wife and between parent and child was seen to obtain, the rural idyll was an integral part of Victorian domestic mythology (Davidoff, 1976; Davidoff *et al*, 1976), giving birth in the twentieth century to Garden Cities, New Towns, and all the trappings of the suburban dream with the 'happy housewife heroine' (Friedan, 1963) as its centre.

If the home was sacred, so, in a way, were women, and although the nineteenth-century emphasis on women's purity can be traced back to the end of the seventeenth century, it was during the Victorian era that it was most persuasively put. It was openly said that both the home and women in it stood for Nature against Culture, an association that invited further intensely gender-differentiated theories about the 'natural' differences between the sexes and their 'proper' social spheres.

But the saccharin pronouncements of Ruskin and others on this question hid a basic contradiction in Victorian attitudes to women. The idealized leisured and prudish dependence of the Victorian lady rested on the labour of her working-class sisters — as factory and mine workers, domestic servants and prostitutes. Labour was good for the working-class soul, but detrimental to the sensibility of the middle-class woman. Factory inspectors and other middle-class reformers were often seen by working-class women as interfering intruders who would reform away the livelihoods of those they 'rescued'. Throughout the Victorian period, most working-class women were employed, as, increasingly, were unmarried middle-class women in the 'respectable' occupations of governess or teacher, nurse, saleswoman, clerk or civil servant. Even in 1881 one in four of the female population was 'gainfully occupied', a figure that remained substantially unchanged until the 1950s. A pit-worker in 1842 described her day:

I have a belt round my waist and a chain passing between my legs, and I go on my hands and feet . . . There are six women and about six boys in the pit I work in: it is very hard work for a woman. The pit is very wet where I work, and the water comes over our clogs always, and I have seen it up to my thighs: it rains in at the roof terribly; my clothes are wet through almost all day long . . . My cousin looks after my children in the daytime. I am very tired when I get home at night; I fall asleep sometimes before I get washed. I am not so strong as I was, and cannot stand my work so well as I used to do. I have drawn till I have had the skin off me; the belt and chain is worse when we are in the family way. My feller has beaten me many a time for not being ready. I were not used to it at first, and he had little patience. [Cited in Neff, 1966, p.72].

This was hardly the same world as that of the 'lady':

I could dawdle about in the nursery, and count the apricots on the wall. I could water plants in a green-house, and pick off dead leaves from the geraniums. I could ask old women about their rheumatisms, and order half-a-crown's worth of soup for the poor. . . . I could even drive out ten miles to dine at a neighbour's, and dress in the fashions of the year before last. I could go to church and keep awake in the great family pew; or go to sleep behind the curtains [Cited in Neff, 1966, pp.206–7].

Patricia Branca (1975) has suggested that the image of the idle lady has been promulgated so uncritically by historians that it is probably applicable to smaller numbers of middle-class women than most people believe. Examination of income and census data indicates that the majority of middle-class families would not have had the income necessary to support the idealized mode of feminine existence; the average income of £100 – 300 a year could not have paid for a governess, for instance, or, indeed, for more than one servant — the ubiquitous 'maid-of-all-work'. (It took £5000 a year to generate the account above.) Nevertheless, the image did approximate to reality for upper-class and upper-middle-class women, and must have been an important influence on the aspirations of the majority.

THE RIGHT OF EVERY WOMAN

Class-specific and sexually inegalitarian ideologies of women became explicit in the Victorian period both as a cause and a consequence of social change. One paradox is that these ideologies experienced a peak simultaneously with, and not prior to, the emergence of feminism as an organized movement.

Did the suffragettes change the position of women? Viola Klein's view that feminism was born, not in the factory or the mine, but 'in the Victorian middle class drawing room' (Klein, 1949, p.262), is contradicted by the evidence of working-class women's political activities throughout the nineteenth century. In the early part of the century female chartists ran their own political unions and pursued questions of female independence, sex equality and political participation. A weaver from Glasgow wrote to the *Northern Star* in June 1838:

Fellow Countrywomen — I address you as a plain working woman — a weaver of Glasgow. You cannot expect me to be grammatical in my expressions, as I did not get an education, like many other of my fellow women that I ought to have got, and which is the right of every human being . . . It is the right of every woman to have a vote in the legislation of her country, and doubly more so now that we have got a woman at the head of the government . . . [Cited in Thompson, 1976, p.123]

It was particularly in the North of England that the tradition of female activism flourished. In the Lancashire cotton towns women were (relative to the country as a whole) well paid and highly organized: in 1896 the 90,000 or so women workers in the cotton unions represented five-sixths of all organized female workers in Britain. These women fought for a whole range of feminist demands, including women's right to work, cooperative rather than family-based childcare, equal pay for women and family allowances for all children. Their campaign, which was frowned on as too radical by most suffragettes, continued throughout the period from 1884 to 1903 when suffragette activity lapsed (Liddington and Norris, 1978).

The campaign for the vote built on these foundations. In 1865 the first woman's suffrage society was formed in Manchester, and the movement spread to London, Birmingham and Bristol. In April 1868, the first public meeting on women's suffrage in Britain was held, in the Assembly Room of the Free Trade Hall in Manchester; the meeting passed a resolution asking for the vote 'on the same terms as it is or may be granted to men' (Rosen, 1974, p.7). Over the next sixteen years the fight for enfranchisement was constantly overcome by other political considerations, not the least of which was the fact that most political leaders were opposed to it, either personally or because they thought their political supporters were. Between 1886 and 1892 the Commons did not even debate women's suffrage. In 1903 the Women's Social and Political Union was formed, and by 1910 suffragettes had succeeded in persuading male politicians that votes for women was more than a platform for jocular remarks and desultory debate. By 1916, Prime Minister Asquith described the women's case as 'reasonable' and 'unanswerable' (Rosen, 1974, p.259). In 1918 the Representation of the People Act, whose main purpose was the extension of the male franchise to the thousands of unpropertied men who had served in the war, also acceded the principle of female suffrage by allowing propertied women over 30 the vote. For how, as Asquith said, could it legitimately be withheld from those women who had worked alongside the men during the long years of the war for the nation's survival?

An important question is, of course, why feminist activity developed at all in the nineteenth century; the fact that a certain group of people is excluded from the exercise of legal and political rights does not explain the emergence of a movement to claim them. One answer is that the contraction of women's opportunities in the early nineteenth century occurred together with the expansion of men's opportunities and at a time when generally liberal and libertarian ideas were in ascendance. The paradox was obvious. Moreover, it is true that many of the important legislative changes preceded, rather than followed, the gaining of political rights. It does not seem to be the case that the vote was 'the germ from which shall spring the reorganization of society' (Bullard, 1969, p.121), but rather that the vote was itself a product of that reorganization. Millicent Fawcett, whose active political life spanned the whole suffragette period from the 1860s to the 1920s, anticipated this in 1886 when she wrote:

Women's suffrage will not come, when it does come, as an isolated phenomenon, it will come as a necessary corollary of the other changes which have been gradually and steadily modifying during this century the social history of our country. It will be a political change, not of a very great or extensive character in itself, based upon social, educational and economic changes which have already taken place. [Cited in Rover, 1967, p.2]

The legal merging of the married woman's personality and property with that of her husband was appropriate to a feudal system of land-based wealth in which the home and the land around it formed the centre of production. The industrial revolution created new forms of wealth: the growth of limited liability companies in the nineteenth century produced economic power divorced from the ownership of land, and land itself became subject to market forces — land went public as the home became private. Legal reform was needed to take account of this changed reality. Thus the British Married Women's Property Act of 1882 acknowledged that husband and wife were separate individuals in the eyes of the law, but was not the milestone in the march of women to equality that it is frequently claimed to be: 'it did little more than save wealthy women from the irksome restraints of holding property through trustees' (Sachs and Wilson, 1978, p.137). Similar qualifications have been suggested as applying to the matrimonial legislation that recognized and remedied some of the more glaring inequalities between husband and wife in access to divorce and its effects. The improvements in women's legal situation which began in America in the 1820s did so in the Southern States where feminism had no influence, and seem to have been inspired 'mainly by the liberal spirit of the times, the progress of equity law, and the desire of male debtors to save their property from seizure' (O'Neill, 1969, p.21).

In view of the widespread character of women's socially imposed disabilities in the nineteenth century, it could be argued that the suffragettes' concentration on the vote was extraordinarily myopic. In fact the question of suffrage only emerged gradually as the priority, and its roots lay in the particular plight of the 'surplus' of unmarried women who suffered especially acutely from the lack of education and employment opportunities affecting middle-class women as a whole. The contribution of the suffragettes was to raise the political status of female suffrage as an issue. But it was, paradoxically as we shall see in the next chapter, the suspension of their militancy during the war that enabled male politicians to sponsor women's enfranchisement without losing face.

FEMALE SLAVERY

Linda Brent, a Mulatto slave born in South Carolina in 1818, described in a remarkable document the double oppression of the female slave:

He peopled my young mind with unclean images, such as only a vile monster could think of. I turned from him with disgust and hatred. But he was my master, I was compelled to live under the same roof with him — where I saw a man forty years my senior daily violating the most sacred commandments of nature. He told me that I was his property; that I must be subject to his will in all things . . . No matter whether the slave girl be as black as ebony or as fair as her mistress. In either case, there is no shadow of law to protect her from insult, from violence, or even from death; all these are inflicted by fiends who bear the shape of men. The mistress, who ought to protect the helpless victim, has no other feelings towards her but those of jealousy and rage. The degradation, the wrongs, the vices, that grow out of slavery, are more than I can describe . . . Slavery is terrible for men, but it is far more terrible for women. Superadded to the burden common to all, *they* have wrongs, and sufferings, and mortifications peculiarly their own [Brent, 1973, pp.26 – 7, 79]

Linda was persuaded to give an account of her life as a slave by a woman abolitionist who saw its purpose as arousing the sympathy of women in the North for the plight of Southern slave women. Emancipation, the word most often used to describe what happened to women in late Victorian and Edwardian Britain, means freedom from possession. Historically, and especially in America, anti-slavery and women's rights campaigns had important linkages. Abolitionism was a field in which women were public figures; abolitionist leaders supported women's rights — at least in theory; Elizabeth Cady, the greatest single figure in the history of American feminism, married Henry Stanton, a noted abolitionist, and Lucy Stone and Henry Blackwell's union was modelled on the same pattern. More than half the signatures on the petitions that forced Congress to take up the slavery question were women's, and feminists appeared to have used abolition as a platform for advocating women's interests, as well as being pointed in the direction of feminism by the practical chauvinism of the male anti-slavery agitators (for a 1960s parallel, see pp.28-30). In 1840, London saw the paradox of an anti-slavery convention at which Lucretia Mott and Elizabeth Cady Stanton both spoke as United States' delegates, but from which women as a category were excluded by a vote taken at the convention.

The analogy of women with slaves is a recurrent theme in both nineteenth- and twentieth-century feminist writing. Wollstonecraft (1929, p.164) talked about women's 'slavish obedience', and argued that the artificial character imposed on women in male society gave them the 'constitution' of slaves and men the occupation of 'slave-masters'. J. S. Mill based his case on the equivalence of women's legal subordination with the institution of slavery calling it a 'milder form of dependence' but one that 'has not lost the taint of its brutal origin' (Mill, 1929, p.223). He considered some objections to his view which it is worth quoting because they remain important criticisms of the feminist viewpoint in the twentieth century. Firstly:

Some will object, that a comparison cannot fairly be made between the government of the male sex and the forms of unjust power which I have adduced in illustration of it, since these are arbitrary, and the effect of mere usurpation, while it [the government of women by men] on the contrary is natural. But was there ever any domination which did not appear natural to those who possessed it? {Mill, 1929, p.229]

Secondly:

it will be said, the rule of men over women differs from all these others in not being a rule of force: it is accepted voluntarily . . . In the first place, a great number of women do not accept it . . . How many more women there are who silently cherish similar aspirations, no one can possibly know; but there are abundant tokens how many *would* cherish them, were they not so strenuously taught to repress them as contrary to the properties of their sex. [Mill, 1929, p.231].

Thirdly:

All causes, social and natural, combine to make it unlikely that women should be collectively rebellious to the power of men. They are so far in a position different from all other subject classes, that their masters require something more from them than actual service. Men do not want solely the obedience of women, they want their sentiments. [Mill, 1929, p.232]

Women's subordination to men is (a) natural, (b) justified because women don't complain, and (c) maintained by the tie of romantic and sexual affection between men and women. The first two of these propositions can now be countered with evidence (see Chapters 3 and 4) about the sources of gender differences and the psychology and happiness of women that was not available in Mill's day — though this does not prevent either still being cited as reasons why equality won't work and/or is contrary to women's interests. The third objection is, in the 1970s, both the most common reason advanced for women's failure to espouse equal opportunities, and the major stumbling block in feminist analyses of women's caste or class-status.

Gunnar Myrdal has noted that women and children share with Negroes both high social visibility and oppression in a manner that cuts across cultural boundaries. The ninth Biblical commandment, associating women, servants, mules and other property, was the principle invoked to define the legal status of the first Negro servants imported to colonial America in the seventeenth century, precisely by extending the status of women and children to Negroes. Both the Negro and women had their place in society rationalized, as Mill correctly observed, by the myth of 'contentment', which obstructed the perception of oppression. And just as white masters were considered 'natural' for Negroes, so male authority was (is) deemed the only kind that women 'naturally' accept. Speaking, one presumes, in his role as a slave-master, Myrdal concludes:

As in Germany it is said that every gentile has his pet Jew, so it is said in the South that every white has his 'pet nigger', or — in the upper strata — several of them. We sometimes marry the pet woman, carrying out the paternalistic scheme. But even if we do not, we tend to deal kindly with her as a client and a ward, not as a competitor and an equal. [Myrdal, 1944, p.1078]

It follows that the most 'oppressed' group of all is the one discriminated against on grounds of both sex *and* race. In modern South Africa 'the black consciousness of "inferiority" ingrained by the colonists . . . is the first imposition; the second is the inferior status imposed by the relationship of the women and men' (Bernstein, 1978, p.8). South African black women are not even allowed the sacred feminine domain of the family, for this sentimental conception is not necessary in a system that exploits cheap black migrant labour and regards women merely as 'appendages'.

As we shall see later in this book, perceiving women as a group disadvantaged by sex in the same way as other social groups are disadvantaged by their ethnic origin throws a great deal of light on women's psychology and on the external pressures that help to shape it. Simone de Beauvoir, in her brilliant and unequalled *The Second Sex*, framed the problem in terms of the predominant sense women have had of themselves as the Other: as creatures seen by, and for, men; the object of men's conceptions, explorations, provisions and articulations, rather than their own. She reflected that sometimes the 'feminine world' is contrasted with the 'masculine universe', but women have rarely constituted a closed and independent society (for an arguable exception see pp.332-3):

. . . they form an integral part of the group, which is governed by males and in which they have a subordinate place . . . they are always compelled . . . to band together in order to establish a counter-universe, but they always set it up within the frame of the masculine universe.

Hence the paradox of their situation: they belong at one and the same time to the male world and to a sphere in which that world is challenged; shut up in their world, surrounded by the other, they can settle down nowhere in peace. [De Beauvoir, 1960, pp.297 – 8]

Getting the vote did not enable women to settle down in peace. Whether, or to what extent, the movement towards sex equality that has characterized the second half of the twentieth century has enabled them to do so, is the next question.

CHAPTER TWO
Liberation

Some of us hoped more from woman suffrage than is ever going to be accomplished. My own large anticipations were based partly upon ignorance of the magnitude of the task which we women reformers so confidently wished to undertake. [Pankhurst, 1924, p.38]

A period of relative silence on the subject of women's rights followed the granting of the suffragettes' demand for the vote in 1920. By 1970 a rebirth of feminist insurgency had established an active women's liberation movement in all but three of the liberal – democracies of the capitalist world.

Nineteenth-century feminism demanded rights and espoused a vision of women as the legal and political equals of men. Twentieth-century feminism continues to argue the necessity of women's rights, but says that an enfranchised woman is still a member of a socially inferior gender, and if men become the norm that women must strive to emulate, society — and women — remain dominated by a masculine ethic. Unless the gender role system itself, together with its economic base, is questioned, what women gain in the way of rights is too easily put to the service of men. A 'good woman' in the 1970s is one who has two careers: one as a wage/salary earner, and one as a home-provider, which includes up-to-date knowledge of the techniques of childrearing, meal-provision and sexual satisfaction. Such an image is not what nineteenth-century feminism rebelled against, nor, presumably, is it the fate they envisaged for emancipated women.

The fact that organized feminism is alive and well today gives rise to a series of interrelated questions:
(1) Why did feminism decline in the years following the First World War?
(2) Why did it re-emerge in the 1960s?
(3) What is the legal, political, social and economic situation of women today?

ANN VERONICA AND THE WAR OF THE SEXES

In 1909 H. G. Wells published a novel about the discontents of an earnest young middle-class woman who was 'eager for freedom and life'. Ann Veronica, the heroine whose name provides the title of the book, finds Edwardian family life under the aegis of a patriarchal father unbearably restrictive, leaves her comfortable suburban home to study comparative anatomy in London, joins the suffragettes and falls in love with a married man, thus generally promoting her own personal fulfilment at a time when women were not supposed to do so. (The novel was banned by public libraries when it first came out for this combination of moral transgressions.)

Ann Veronica first meets the suffragettes' ideas in the person of Nettie Miniver

a slender lady of 30 or so in a dingy green dress . . . . Miss Miniver looked out on the world through large emotional blue eyes that were further magnified by the glasses she wore, and her nose was pinched and pink . . . On her lapel was an ivory button, bearing the words 'Votes for Women'. [Wells, 1943, p.27]

Nettie Miniver tells Ann Veronica that Edwardian England is a man-made society in which man-made institutions exploit all women. Her views are based on a wide-ranging theory:

'We are the species', said Miss Miniver, 'men are only incidents . . . Only in man is the male made the most important. And that happens through our maternity; it's our very importance that degrades us. While we were minding the children they stole our rights and liberties. The children made us slaves, and the men took advantage of it . . . Women, to begin with were the rulers and leaders; they owned all the property, they invented all the arts. The primitive government was the Matriarchate. The Matriarchate! The Lords of Creation just ran about and did what they were told.'

'But is that really so?' said Ann Veronica.

'It has been proved', said Miss Miniver, and added, 'by American professors.'

'But how did they prove it?'

'By science,' said Miss Miniver, and hurried on, putting out a rhetorical hand that showed a slash of finger through its glove. 'And now, look at us! See what we have become. Toys! Delicate trifles! A sex of invalids. It is we who have become the parasites and toys'.

It was, Ann Veronica felt, at once absurd and extraordinarily right. [Wells, 1943, p.30 – 1]

Contemporary feminist analyses have subsequently borne out Nettie Miniver's theory about the oppressive social character of reproduction — though not the enticing notion of primitive matriarchy (see pp.310-15). At any rate it was sufficient to persuade Ann Veronica. She campaigns with the suffragettes and is imprisoned with them, but undergoes a strange *volte face* during her contemplative months in prison. 'One day the idea of self-sacrifice came into her head' (p.209). She sees how her recent conduct has been motivated purely by self-interest and without any thought of the cost to others. In accordance with this fresh moral insight, she returns home to her obdurate father, and the end of the book finds her married to her (now divorced) lover, mistress of her own home, and on the brink of the maternity that in Nettie Miniver's eyes sets so final a seal on women's chances of liberty.

H. G. Wells ends Ann Veronica's dilemma with what Ehrenreich and English (1979) have called the 'romantic' solution to the Woman Question. The problem of women's nature and proper destiny is solved by regarding them as the antithesis of men, a view that allows the full-blown ethic of romantic love to come into play. When Ann Veronica 'discovers' the value of self-sacrifice and 'chooses' marriage and motherhood, her actions are compatible with the tone and political context of her feminism.

The saga of Ann Veronica was a warning of developments to come. What happened to Wells' heroine happened to many women who, during and after the First World War, saw self-sacrifice as a higher duty than the feminist struggle. War always has a special tendency to highlight paradoxes in the position of women. When male workers leave their jobs to fight, women's capacities as substitute productive workers become a matter of national emergency. But once the war ends, the returning heroes must be reabsorbed into the labour force. Furthermore, the exigency of replacing those who have died focuses attention on women as reproducers in whose hands (wombs) lies the future of the birth rate — a national crisis of a different, but no less forceful, kind.

Within days of the outbreak of the First World War in August 1914, the women's suffrage campaign suspended its militancy and many suffragettes began actively to campaign for women's recruitment as war workers. The London Society for Women's Suffrage in Britain promptly changed its name to Women's Service. The leader of the

National Union of Women's Suffrage Societies, Millicent Fawcett, declared 'a time for resolute effort and self-sacrifice on the part of every one of us to help our country' (Marwick, 1977, p.27). Christabel Pankhurst reappeared at the London Opera House after her long exile to give a speech, not on women's enfranchisement, but on 'The German Peril'. Her mother toured the country making recruiting speeches. The *Suffragette* newspaper was renamed *Britannia*. When not actively recruiting, most suffragettes expended their energies on relief work, dealing with the social problems of inadequate separation allowances, malnutrition among mothers and infants, the provision of clinics and nurseries for both employed and non-employed mothers and their children, and, a constant theme, the misery of rising prices. In February 1915 flour cost 75 per cent more than a year before, meat was 12 per cent up, coal 15 per cent and sugar 72 per cent: 'Labour members in Parliament stated that many labourers were getting only one good meal a week; they did not say whether the labourers' wives or children were getting even that' (Marwick, 1977, p.37).

The replacement of male by female workers intensified the burning issue of 'dilution' — the substitution of unskilled and semi-skilled for skilled workers. This was a process that industry had been undergoing since the 1880s, but there was no doubt that some industrialists saw the war as an opportunity to strengthen their hand against the unions. Unskilled women workers took over men's jobs — as bank clerks, bus drivers, furnace-stokers, shipbuilders, plumbers, gravediggers, for example — and their consequent unpopularity with male workers was one thread in the antagonism the war bred between the sexes. Between April 1915 and July 1918, 1,659,000 women were added to the workforce. By 1918 1,816,000 women were directly replacing men.

Everyone seems to have appreciated women's war work, and the War Office in September 1916 paid them the dubious compliment that they had 'shown themselves capable of replacing the stronger sex in practically every calling' (Rosen, 1974, p.256). The official object lesson of this was not, however, considered to be one about the true capabilities of women; rather, it was that publicizing the success of women as substitutes for male workers might persuade more employers to release more men for active service. It was continually emphasized that whatever was learnt (by women, men, employers, workers or government) during the war about women's roles as workers was to be confined to the war period. All that women were allowed to think they had proved was their ability to 'temporarily substitute' for men. This had the backing of the law in the shape of the Pre-War Practices Act, which required employers to give men their jobs back and represented the terms of the trade unions' agreement with the government on the matter of 'dilution' — that it would end when the war did.

Of the two major events in British women's history which took place in 1918 — the granting of the vote to six million women and the return of men to the labour force — it was the latter that was most immediately influential. Ray Strachey, in her history of the women's movement published in 1928, describes the demobilization of women war workers in these terms:

thousands upon thousands of women workers were dismissed and found no work to do . . . it was terribly hard on the women. Everyone assumed, of course, that they would go quietly back to their homes, and that everything would be as it had been before; but, apart altogether from anything the women might wish, this was sheerly impossible. The war had enormously increased the number of surplus women, so that very nearly one woman in every three had to be self-supporting; it had broken up innumerable homes and brought into existence a great class of 'new poor'. Prices were nearly double what they had been in 1914, and the women who had been able to live upon their small allowances or fixed incomes could do so no more. All these facts, however, were forgotten. Public opinion assumed that all women could still be supported by men, and that if they went on working it was from a sort of deliberate wickedness. The tone of the Press swung, all in a moment, from extravagant praise to the opposite extreme, and the very same people who had been heroines and saviours of their country a few months before were now parasites, blacklegs and limpets. Employers were implored to turn them out as passionately as they had been implored to employ them . . . [Strachey, 1928, pp.370 – 1]

Anti-suffragette opinion resurfaced despite (or because of) the imminent female franchise; Lord Curzon, a well-known chauvinist, declared that the first duty of the country was to return women to the home and resume 'a more healthy condition of social and domestic life' (Harrison, 1978, p.230). Left-wing politicians joined him, and the labour movement responded sympathetically when an unemployed ex-service man in Bristol smashed the windows of tramcars and attacked conductresses in protest against women's employment in the public services.

The women's press rapidly moved from the nostalgic position of *Vogue* magazine in November 1918:

for many [women] the end of the war must necessarily imply the closing of a stimulating chapter of experiences . . Many a chauffeuse in navy blue or military khaki will regret the Mercedes in which she came to have almost a proprietary interest . . . To many . . . the war has brought responsibility and conspicuous service . . . . [Cadogan and Craig, 1978, p.38]

to the renegade moral pronouncements of *Woman's Life* in February 1920:

. . . the sex is returning to the deep, very deep sea of femininity from which her newly acquired power can be more effectively wielded. [Cadogan and Craig, 1978, pp.38 – 9]

Such advice played an important part in creating public opinion. The social and economic changes of the war itself profoundly affected the women's magazine industry, and it was in the years 1920 – 1939 that the present domestic orientation of the big-selling women's magazines solidified. As Cynthia White phrases it in her history of women's magazines:

[Editors] expatiated in unison on the sacrificial joys of being a wife and mother . . . elevated housewifery into a craft, gave it the status of a profession, and sold it to readers on the most attractive of terms, thereby nullifying all that had been achieved by the women's rights movement. [White, 1970, p.104]

A perfect climate was created for the selling of every kind of household commodity. A baby food advertisement of 1920 asked:

Do you realise, Mother of a Baby — that you can be one of the greatest creative artists in the world? — Just like every other artist a mother must study her Art — the greatest Art of all — the great Art of creating strong, straight, noble men and women. [Quoted in White, 1970, p.104]

The war and the vote both presented problems of future strategy to organized feminism. The first issue divided suffragettes into two camps: the majority who gave up pursuit of the franchise or women's advancement for war work, and a minority who repudiated the war and continued to work for women's issues. When the vote was won the movement was further divided. There were some who thought it should exist primarily to promote feminist causes — of which there were still plenty, even though the principle of women's suffrage had been acceded. Others wanted to use their political power for all the general humanitarian causes that they had cited as reasons for obtaining the vote: spheres like the promotion of international understanding and the improvement of health education and sanitation in which they saw a need for the special contribution women might make. In the end this latter view prevailed. The National Union of Women's Suffrage Societies became the National Union of Societies of Equal Citizenship, with a broad and not specifically feminist brief. Although other, more feminist, women's organizations continued to exist for a time, the war's legacy of a complex coordinating machinery designed to unify the efforts of all the various societies proved a bureaucratic obstacle to any real progress. Christabel Pankhurst's programme for 'The Women's Party', the new title adopted by the Women's Social and Political Union in 1917, combined an intensely reactionary xenophobia (the Empire to be kept under 'strictly British ownership', etc.) with a wide-ranging list of reforms in the status of women and children — from equal pay for equal work to better food and living conditions for pregnant and lactating mothers, from medical care for all children to nursery schools and centralized laundries. Christabel herself took to religious evangelism, while her sister Sylvia continued with her social work among poor women and later became a partisan of Ethiopian independence. Their mother lectured on moral hygiene in Canada. She died in 1928, appropriately the year the restrictions of the 1918 Act were lifted, but shortly after her paradoxical adoption as a Conservative candidate in the East End of London.

In America, the passing in 1920 of the Nineteenth Amendment to the Constitution granting women the vote had a similarly paralysing and divisive effect on the women's movement, whose development until that time had broadly paralleled that in Britain. The League of Women Voters evolved out of the right wing of the movement and concerned itself with the same humanitarian pursuits as were preoccupying many ex-suffragists in Britain — pacifism, general living conditions, child labour laws. The militant National Women's Party took the view that the vote was only a beginning, and said that women were still 'subordinate to men before the law, in the professions, in the Church, in industry and in the home' (Deckard, 1979, p.287). Its members pledged themselves to work for full equality, and indeed were able to get an equal rights amendment introduced in Congress in 1923 — and every succeeding year until 1972 when it was passed, although it has yet to be ratified. But the membership of the Women's Party was small (8,000 in 1923, down from 50,000 in 1920) and from the 1920s to the 1960s its battle was waged against enormous odds. Having to fight the extra attack of communism did not help. (Ex-senator Weeks who had been defeated by women voters sponsored a campaign to show how all women's groups were part of a 'spider web' directed from Moscow [Deckard, 1979, p.305].) Those women's groups that did survive became increasingly conservative and oriented to general educational or reform issues, some even adopting the ex-senator's line and joining him in a communist witch-hunt. By 1923 the women's movement as such had disappeared.

The British and American experiences were part of a general wave of anti-feminism that swept Europe after 1918. Democratic societies became reactionary on the issue of women, and in totalitarian or Catholic countries the reaction was even more pronounced. By taking over men's jobs, becoming breadwinners, supporting and bringing up children on their own, discovering and enjoying the benefits of economic independence and domestic freedom, women threatened men's views of femininity and masculinity and the proper relation between them. The pace of change was simply too fast and its depth too disturbing.

Nevertheless, the post-war years did see the quiet passage of some important legal reforms. Feeling somewhat uncomfortable about the way women had been forced to retreat from their wartime employment, and about the death of a wide-ranging Private Member's Emancipation Bill in the House of Lords in 1919, the British government conceded the right of women to become members of the House of Commons and passed the Sex Disqualification (Removal) Act of 1919, which allowed women to exercise any public function, judicial office or profession, and enabled them to serve as jurors. In 1921, and after a long fight, the civil service agreed to admit women, though they appeared to be in no hurry to implement this decision.

On the domestic front, the Law of Property Act of 1922 made husbands and wives, mothers and fathers, and sons and daughters, equal in cases of intestacy. In 1920 it became for the first time legally possible for husbands and wives to steal from each other when they were living apart. A number of maintenance Acts codified fathers' responsibility towards both legitimate and illegitimate children. The 1923 Matrimonial Causes Act corrected the anomaly of sex-differentiated grounds for divorce, and infidelity became a ground for divorce for both sexes. Before this date a woman had to prove her husband's desertion or cruelty in addition to his adultery. An immediate increase in undefended suits followed. In 1925 Caroline Norton's attempts fully to equalize the rights and responsibilities of both parents with regard to the guardianship of their children finally bore fruit with the Guardianship of Infants Act. The Administration of Estates Act, 1925, said that for the purpose of distributing or dividing property, husbands and wives were in future to be treated as two persons. Another Law of Property Act in the same year followed this precedent and remedied the unjust situation whereby if a gift of land were made to a husband and wife and a third party, the husband and wife counted as one person and received half only. The Criminal Justice Act of 1926 applied the new legal doctrine of husbands' and wives' separate existence to the traditional legal maxim that married women committing criminal acts necessarily do so under the coercion of their husbands.

The second women's franchise act was passed in 1928. This was regarded by many people at the time, and by many historians of the nineteenth- and early twentieth-century women's movement, as the abolition of the 'last glaring inequality in the legal position of women' (Strachey, 1928, p.384). Hansard for 19 March 1928 reports Prime Minister Stanley Baldwin as saying:

The subjection of women, if there be such a thing, will not now depend on any creation of the law, nor can it be remedied by any action of the law. It will never again be possible to blame the Sovereign State for any position of inequality. Women will have, with us, the fullest rights. The ground and justification for the old agitation is gone, and gone for ever. [Cited in Strachey, 1928, p.384]

PRONE WOMEN AND THEIR FOUR DEMANDS

He was wrong, of course. Out of the radicalism of the student left, the civil rights struggle and the peace movement in the 1960s, the women's liberation movement was born. From its beginning this movement has seen the position of women in a different light from earlier feminists. It has taken up some of the early more radical themes — the bondage

of marriage, the economic and emotional poverty of housework —
but has advanced these and the more specific documentation of
institutional discrimination in two main ways. In the first place, it has
sought for a theoretical understanding of why women are oppressed.
In the second place, it has seen this oppression as existing within
attitudes and ideologies as much as in actual behaviour. This means
that women are in one sense collaborators in their own oppression, an
insight that has had far-reaching implications for the politics of the
modern women's movement (see Chapter 12).

The 1930s, 1940s and 1950s were a bad time for women. Led to
believe they possessed equality, they found that they did not. The post-
First World War reactions against socio-economic change persisted
beneath the superficially seductive glitter of the jazz age and the
apparently liberating new sexual morality. It was certainly part of the
conventional wisdom of the time that women's sexual behaviour had
changed, and the Kinsey report seemed to confirm this (Kinsey *et al*,
1953). The biggest change appeared to be the rise in pre-marital
intercourse among young middle-class women in the decade following
the end of the First World War; this, together with an increased
incidence of pre-marital petting, was regarded by the authors of the
Kinsey Report as the greatest post-war change in sexual mores.

Pioneer sexual ideologists regarded freedom of sexual expression
for women as a significant advance. It fitted in with the general
relaxation of manners that younger women were experiencing:

skirts grew shorter and shorter, clothes grew more and more simple and
convenient, and hair, that 'crowning glory of women' was cut short — with
one bound the young women of 1919 burst out from the hampering
conventions, and with their cigarettes, their motor cars, their latch keys, and
their athletics, they astonished and scandalised their elders. [Strachey, 1928,
p.389].

The trouble was that such changes merely skimmed the surface. Even
Kinsey and his colleagues noted that the rising numbers of young
unmarried women who had intercourse were accompanied by an
unchanging proportion who had (or said they had) orgasms. One
result of the increased awareness of female sexuality was a rise in
teenage marriage, not a particularly liberating consequence for
women. Moreover, the pioneers of sexual freedom did not anticipate
the effects of Freudian theory, which has undoubtedly been one of the

two most influential reactionary ideologies affecting women in the last half century. At first Freudians were interpreted as favouring sexual promiscuity, but a conservative portrayal of women quickly seeped through the sieve of this interpretation; Kate Millett evaluates this development thus:

By an irony nearly tragic, the discoveries of a great pioneer, whose theories of the unconscious and of infant sexuality were major contributions to human understanding, were . . . invoked to sponsor a point of view essentially conservative. And as regards the sexual revolution's goal of liberating female humanity from its traditional subordination, the Freudian position came to be pressed into the service of a strongly counterrevolutionary attitude. Although the most unfortunate effects of vulgar Freudianism far exceeded the intentions of Freud himself, its anti-feminism was not without foundation in Freud's own work. [Millett, 1971, p.178]

Women thus came again to be seen as incurably unequal through their biological difference from men.

Economically, the theme of women's status as a reserve labour force was repeated during the depression of the 1930s and again after the Second World War. Women's gains during this period were, not surprisingly, disappointing. In America, women made up a smaller proportion of college students in 1950 (30 per cent) than they did in 1920 (47 per cent). In 1920 women earned one out of every six doctorates, compared with one out of ten in 1956. Occupational sex segregation stayed more or less unchanged from 1900 to 1960 (Gross, 1968). In 1940 Margaret Mead summed up the situation as one of 'private license' rather than 'institutionalized powers' for women (Mead, 1940). The advance in England was similarly depressing — indeed, as Juliet Mitchell (1971) points out, all the countries where women's liberation movements arose in the 1960s could point to parallel patterns of discrimination. Women made up about a third of the labour force, were paid half to three-quarters the male wage, and worked mostly in unskilled jobs. Whereas many countries had been 'committed' to equal pay for some years, nowhere had women come anywhere near achieving it. Between a quarter and a third of women students (except in America) were female, and their opportunities for further training, apprenticeship or day-release schemes were not equivalent to those available to men. Legal discrimination, often disguised as 'protective legisation', operated in many places.

Women's rise in formal male politics — either as a goal in itself or to achieve those far-ranging ends the suffragettes envisaged — had been paltry, as had their infiltration into the professional elites. Contraception and abortion, prerequisities of women's freedom, were not easily available, safe or under the control of women themselves. One apparent change was the rise in married women's employment.

In 1961 more than one-half of all the women in paid employment in the United Kingdom were married. The proportion had been rising steadily for over a decade. It is now higher than the figure reached during the peak years of employment during the Second World War; the highest, indeed, in Britain's industrial history, and probably the highest in the Western world. [Titmuss, foreword to Jephcott, 1962]

Some of this rise is explained by the falling age and increasing popularity of marriage, but there was also a clear trend towards the reintegration of older married women into the labour force. Sociologists put a label on this dilemma of women's confinement to the home and determined effort to escape it. They called it 'women's two roles' (Myrdal and Klein, 1956). While urging people to accept married women workers as a new and permanent social phenomenon, they regarded it as important to ask why women want to work and what consequences women's employment has for their husbands, homes and children. They did not ask (at least not until the late 1960s) what this dual role did to women themselves.

Freudian ideology and theories of maternal deprivation encouraged a conspiracy of silence among women about their dissatisfactions. In 1963 an American journalist – housewife wrote a book that put another label on the reactionary era of the 1950s and 1960s: *The Feminine Mystique* (Friedan, 1963). 'The whole world lies open to American women', wrote Friedan with an honest air of puzzlement. 'Not long ago, women dreamed and fought for equality, their own place in the world. What happened to their dreams?' (Friedan, 1963, p.36). Like 'Diogenes with his lamp' she went from suburb to suburb searching for fulfilled housewives. One of the most revealing passages in her book concerns an upper-income development where she interviewed 28 apparently satisfied wives. Only one was employed; the rest were dedicated to motherhood, and many, at or near 40, were pregnant again. In this community the mystique of feminine domestic fulfilment was so literally followed that if a little girl said she wanted to be a doctor, her mother corrected her and said '"No dear . . . You're going to be a wife and mother, like mummy"' (Friedan, 1963, p.235). Probing beneath the surface of this suburban dream Friedan found that mummy was really not very happy at all: 16 of the women were in analysis; 18 were taking tranquillizers; several had tried suicide; and some had been hospitalized for depression or psychotic states. One who breastfed her baby (breastfeeding and natural childbirth were seen as a necessary part of the feminine mystique) did so until the child suffered from malnutrition and her doctor intervened by force. Twelve women were having extramarital affairs either 'in fact or in fantasy'. Bread-making, the chauffeuring of children, community work and the servicing of husbands in the kitchen and in bed — these did not seem to be the universal panacea they were believed to be.

In England, people began to make the same discovery as Friedan — though a little later, and in a more moderate fashion. Writing about *The Captive Wife*, Hannah Gavron, for example, said with typical sociological understatement: 'the situation at present is one of conflict and stress' (Gavron, 1966, p.145).

The publication of Friedan's book made her a 'leper' in her own suburban neighbourhood. Her children were ostracized and she and her husband were no longer invited to dinner parties. She felt as though she were being 'burnt at the stake' (Friedan, 1977, p.89). It was, however, some consolation to her that her book provided a prod for the organization of one branch of the American women's movement. The National Organization of Women (NOW) was formed in 1966 and adopted a Bill of Rights at its first national conference in 1967. This asked for:

1.   An equal rights constitutional amendment.
2.   The enforcement of the law banning sex discrimination in employment.
3.   Maternity leave rights in employment and in social security benefits.
4.   Tax deduction for home and child-care expenses for working parents.
5.   Child day-care centres.
6.   Equal and nonsegregated education.
7.   Equal job training opportunities and allowances for women in poverty.
8.   The right of women to control their reproductive lives.
[Walum, 1977, p.203]

The immediate prelude to NOW's formation was the strange

episode of Title VII of the 1964 Civil Rights Act. Representative Howard Smith introduced an amendment to include sex as an illegal ground for discriminaton, hoping to split the liberal vote and dispose of the civil rights bill. Through concerted action on the part of various individuals, the amendment was passed (although it remains unratified), to be described as a 'fluke . . . conceived out of wedlock' by the director of the Equal Employment Opportunity Commssion, the agency responsible for its enforcement (Walum 1977, p.202). NOW represented an attempt to get some enforcement by official agencies of this important constitutional amendment — one that Britain did not acquire for another eleven years.

Even after the passing of the Civil Rights Act, the role of women in socialist, peace, student and black movements remained a traditional one, in accordance with Stokely Carmichael's famous dictum that 'the only position of women [in the civil rights movement] is prone' (Deckard, 1979, p.332). The first stirrings were in 1964 when a small group of women in the Student Non-Violent Co-Ordinating Committee (SNCC) began to discuss the limitations of their role in that organization. When they started to air their discontent, they were greeted with 'catcalls, storms of ridicule and verbal abuse' — 'she just needs a good screw!' (Deckard, 1979, p.332). The realization that 'people don't get radicalized fighting other people's battles' (Jones and Brown, 1970, p.364) led to the formation of many women's groups — helped by the expulsion of white men and women from the SNCC, which suggested the crucial and timely analogy of women being in charge of their own liberation. By 1968 there was a recognised, if heterogeneous, women's liberation movement in America. The Radical Women's protest at the Miss America Contest in September of that year was the first feminist activity to get front page coverage. A Freedom Trash Can was provided to receive 'bras, girdles, curlers, false eyelashes and wigs', and a sheep was crowned Miss America.

According to Juliet Mitchell (1971), rumours of an emerging women's movement in America and Europe reached England in 1967; Sheila Rowbotham puts the date as autumn 1968. Recollecting the chronology of events, she says

We had only a hazy idea of what was going on. No-one I knew then had actually read anything which had been produced by the women's groups. All we knew was that women had met together and had encountered opposition within the left . . . In the diary I kept in 1967 there are persistent references to incidents I'd seen and books I'd read from a women's liberation point of view. I can remember odd conversations with women who were friends of mine, and particularly very intense moments when I was hurt and made angry by the attitudes of men on the left. But it was still at an intellectual level. We didn't think of meeting consciously as a group, far less of forming a movement. [Rowbotham, 1973, p.91]

By 1969 most major British towns had women's liberation groups, the core of a movement that came together in March 1970 at a national conference to determine an overall programme of action. The conference, held in Ruskin College, Oxford, formulated four 'demands':

(1). Equal pay.
(2). Equal education and opportunity.
(3). Twenty-four hour nurseries.
(4). Free contraception and abortion on demand.

A manifesto was produced, identifying a belief

that women in our society are oppressed. We are economically oppressed: in jobs we do full work for half pay, in the home we do unpaid work fulltime. We are commercially exploited by advertisements, television and press, legally we often have only the status of children. We are brought up to feel inadequate, educated to narrower horizons than men. This is our specific oppression as women. [*Shrew*, Vol.3, no.6, July 1971]

WE'VE BEEN WAITING A LONG TIME

Sheila Rowbotham was born in 1943 and grew up in the 1960s, a period whem many of us — middle-class girls educated to apparently liberated horizons — were discovering how the contradictions of advanced capitalist society stifled the position of women. In her partly autobiographical account of the emergence of the women's liberation movement, she describes the stereotype of the nineteenth-century feminist that was bred into us in history lessons, an image that we suspected had a vague relevance to the blatant sexism of popular culture, although we could not, at the time, quite pin it down.

When I was seventeen feminism meant to me shadowy figures in long old-fashioned clothes . . . From dim childhood memories I had a stereotype of emancipated women: frightening people in tweed suits and horn-rimmed glasses with stern buns at the backs of their heads . . . Feminism seemed the very antithesis of the freedom I connected with getting away from home and school . . . My recognition of women as a group was as creatures sunk into the very deadening circumstances from which I was determined to escape . . . .

On the other hand, the 'mystique' was very much part of my own life. There was pop music for example. My own sense of myself as a person directly conflicted with the kind of girl who was sung about in pop songs. When I was sixteen I remember feeling really angry about 'Living Doll' ['I got myself a sleeping, walking, crying, talking, Living Doll' — Cliff Richard, 1959] because it cut away from all my inside efforts towards any identity. It hurt me particularly because when I tried to argue about it with a boy I really liked I felt terribly constrained by his contempt when he said that was how he liked girls. [Rowbotham, 1973, pp.12 – 13]

Before the women's liberation movement could be born, there had to be the recognition among women of a shared female condition — a condition that constrained all women, regardless of their individual circumstances. The problem was, as Rowbotham says, that mirrors everywhere distorted the image, reflecting the post-war portrait of women as people whose satisfactions stemmed from the home (and were therefore automatically fostered by the growing economic prosperity). The genesis of the movement thus lay, not in the identification of a particular goal for which political organization among women was needed, but in the personal experience of women whose dissatisfaction was not the image thrown back at them by the mirror. From believing that we were each individually sick — incapable of adjusting to the proper standard of feminine normality — we came to see how our authenticity was jeopardized by the social relations and expectations that surrounded us.

In the last ten years the women's liberation movement has produced a body of theory to account for the persistently disadvantaged situation of women, based on two axes of discrimination: economic and psychological. Firstly, a double role as reproducers — of children in the biological sense and of the labour force in the wider social sense of supporting and servicing male breadwinners — means that women's own economic autonomy is reserved for the 'exceptional' case of the woman who is not living in a relationship with a man. But even these women are not free from oppression, because economic gender divisions are represented in the psychological construction of femininity and masculinity. The very identity of men and women is predicated on the secondary nature of women, and these mental maps are written on the cultural institutions that surround us. The effect of this diagnosis is to define the capitalist system of production as an oppressor of women, whereas many nineteenth-century feminists saw it as a liberator, offering possibilities of professional advancement for women who rejected a narrowly domestic role.

Secondly, the institutions of marriage and the family are today seen as the prisons in which women's psychological inferiority is imbibed and ensured. Although some nineteenth-century feminists such as Charlotte Perkins Gilman labelled the home the prison of women, current feminist perceptions of the family's twin ideological and economic functions in the construction of womanhood take the older insight a good deal further. Modern feminists see the family as part of a wider gender role system. This brings men into the discussion, for if the ideology of femininity constrains women, so, presumably, does the ideology of masculinity constrain men. The desire to be freed from these limitations has led to the formation of men's liberation groups whose function appears to parallel those of women. But one basic difference between the two is, of course, that, while men may be psychologically limited by their masculinity, women are socially and economically oppressed by their femininity.

Feminist theory is heterogeneous (see pp.335 – 8) and I have simplified in order to bring out the main differences between liberationist and older 'emancipatory' diagnoses of the reasons for women's subjection. Today there is, in fact, considerable disagreement among feminists about how economic and psychological modes of oppression interact: which is primary, and what are the mechanisms that cause them to be patterned in the same way? One theme that has persisted is the close relationship between the fate of women and that of ethnic minority groups. In America, nineteenth-century feminism was born out of the realization that women as well as Negroes were oppressed, and the women's liberation movement of the 1960s and 1970s was a reaction against the sexist politics of the black rights movement. Sex equality legislation was the daughter of race equality legislation. In Britain in the 1970s a new legal package for women promising them the final eradication of institutional inequalities grew out of a promise that was first made to oppressed ethnic minorities; it was redrawn to fit the special requirements of women — the disadvantaged 51 per cent majority.

In Britain the Race Relations Acts of 1965 and 1968, consolidated and amended in the Race Relations Act 1976, provided a model for outlawing the victimization of individuals on 'irrelevant' biological grounds. The demand for women to be included in this legislation was first heard in 1968, when an amendment was moved to subsume sex discrimination under the heading of the 1968 Race Relations Bill. It was unsuccessful, as were a whole series of Private Member's bills subsequently introduced. In 1971 a bill defeated in the Commons was referred to a Select Committee in the House of Lords, and two years later, after hearing a vast amount of evidence, the Committee came out in favour of sex discrimination legislation; this was followed by a House of Commons Select Committee set up in 1973. By this time, in the climate of an increasingly vociferous women's movement, the proposal to legislate against sex inequality had support from both left- and right-wing politicians; on one critical vote in favour of establishing a Sex Discrimination Board with powers to investigate discrimination and promote equality, the Conservative chairman of the House of Commons Select Committee voted against his party. 'In six years, an idea which had been thought unimportant had become a matter of government policy' (Rendel, 1978, p.900). When the Conservative government fell in March 1974, the new Labour government was committed to fostering both race and sex discrimination legislation. Their White Paper *Equality for Women* (Home Office, 1974) proposed an enlarged scope for such legislation, the establishment of an Equal Opportunity Commission and somewhat strengthened enforcement procedures. The Bill became law on 29 December 1975, the same day as the provisions of the Equal Pay Act passed by Parliament in 1970 came into force.

In America, a lacuna between 1919 and the 1960s marked attitudes to the removal of sex inequality by legal means. As we have seen, by a strange accident, Title VII of the Civil Rights Act of 1964 predated the new women's movement. In 1963 America also passed an Equal Pay Act. American practice remained in advance of that in Britain throughout the period, in part because the equal rights amendment never quite died as an issue from the early 1920s on, and because there was the example of a radical political tradition with which women could identify. The Equal Rights Amendment to the Constitution was passed in 1972, but required the approval of 38 states for ratification. By 1977, 35 of the necessary 38 states had voted for its ratification. Although Supreme Court decisions on sex discrimination in the early 1970s revealed 'hope and then ambivalence, if not outright regression' (Sachs and Wilson, 1978, p.211), American feminists were contending the interpretation and enforcement of equal rights at a time when British feminists were still trying to work out what sex discrimination legislation might represent and achieve.

In the 1960s and 1970s what we have seen, therefore, is a return to the idea that the injustices of women's station in society can be remedied by using the law as an instrument of liberation. What has this legal reform in fact achieved?

In Britain, women's pay has increased faster than men's since 1970, moving from 65.4 per cent of men's pay in 1970 to 73.8 per cent in 1977 (Equal Opportunities Commission, 1978–9, p.51). A few women have received large pay increases or obtained jobs they would otherwise probably not have done. The biggest post-war change in women's employment is the employment of married women, which continues to rise — from 42 per cent in 1971 to 49 per cent in 1976 (Equal Opportunities Commission, 1978–9, p.38). The most marked growth sectors for employed women are part-time work, the service industries and unemployment. Among managerial and professional workers, women remain a small proportion — 1 per cent of bank managers, 2 per cent of chartered accountants and university professors, 5 per cent of architects (Equal Opportunites Commission, 1978–9, p.47). This is paralleled in the educational system: while the relative proportions of males and females in education have changed somewhat, their subject-specializations on the whole have not. The political world has shown no tendency vastly to increase female participation rates. While the 1979 election provided the phenomenon of a female prime minister, it did so against the tide of a fall in women's membership of the House of Commons to the level obtaining in 1951. In the domain of public power generally, women have failed to advance. Membership of royal commissions is a male preserve, as is membership of the boards of nationalized industries and the judiciary. The percentage of women members of some professional institutes such as the Institute of Structural Engineers and the British Dental Association has risen slightly, and trade union female membership increased from 22 per cent in 1966 to 29 per cent in 1976.

The American experience has been somewhat similar, although in politics women have been more successful and notably better organized — a National Women's Political Caucus was founded in 1971.

The sex equality legislation of the 1970s rested on the philosophy that inequality derives from discrimination in the public world outside the home. In Britain, the Equal Pay Act, 1970, and Sex Discrimination Act, 1975, tackle gender discrimination in the public arena of employment with regard to entry, pay, conditions, promotion and firing, but exempt national insurance and social security, existing 'protective' labour legislation, work where a 'material difference' from male jobs can be demonstrated, and 'special treatment' of women connected with their reproductive role. Coverage of educational discrimination is limited by the provision that single sex schools are allowable, and by the requirement that complaints against schools maintained by local education authorities must be referred first to the Secretary of State for Education, the price the Department of Education and Science exacted for the inclusion of education with the terms of the Act.

Reproduction is covered by the Employment Protection Act, 1975, which contains the first statutory entitlement women in Britain have had to maternity leave. It establishes the principle that dismissal on grounds of pregnancy is unfair, and requires employers to give mothers their jobs back within 29 weeks of childbirth. (It does, however, exempt part-time workers, applies only to women who have been in the same job for two years, and only provides for six weeks' pay at 90 per cent of the basic rate.) Since paternity is omitted, the Employment Protection Act strictly speaking comes under the heading of 'protective' rather than sex equality legislation.

The remaining piece of legislation, the Social Security Pensions Act, 1975, abolishes some of the more blatant items of discrimination against married women within the social security system. For example, the lower rates of sickness and unemployment pay to which married women (paying the full contribution) have been entitled are abolished, as also is the iniquitous 'half test' rule, whereby married women paying full contributions are entitled to a pension in their own right only if they have paid contributions for at least half the years between marriage and retirement. But employed women will still not be able to claim benefit for their children in the event of unen ployment or sickness, and a recent EEC directive on sex equality in social security will not achieve this in the near future, since the British government's specially chauvinist contribution was to get the EEC provisions watered down so they would have almost no impact on the British social security scheme: child additions to unemployment/sickness benefit have been deferred until the magic date of 1984.

Even without such obstructions, several important shortcomings of the British sex equality legislation have been evident for some time. In the first place, provisions for its enforcement have been far too weak. The Equal Opportunity Commission (EOC), the body set up to aid, review and play a positive role in the application of both the Equal Pay and Sex Discrimination Acts, has been described as a 'rather wet, ladylike body too concerned with holding its skirts down against the rude winds to have a go at entrenched masculine strongholds' (*Guardian*, 19 March 1979). Its provincial location (in Manchester) and slowness to get down to work have been construed as rearguard actions on the part of those opposed to sex equality legislation. By 1977, when the National Council for Civil Liberties reviewed the contribution to sex equality made by the legislation, the EOC had promoted only one research investigation and had issued not one 'non-discrimination notice' (Coussins, 1977). (This latter strategy constitutes one of the powers of the EOC and can be followed by a court injunction in the event of non-compliance.) *The Equality Report* noted that, of the EOC's fourteen commissioners, six represented the Trade Union Congress or the Confederation of British Industries, and none was aged under 35 or had any experience of working in the women's movement. And, of course, the means available to the EOC for enforcing non-discrimination reflect the very practices the legislation is trying to discourage: in 1976–7, only 28 per cent of tribunal members concerned with equal pay/sex discrimination cases were women (Coussins, 1977, p.43).

Unlike its American equivalent, the British legislation requires individual and not corporate actions to be taken in cases of alleged discrimination. This raises the cost and reduces the chances of success. A comparison of American with British practice noted that

In the whole of the past three years, industrial tribunals in England, Scotland and Wales have awarded a total of £16,341 in loss of earnings, and other forms of compensation to women under the Equal Pay and Sex Discrimination Acts. In one single action, settled out of court in 1973, one giant American corporation paid out $35 millions [£17.5 million] to its women employees in back pay alone. [*Guardian*, 4 December 1978]

Although individual women do not get rich in this process, the cost to the big corporation is large enough to induce more than cosmetic steps towards equal employment opportunity. This is a prod to the kind of *positive* discrimination in women's favour that is missing from the British scene. In Britain, too, the fact that non-employment cases have to be taken to the county courts rather than to industrial tribunals provides a further and expensive complication, rendering the Sex Discrimination Act much less useful in practice than it might be, and certainly than feminists hoped it would be.

Aside from the weaknesses of enforcement procedures, the exemptions laid down for the British sex equality legislation are also bound to dilute its effect as an instrument of change.

Thirdly, and following from the presumption that legislation can only tackle instances of public discrimination, the underworld euphemistically referred to as 'the private relationships of citizens' (Home Office, 1974, p.1) is preserved as a domain where public intervention is not allowed. The trouble is that it is in this area of relationships with men — sexual, domestic and reproductive — that women's disabilities are bred. In this sense, the analogy between racism and sexism has to be mistaken (Nandy and Nandy, 1975; Oakley, 1975). Women cannot be liberated to the kind of roles that men have traditionally played in the public fields of education, employment and so forth, unless they are also liberated from their responsibility for reproducing the labour force. But the public/domestic distinction is enshrined in the Sex Discrimination Act's differentiation of 'direct' discrimination (which is always illegal) and 'indirect' discrimination, which means applying a particular requirement or condition that places one sex category at a relative disadvantage: here the employer may argue that the discrimination is 'justifiable' and therefore not unlawful. A notorious case in the early years of the Sex Discrimination Act's life was of Linda Price, a 35-year-old civil servant who was ineligible for promotion to the Executive Officer grade because of an imposed age limit of 28 years.

She argued that this amounted to indirect discrimination since the different pattern of women's employment (taking time off work to have, and rear, children) means that women tend to climb the career ladder more slowly than men. The tribunal refused to accept the argument, and Linda Price lost her case.

Behind this refusal to confront 'the private relationships of citizens' the sex equality legislation in Britain and, to a lesser extent, in America, has subscribed to a particular ethic of sex differences. Social differentiation is confused with biological differentiation so that what is, or is not, discrimination has to be referred to an underlying biological substratum whose contours are conveniently unclear. The key question is the much discussed 'genuine occupational qualification' clause. In the Sex Discrimination Act, this is extremely ill defined, with reliance on vague terms such as 'essential nature of the job', 'authentic male characteristics', the need for 'decency' and 'privacy' and the inclusion of a 'reasonable objection' escape route. In the White Paper whose principles the Act espouses, there is reference to 'objective differences' between the sexes and an appeal to 'scientifically demonstrable grounds' for treating men and women differently (shades of Nettie Miniver). To pile confusion on confusion, the White Paper also notes that 'common sense' on the topic of sex differences must be allowed to determine standards of justice and does not constitute 'prejudice'. In terms of the actual provisions of the legislation, some consequences of this argument are that different heights for men and women are still allowable as criteria for entry to the police force; men are entitled to govern women's prisons and take up midwifery; 'femaleness' has acquired the status of a genuine occupational qualification for foster-parenting; and insurance agents are still allowed to do different sums for men and women.

In the United States, Title VII of the Civil Rights Act contained the exception of a 'bona fide occupational qualification reasonably necessary to the normal operation of that particular business or enterprise' (Deckard, 1975, p.166), which has proved a major problem in interpreting the scope of the anti-discrimination provision. Much of the difficulty has been the apparent nullification by state protective labour laws of the injunction not to discriminate on grounds of sex. In August 1969 the Equal Employment Opportunity Commission declared that Title VII superseded the state laws and that the only exceptions where the authenticity of one sex is allowable are acting, modelling and wet nursing. -

Clearly, legislation against sex discrimination and promoting financial, employment, educational and legal equality is necessary in order to bring women into full citizenship. It is also, as yet, in Britain and other countries, incomplete — one reason being that it is only a necessary and not a sufficient condition for liberation. Although sex equality legislation in the 1960s and 1970s carried much further the infant impulses of Victorian legislators who turned to the law as a way of redressing the wrongs of women's situation, the law as it has been used to date has limited power to change attitudes, and itself arises as a superstructure of an essentially masculinist social order.

Only one model of sex equality is possible in such a society, and that is the one that says women must be made equal to men. It does not say men must become equal to women (partly because women's traditional preoccupations are seen as weaknesses, not as strengths), and it does not question the present gender dichotomy by devising a new, more radical and more equitable standard of citizenship for both men and women. The standard myopic view of sex equality cannot embrace the full-blown vision of liberation that the modern women's movement has bequeathed to the history of feminism. For liberation is, according to one personal testimony of a British feminist in the 1970s,

understanding the complete horror of ourselves, the parts that never grew, deformed, maimed, infiltrated by the social relations around us.

The needs of a system of exploitation based on the division of labour demand that people have roles, that we cannot be whole . . . the system needs exploiters and exploited, active and passive, bread-earner and child-minder, man and woman.

One part of our schizophrenia is the gap we experience between these roles and the people we are . . . between the image we and others have of ourselves and our 'self' . . . .

Liberation is the liberation from passivity — a slow realization that we have in us all possibilities, that we can all write, act, paint, dance, mend fuses, talk in meetings . . .

Liberation means liberation from fear, from the doubts that make us see the will to freedom as selfishness, freedom as hardness and love as a trap . . .

We need to grow as trees need the sun and the water and air to breathe.

We've been waiting a long time . . . . [*Shrew*, undated]

The Making of a Woman
What makes a woman?

CHAPTER THREE

Genes and Gender

It is nature, they say, that makes us get married. Nature, they say, that makes us crave to have babies . . . . It's nature that makes us love our children, clean our houses, gives us a thrill of pleasure when we please the home-coming male.

Who is this Nature?

God?

Or our disposition, as laid down by evolutionary forces, in order to best procreate the species?

I suppose, myself, that it is the latter.

Nature does not know best, or if it does, it is on the man's side. Nature gives us painful periods, leucorrhoea, polyps, thrush, placenta praevia, headaches, cancer and in the end death.

It seems to me that we must fight nature tooth and claw . . .

Nature does not know best; for the birds, for the bees, for the cows; for men, perhaps. But your interests and Nature's do not coincide.

Nature our Friend is an argument used, quite understandably, by men. [Weldon, 1978, pp.140 – 1]

Whatever nature does or does not determine in the psycho-sexual differentiation of females and males, many people today believe that innate genetic qualities of individuals are extremely important in shaping gender-differentiated behaviour. This draws attention to a central conceptual distinction I have already used in this book: that between 'sex' and 'gender'. 'Sex' refers to the biological division into female and male; 'gender' to the parallel and socially unequal division into femininity and masculinity (Oakley, 1972; Stoller, 1968). This usage is now well established, though, as Tresemer (1975) notes, the opposition between the two terms presupposes a degree of prior certainty about the separation of innate and environmental differences. Can we be certain?

WHAT MAKES A MALE?

Most remarkably, the question is not 'what makes a female?' but 'what makes a male?' In every other field discussed in this book (for reasons reflecting current ideology), the issue is framed as one of women's differences from men: women are seen as a 'problem', a special group, a disadvantaged minority, and so forth. In the biological field our vision has to shift. In the first place, of the 46 chromosomes coding the genetic inheritance a child receives from its parents, only two relate directly to its sex. Secondly, men have only themselves to blame for creating a second sex. All female ova contain one of the sex chromosomes, the X chromosome, and the original battle of the sexes takes place in the discharge of paternal sperm, which are divided into those bearing the X (female-determining) and those bearing the Y (male-determining) chromosome. The Y chromosome has been described as an incomplete X, one-fifth of its size: 'the shape of a comma, the merest remnant, a sad-looking affair' (Montagu, 1968, p.73). One specialist has put it like this:

The X-chromosome in man [sic] is of medium size, containing about 5 or 6% of the genetic material in a haploid set of human chromosomes. On the basis of recognised traits, it seems to carry about that same proportion of genetic information, including known genes affecting every major body system. The Y chromosome, on the other hand, is one of the smallest chromosomes, and, as far as is known, carries only the genetic instructions for maleness. [Lehrke, 1973, p.173]

'No abortus or stillbirth or person has been known to exist without at least one X chromosome' observe Ounsted and Taylor in their *Gender Differences*.

Half the species has no Y chromosome. To us this seems the strongest, but most undervalued evidence that it is unlikely to carry much significant genetic information . . . . The Y chromosome cannot therefore be considered to be fundamental to organismal development. [Ounsted and Taylor, 1972, p.249]

The development of the fertilized ovum is basically female. Until about seven weeks of pre-natal life the internal and external genitalia look the same in both 'sexes'. Indeed, even in this crucial respect, men and women remain similar: the penis is an analogue of the clitoris, the scrotal sac of the female labia. This aspect of female sexuality charted by embryologists lay buried in the mystiques of Victorian prudery and

Freudian dogma for a long time, being rediscovered by Kinsey in the 1950s and then by Masters and Johnson in their original laboratory work a decade later (Kinsey *et al.*, 1953; Masters and Johnson, 1966). The fact that the basic human form is female and maleness represents an addition to this structure has been dubbed 'the natural superiority of women' (Montagu, 1968). It is a cause for celebration among modern feminists who live in a society where maleness is the accepted human standard:

It was . . . a shock equivalent to a theological declaration that God was a woman [see p.320] when embryologists discovered that the basic pattern of the embryo was neither male nor undifferentiated nor, as Freud believed, bisexual, but female in structure . . . In terms of the biblical model of special creation, it would be like saying that God created Eve first, then added to her body an androgen-soaked rib to produce a belated Adam. [Adler, 1975, p.35]

It certainly appears to be the case that many of the male's troubles are due to the fragility of his biological status as an addition to the basic female groundplan. Physically, maleness is brought about when the embryonic gonads (the glands that become either ovaries or testes) start to produce the male hormone testosterone at around seven weeks of intrauterine life. This causes the genitals to assume the male form and is later responsible for the secondary sexual characteristics of puberty. (If the embryo is chromosomally female, it appears that no such production of hormones in early intrauterine life is necessary for its development: ovarian differentiation takes place later in foetal life, at around twelve weeks — Jost, 1972.) Whether the gonads develop into ovaries or testes is determined by the embryo's chromosomal constitution, decided at conception.[1] Without testicular tissue, a female child will develop, and experiments with a variety of mammals show that if the embryonic gonads are removed prior to the critical period of sexual differentiation, the embryo will differentiate as female regardless of genetic (chromosomal) sex. Individuals who, through a genetic error, have only one sex chromosome (XO —

---

[1] A gene, or group of genes, on the Y chromosome makes a molecule that sits on the surface of the gonadal cells, signalling these to develop into testes via a male-specific plasma membrane protein known as the H-Y antigen (Wachtel, 1979).

Turner's syndrome) have external female genitalia and an incomplete female internal anatomy. Not surprisingly, they are usually reared as girls.

The lack of the second X chromosome, and its replacement by the Y chromosome, puts men at a biological disadvantage. In the first place, this is the mechanism by which men express sex-linked diseases in greater numbers than women do. Some of these can only be passed by fathers to sons via the Y chromosome. Yet other diseases and disabilities are more likely to occur in males simply because if they are carried by one X chromosome there is no second X chromosome to counteract this effect. Haemophilia and red – green colour blindness fall into this category, and are among the 100 or so known disorders that are sex-linked and found mostly in males. (They only occur in females in the rare case of the father being affected and the mother also acting as carrier of the gene.)

Being male is associated with higher mortality during gestation and afterwards, throughout childhood and adult life. 'Take 20,000 newborn babies, equal numbers of boys and girls, and apply current mortality rates: after 70 years there would be 5743 men and 7461 women still alive' (*British Medical Journal*, 18 June 1977). In 1971 – 3 British men and women aged 60 could expect to live to 75 and 80 respectively; this difference in life expectancy is typical of many countries. At the other end of the life cycle, more males are miscarried and stillborn than females. More males than females are usually born (about 106:100) — though this sex ratio varies between different societies, probably reflecting environmental influences on pregnancy loss and perinatal mortality (*Race Today*, November 1969, p.221).

Many diseases of childhood and adult life are more common in males than females, and it appears to be the case that, exposed to the same biological stress, men are more vulnerable than women. Out of seven causes of perinatal death, boys preponderate in six; the sex imbalance is particularly marked in birth trauma, alveolar haemorrhage and cerebral intraventricular haemorrhage (Butler and Alberman, 1969, p.172). During the first year of life, one-third more males than females die, primarily from infectious diseases (Barfield, 1976, p.67). Boys are more often the victims of childhood accidents — both in and outside the home — and 'violent deaths' in adulthood are a male speciality (Brown and Davidson, 1978; Office of Health Economics, 1978). In middle age, men are 1.95 times more likely than women to die of heart disease, cancer, chest illnesses, kidney diseases and digestive disorders (*New England Journal of Medicine*, 20 October 1977, p.863).

The reasons for men's pronounced physical vulnerability are, in part, biological, though it is not known exactly what mechanisms are involved. It seems likely that resistance to infectious diseases has a genetic component, and it has been suggested that the synthesis of immunoglobulin is affected by genetic loci on the X chromosome, so that the female with two X chromosomes is better off than the male with one (*Lancet*, 18 October 1969, p.826). Whilst in females one of the two X chromosomes is inactivated, greater protection against death, disease and disability is given by the fact that either X chromosome may be inactive in different cells of the same individual.

Other physical differences between males and females, such as the male's greater size and weight, may be implicated in the disease-and mortality-differential — for example in the greater male susceptibility to birth trauma. It is known that even in infancy the male metabolic rate is higher (Garai and Scheinfeld, 1968) and, in adulthood, males have a higher blood pressure than females (Hutt, 1972). In general, females mature faster: at five months of pregnancy, females are two weeks ahead of males; at birth they are four weeks ahead. Thus, among premature infants, for whom the greatest danger is death from respiratory distress syndrome, girls are better off than boys since their lungs are likely to be more mature. Presumably females' earlier maturity at such developmental tasks as walking and motor coordination provides some insurance against accidents. Disabilities such as speech defects and reading difficulties, which do not result in death but show a similar preponderance among males, may also be related to the male's increased susceptibility during the course of a longer maturational period.

But it is too simplistic to attribute even these sex differences in physical life chances exclusively to a biological cause. For example, it has been suggested that one reason why adult men die more often than women is because they seek medical help less readily — help-seeking is not concordant with the ideology of the masculine role (*New England Journal of Medicine*, 20 October 1977, p.863). Some male mortality and disease is occupationally related: heart disease to dietary and activity patterns that may be more pronounced in masculine occupations; certain types of cancer to contact with industrial chemicals or radiation.[2] Men are also more prone to diseases of the lung related to smoking, until relatively recently a masculine rather than feminine habit. Where it is possible to compare the disease patterns of men and women with similar life-styles, some of these differences are reduced. In a study of men and women living in religious cloisters with similar diets, housing, occupation, etc., life expectancies were raised in both sexes, but women still fared better, especially in relation to degenerative diseases (such as heart disease) (Madigan, 1957).

It is generally supposed that men's and women's lives are more alike now than they used to be twenty years ago. So is the gap between their physical vulnerabilities narrowing?

There is certainly a rise among women of certain types of 'masculine' behaviour known to be related to the mortality differential. They drink more, smoke more and go out to work more. In the last ten years in Britain the ratio of women to men alcoholics has increased from about 1 in 8 to at least 1 in 3, and is paralleled by a rise in other countries, including the United States, France, Germany and the Netherlands (National Council of Women, 1976; Alcoholics Anonymous, 1980). More women are convicted of drunkenness, and more are labelling themselves as alcoholics. A rise in the risk of developing alcohol-related diseases (cirrhosis of the liver, peptic ulcer, peripheral neuritis, anaemia, etc.) is occurring among women, and it has been suggested that apparently unrelated illnesses such as breast cancer are also stimulated by increased alcoholic intake (United States National Institute of Health, cited in National Council of Women, 1976, p.13). Women alcoholics are said to be more prone than male alcoholics to cirrhosis of the liver and death from alcohol-related diseases, though at the same time a genetic influence on alchohol dependence has been proposed for men but not for women (*British Medical Journal*, 26 November 1970, p.1371).

Reports of the statistics on female alcoholism in the press and in specialist publications over the last few years attribute the increase in 'lace-curtain drinkers' (as female alcoholics have been caricatured) to 'social pressures', such as

---

[2] The possibility of female mortality being occupationally related in this way is less easy to research (and has received much less attention) because of the common statistical practice of associating women with their husband's occupation.

the advent of 'women's lib', domestic stress, especially the isolation and depression experienced by many women and those 'trapped' by children, frustration at having to suppress their own ambitions and desires to fit in with the family's and husband's desires and needs, and the fact that it was now easier for women to buy drink, for example in a supermarket while shopping. [*Times*, 19 January 1976, commenting on a report on *Female Alcoholics* by The Helping Hand Organization]

Smoking accounts for almost half the cancers occurring among British males (Doll *et al.*, 1966). One calculation attributes an excess of 33,862 male deaths in Britain in 1971 to smoking-related diseases, including respiratory cancers, bronchitis and emphysema and ischaemic heart disease. The article in which this calculation appeared concluded: 'Whether men will live longer or women die younger in the future will depend quite largely on whether men smoke less than they do now, or women smoke more' (Preston, 1974, p.763). In tune with this prediction, an analysis of World Health Organization computer data for nine industrialized nations, published in 1977, showed dramatic increases in lung cancer mortality in women in eight of these countries over the period 1965 – 72. The increases ranged from 39 per cent in the United States to 16 per cent in Poland and Japan, with 19 per cent for England — a change that is interpreted as a trend among women away from 'social' and towards 'addicted' smoking (*Lancet*, 30 July 1977). There appears to be no doubt that, at least over the period 1972 – 78 in Britain, cigarette smoking fell more among men than among women; among older women it hardly fell at all (Office of Population Censuses and Surveys, 1979).

Heart disease among women, especially under 45, is another area where the male-female gap has narrowed. Between 1958 and 1970, the mortality rate for ischaemic heart disease in women under 45 increased by 50 per cent. Amongst those aged 45 – 54, it also increased, but not so markedly, while among women aged 55 – 64 the rate was more or less level (Oliver, 1974). Smoking was prominent among the risk factors involved in the detailed study of 150 women suffering from heart disease from which the above figures are taken. This study concluded with typical medical caution:

. . . the incidence of ischaemic heart disease in young women seems to be on the increase, but the cause of the rise in mortality in the years 1958 – 70 is unexplained. The striking increase in the percentage of young women who smoke cigarettes and the increase in the number of cigarettes smoked may be a major contributor. If so, we can expect a steady increase in myocardial infarction in young women. [Oliver, 1974, p.259]

It is arguable whether these trends are unintended consequences of women's 'liberation' or signals of stress pointing to the *failures* of our society in this direction. But what they do demonstrate is an interaction between the protective effect of biological femaleness and the corrosive impact of participation in a socially stressful world.

Changing social mores influence biological indicators of gender differences. These biological indicators themselves are associated with one complex group of factors I have so far avoided discussing in this chapter: hormones. Many attributions of biological cause and social effect in everyday life appeal to hormones as a Pandora's box of explanations. In the next few pages I attempt a short summary of the current status of 'scientific' work on the matter of hormonal explanations of gender-differentiated behaviour, with particular reference to those areas from which it is possible to argue a 'biological' theory of women's oppression. The last section of the chapter places this work in the important context of the politics of sex differences research.

OF MICE AND MEN

'Hormones' are secretions of the endocrine glands (the pituitary, adrenal glands, thyroid, pancreas, ovary and testis). The number and range of hormones circulating in the bodies of males and females is virtually the same, but women produce a preponderance of what are somewhat incorrectly dubbed the 'female' sex hormones, oestrogen and progesterone, and males a preponderance of testosterone and the general group of hormones known as androgens or 'male' sex hormones. Individual variations mean that it is not uncommon to find women with higher androgen levels than those of the 'average' man, and men with higher oestrogen levels than those of the 'average' woman. Androgen and oestrogen are also interconvertible in normal body processes. In both men and women the sex hormones are manufactured not only by the ovary and testis, but by the adrenal glands as well. Their function is primarily to ensure the differentiation of reproductive anatomy and physiology. But other effects are possible, and three of these have been singled out in sex differences research: their impact on the central nervous system, on aggression and on the periodicity of women's state and behaviour.

(i) It's all in the mind

During embryonic and fetal life, when different hormone profiles distinguish between male and female sexual development, there is also an effect on the brain. The hypothalmus (the brain's control centre for several basic bodily systems) is converted either to a cyclical female or acyclical male rhythm. Like much evidence in this field, this demonstration of an effect on the central nervous system (CNS) is derived from animal experiments that indicate another effect of intrauterine sex hormones — a differentiation of adult sexual behaviour. For example, rats display 'normal' female and male mating behaviour only if they are exposed to the 'correct' hormones in the critical developmental period. If female rats are exposed to androgens in the sensitive neonatal period (in some mammals, unlike humans, the sensitive period is just after birth), they behave in inappropriate ways: 'the animal might accept the male, but on a bizarre schedule, such as on 9 consecutive days' (Money and Ehrhardt, 1972, p.68), i.e. she loses her cyclic oestrus. In the presence of normal animals, androgenized females try to mount them (apparently normal females do this too from time to time, thus demonstrating for rats the underlying bisexual potentiality Freud wrote about). Male rats given oestrogens neonatally have lowered intromission and ejaculation rates, and are inept mounters: 'the animals tried to mount from the head, the side, or high up on the back of the receptive female' (Money and Ehrhardt, 1972, p.72). Male rats that are castrated and given no exogenous hormones are simply sexually indifferent. Though rats seem to be the favoured 'guinea pigs' in these experiments, guinea pigs themselves are also used, along with rabbits, hamsters, rhesus monkeys and beagle dogs, but not, of course, humans.

These are long-term consequences of pre-natal/neonatal sex hormones. The fact that in animals some areas of the brain are clearly sensitive to hormones pre-natally raises the question whether there is some more general effect that might account for documented differences in functioning between the sexes in human beings. One such area intensively investigated is that of intellectual functioning. Sex differences here, it is now generally (though not incontrovertibly) agreed[3], relate not to general intelligence but to specific skills. From puberty onwards, females exceed males in verbal ability, and males are slightly better than females at visual – spatial tasks (Maccoby and Jacklin, 1974).

The hypothesis about the relevance of pre-natal brain differentiation to these sex differences goes as follows: the left side of the brain controls language function and the right side is responsible for spatial and non-verbal functions. The left side is usually dominant in both sexes after about the age of 2. But this dominance is more complete and develops at an earlier age in females, accounting for their verbal superiority, and for the superiority of visual – spatial ability in males. The sex-differentiated pattern of dominance results from the pre-natal influence of sex hormones on the brain (Buffery and Gray, 1972; Gray and Buffery, 1971).

Evidence relevant to this hypothesis comes from various kinds of studies, and is ambiguous, even contradictory. For instance, Levy (1972), Sperry (1974) and Witelson (1976) contend that women's spatial-task inferiority is due to a *lesser* degree of lateralization — not, as Buffery and Gray would have it, to a *higher* degree of lateralization. Exposing 4- and 5-year-old children to verbal and non-verbal noises resulted in the conclusion that children of above average IQ from professional homes did not show sex differences, but among less-advantaged children there was a sex difference in the direction predicted by the hypothesis (Kimura, 1963a, b).

Yet another problem is that the 'package' of skills localized in each hemisphere does not correspond to the 'known' sex difference in abilities. This is not entirely surprising since, as Star (1979, p.64) explains, the idea that brain functions are totally specialized into spatial ability (right hemisphere) and verbal ability (left hemisphere) arose as a *theory* among researchers in the early 1960s and has subsequently been taking up as proven fact. One among many possible revisions of the Buffery – Gray argument is that girls' earlier verbal development orients them towards verbal methods of problem-solving and eliminates the need for spatial thought. In this case the male specialization in spatial thought is an 'opting out' strategy (Maccoby and Jacklin, 1974, pp.126 – 7; see also Star, 1979).

The debate about sex differences in cognitive abilities lacks

---

[3] See the discussion in Griffiths and Saraga (1979).

documentation derived from experimentation on human subjects for obvious ethical reasons, but nature herself provides some fascinating and instructive experiments. These consist of individuals whose biological sex deviates from the model of normal female-male dimorphism, in that they were deprived of the usual pre-natal hormonal differentiation. John Money and Anke Ehrhardt (1972) have described a follow-up study of 25 fetally androgenized girls who had either been masculinized by the administration of hormones to the mother in pregnancy (to prevent miscarriage) or by inheritance of a genetic defect called the adrenogenital syndrome: in these girls, the adrenal glands to not produce their proper hormones, cortisol, and this lack causes a rise in the production of male sex hormones. In both cases the internal reproductive anatomy is normal, but the external genitalia have a male appearance. Usually the anomaly is diagnosed at birth, in which case the child will be reared as a girl and receive surgical correction of her inappropriate appearance and also cortisone therapy throughout her life to prevent the development of masculine secondary sexual characteristics.

Money and Ehrhardt compared the development of these girls with those in a control group matched for IQ, socio-economic background and race. Some of their findings were, in the androgenized group:
(1) a greater incidence of 'tomboyism';
(2) a preference for athletic games;
(3) a preference for 'practical' rather than 'feminine' clothes;
(4) more indifference to dolls, and choice of cars, trucks and guns as toys in childhood; less interest in infants later on;
(5) more enthusiasm for 'non-marital' careers;
(6) higher IQ.[4]
This last finding in particular has attracted a great deal of interest. Dalton's work in England pointed in the same direction, and an IQ effect of pre-natally administered progesterone (for toxaemia of pregnancy) was claimed (Dalton, 1968). Does this then mean that there is a direct relationship between male sex hormones and intellectual ability?

So far as Dalton's research is concerned, more recent analysis has shown no improved intellectual attainment in progesterone-treated

---

[4] See Fried (1979) for an important discussion of the selective language in which these 'findings' are communicated.

children (Lynch, Mychalkind and Hutt, 1978). Re-analysis of Dalton's own data has shown statistical errors, which account for her 'finding' of raised IQ among hormonally masculinized children (Lynch and Mychalkind, 1978). Examination of the normal sisters of girls in Money and Ehrhardt's fetally androgenized group some years after the report of the first finding, showed that these also had raised IQs (Ehrhardt and Baker, 1973). Thus, the most likely explanation is that a selective factor is operating, such that children who receive unusual doses of hormones pre-natally are more often found in families with high IQs.[5]

The significance of Money and Ehrhardt's other findings has been questioned on the grounds that the data are derived from mothers' reports, and the mothers were of course aware of their children's medical histories (Maccoby and Jacklin, 1974, p.217).

Whatever the biological basis of observed gender differences, adult gender identity and role vary between cultures and within the same culture according to ethnic and socio-economic group. Margaret Mead's famous study of *Sex and Temperament in Three Primitive Societies* (1935) is not the only anthropological research to document this, though it is by far the best known. She found three societies exhibiting three different gender patterns: the Arapesh where both sexes were gentle and 'maternal', the Mundugumor where hostile, vigorous and unmaternal personalities were the norm for both sexes, and the Tchambuli where the traditional western model was reversed, and assertive, business-minded women with shaved heads were complemented by 'skittish', gossipy, adorned male-housewives (Mead, 1962, p.107). Reviewing the literature on the anthropological perspective more recently, Strathern has said that

---

[5] The existence of a sex-linked recessive spatial gene may also be relevant. One estimate is that 25 per cent of women compared with 50 per cent of men will have this trait (Bock and Kolawski, 1973). But spatial ability is genetically and culturally multi-determined. Cross-cultural work on intellectual abilities has found very large differences between cultures. A comparison of 'traditional' and 'transitional' (to the modern industrialized life-style) peoples has shown higher spatial scores in this latter group (Kagan and Kogan, 1970), and has identified a relationship between spatial abilities and amount of autonomy allowed in childhood: the more autonomy, the higher the spatial test scores (Berry, 1966; MacArthur, 1967).

. . . while attention to gender is universal, in many societies a major preoccupation, there are a handful of cultures which do not seem to utilize it to any great extent. This should alert us to the question of what its uses might be. [Strathern, 1976, pp. 51 – 2]

Aside from conveying a moral about the plasticity of human 'nature', the cross-cultural evidence alerts us to the importance of *socialization* as a major pathway to adult gender identity. Parents are influential in this process (though not omnipotent, as we shall see in Chapter 5); hence the mothers and fathers of the hormonally masculinized girls in Money and Ehrhardt's study are likely to have been instrumental in conveying to their daughters notions of femininity revised to fit their medical biographies.

It is from such natural experiments as the subjects in Money and Ehrhardt's study that much has been learnt in recent years about the relative importance of biological sex (chromosomes, reproductive anatomy and hormone profiles) vis-à-vis the social perception and inculcation of femininity and masculinity. Among the substantial group of cases examined and discussed by researchers since the 1960s, by far the most amazing, horrific and persuasive is that of the identical male twins reported by Money and Ehrhardt. At 7 months the twins were circumcised by electrocautery; the electrical current used on one twin was too powerful and it burnt off his penis entirely. Naturally stunned by this surgical mishap, the parents agonized about what to do until a consultant plastic surgeon recommended reassignment as a girl. When the child was 17 months old, the parents changed 'his' name, clothing and hair style; four months later surgery to reconstruct his genitals as female was initiated. In the six subsequent years both twins appeared to develop 'normally' — one as a boy, one as a girl. When the twins were 4½ years old, their mother said of the 'girl':

One thing that really amazes me is that she is so feminine. I've never seen a little girl so neat and tidy as she can be when she wants to be . . . She is very proud of herself, when she puts on a new dress, or I set her hair. She just loves to have her hair set; she could sit under the drier all day long to have her hair set. She just loves it. [Money and Ehrhardt, 1972, pp.119 – 20]

As Money and Ehrhardt observe, it is 'abundantly clear that nature has ordained a major part of human gender-identity differentiation to be accomplished in the postnatal period' (Money and Ehrhardt, 1972, p.18; see also Green, 1974 and Stoller, 1968).[6]

(ii) A male problem
Although the boy twin reassigned as a girl in the above case moved from a position of physical dominance over her brother to one of 'mother hen' (Money and Ehrhardt, 1972, p.122) following her new gender categorization, she remained a 'tomboy' in her mother's eyes. Greater physical activity, strength and aggression in males have represented a stereotype of enormous importance in the evolution of sex differences research. In social terms, aggression (however defined, and it often is not) is a male problem: men beat and rape women rather than vice versa; most crimes of violence are committed by males; men are more likely to engage in dangerous and violent sports than women; and so on. Jessie Bernard has put the position (from women's point of view) in a nutshell: 'I think I have no hang-ups about sex differences. I am quite willing to concede male superiority in offensive aggressiveness' (Bernard, 1975, p.23).

In Maccoby and Jacklin's review of sex differences research, aggression emerges as one of three sex-differentiated traits (the others are visual – spatial and verbal ability) for which there is reasonably sound evidence. Before the age of about two years most studies show no sex difference. There is clear evidence that aggression is a learned capacity (Bandura, 1973; Patterson *et al*, 1967; see also Scherer *et al*, 1975). There is also evidence that hormones play a role. Genetic females hormonally masculinized in the womb have elevated levels of threat behaviour and rough-and-tumble play, an effect that has been demonstrated in humans, monkeys and rats. But for both humans and animals it is too simplistic to say that individual differences in aggressive behaviour correlate with different levels of male hormones. In monkeys, dominant males have higher testosterone levels than non-

---

[6] A recent television programme (*Open Secret*, BBC 1, 19 March 1980) questioned the success of this particular gender reassignment. The 'evidence' presented came from psychiatrists who had been called in by the family and were not part of the original advisory team. They were of the opinion that the 'girl' twin looked masculine, behaved in a masculine way, had masculine ambitions, and was a rather troubled person. The last observation is hardly surprising; the others are subjective assessments for which no supporting data were presented.

dominant males, but this is affected by social context, and low-dominance males caged with females show markedly raised testosterone levels (Rose *et al* 1972).

The tempting hypothesis that male criminal behaviour was under direct genetic control was raised in the early 1970s by the discovery of a number of male prisoners with an XYY chromosome constitution.[7] However, when the excitement died down, it became apparent that while a small number of XYY males may be in prison or mental institutions, the majority are not (Meyer-Bahlburg, 1974). The XYY condition is not itself associated with higher androgen levels. Strikingly, men with an XXY condition, who possess an extra *female* chromosome and low androgen levels, are found in roughly the same proportion as XYY men both in the general population and in mental and penal institutions. John Money suggests that it is the possession of the extra chromosome that pre-disposes toward deviance, and observes the inherent political unacceptability of the idea that XXY males are as aggressive as XYY ones:

. . XXY has none of the fake, supermale magic of an extra Y chromosome relentlessly dictating its possessor to be the victim of his superaggressiveness. The male stereotype in the popular imagination cannot tolerate the idea of the extra X chromosome of the female making the man who possesses it more aggressive. [Money, 1970; cited in Weitz, 1977, p.20]

Summarizing their review of the evidence on the biological predisposition to aggression in males, Maccoby and Jacklin comment that

We have been emphasizing male aggression to the point of allowing females to be thought of, by implication, as either angelic or weak. Women share with men the human capacity to heap all sorts of injury upon their fellows. And in almost every group that has been observed, there are some women who are fully as aggressive as the men. Furthermore, an individual's aggressive behaviour is strengthened, weakened, redirected, or altered in form by his or her unique pattern of experiences. [Maccoby and Jacklin, 1974, p.247]

Accordingly, as these experiences change, so ought the social record of gender patterns in aggression. Beginning in the 1960s, there are suggestions that women are becoming more involved in 'criminal'

---

[7] In France, the issue of genetic determinism in criminality was even offered as a legal defence in one case (Weitz, 1977, p.19).

types of activity. For example, in the United States between 1960 and 1974 there was a 108 per cent increase in arrests among females, compared with a 23 per cent rise among males (Crites, 1976, p.33), and, in Britain, a 225 per cent rise in violent offences committed by women over the period 1965 – 67 (100 per cent for men) (Smart, 1979).

Whatever the 'real' change in women's behaviour, the altered disposition of law-enforcing agencies to find more women guilty of criminal behaviour is important. To assume a direct causal relationship between the rise of the women's liberation movement and a desire on the part of women to emulate the male pattern of criminality is problematic, as Crites (1976) and Norland and Shover (1977) have pointed out. Moreover, in the United States at least, the crime figures are capable of a different interpretation, which is that there have been some gender shifts between crime categories but no sudden marked rise in the overall percentages of crimes committed by women (Steffensmeier, Steffensmeier and Rosenthal, 1980). Most female offenders are poor and commit crimes in order to survive economically; they are very unlikely to have direct contact with the women's rights movement.

No one seems to have investigated the chromosome constitutions of female criminals. The most probable reason is that for women criminals a different and more gender-appropriate version of the biological model has operated: the view that women's behaviour is controlled by the hormones of their menstrual cycle.

(iii) The curse of women

Three football players decided to get married on the same day and to spend the wedding night at the same motel. They had worked out signals in advance: At the moment of climax, the players were to yell, 'Touchdown!'

The big night finally arrived. From the star quarterback's room, after five minutes, came the yell 'Touchdown!' Five minutes later, the all-state tackle yelled, 'Touchdown'.

In the center's room, all was silent. Finally, the other two players heard the center muttering, 'Game postponed. Muddy field'. [Delaney *et al*, 1977, pp.96 – 7]

Beside being a muddy field for bedmates (whether football players or not) and the 'curse' that typically taboos sexual intercourse, menstruation has been a muddy field throughout women's history. In the nineteenth century, it was (as we shall see in Chapter 6) the reason doctors gave why women could not expect (or hope) to live the same sort of life as men. In the twentieth century, less overt biological determinism has predominated among 'experts', but there is still a widespread suspicion that the periodicity of women's hormone levels makes them unequal citizens. In the first place, as Bardwick puts it, the theory is that

The menstrual cycle and pregnancy reinforce an awareness of internal reproductive functions . . . women have a close psychological relationship to their reproductive system, which is a frequent site for the acting out of impulses, especially aggression, and its derivative, sex anxiety, and maternity – pregnancy fears. [Bardwick, 1970, pp.3 – 4]

This mirroring of the anatomy in the psyche is a major component of Freudian theory. In the second place, women are held to be victims of the recurrent 'normal crises' of menstruation, exemplifying in their moods and behaviour the ebb and flow of their hormones. This is the reproductive machine model of women, according to which the body – mind connection is so close that women's behaviour can only be explained in terms of their possession of a uterine physiology (Oakley, 1980). Menopausal and post-menopausal women do not escape from this distorted view but are special victims, since the menopause is seen both as something really terrible and as an invented feminine neurosis: moreover, it provides a convenient excuse for the behaviour of all middle-aged women (Weideger, 1978).

The menstrual hypothesis of gender differences boils down to the description and consequences of something called the pre-menstrual syndrome. This was introduced by Frank in 1931 as a feeling preceding menstruation of 'indescribable tension', irritability and 'a desire to find relief by foolish and ill-considered actions' (Frank, 1931, p.1054). The pre-menstrual syndrome has since been associated in a proliferation of studies with such varying types of behaviour as violent crimes (Cooke, 1945; Dalton, 1961; Morton *et al.*, 1953; Ribeiro, 1962), death from accident or suicide (MacKinnon and MacKinnon, 1956; Mandell and Mandell, 1967), accidents (Dalton, 1960a), admission to hospital with acute psychiatric illness (Dalton, 1959; Janowsky *et al*, 1969), taking a child to a medical clinic (Dalton, 1966), and loss of control of aircraft (Whitehead, 1934).

This seems an impressive record. However, the problem lies not so much in the women but in those who have researched them. Five main problems are identified by Mary Brown Parlee (1976) in her critical review of these studies.

(1) Many are correlation studies, which do not establish causal relationships. Gynaecologists observe that psychological/emotional factors affect the timing of menstruation (Lloyd, 1970, p.473; Benson, 1964, p.573), and many women can confirm this from their own experience. Moreover, showing that, for example, women who commit crimes are more likely to be in the latter part of their menstrual cycle does not justify the generalization that women in this phase of the cycle are more likely to commit crimes.

Many correlation studies are vague or weak on the issue of establishing the timing of menstruation. Frequently, a definition of the 'pre-menstruum' or 'paramenstruum' is taken that is either not spelt out by the investigator or so broad that a fair proportion of the female population would be expected to be in that phase of the menstrual cycle anyway. This difficulty weakens Dalton's well-known work on the relationship between schoolgirls' test performances and menstruation (1960b), which concluded that for 27 per cent there was a fall in intellectual performance in the pre-menstrual phase of the cycle. (For 17 per cent there was an improvement pre-menstrually, and for 56 per cent no change was found.)

(2) Where actual data on pre-menstrual symptoms are collected, the manner of collection usually leaves a great deal to be desired. For example, how do symptoms experienced by individual women prior to menstruation compare with those experienced at other times in the cycle? What *are* the symptoms of the pre-menstrual syndrome? Over 150 are mentioned in the literature: this seems rather a lot. A small study undertaken by Zimmerman and Parlee tested fourteen schoolgirls throughout the menstrual cycle on arm and hand steadiness, galvanic skin response, ability to judge the passage of time and problem-solving ability, and found that only arm and hand steadiness corresponded roughly to the stereotype of the pre-menstrual syndrome, with greater unsteadiness during menstruation, followed by the pre-menstruum. On the other measures there was no consistent correlation with stage of the cycle; and on problem-solving, pre-menstrual scores were as high as those mid-cycle (Zimmerman and Parlee, 1973). Neither analysis of unstructured verbal material nor self-recording of cycle symptoms is free from the bias of living in a

culture in which women's behaviour is widely expected to vary with stage of the menstrual cycle. With appropriate confusion, Dalton's study of punishment records in prisons and schools failed to show 28-day cycles for males, but did show them for female prisoners and schoolgirls — both those who were menstruating and those who had not yet begun to menstruate (Dalton, 1964). When Koeske and Koeske (1975) gave information about a hypothetical female student to a sample of men and women, they included data on her psychological state, external life-events and menstrual cycle phase. The onset of negative moods was uniformly attributed to menstrual cycle phase and the influence of external events discounted.

(3) In a study by Paige (1971) of pill-users and non-pill-users, severity of bleeding turned out to be a better predictor of pre-menstrual anxiety in all the women, suggesting the common-sense conclusion that some pre-menstrual anticipation is due to the inconvenience and discomfort of the physical event of menstruation itself. Women with menstrual problems often have difficulty in getting doctors to recognize the existence of a physical problem. Like many physical problems occurring after childbirth, menstrual difficulties are ascribed to psychic state (Weideger, 1978).

(4) Most of the studies of the pre-menstrual syndrome are consistent with an interpretation of a mid-cycle peak having positive traits, as well as of a pre-menstrual syndrome of negative symptoms. So why is there such an exclusive emphasis on *negative* symptoms?

(5) Men have moods too. Human beings experience various cyclical physiological phenomena (Luce, 1970), and Hersey (1931) found cycles of emotionality in males ranging from three-and-a-half to nine weeks in length. Since then, monthly cycles in men have been reported for body temperature (Kuhl *et al.*, 1974), weight (Luce, 1970), beard growth (Harkness, 1974) and pain threshold (Smolensky *et al.*, 1974). Male cycles have also been documented in schizophrenia, manic-depression and epilepsy (Richter, 1968). In Denmark researchers charting urine levels of male hormones in a sixteen-year study found a pronounced 30-day rhythm (Luce, 1970, p.111). Finally, Persky (1974) tested the moods of 29 women at three points in the menstrual cycle and compared them with those of a male control group. He found the average values for all psychological variables closely similar.

THE POLITICS OF 'SEX DIFFERENCES' RESEARCH

A curious relationship between the size of people's feet, their sex, and whether they are left- or right-handed has been discovered by American researchers. After measuring the foot sizes of 150 individuals, they were able to show that there was a strong association between right-handedness and a right foot bigger than the left — and vice versa — in men. In women, the reverse is true: right-handed women tend to have bigger left feet, and vice versa. [*Sunday Times*, 25 June 1978]

Unless this research were prompted by some charitable intention on the part of shoe-manufacturers and retailers to sell different-sized shoes to accommodate people's different-sized left and right feet, it is difficult to see what relevance it could have to any aspect of social or personal life. Like most of the 'scientific' research on sex and gender differences on which this chapter has had to draw, it is based on the assumption that sex differences matter — and that they matter more than sex similarities. In this way scientific work starts from and reinforces the status quo of everyday beliefs about the roles of men and women. In the closing section of this chapter I add some important caveats to the 'evidence' summarized in the preceding pages.

Firstly, the search for sex differences inevitably serves to magnify them and 'obscures the fact that they may be the conveniently stereotyped extremes of broadly overlapping potentialities and functions' (Star, 1979, p.63; see also Lloyd, 1976). Even in the case of biological sex polarity, around half a per cent of the population is markedly intersexual (Overzier, 1963). The large overlap between the sexes on all characteristics of personality and behaviour is veiled by the common strategy of investigating some trait (e.g. cyclical mood variation) in single sex groups. Where dual sex groups of subjects are taken, some 'sex differences' are bound to occur for statistical reasons. In one longitudinal study in which 35 categories of behaviour were rated yearly for 57 females and 58 males, 7 per cent of 442 female – male differences achieved the 5 per cent level of significance. This is hardly greater than the number of 'findings' that would have been expected to occur by chance (Tresemer, 1975).

Secondly, socialization processes are quite sufficient to account for most of the observed and 'documented' sex differences. The socialization effect cannot be dismissed even from research on neonates, one of the two fields to which sex differences researchers have most hopefully looked for 'pure' data (the other field is the cross-cultural one). One striking omission is that much of this research does not control for the impact of circumcision, which is an injury inflicted on 80 – 90 per cent of North American male babies with relevant identifiable behavioural consequences in the direction of altered arousal levels, more wakefulness and more irritability (Richards *et al.*, 1976).

Thirdly, much sex differences research is conducted on the assumption that conclusions about human behaviour may be drawn from studies of animal behaviour. Such extrapolations ignore (a) the importance of learning in humans, (b) the much greater complexity of humans' verbal communication, and (c) the tremendous extent to which humans are able to manipulate their environment.

Fourthly, biology is not a 'given', a cultural constant. The biological body and its 'natural' divisions are not perceived in the same way in all cultures, or by different social groups within the same culture (S. Ardener, 1978; see also E. Ardener, 1971, 1977; Williams, 1975). One reason why the nature versus nurture debate is outmoded, in other words, is because nurture affects nature.

Last, but by no means least, the status quo that much scientific research on sex differences claims to discover is one that legitimizes the social inferiority of women. Jessie Bernard asks:

How does it happen that so much is made of the fact that the blood of males has more androgen than that of females, but nothing is made of the fact that it also has more uric acid? And how does it happen that the net effect of the vast corpus of research leads to the conclusion that men are superior to women on all the variables that are highly valued in our society, namely: muscular or kinetic strength, competitiveness, power, need for achievement, and autonomy? In brief, the components of the archetypal macho variable, offensive aggressiveness? These are the variables that interest men. These are the variables they judge one another by. These are the variables that are rewarded in our society. [Bernard, 1975, p.10][8]

---

[8] Those who make this observation tend to be female. Lehrke (1973) notes that, of those researchers accepting the hypothesis of greater male variability in intelligence, all have been males, whereas all who have rejected it have been females. The issue is not one of bias, but one of the contrasting perspectives that 'opposite' sexes are bound to bring to the same question.

Among the stimuli within the scientific community that led the debate about sex differences to assume the form it did in the late 1970s were: (1) the counting of chromosomes first made possible by the work of Tjio and Levan in 1956; (2) the development of the radio-immunoassay method of measuring body hormones in the late 1960s; (3) the demonstration of cellular uptake of radioactively labelled oestrogen in individual brain cells in the early 1960s (Michael and Glascock, 1963), which paved the way for speculations about the hormonal basis of adult gender differences. These can hardly be considered to be completely accidental discoveries. They occurred in the political context of a sexist medical – scientific community with a shared ambience and shared standards of rewarded achievement (Kuhn, 1962), and were publicised in a society in which the position of women had come, once more, to be regarded as something of a riddle.[9] In the nineteenth century, a nascent feminist uneasiness produced scientific theories of great biological simplicity. In the 1900s, the era of the suffragettes, a concern with the relative intelligences of men and women flourished. Today, the issue is one of the origin of the present gender role system. From the emphasis on cultural factors evident in the 1950s and 1960s, we have moved through the middle ground of an interactionist line back towards outright biological determinism as the assertiveness of women shows no sign of abating. For, as Crook (1970) has pointed out, in situations of social change, biological explanations may assume the role of an ethical code akin in their moral persuasiveness to religion. They provide powerful, easily understood arguments about the undesirability of change by fuelling a retreatist emphasis on the immutability of the natural world.

---

[9] The same is true of research on ethnic differences (Lynn, 1978).

CHAPTER FOUR

A Kind of Person

The typical female: 'someone who: does not use harsh language; is talkative, tactful, gentle; is aware of the feelings of others; is religious, interested in her own appearance, neat in habits, quiet; has a strong need for security, appreciates art and literature, and expresses tender feelings'. [Fransella and Frost, 1977, p.43]

Women are human beings. But a society organized around gender divisions does not yield a concept of normal or ideal personality applied equitably to both genders. The first section of this chapter examines how women are defined in relation to the prevailing masculine standard of normality. The next four look at key components of the feminine personality stereotype: passivity, instability, materiality and maternalism. In a final section I set these in the context of women's development as a subordinate group within a culture dominated by the interests and perspectives of the 'opposite' gender. Chapter 5 takes up the question of the way in which feminine personality arises: what social influences amplify the biological division so as to produce special personalities in women?

HOMO SAPIENS

The name of the race is Man. Homo erectus became homo sapiens, the noun 'embracing' woman but relegating her to a sub-group, its adjectival qualification suggesting that the wisdom marking Man's descendancy from animals is a male trait. The labelling habits of the nineteenth-century evolutionists were contiguous with the conventions of their culture: men represented the norm with which women were (usually invidiously) compared (E. Morgan, 1972). They still do. Femininity is defined in relation to masculinity, not the other way around: the media offer special programmes or features for women, but not for men, since men are the general audience at whom the bulk of media provision is aimed; in textbooks on sex roles, aggression appears first and is discussed as a positive trait, while feminine passivity comes second and is negatively valued (e.g. Weitz, 1977);

questions about inequality in patterns of female and male employment are phrased as questions about the 'failure' of women to make use of their opportunities, in terms of the 'under-achievement' of women (what about the under-achievement of men in the home?). This last example is particularly telling, since it points to the devaluation of femininity: those concerns with which women have traditionally occupied themselves and for which their personalities are supposedly most suited, count for nothing when goals of equality and equity are formulated.

In a very important sense, it is normal to be a man and abnormal to be a woman. Rosenkrantz and his colleagues (1968) asked 154 people to rate 122 bipolar personal qualities (e.g. 'not at all aggressive' versus 'very aggressive') in terms of their relevance to the 'average female' and the 'average male'. A third of the qualities were differentiated by gender in the sample's ratings, and 71 per cent of these 'stereotypic' items had the masculine pole designated as more socially desirable. The stereotype of the typical female produced by the study was quoted at the beginning of this chapter. By comparison, the typical male emerged as

someone who: is aggressive, independent, unemotional, or hides his emotions; is objective, easily influenced, dominant, likes maths and science; is not excitable in a minor crisis; is active, competitive, logical, worldly, skilled in business, direct, knows the ways of the world; is someone whose feelings are not easily hurt; is adventurous, makes decisions easily, never cries, acts as a leader; is self-confident; is not uncomfortable about being aggressive; is ambitious, able to separate feelings from ideas; is not dependent, nor conceited about his appearance; thinks men are superior to women, and talks freely about sex with men. [Fransella and Frost, 1977, pp.43 – 4]

In a second study, the Rosenkrantz questionnaire was given to 79 mental health clinicians (Broverman *et al.*, 1970). The hypothesis was that personality traits regarded as socially desirable are positively related to ratings of normality, mental health and adjustment. The clinicians were divided into three groups: the first group was asked to fill in the questionnaire with normal adult men in mind, the second group for normal adult women, and the third group was asked to describe a 'healthy, mature, socially competent person'. Socially desirable masculine characteristics were seen as healthier for men than for women. Healthy women were more submissive, less aggressive, less competitive, more excitable, more easily hurt, more emotional, more conceited about their appearance and less objective than healthy men. This, say Broverman *et al*, is a powerful negative assessment of feminine personality and 'seems a most unusual way of describing any mature, healthy individual' (Broverman *et al*., 1970, p.5). It points to a double standard of mental health. For a woman to be considered mature and healthy, she must behave in ways that are socially undesirable and immature for a competent adult. The conflict is unavoidable, for if women 'choose to act in the more socially desirable and adult ways preferred by their culture, they risk having their femininity questioned. If, however, they choose to act in the prescribed feminine way, they are accepting a non-adult status' (Walum, 1977, p.10).

This conflict, between being a woman and being a person, is central to women's psychological development. The 17-year-old Sylvia Plath wrote:

I want to be free — free to know people and their backgrounds — free to move to different parts of the world so I may learn that there are other minds and standards besides my own. I want, I think, to be omniscient . . .

In the same piece, 'Reflections of a Seventeen Year old', she also said,

I have a terrible egotism . . . I am 'too tall' and have a fat nose, and yet I poke and prink before the mirror . . . I have erected in my mind an image of myself — idealistic and beautiful. Is not that image, free from blemish, the true self . . . [Plath, 1977, pp.37 – 8]

In terms of outward appearance, Sylvia was a very feminine person. But she was also a very determined person, with a strong commitment to a writing career. Between the ages of 17 and 24 she had many minor publishing successes and added a long list of scholastic achievements to an already impressive record. A suicide attempt at 21 followed some minor setbacks; she convinced herself she would never succeed as a writer. Readjusted with psychiatric help, which she later satirized in her autobiographical novel *The Bell Jar* (' "Suppose you try and tell me what you think is wrong" ', said the psychiatrist. 'What did I *think* was wrong? That made it sound as if nothing was *really* wrong, I only *thought* it was wrong' — Plath, 1963, p.137), Sylvia continued her search for freedom, omniscience and femininity. In 1956, on a Fulbright scholarship to Cambridge, she told her mother 'I would smother if I didn't write . . . Writing sharpens life; life enriches writing', adding, as reassurance,

> Don't worry that I am a 'career woman', either. I sometimes think that I might get married just to have children if I don't meet someone in these two years . . . I am definitely *meant* to be married and have children and a home . . . [Plath, 1977, p.232]

In Cambridge she met and later married a fellow poet, Ted Hughes. During the courtship she described the flavour of the relationship and its impact on her personal ambitions to her mother thus:

> Last night while I peeled mushrooms to go with our dinner of sweetbreads, he read me aloud from a book of Celtic tales we just bought and from Dylan Thomas' story book, *Portrait of the Artist as a Young Dog*. I can't tell you how wonderful it is to share so completely my greatest love of words and poems and fairy tales and languages . . . I shall be one of the few women poets in the world who is fully a rejoicing woman, not a bitter or frustrated or warped man-imitator, which ruins most of them in the end. I am a woman and glad of it, and my songs will be of fertility, of the earth . . . I shall be a woman singer, and Ted and I shall make a fine life together. [p.291]

They had a fine life together for six years. Sylvia housekept in a three-room rented flat ('I'll make it like an ad out of *House and Garden*' — (p.324)), and finally in a rambling Devon farmhouse. When Ted's first book of poems was accepted for publication she said

> I am more happy than if it was my book published! I have worked so closely on these poems of Ted's and typed them so many countless times through revision after revision that I feel ecstatic about it all.
>
> I am so happy *his* book is accepted *first*. It will make it so much easier for me when mine is accepted . . . I can rejoice then, much more, knowing Ted is ahead of me. [p.340]

In 1957 her comment, in a letter to her mother, was

> I envision myself as writing in the morning and reading widely and being a writing-wife. I am simply not a career woman, and the sacrifice of energy and lifeblood I'm making for this job [a temporary teaching position at Smith college] is all out of proportion to the good I'm doing in it. My ideal of being a good teacher, writing a book on the side, and being an entertaining homemaker, cook and wife is rapidly evaporating. I want to write first, and being kept apart from writing, from giving myself a chance to really devote

myself to developing this 'spectacular promise' that the literary editors write me about when they reject my stories, is really very hard. [p,377]

At the beginning of 1960 her first child was born; a little while later Ted began to use a room in someone else's house because

It is impossible for him to work in this little place with me cleaning and caring for the baby, and when he is out, I have the living room and desk to myself and can get my work done . . I find my first concern is that Ted has peace and quiet. I am happy then and don't mind that my own taking up of writing comes a few weeks later . . .' [pp. 443 – 4]

Later still they began to share the use of this room and the care of the baby: 'the mornings at the study are very peaceful to my soul, and I am infinitely lucky we can work things out so I get a solid hunk of time off, or rather time on, a day' (p.449). She did all the housework, trying to fit it into a schedule so that it did not intrude into her writing time. She discovered a 'new and exciting hobby' — making clothes for little Frieda: 'I don't know when anything has given me as much pleasure' (p.461), an interest in domesticity that was heightened by the move to Devon and the birth of her second child. 'Ted's a saint,' she wrote to her mother, 'minding Frieda all day, making me mushrooms on toast, fresh green salads and chicken broth. I hope when you come [on a visit from the States] we can give him a six week holiday from any baby care' (pp. 523 – 4). She herself felt exhausted; as the new baby slept more, she took over the care of Frieda and said, wistfully, 'Perhaps at the end of the month I shall be back in my study again' (p.525). She was:

I am enjoying my slender foothold in my study in the morning again. It makes all the difference in my day. I still get tired by tea time and have spells of impatience for not doing all I want in the way of study and reading. But my mornings are as peaceful as church-going — the red plush rug and all and the feeling that nothing else but writing and thinking is done there. [p.530]

At about this time, Ted Hughes started a relationship with another woman and four months later he left Sylvia. The separation was a relief for her in some ways, because it freed her from the strain of living in a disintegrating marriage, and because it restored to her the idea that she was an independent person. She bought new clothes, had her hair restyled ('It is amazing how much my new hairdo and new clothes have done for my rather shattered morale' — p.380), voiced optimism about her future as a writer, and generally reconstructed her identity. In practice, however, managing without Ted proved difficult: housing and money problems, the bitterly cold strike-ridden winter of 1962 – 3 and her own and the children's ill-health wore her down. Some weeks before her death from suicide she said

It is so frustrating to feel that with time to study and work lovingly at my books I could do something considerable, while now I have my back to the wall and not even time to *read* a book . . .
I just haven't felt to have any *identity* under the steamroller of decisions and responsibilities of this last half year, with the babies a constant demand . . .
How I would *like* to be self-supporting on my writing! But I need *time*.
I guess I just need somebody to cheer me up by saying I've done all right so far. [pp.570, 583 – 4]

Although she lived in the shadow of Ted Hughes, death made Sylvia Plath famous. The women's liberation movement in particular adopted her as a martyr, a symbol of man's oppression of woman. [1] I have described her life here because it illustrates the opposed pull of the two motivations in women's personalities: to become and be a person, making a contribution to society based on individual worth, and to become and be a woman, matching conventions of femininity. The battles fought in her life were those between, on the one hand, ideals of femininity — a 'nice' girl, a devoted wife, a good mother, an imaginative and efficient housewife — and, on the other, the urge that she had to write, to publish and to be publicly acclaimed a success for her talent and the hard work she had put into its realization. The battles were intensified by the fact that both kinds of ambition — the feminine and the individual — were part of her personality.

Of course, Sylvia Plath's life also illustrates a great many other relevant aspects of women's lives: the frustration of creativity by domestic responsibility; the function of mental illness as an acceptably feminine escape route; the economic vulnerability of women and children as dependents of men. But these also are related to the structural *ambivalence* surrounding the character and position of

---

[1] This is, of course, an oversimplification — her life and death signify much more than that. In the same way, attempts to psychoanalyse her life around the twin themes of obsession with her father and ambivalence about being a woman (e.g. Butscher, 1977) mystify what it was she felt she was struggling against, and what she was trying to make of her life.

women in industrial society (Oakley, 1974a, pp.80 – 90). In *Thinking About Women* (1968), Mary Ellmann makes the crucial point that every virtue in the stereotype of feminine character implies a feminine vice: chastity entails frigidity, intuition is counterposed by irrationality, motherhood involves domination, and so on. Thus women's characterization as feminine can be dissected into certain key qualities, each of which is capable of both negative and positive valuation. We find these qualities portrayed both in stereotypes of femininity and in women's actual behaviour and self-perceptions. Four of these central qualities are passivity, instability, materiality and maternalism.

STANDING (OR LYING) STILL: FEMININE PASSIVITY

In *Ways of Seeing*, John Berger describes the representation of women in art, the passive female contrasting with the active male; it is of course significant that he places men first:

A man's presence is dependent upon the promise of power which he embodies
. . . A man's presence suggests what he is capable of doing to you or for you . . .
By contrast, a woman's presence expresses her own attitude to herself . . .
Her presence is manifest in her gestures, voice, opinions, expressions, clothes, chosen surroundings, taste . . .
One might simplify this by saying: *men act* and *women appear*. Men look at women. Women watch themselves being looked at. This determines not only most relations between men and women but also the relation of women to themselves. The surveyor of woman in herself is male: the surveyed female. Thus she turns herself into an object — and most particularly an object of vision: a sight. [Berger, 1972, pp.45 – 7]

The idea that women are naturally passive has a long history.

Men have been generals, kings, writers, composers, thinkers and doers; women have been wives, mistresses, companions, friends, and helpmates. The very word woman, in fact, emphasizes this dependent anonymous position. It derives from the Anglo Saxon *wifman*, literally 'wife-man'. [Bullough, 1974, p.3]

However, as Bullough points out, we do not really know whether or how women experienced this passivity, since most historical records are written by men. In such records it is often sexually scandalous behaviour on the part of women that ensures their notoriety: Cleopatra, Lucrezia Borgia, Eleanor of Aquitaine, Catherine the Great of Russia — these 'leaders' of 'men' have their places in history defined by their active and unusual sexuality. Elizabeth I of England, who was not sexually scandalous in this way, puzzled historians with her unconsummated love affairs and refusal to marry; some, therefore, concluded she was really a male in drag (Bullough, 1974, p.4).

There is no doubt that two processes have exacerbated this tendency to cast women in a mould of necessary inactivity. The first is the assurance with which many religious ideologies have defined women's place. The second is the massive upheaval in gender roles and perceptions that has accompanied the industrialization of work.

The expulsion of Adam and Eve from the Garden of Eden is not exactly the latest news, but few contemporary happenings have affected women of today any more directly [says Merlin Stone in *The Paradise Papers*]. The image of Eve, created for her husband, from her husband, the woman who was supposed to have brought about the downfall of humankind, has in many ways become the image of all women. [Stone, 1976, pp.1 – 2]

Christian conceptions of womanhood have changed in the course of their evolution. While in the Pre-Reformation Church, Catholicism used a combination of misogyny and asceticism to issue the formula 'women are evil', with the Protestant Reformation this attitude was tempered somewhat, because Protestants believed that everyone shared the right to true belief and the protection of God. Celibacy was attacked on the grounds that the 'family man' was as good as any other; bishops began to marry, if somewhat cautiously, as in the case of Henry VIII's Thomas Cranmer, who wed a German lady and had her carried round in a chest with air holes in it whenever she left the house.

Protestantism drew attention to the importance of living the whole of one's life in a Godly fashion. Hence the priority of surveying family life, which began to be conducted from the ideological vantage point of two kinds of family in particular: those of the 'industrious middle sort', who made up most of the preachers' congregations, and the patriarchal families of the old Testament, who were considered to set the most relevant example. Preachers regarded it as essential to lay down the rules for all aspects of family life: these centred in the proper relationship of husband and wife, which had to be at one and the same

time that of loving companions and unequal partners, the woman acting as a vessel for the relief of her husband's concupiscence and submitting to his dominance in all sexual, domestic and public matters.

Protestant ideology both improved and limited women's status. While it freed them from some of Catholicism's worst taints, it was much more precise about their character, and about the proper location and expression of this character in the family. The woman acquired a 'live-in spiritual advisor' — her husband (Hamilton, 1978, p.69). Masculine authority entailed feminine inferiority, which was rationalized by appealing to biological analogies. A proper wife was the paradigm that replaced that of the evil woman. It was therefore Protestantism that turned an active and aggressive image — that of women's sexuality — into a passive one: women's place is in the home, dependent on, and submissive to, men.

Capitalism and Protestantism are connected 'revolutions'. The Protestant idealization of the home and the family (and women) was 'an inheritance given substance by the capitalistic division of the world into work and home' (Hamilton, 1978, p.22) and, reciprocally, Protestant ideology gave capitalists the tool with which to mythologize the activity of women. What was most important about this mythology was its fabrication of a natural feminine passivity, a tradition that Freud, who has done more than anyone else to equate female biology with feminine passivity, himself inherited. The families into which he was born and which he founded were models of conventionality — wife – mother kept house, reared the children and was submissive to the male head of the household (Puner, 1947). Freud was bitterly attacked by the Church for his irreligious 'science' of psychology, and yet his theory really represents the secularization and apotheosis of Protestant ideology on the subject of the human, and especially the feminine, character.

Freud observed (incorrectly): 'The male sex-cell is actively mobile and searches out the female one, and the latter, the ovum, is immobile and waits passively. The behaviour of the elementary sexual organism is indeed a model . . .' (Freud, 1964, p.114). Noting three meanings of 'masculinity' and 'femininity' in everyday language — the equation with activity – passivity, the biological and the 'sociological' — he was in no doubt as to their relative importance: 'The first of these three meanings is the essential one' (Freud, 1962, p.85). The distinction

between masculine activity and feminine passivity was absolutely central to his work. It enabled him, for example, to characterize women as constitutionally passive, to say that auto-eroticism in women was phallic in nature, and to construct the libido (sexual drive and life-force in general) as 'regularly and lawfully of a masculine nature whether in the man or the woman' (Freud, 1933, pp.612 – 3).

As pure description the Freudian paradigm has a certain merit. The prescription to be passive is to some extent internalized in the social system of which Freud writes and women tend to experience themselves as passive, as objects of other people's experiences rather than subjects of their own.

The passive victim lacks a voice of her own — inarticulateness is the mark of an oppressed group. Patterns of verbal communication are thus one way in which the stereotype of the feminine character is expressed in the reality of female behaviour. D. W. Addington asked two men and two women to read the same passage in a number of different ways. They varied their pitch, rate of speaking and voice qualities — breathy, tense, thin, flat, throaty, nasal and full. A group of listeners (men and women) rated the speakers on 40 personality traits. Female and male listeners were agreed as to which were 'feminine' and which were 'masculine' traits. The same quality in a male voice and in a female voice did not give rise to the same personality description. For example, increased breathiness in a male voice produced a rating of greater youth and artistry, whereas females were seen as more feminine, prettier, smaller, more effervescent and more highly strung. Flatness in both female and male voices was perceived as being more masculine, sluggish, cold and withdrawn. Tenseness in a male voice signified age and cantankerousness; in a female voice, youth, emotion, femininity and lower intelligence. Throatiness made men (predictably) older, mature, sophisticated and well-adjusted, but females with throaty voices were stupid, lazy, boorish, unemotional, ugly, sickly, careless, quiet, uninteresting, apathetic and generally 'cloddish or oafish' (Addington, 1968, p.502).

The moral seems to be, if you're a woman, don't have a throaty voice. There is a biological consideration here: women and men have on average differently sized vocal tracts and females usually have higher-pitched voices than males because their vocal bands are shorter and thinner (Eakins and Eakins, 1978, pp.90 – 1). But research on female – male acoustic differences yielded the conclusion that the

gender gap is much sharper than could be accounted for by biology alone: 'In other words, men tend to talk as though they were bigger and women as though they were smaller than they actually may be' (Sachs *et al.*, 1973, p.75).

Women specialize in what Lakoff has termed 'tag questions' (for example, 'I did lock the door, *didn't I?*'). These are used 'when the speaker is stating a claim, but lacks full confidence in the truth of that claim' (Lakoff, 1975, p.15). A related device is the feminine intonational pattern of a rising inflection at the end of an answer to a question, for example,

'When will dinner be ready?'

'About six o'clock?'

'The effect is', says Lakoff, 'as though one was seeking confirmation, though at the same time the speaker may be the only one who has the requisite information' (Lakoff, 1975, p.17).

Women's reticence is balanced by men's assertiveness. Power is reflected in speech. Barbara and Gene Eakins (1978) taped a year's worth of university faculty meetings, counting 'speaker turns'. The males surpassed the females in number of turns taken, and they spoke for much longer (average *longest* female turn, 10 seconds; average *shortest* male turn, 10.66 seconds). Moreover the number of turns followed a hierarchy of power or status, according to rank, importance or length of time in the department. A study by Zimmerman and West (1975) looked at 'overlaps', interruptions and silences in same-sex and dual-sex conversations recorded in coffee shops, drug stores and other public places in a university community. In same-sex conversations, interruptions and overlaps (an intrusion at the end, rather than in the middle, of a statement) were equally distributed between both speakers. But in female – male conversations 96 per cent of the interruptions and 100 per cent of the overlaps came from males. Eakins and Eakins found a similar pattern in their study: the person who was interrupted most in faculty meetings was a woman, the only member of the department without a PhD; the person who was interrupted least was the male departmental chairman.

Most silences, in Zimmerman and West's study, occurred in female – male conversations, and two-thirds of these followed three moves on the part of the man: an overlap, an interruption and a 'delayed minimal response'. Women may thus be literally reduced to silence by masculine communication strategies. 'Hmmhmm' is a feminine marker linked to this inarticulateness: women in another study each produced more of these than all the men put together (Hirschman *et al.*, 1975).

Such feminine – masculine polarities are apparently at a premium in intimate relationships, and the more intimate the setting (e.g. in bed), the bigger the difference. Pamela Fishman set up a tape recorder in the apartments of three couples and analysed 52 hours of tape-recorded conversation. Some of her findings were:

(1) The men were consistently successful in initiating interactions, while the women's attempts often failed because the men didn't respond — didn't do any 'interactional work'.

(2) The women asked two and a half times more questions than the men did.

(3) The women used attention-getting devices (such as 'Do you know what?') and the men didn't.

(4) The men more often used monosyllabic responses (e.g. 'yeah'). When women used them they did so to punctuate a masculine stream of talk: 'support work'.

A relevant point is that all the participants had 'feminist' sympathies. Fishman called her article 'Interactional Shitwork', and concluded that interactional work is tied up with feminine identity: 'It is not seen as something we do, but is part of what we are' (Fishman, 1977, p.101).

Similarly with humour. Women's humour is essentially passive and consists of laughing at (men's) jokes rather than making them. It is of course important that, as Lakoff notes, our culture contains

a whole genre of antiwomen jokes, based on sexual stereotypes as antiethnic jokes were (and are) based on ethnic stereotypes: women as a group and any woman because of belonging to that group are vain, fuzzy-minded, extravagant, imprecise, long-winded . . . and numerous variants on those themes, concerning jealousy of other women, hat buying, driving, and so on. There are to my knowledge no parallel joke types based on stereotypes of men in general. Even female comediennes don't tell such jokes, probably because men make up the jokes, or at least men seem to establish what constitute acceptable topics for joking about. [Lakoff, 1975, pp.81 – 2]

But even given this, the use of laughter in conversations has a political character. Rose Coser noted the appearance of laughter in the staff meetings of a mental hospital over a period of several months, and found that hierarchy counted. Of 90 witticisms made by staff, senior staff made an average of 7.5 jokes each, junior staff 5.5 each and paramedics 0.7. Witticisms directed at a person were never directed at someone higher in the hierarchy than the person making the joke, and usually the target was someone of lower status (so that paramedics were reduced to making jokes about themselves). Men made most of the jokes (99 out of 103) but women laughed harder, according to the formula 'The man provides; the woman receives' (Coser, 1960, p.85).

How women use their voices and their eyes is part of their general demeanour as feminine people, part of what Henley (1977) has called 'body politics'. Women's passivity appears to consist of a lack of initiation, in a tendency to be the object responding to, rather than the subject constructing, a social situation. This characteristic of responsiveness, which is positively valued by masculine culture, has its negative side in women's instability.

RESPONDING WELL: FEMININE INSTABILITY

Stephen Spender once compared Sylvia Plath's poetry with that of Wilfred Owen, the British war poet

being a woman, her warning is more shrill, penetrating, visionary than Owen's. Owen's came out of the particular circumstances of the trenches, and there is nothing to make us think that if he had not been on the Western Front — the mud and blood into which his nose was rubbed — he would not have warned anyone about anything at all. He would have been a nice chap and a quiet poet. With Sylvia Plath, her femininity is that her hysteria comes completely out of herself, and yet seems about all of us. And she has turned our horrors and our achievements into the same witches' brew.[Spender, 1966, p.26; cited in Ellmann, 1968, pp.84 – 5; see pp.325 – 9 on the importance of the witch in feminine imagery]

As Mary Ellmann notes, the two interpretations are that Owen's 'disturbance' resulted from his appalling war experiences, while Plath's resulted from her 'nature' as a feminine woman. The gulf is in part caused by the blindness men (including Spender) have conventionally had about women's lives; so that if women are appalled by their lives, this fact is often not revealed. But the basic conundrum is wrapped up in the Greek word 'hysteria':

A functional disturbance of the nervous system, characterised by anaesthesia, hyperaesthesia, convulsions, etc, and usually attended with emotional disturbances or perversions of the moral and intellectual faculties. Women being more liable than men to this disorder, it was originally thought to be due to a disturbance of the uterus. [OED]

In other words, women were considered to be emotionally unstable for biological reasons.

Despite the demise of the ancient Greeks, this remains a prominent theme in the feminine stereotype. We saw in Chapter 3 how the impact of the menstrual cycle on women's social and psychological functioning has been researched so as to construct an image of women as unreliable, reproductive machines. In very many aspects of life the view prevails that women can't be trusted because they have poor control of their emotions. Hence employers cite their unsuitability for technically demanding work (Thorsell, 1967); doctors define women as more 'troublesome' patients because of their tendency to consult with emotional difficulties (Stimson, 1976). Feminine instability is seen as a core female trait (Holter, 1970, p.124) and is one of the commonsense understandings about women in industrial societies, expressed in such everyday epithets as 'It's a woman's privilege to change her mind' and in the attribution of 'moods' as explanations of women's behaviour.

In an interesting analysis of reviews of Emily Brontë's *Wuthering Heights*, Carol Ohmann has explored the different characterizations associated with male and female authorship. *Wuthering Heights* was first published under a male pseudonym (Ellis Bell), as were all the Brontë sisters' works. Charlotte later noted the reason, still appropriate today,

We did not like to declare ourselves women, because — without at that time suspecting that our mode of writing and thinking was not what is called 'feminine' — we had a vague impression that authoresses are liable to be looked on with prejudice; we had noticed how critics sometimes use for their chastisement the weapon of personality, and for their reward, a flattery, which is not true praise. [Cited in Ohmann, 1971, p.906]

Ohmann shows how differently *Wuthering Heights* was interpreted when written by Ellis Bell as opposed to Emily Brontë. With the former author, the novel was taken to be a representation of brutality and violence, a celebration of masculine sexual power. One reviewer described the author as 'a rough sailor [with] a powerful imagination' (George Washington Peck, cited in Ohmann, 1971, p.908). He said that the author pretended to understand women but only really understood his (male) view of them. In the reviews of the second edition, when Emily Brontë was its author, the word 'original' — prominent the first time around — is missing; it became a work of 'female genius', a tale typical of women's imagination and peopled by male monsters whose creation was due to the fact that their female author did not understand men. It became principally a love story concerned with the portrayal of emotion, a task for which female writers were of course specially equipped.

Mary Hiatt has looked at the stereotype and reality of emotionality in women's writing generally. She used a computer to analyse passages out of 100 books, half written by men and half written by women, half fiction and half non-fiction. Taking various indices of emotionality (for example the use of exclamation marks and different kinds of adverbs), she found that there were differences between the way women and men write, but that these did not fit the common stereotype. For instance, the men used twice as many exclamation marks as the women, and they used them either as part of their own style or in the speech of male characters. Women used more adverbs of emotion (e.g. 'abjectly', 'happily') than men, and men used more adverbs of pace ('quickly') than women. Women used 'really' much more in both fiction and non-fiction 'in an apparent effort to be credible in the face of disbelief' (Hiatt, 1977, p.106). Verbs suggesting intuition (e.g. 'feel') were used slightly more often by the women, but those suggesting reason or logic were used equally by both sexes. The women's writing proved more stylistically complex and logical than the men's and they were not more longwinded — another prevalent feminine stereotype; woman averaged 21 words per sentence (range 13 – 23) and men 23 (range 13 – 30), but twice as many short (less than six-word) sentences were found in the women's writing as in the men's.

Another mark of women's instability is the tendency of women to specialize in mental illness. This is a proven fact in most industrialized societies (see Table 4.1). Many more women than men are classified as having 'neurotic' disorders and females predominate in all psychosomatic disorders (Silverman, 1968). Weissman and Klerman (1977), surveying 37 reports from a wide range of countries, conclude that the female preponderance in depression is almost universally 2:1. (The exceptions were parts of developing Africa and India. Cross-cultural research is inadequate in this field, as it is in most others discussed in this book.[2])

TABLE 4.1 Admissions by sex and diagnostic groups, mental illness hospitals and units in England, 1977

Diagnosis	Female	Male	Total
All diagnoses	104336	71086	175422
Schizophrenia	14683	14376	29059
Depressive psychoses	15378	7065	22443
Senile psychoses	7111	3134	10245
Alcoholic psychosis	630	1049	1679
Other psychoses	8872	5298	14170
Personality and behaviour disorders	9887	8393	18280
Alcoholism	2955	7667	10622
Drug dependence	484	960	1444
Psychoneuroses	14886	6887	21773
Mental handicap	452	402	854
Other psychiatric conditions	3065	2112	5177
All other conditions*	25933	13743	39676

* Including depression not specified as psychotic or neurotic, epilepsy, undiagnosed cases and admissions for other than psychiatric disorders.
Source: Department of Health and Social Security (1977b). Crown copyright.

If 'depressive psychoses' and 'psychoneuroses' are categories in which women cluster, the social situation of those thus afflicted contains some clues. Gove (1972) and Gove and Tudor (1973) have shown how mental illness statistics reveal a pattern of higher male rates in never-married, divorced and widowed categories and higher female rates in the married population. One study by Hinkle and Wolff (1957) related health to life stress over a number of years and found that the healthiest group on their measures were middle-aged unmarried women.

---

[2] See Murphy (1962) and Leighton *et al.* (1957) for two contradictory sets of findings.

Since only a proportion of those diagnosed as mentally ill become hospital in-patients, GPs' experiences of treating mental illness are highly relevant. Over half of all psychiatric disorders seen by GPs are neuroses (Shepherd *et al.*, 1966). Using twelve-month records from a sample of London GPs, Shepherd and his colleagues found that 18 per cent of the women in the practices had visited their doctors and been given some kind of psychiatric 'diagnosis', compared with 10 per cent of the men. More of the women than the men who were given a psychiatric diagnosis were classed as neurotic. Mood-altering ('psychotropic') drugs are more often given to women than to men by GPs. Looking at repeat prescriptions in general practice in 1970, Balint and others found that three-quarters of these drug users were women (and in the ten years between 1957 and 1967 consumption of these drugs rose by 70 per cent). A more recent study of five group practices showed that 9.7 per cent of the men in the patient population and 21 per cent of the women received at least one psychotropic drug in the year surveyed. Among women aged 45 – 59, 33 per cent received a psychotropic drug (Skegg *et al.*, 1977).

There is little evidence that such drug treatment of depressed women by GPs is effective in curing depression. One controlled trial of imipramine, a very commonly used anti-depressant, found no superiority over a placebo (a drug-free pill) in bringing about a remission (Porter, 1970). This question of the curative capacity of medical treatment in the case of depression is highly relevant to a discussion of feminine personality stereotypes. For, if medical treatment does not cure depression, then it is a way of exercising control over the social functions of women — of ensuring that women conform in practice to the image of femininity that is the stereotyped ideal. Michèle Barrett and Helen Roberts (1978) studied the consulting patterns of middle-aged women and found that GPs often attributed women's anxiety and 'depression' to their inadequate adjustment to domesticity, and that 'readjustment' to domesticity was the dominant aim of treatment. This fits in with what Broverman *et al.* described as clinicians' standards of feminine normality: healthy women are emotionally volatile and in need of protection and help. Accordingly, the commercial promotion of psychotropic drugs relies on a heavily reactionary mythology of women. One advertisement in an Australian medical journal shows a typical 'before' and 'after' situation in which a lethargic, sedentary housewife nursing an inactive hoover is transformed into a bright, cheerful, hoover-pushing housewife via the medical administration of a magic potion (Chapman, 1979).

It is equally clear that many female users of psychotropic drugs are under no illusion as to their prime function in bringing about 'adjustment' to a socially stressful situation. Cooperstock and Lennard found in their Canadian survey of valium that even if its initial use had a physical referent for some users, its continuing use could only be understood 'in terms of "permitting" them to maintain themselves in a role or roles which they found difficult or intolerable without the drug' (Cooperstock and Lennard, 1979, p.335). For male ingesters of valium the problematic role was that of paid employment; for women, it was the domestic role — or, rather, roles, for that was one of the problems. Cooperstock and Lennard summed up the typical female valium-user as experiencing extreme role-strain and an inability to comply with traditional female role expectations, at the same time as feeling it illegitimate overtly to express dissatisfaction and quite impossible to escape the situation. One mother of four teenage children said:

I take it to protect the family from my irritability because the kids are kids. I don't think it's fair for me to start yelling at them because their normal activity is bothering me . . . So I take the valium to keep me calm. That's what my husband wants . . . One of these days I'm going to leave the whole kit and kaboodle and walk out on him. Then maybe I won't need any more valium. [Cooperstock and Lennard, 1979, p.336]

Brown and Harris's recent work on depression in women has made an important contribution to this picture (Brown and Harris, 1978). Looking at an urban population, they found that a third of all women could either be classified clinically as suffering from a psychiatric disorder or were borderline in terms of accepted clinical criteria. Almost all the psychiatric diagnoses were of depression. Examining the women's social situations, both past and present, Brown and Harris found significant associations between life-events and long-term difficulties and the genesis of depression. Four factors in particular made women more likely to react with a depressive disorder to stress: having three or more children under 14, lacking an 'intimate' relationship with a spouse or other adult, loss of mother before the age of 11, and not having employment outside the home. The relationship between these and the severity of life-events and chronic difficulties in the women's lives provides convincing evidence that depression is socially caused, even if it is not thus interpreted by those who diagnose and treat it. Much the same could be said about many cases of depression occurring after childbirth. Childbirth is a life-event that can lead to unhappiness and 'adjustment' difficulties, especially when it occurs in difficult circumstances, though its accompanying hormonal changes suggest to those espousing a 'reproductive machine' model of women that the breakdown is an internal one (Oakley, 1980).

Brown and Harris's work is illuminating on two other counts: firstly, they show why and how depression is concentrated among poor women (23 per cent of the working-class women in the sample as against 6 per cent of the middle-class sample); secondly, they demonstrate how much depression among women remains hidden — half of those in their sample with a definite psychiatric disorder were not being treated for it, and two-thirds of those assessed as 'borderline' had not taken their symptoms to a doctor.

Women's energies in our kind of society appear to be devoted to 'doing good and feeling bad'. Masculine culture delegates to them the care of not only humanity's lowest needs (the 'lavatorial' function of housework, the cleaning of small children, etc.) but its 'highest necessities' — 'the intense, emotionally connected co-operation and creativity necessary for human life and growth' (Miller, 1976, pp.25 – 6). Sociologists have called this the 'expressive' role and seen its performance by women as essential to the stability of the family and society. Yet it is the very *sensitivity* of women to other people's needs that is likely to produce the appearance and the consequence of mental instability — women's instability stabilizes the world.

Depression and oppression are thus linked. Feminine hysteria and depression are reflections and projections of a sex-divided society.

COSMETIC AND COSMIC DISASTERS: FEMININE MATERIALITY

She is too short or too tall, too fat or too thin; her breasts are too small or too big; she has a mole on her face; her nose is too big or crooked; her ears stick out. When beauty becomes the one and only passport to happiness, a morbid sort of self-consciousness results. A girl becomes sure that a flaw so minor no one notices it completely ruins her looks and thus her life. A pimple becomes a cosmic disaster. [Deckard, 1979, p.45]

Such disasters are, as Deckard observes, good for the economy since women's preoccupation with their looks is extremely profitable and the cosmetics industry trades on the probability that no woman will ever be entirely satisfied with her appearance. The careful watching of one's body and its fabrication as a public viewing object, is one of the aspects of femininity Freud referred to when he identified women as narcissistic. Narcissism is not a universal and exclusive characteristic of females: the history of our own society tells us that. *Men's* preoccupation with the bedecking and sexualizing of their bodies is evident (in paintings, for instance) up until the early nineteenth century. Moreover, the question of women's constitutional fixation on beauty is settled for us by anthropologists who have described many cultures where the women go 'unadorned, managing and industrious' and the men 'decorative and adorned' (Mead, 1962, p.69).

Women's obsession with their physical appearance is especially encouraged within a cultural context in which they are parasitic on the work and status of men. Olive Schreiner, a South African writer and feminist, argued this thesis in her *Woman and Labour*, first published in 1911. She observed that the reduction in women's reproductive role, coupled with their exclusion from the process of production (actual and ideological, as in the Victorian precept that 'ladies' do not 'work'), had made women 'parasites' and that 'an intense love of dress and meretricious external adornment is almost invariably the concomitant and outcome of parasitism' (Schreiner, 1978, p.185). Schreiner believed that as women came to play a larger part in production they would adopt a more 'rational' attire and cease to be so concerned with external ornamentation.

The history of women's clothing certainly shows an adaptation to their changed social circumstances. Where the social roles of men and women are highly differentiated, as in nineteenth-century Britain and America, their clothes function as an 'identity kit' (Goffman, 1961, p.20) in the signification of gender. [3] (This is the reason why small children are often unable to name a person's sex unless he or she is

---

[3] This does not mean that non-gender-differentiated clothes (as in the 'unisex' phenomenon) necessarily prove an *absence* of gender divisions.

clothed: the clothes indicate gender, and it is gender not sex that is the salient social fact — Lewis, 1968, p.16).

In the Victorian period, women's dress projected the values of frivolity, delicacy, inactivity and submissiveness. Sleeves fashionable in the late 1830s and 1840s were set so low over the shoulder and so tightly encased the arm that 'it was virtually impossible to raise the arm to shoulder height or make an aggressive or threatening gesture' (Roberts, 1977, p.557). Crinolines turned women into caged birds surrounded by hoops of steel, and boned corsets painfully reduced normal waists to an incredible 14 inches. Artifices of this kind undoubtedly contributed to the lack of vitality many Victorian women felt — culturally-prescribed narcissism induced passivity by mechanical means.

During periods of feminist rebellion, there is usually a change in clothing style. In the late 1880s and 1890s, for example, there was a move towards plainer and more masculine female dress. The new public schoolmistresses and the students and teachers in the new Oxbridge women's colleges adopted an austere style of dress, rejecting ornamentation in order to indicate their serious purpose. In the 1960s and 1970s clothing is self-consciously defeminized among women's liberation movement members. Joan Cassell, a sociologist describing the structure, organization and ideology of the women's liberation movement in the early 1970s, observed:

From the lesbians through radical to reform feminists, demeanour could be arranged on a continuum — the more radical the ideology, the more recognisable the demeanour. Lesbian feminists generally wore jeans or denim workmen's overalls, the baggy kind that hid the shape of the wearer. The pants might be topped by a man's T shirt or workshirt. It was apparent that they were not wearing bras. Their hair was not so much styled as there; they wore no cosmetics; steelrimmed glasses or sunglasses were frequent; footgear was comfortable, with a predominance of heavy men's workboots or sneakers; and jewellery was rare, with the exception of political buttons or women's liberation pendants. Associated with this costume was a recognisable deportment and bearing, a freedom of stride, of stance, of language. These women talked back to street hecklers; carried heavy loads with pride; changed their own tyres; repaired and operated their own public address systems. [Cassell, 1977, pp.82–3]

She compared this with the uniform of women belonging to the much less radical National Organization of Women; members of this wore cosmetics, attractively styled hair, stockings and highheeled shoes. Outfits ranged from unobtrusive pants and tops through dresses and long skirts, to a conspicuous and seductive style of dress associated with vacation resorts for 'singles'. This involved an elaborate hairdo dyed blonde, red, or black, lavishly applied cosmetics, false eyelashes, much jewellery, and skin tight knit pants with a tight knit shirt, emphasizing a cantilevered bra . . . [Cassell, 1977, p.85]

When Susie Orbach (1978) wrote that 'fat is a feminist issue', she drew attention to the need for women to confront the artificiality of these narcissistic images. Many studies (e.g. Kurtz, 1969; Douty *et al.*, 1974; see also Wooley *et al.*, 1979) show how women's attitudes to themselves are bound up with their perceptions of how they look. The young Sylvia Plath reflected on this (p.65), and female asolescents are typically engaged in a dialogue with themselves about the ideal and reality of their physical appearance. Many women are dissatisfied with their weight (Fransella and Crisp, 1974), and although theories about the causes of the highly distressing condition of anorexia nervosa proliferate, there can be no doubt that, in part, over-dieting is an extreme form of a 'formal' feminine response. Femininity has traditionally meant the denial or suppression of all physical appetite. Neither sexuality nor food must be eagerly desired, or the feminine standard (passive sexuality, physical thinness) will be transgressed. Hence Orbach's interpretation that fat women are fat because they are trying to avoid being seen as the ideal woman.

Goldblatt *et al.* (1965) have shown that, as women themselves suspect, obesity has considerable social ramifications. Analysing the weights and social statuses of an American sample, these researchers found 'thin' women distributed unevenly in three social classes. In the high socio-economic status group 37 per cent of women were thin compared with 19 per cent in the middle group and 9 per cent in the low group. Since the percentage of thin men in each group was about the same (10 per cent in the low, 9 per cent in the middle and 12 per cent in the high group) the answer is not simply that poor people overeat a high carbohydrate diet as a stress response to their social deprivation. The answer suggested by the authors is that thin women are preferentially selected for high status positions at home and at work. The packaging of women's fatness or thinness has had another important function in masculine capitalist society: the public display of wealth. Women, their clothes and adornment, have been the property of men (as fathers or husbands) — one is a vehicle for publicising the other. In *The Second Sex*, Simone de Beauvoir points out the connection between the 'show' of a woman's appearance and her duties in the home:

in the first place, she must 'make a good show' where she is herself concerned; in the house, attending to her work, she is merely clothed; to go out, to receive, she 'dresses up'. Formal attire has a double function: it is intended to indicate the social standing of the woman (her standard of living, her wealth, the social circles to which she belongs), but at the same time it is feminine narcissism in concrete form; it is a uniform and an adornment; by means of it the woman who is deprived of *doing* anything feels that she expresses what she *is*. To care for her beauty, to dress up, is a kind of work that enables her to take possession of her person as she takes possession of her home through housework; her ego then seems chosen and recreated by herself. [De Beauvoir, 1960, p.237]

Women's culturally induced preoccupation with external appearances gives rise to the fiction that women's materiality is women's nature. Such a fiction is an essential element in that other construction of femininity: domesticity. Psychiatrist John Cooper developed an inventory of 69 questions designed to assess obsessional traits and symptoms and found that 'houseproud housewives' (women nominated by health visitors as 'unusually houseproud or perfectionist in their approach to housework and childrearing' — Cooper, 1970, p.48 — but otherwise 'normal') had symptom and trait scores similar to those of patients suffering from an obsessional illness. Also significantly, 'normal women' had higher scores than normal men. The questions covered such subjects as attitudes to dirt and contamination, personal and household cleanliness and tidiness, order and routine, repetition, 'over-conscientiousness', moodiness, irritability, pedantry, punctuality and hoarding. Commenting on the fact that symptom scores were a better differentiator between the different sample groups than the trait scores, Cooper deemed it 'disappointing . . . that the houseproud housewives are not better differentiated . . . from the normals' (Cooper, 1970, p.56). In other words, it is 'normal' for women to be houseproud housewives.

MOTHER FIGURES: FEMININE MATERNALISM

Of all the things women are supposed to be, mothers come first. Here the connection with nature is indubitable: *only* women can be mothers.

Women's reproductivity is as powerful a cultural myth as (in the post-capitalist West) their non-productivity. Becoming and being a mother is held out as the primary feminine goal — in the 1980s, as in the 1920s or the 1850s. Two women who became mothers in 1975 said:

It's made me feel more fulfilled. It's given me something in life; I feel that I've *achieved* something now. Whereas before, I mean work and everything, maybe it was the jobs I had, but I always felt like I was in a rut and was never *achieving* anything. But I feel as though I've done something *useful* . . .

I feel older; you're more responsible: you've got someone to be responsible *for*. I suppose when you work, you just pop out for a drink lunchtime, yet I wouldn't *think* of doing something like that now. It's really like living in a different world. [Oakley, 1979, p.263]

Motherhood settles women down and provides a focus for feelings of feminine responsibility. It is 'fulfilling' — both of the social expectation and of the personal desire — though its capacity to satisfy the latter is not so great in reality as in anticipation (when babies are clothed in a mystique that red and squalling infants do not have). As I have argued elsewhere (Oakley, 1974a, 1980), the *glorification* of motherhood is perhaps the most important aspect of capitalist ideologies of femininity. It justifies the restriction of women to the home and is interpreted as a rationale for every facet of husband- and home-work. More than this, the very sentimentalization of motherhood is a problem for women in becoming and being mothers, since it poses the insoluble dilemma of reaching perfection in imperfect circumstances.

It is, however, the symbolic power attached to the idea of women-as-mothers that has a longer and more influential history than either of these dimensions of motherhood's glorification. Although the first mother in Christianity was Eve, the evil temptress, the second was Mary, the chaste and charitable Virgin. Mary symbolizes goodness, purity, gentleness and submission and, beyond a simple representation of the nobility of motherhood, stands for the ideal woman. All women are potential mothers: mothers are good women and good women are mothers. Marian iconography expresses the totality of women's supposed instinctive, tender and asexual devotion to their children. For so contrary to logic and rationality are the demands of mothering that they can only be met by instinct. Donald Winnicott, a prominent child analyst, wrote a book for mothers in which he referred to this. He said

In the ordinary things you do you are quite naturally doing very important things, and the beauty of it is that you do not have to be clever, and you do not even have to think if you do not want to. You may have been hopeless at arithmetic at school, or perhaps all your friends got scholarships, but you didn't like the sight of a history book, and so failed and left school early . . . . But all this does not matter, and it hasn't anything to do with whether you are a good mother or not. If a child can play with a doll, you can be an ordinary devoted mother, and I believe you are just this . . . Isn't it strange that such a tremendously important thing should depend so little on exceptional intelligence! [Winnicott, 1964, pp.16 – 17]

The myth of the maternal instinct has been a long time dying, and is not dead even yet. Of a sample of mothers interviewed in 1975 – 6, 61 per cent believed in it, though 36 per cent of these found that in practise they did not have 'it' when they came face to face with their babies (Oakley, 1979, p.243).

Also central to the paradigm of ideal motherhood is the notion that it absorbs physical energy of a definitely non-sexual kind. Marina Warner notes in her book about the cult of the Virgin Mary how the dominant representation has been of Mary's pregnancy and delivery as spiritual acts. St Bonaventure in the fourteenth century put it nicely, if incredibly:

The Virgin rose and stood erect against a column that was there. But Joseph remained seated . . . taking some hay from the manger, placed it at the lady's feet, turned away. Then the Son of the eternal God came out of the womb of the mother without a murmur or lesion, in a moment . . . . [Cited in Warner, 1976, p.45]

The aphorism is that religions work 'like washing machines: men construct them and women run them' (Ellmann, 1968, p.93). It has taken those twentieth-century sex researchers, William Masters and Virginia Johnson (1966), to show just how nakedly sexual the experience of reproduction can be to real women. Pregnancy, birth and breastfeeding in fact involve all the physiological pathways to erotic pleasure that come into play during masturbation or coitus.

Masters and Johnson investigated the effects of pregnancy on sexual behaviour in 111 women, and also in six pregnant women who agreed to become laboratory subjects and have their physical responses monitored. In general, higher levels of sexual tension were found during pregnancy. The state of the genitalia in pregnancy resembled that during sexual excitement even when no sexual stimulation had occurred. Two of the six women who were studied in the laboratory developed the capacity for multiple orgasms for the first time during their pregnancies. The normal process of relief of pelvic vasocongestion after orgasm did not occur, so that sexual tension was chronic and unrelieved by orgasm. After birth there was a relationship between eroticism and breastfeeding, with the breastfeeding mothers reporting that suckling was sexually stimulating (even occasionally to orgasm) and that they felt guilty about this; they were therefore anxious to resume 'normal' marital relations as soon as possible. If the female nipple is sexually stimulated when men (or other women) suck it, it is not surprising that the same effect occurs when babies do. This is an aspect of motherhood that is omitted from the advice literature and from many women's own conscious knowledge of maternal behaviour. Motherhood and the mother – child relationship are not interpreted as sexual activities except, of course, by psychoanalysts, who take, as we have seen, a partial view of how any physical feelings that might occur may be explained.

DOMINANT STANDARDS

Most research on ideas of feminine personality has been done using white, middle-class and university-educated populations. Yet there are likely to be significant social class and ethnic differences. For example, Turner and Turner (1974) found in a study of black and white students that white men differed from black men, white women and black women in rating 'most women' especially low on the effectiveness/efficiency dimension. They suggest that this is because of sub-cultural differences in the role of women, which in black culture has traditionally been a great deal more 'instrumental' than the role of women in white culture.

Predictably too, investigations of ethnic differences have rarely moved beyond the confines of the industrialized West. One study that did this was that by Huang (1971). She asked some Chinese students (again, the student bias) from Taiwan and some American students to complete Rosenkrantz's questionnaire (see p.64). There were many similarities in the ratings made by both sexes of feminine and masculine characteristics in the two samples, but some differences emerged. By comparison with the American women, the Chinese women saw women as

having a poorer sense of humour and a weaker personality; less conscientious and less resourceful; more selfish; giving up more easily; less dominant; less adventurous, less inclined to act as leader; and more timid, more afraid to be different, and less creative. [Fransella and Frost, 1977, p.46]

Chinese men were even more negative about women, and the gulf between the sexes was much bigger than in the American sample.

One important aspect of research on gender stereotypes is that, when comparing their notions of normal femininity and masculinity with their ideas about themselves, many men and women emerge as conspicuously less gender-typed. In Rosenkrantz's study, for instance, the women saw themselves as 'less female' and the men saw themselves as 'less male' than their stereotypes (Rosenkrantz *et al.*, 1968). This is a remarkably consistent finding across the whole field of gender perceptions. It is also the case that women see themselves as less feminine than they think men would like them to be — though no research appears to have taken up the challenge and found out whether the women are right about this.[4]

Women's personalities, self-perceptions and feminine ideals are formed as part of a male-dominated culture. They have historically been subject to many of the same sorts of social, economic and psychological discrimination as have black people. This means that their psychology and the idealized construction of feminine personality can very largely be seen as an embodiment of subordinate group status.

Jean Baker Miller has put this interpretation in *Toward a New Psychology of Women*. Examining the relations between men and women under the more general titles of 'dominants' and 'subordinates', she shows how both the designated roles of women and their personality types flow from the dominant – subordinate relation. Personality characteristics of subordinate groups form a familiar cluster:

---

[4] I know of no study that looks at whether men think they are less masculine than women would like them to be.

submissiveness, passivity, docility, dependency, lack of initiative, inability to act, to decide, to think and the like. In general this cluster includes qualities more characteristic of children than adults — immaturity, weakness and helplessness. If subordinates adopt these characteristics they are considered well-adjusted. [Miller, 1976, p.7]

A further implication is that the dominant group's model of itself becomes the paradigm of 'normal' human personality and relationships.

The dominant — subordinate split makes for the over-valuation of some aspects of the human potential and the under-valuation of others. Perhaps the most important point is, as Miller puts it, that women as subordinates have become 'the "carriers" for society of certain aspects of the total human experience — those aspects that remain unsolved, (1976, p.23). These have to do with emotional connections between individuals, which are an essential part of human social life and individual psychic health. Connectedness is not possible without the qualities of vulnerability, weakness, helplessness and dependency. It is immediately obvious that the central paradox is that these qualities are negatively described as constitutionally feminine and thus necessarily undesirable (from the dominant group's point of view). Women's involvement in this kind of emotional work has been at great cost to themselves — they have been led to believe that effective thought and action will jeopardize their chances for satisfying emotional experience. The capacity and need for emotional connection becomes a liability, not an asset: women experience powerlessness and low self-esteem and are unable to regard their traditional activities as enhancing self-development and self-fulfilment — 'real work' in the dominant group's paradigm is something that a person does for himself and for money that rewards his effort.

Another significant implication of the construction of femininity within this dominant — subordinate framework is that because women embody the dominant culture's unsolved problems, and because they are the source of life itself, their very existence confronts and challenges men. The result is a powerful mythology of feminine evil centred around two figures in particular: the shrew and the witch.

Shrew A woman given to railing or scolding or other perverse or malignant behaviour; a scolding or turbulent wife.

Witch A female magician; sorceress; a woman supposed to have dealings with the devil or evil spirits and to be able by their co-operation to perform supernatural acts. [OED]

Both appellations convert benign femininity into malignant aggression. Neither shrews nor witches are passive and maternal, and in both stereotypes a wholly suspect active power is substituted for conventional feminine capabilities. In fiction, in historical records and analyses, and in the everyday conceptual frameworks of men and women, both have been, and are, compulsive ways of describing women. Mary Douglas portrays witches as

social equivalents of beetles and spiders who live in the cracks of the walls and wainscoting. They attract the fears and dislikes which other ambiguities and contradictions attract in other thought structures, and the kind of powers attributed to them symbolize their ambiguous, inarticulate status. [Douglas, 1970, p.124]

The powerless position of women is a focus for men's unease. In turn, the prevalence of the witch image robs women of appropriately positive models for their development as individuals. To call a woman a witch was in the past an effective way of denigrating female initiative and independence; today we have substituted more subtle stereotypes, such as that of a 'career-woman', an epithet conveying the same judgement of feminine abnormality and calling up a familiar spectre of illegitimately wielded authority. Yet if women are to protest against accepted stereotypes of femininity, they have to appear to turn themselves into shrews and witches: this is why, in Britain, there is a woman's liberation magazine called *Shrew* and a feminist publishing house called 'Virago' ('A man-like, vigorous and heroic woman' — OED). Virginia Woolf found herself turning into a destructive witch when she confronted the submissive, self-sacrificing feminine stereotype within the thought structure of her own highly creative writing:

And while I was writing this review, I discovered that if I were going to review books I should need to do battle with a certain phantom. And that phantom was a woman, and when I came to know her better I called her after the heroine of a famous poem, The Angel in the House. It was she who used to come between me and my paper when I was writing reviews. It was she who bothered me and wasted my time and so tormented me that at last I killed her . . . I turned upon her and caught her by the throat. I did my best to kill her. My

excuse, if I were to be had up in a court of law, would be that I acted in self defence. Had I not killed her she would have killed me. She would have plucked the heart out of my writing. [Woolf, 1942, pp.236 – 8]

It is in these ways that the kind of people women are supposed to be interferes with the flowering of their initiative. A paralysing incapacity to act outside the closed circle of family relations is the legacy of femininity women inherit.

CHAPTER FIVE

Childhood Lessons

Doctor: 'Come on junior. Only a lady could cause so much trouble. Come on, little one [baby is delivered]'.
Mother: 'A girl'.
Doctor: 'Well, it's got the right plumbing'.
Mother: 'Oh, I'm sorry, darling'.
Father (laughs)
Doctor: 'What are you sorry about?'
Mother: 'He wanted a boy'. [Macfarlane, 1977, p.63]

Conversations of this kind set the scene for a lifetime's lessons. Gender is in most situations the most salient social fact about an individual, both because of its presumed relationship to eroticism and because in the culture of capitalist societies social differences between females and males are a basic structural theme.

Gender is assigned at birth when parents and medical staff view a baby's external genitals. They bring to this occasion all their own preconceptions about the social content and psychic meaning of boyhood/girlhood and manhood/womanhood, matching their categorization of the newborn's genitals with this determination of gender. It is therefore long before she reaches adulthood that a female experiences the full extent of her cultural definition as a secondary feminine being.

IT'S A BABY

Moss (1967) looked at the way mothers and their first-born infants behaved in the first three months of motherhood.[1] Dimensions of behaviour examined included crying, fussing and sleeping in the infant, and holding, feeding, rocking, talking to and stimulating in the mother. He found that male babies 'fussed' more and that the mothers of sons held, attended to, stimulated and looked at their

---

[1] Most research on newborns' behaviour has concentrated on mothers — not because mothers are necessarily the most important influence, but because they are believed to be.

babies more than the mothers of daughters, who characteristically imitated their daughters' vocalizations more than did the mothers of sons. Mothers also hovered over male babies more, trying to anticipate a restlessness that might need maternal intervention; in males discomfort was less easily cured than in females, who 'quieted and restored themselves to a state of equilibrium' more often, thus relieving their mothers of the need to do so. Moss summed up his findings as indicating that

male infants tend to function at a less well-organized and less efficient level than do female infants. The males were more irritable and seemed less facile than females in responding to learning contingencies, particularly in regard to social stimuli. [Moss, 1974, p.151]

A number of questions can be asked about such a study. Do differences in maternal behaviour merely parallel 'natural' differences between female and male infants? Do first-borns behave differently from second or subsequent children? How do fathers behave? Moss looked at the first possibility by statistically controlling for the variance in scores associated with fussing and crying. Some of the maternal differences disappeared when this was done, but the two differentiators of stimulating/arousing male infants more and imitating females more remained. In a similar study (cited in Moss, 1974, p.156) first and second children and maternal and paternal behaviour were compared. First-born children emerged as more irritable than second-born ones, and working-class infants were more irritable than middle-class infants. So far as parental behaviour was concerned, both mothers and fathers spent longer trying to make girls than boys vocalize, but mothers spent longer than fathers on the somewhat different, and more 'masculine', requirement of getting the baby 'to grab for a bell'; fathers spent longer than mothers with both sexes attempting to elicit the desired behaviour.

These findings suggest the complexity that surrounds the task of determining how femininity and masculinity are learnt. Infants are not *tabula rasa* on whom parents inscribe easily decipherable gender messages. As we saw in Chapter 3, males inherit a certain biological disadvantage along with their chromosomal constitution. But what parents do and how babies behave, reflect a two-way influence of biological potential and cultural determinism in which biological and cultural inputs are not likely ever to be clearly identified.

TABLE 5.1 *Sex preferences and reactions*

Wanted girl	22%
Wanted boy	54%
Didn't mind	25%
Had girl: pleased	56%
Had boy: pleased	93%
Had girl: disappointed	44%
Had boy: disappointed	7%

Source: Oakley (1979) p.118.

Let us, nevertheless, look at some of those factors known to be responsible for the development of gender identity. Few parents, in the first place, are indifferent to the sex of their child. In my own study of London women having their first babies in 1975 – 6, three-quarters said in pregnancy they had a definite sex preference and many of those who said they 'didn't mind' added after the child was born that they had minded, but hadn't wanted to voice a preference for fear of being disappointed, or because to do so is regarded superstititously as bringing bad luck. Table 5.1 shows how many women wanted boys and girls and what their reactions were: 93 per cent of those who had boys were pleased; 44 per cent who had daughters were not (as in the delivery room scene above). Whatever treatment girls receive in childhood to point them in the direction of femininity, it is clear that they are more likely to start off as a disappointment to their parents. Dana Breen (1975) found more cases of postnatal depression occurring among mothers of girls than mothers of boys, and in my own study daughters were likely to provoke less positive and more negative feelings in their mothers than sons. And,

In studies of preferences for sons or daughters, it has consistently been found that there is a preference for more males than females and a preference for the firstborn to be male . . There is also some tendency for women with only daughters to intend and have more subsequent children than those with only sons. [Westoff and Rindfuss, 1974, p.633]

Since children asked which sex children they would like to have prefer those of their own sex (Hartley *et al.*, 1962), the question arises whether adult women's stated preferences are theirs or those of their male partners. Do they really want boys, or do they want boys because men do and they want to please men? Elena Belotti in *Little Girls* (1975) discusses 'old wives' tales' predicting the baby's sex ('carrying at the back'/a difficult pregnancy or labour means a girl, etc.) and comments that those indicating femaleness are usually negative evaluations. It is also common, in line with cultural standards, for pregnant women to perceive activity as a male characteristic — so late fetal movements and a slow heartbeat presage a girl. (Bourne points out that the opposite in fact appears to be the case: 'A heart rate which is persisently below 140 beats per minute is usually male, whereas one which is persistently above 140 beats per minute is usually female — 1972, p.64.)

Sex preferences are conscious; gender-differentiated treatment of children often is not. Lake (1975) gave five young mothers Beth, a six-month old in a pink frilly dress for a period of observed interaction; five others were given Adam, a six-month old in blue overalls. Compared to Adam, Beth was smiled at more, offered a doll to play with more often and described as 'sweet' with a 'soft cry'. Adam and Beth were the same child.

CONCEIVING GENDER

Freud thought that gender was determined and also expressed at the moment of conception when active sperm met immobile ovum. As we have already seen in Chapter 3, the position of women cannot be reduced to such a simple biological formula. But the question remains: how do women come to think of themselves as feminine people?

Money and Ehrhardt (1972) have suggested that a relevant analogy for the development of gender identity is that of bilingualism. A child growing up in a bilingual environment is presented with two languages that require two different sets of behavioural responses. So with gender: there are two sets of stimuli to be programmed by the brain into two different complexes of behaviour. The child's task is to identify with one and reject the other; the parents' conscious or unconscious duty is to provide the means whereby little girls identify with the feminine model and little boys with the masculine one.

'Identification' is the key concept. Most theories of gender-identity development reserve an important place for it. Because it implies the idea of a 'model' with whom identification can take place, most theories also stress the importance of parents as the primary teachers of gender. The three main theories are the cognitive – developmental, the social learning and the psychoanalytic.

The first of these builds on the work of Piaget (1952) and says that gender is based on genital sex and so is a physical property of people that has to be learnt in the same way as other unchanging physical properties. Children below the age of 4 or 5 years cannot appreciate the unchangeable character of physical objects: cats can become dogs at will, water poured into different-sized glasses has changed its volume; girls can become boys. Thus a little girl first of all develops the idea that she is a girl and later (by the age of 5 or 6) appreciates that gender is invariant, that everyone has a gender and that gender is primarily a question of physical sex differences. Once the idea of a stable feminine gender identity is developed, she begins actively to prefer feminine activities and objects. The thinking is: I am a girl; therefore I like girl things; therefore doing girl things is rewarding (Kohlberg, 1967; Kohlberg and Ullian, 1974).

The second theory, that of social learning, contends that the development of gender identity involves a learning process that is essentially the same as other learning processes. A little girl observes her parents performing feminine and masculine roles, but when she imitates the various behaviours she sees, she is only rewarded for those considered appropriate to her gender. Through such differential reinforcement, feminine behaviours come to be positively evaluated and masculine ones rejected: I want rewards; I am rewarded for doing girl things; therefore I want to be (am) a girl. The result is a generalized tendency to imitate all same-gendered 'models' (Mischel, 1967, 1970).

Thirdly, we have the psychoanalytic view of gender – identity development, which has already been referred to at various points in this book. In this, awareness of genital difference comes first and paves the way for an identification with the parent who has a similar set of genitals. The formula runs: I do not have a penis; therefore I am a girl. Freud did not concern himself with the notion of 'gender identity' since he regarded genital – sexual identity as entirely synonymous with the cultural meaning of femininity and masculinity. The manner in which the anatomical sex difference is reflected in the different psychic constitutions of men and women is determined in

Freud's theory by one crucial and cultural mediating factor: the structure of the family.[2] Because women rear children, the love of both girls and boys is originally centred on the mother. This, combined with an early unawareness in small children of the genital difference, means that at first the psychological development of females and males is the same. But when the girl discovers that she has no penis she also recognizes that her mother shares the same fate and blames her for her disadvantaged condition.[3] This leads to a rejection of the mother as a love object; the girl turns to her father instead, a move that lays the foundation for her adult sexual attraction to males and her desire to bear male children. When she realizes the futility of seeing her father as a love object and its threat to her mother's attitude towards her, she is again inclined to a maternal identification. The discovery of the missing penis is thus the event that, in a complex series of stages, determines the feminine character with its three special qualities of masochism (a permanent sense of being castrated), passivity (the reluctant acceptance of the clitoris as an inadequate analogue of the penis) and narcissism (women's overvaluation of their superficial physical charms as compensation for their inferior genital equipment).

All three theories — the cognitive–developmental, the social–learning and the psychoanalytic — take the actual processes that are involved in the emergence of adult femininity and masculinity as in need of explanation. All assume that some identification with the same-sexed parent has to take place and is the main precursor of the desire to be seen as feminine or masculine. This 'motivational consequence' is not only a necessary element in the continuing gender socialization of children ('self-socialization'), but is, of course, an absolutely central means for the cultural transmission of gender concepts from one generation to another. Lessons learnt in childhood become the lessons that parents want their own children to learn.

The following points summarize some of what has been written on the relevance of the different theories, particularly Eleanor Maccoby

---

[2] Freud took the structure of the family as a universal given, and did not, so far as I know, comment on the impact of different types of family system on the individual's psychology.

[3] It is difficult to see how blaming the mother logically follows from the discovery of shared genitals in mother and daughter.

and Carol Jacklin's (1974) careful and comprehensive review of the literature on gender differences.

(1) Children know their own gender — they describe themselves accurately as boys or girls and choose gender-appropriate toys and and activities — before they are able to relate this to genital sex differences (Kohlberg, 1967).

(2) Understanding of gender invariance follows rather than precedes the establishment of 'correct' gender preferences in toys/activities (Sears *et al.*, 1965).

(3) Gender identity is irreversibly fixed in the first two years of life. After this point in individuals whose gender has been incorrectly assigned because of some physical ambiguity, gender reassignment is not likely to be successful (Money and Ehrhardt, 1972). (See p.53 for a male twin successfully reassigned as feminine at the age of 17 months.)

(4) *Parents'* distinctions between boys and girls are not wholly sufficient to explain the gap between the feminine and masculine self-concepts that are developed. There *are* differences in how parents treat boys and girls (chiefly less aggression, less praise, less criticism and less discouragement of gender inappropriate behaviour for girls), but there are also similarities: independence appears to be equally encouraged, and displays of aggression equally condemned (Maccoby and Jacklin, 1974, p.362).

(5) Children do not tend to identify with same-gendered models, even after the age at which quite rigidly differentiated gender identities are formed (Hetherington, 1965; Maccoby and Jacklin, 1974, pp.293 – 7).

(6) Parent – child similarities on a range of attributes are not strong, and in particular there are no stronger correlations between children and same-gendered parents than between children and parents of the other gender (Roff, 1950; Lazowick, 1955; Rosenberg and Sutton-Smith, 1968; Mussen and Rutherford, 1963; Hetherington, 1965; Fling and Manosevitz, 1972).

(7) The activities preferred by children, though gender-differentiated from nursery school age on, often do not follow any pattern that they have been exposed to in their own families. (Daughters play hopscotch but mothers don't; sons of male office workers

manipulate trucks and building bricks. The daughter of a doctor ardently declares only men can be doctors when her own mother is one — Maccoby and Jacklin, 1974, p.364.)

The cognitive – developmental view is supported by points 1,4,5,6 and 7, and is not supported by points 2 and 3. In other words, this theory is quite compatible with the fact that modelling specifically on *parental* behaviour may not be the core phenomenon; the problem is that gender identity in many senses happens before the idea takes root that gender is a fixed attribute. The social learning view is contradicted by points 4,5,6 and 7 but supported by points 1 – 3. In this approach the importance of parents as models and as differential reinforcers of gender-appropriate and gender-inappropriate behaviour is critical. The fact that parents do not have, or at least do not seem to exercise, this kind of power over the construction of gender in children is a significant criticism, as is the fact that gender identity is apparently firmly established at an age when much conscious learning of gender still remains to be accomplished. However, the social learning theory takes account of the slowness with which children base gender in genital sex differences and come to regard it as an unchangeable characteristic of people.

Finally, the psychoanalytic interpretation is really not supported by any of these findings. Physical sex differences are not the most salient determinant of gender identity for children. (It is not irrelevant that blind children develop stable gender identities — Person, 1974.) Identification with a parental model is not, apparently, the most powerful force establishing adult gender differences. Most persuasive of all, children regard themselves as feminine or masculine at an age at which Freud has them still in a state of ignorance.

PENIS AND OTHER ENVIES

It is significant that feminist descriptions of the imprisonment of women in a feminine mould blame 'society' in general for their captivity. Particular individuals are not usually identified as the teachers of femininity; it is the wide range of cultural pressures all acting in the same direction — the 'overdetermination' of gender — that is implicated. In Simone de Beauvoir's words,

One is not born, but rather becomes, a woman. No biological, psychological, or economic fate determines the figure that the human female presents in society; it is *civilisation as a whole* that produces this creature, intermediate between male and eunuch, which is described as feminine. [De Beauvoir, 1960, p.8; italics added]

'Civilization' is not feminine; it is 'a man's world'. Of all the lessons girls learn, this is the most important one. Freud, from his enviable position of masculine hegemony, called it penis envy, but it is not the penis that women want. Clara Thompson, one of the small band of female analysts who challenged Freud's thinking, wrote

one can say the term penis envy is a symbolic representation of the attitude of women in this culture . . . the penis is the sign of the person in power in one particular competitive set-up in this culture, that between man and woman. The attitude of the woman in this situation is not qualitatively different from that found in any minority group in a competitive culture. So, the attitude called penis envy is similar to the attitude of any underprivileged group toward those in power . . . [Thompson, 1974, pp.53–4]

Women envy men their power. Small children learn effortlessly about masculine power within the asymmetrical nuclear family. Father leaves the house each day as the family's representative in the public world and returns with proof (money) of the valuation of his labour; his status in the household and in society is clearly different from that of mother. But in fact, and paradoxically, dominance and nurturance are the two adult qualities that most attract children to identify with parents (Bandura and Huston, 1961; Hetherington, 1965; Hetherington and Frankie, 1967). Such an inherent contradiction throws light on many of the difficulties men and women have in adjusting their identities to fit the standard gender formulae.

When Florence Nightingale was born, she was the second daughter, intended to be a son, of ill-matched parents. Fanny Nightingale was six years older than her husband, a dedicated hostess married to an indolent and charming dilettante. Florence's biographer, Cecil Woodham-Smith, comments:

She did not attach herself to her mother. The companion of her childhood was W.E.N. [as her father was known] . . .
    W.E.N. was a man to enchant a child. He loved the curious and the odd, and he loved jokes; he had a mind stored with information and the leisure to impart it. He had great patience, and he was never patronising. Partly as a

result of marrying Fanny, partly by temperament, he was a lonely man, and it was with intense pleasure he discovered intellectual companionship in his daughters. Both were quick; both were unusually responsive; both learned easily, but the more intelligent, just as she was the prettier, was Flo. [Woodham-Smith, 1952, pp.7 – 8]

He educated both Florence and her elder sister Parthenope (Parthe) himself, teaching them Greek, Latin, German, French, Italian, history and philosophy. Parthe rebelled and joined her mother in domestic activities. Florence and her father 'were deeply in sympathy. Both had the same regard for accuracy, the same cast of mind at once humorous and gloomy, the same passion for abstract speculation'. Affection for her father and resentment of her mother (and her sister) were the dominating passions of her life.

Florence found the life of a Victorian lady boring, debilitating and depressing; her two havens were her father, who had some understanding of his daughter's need to find an outlet for her energy, and her father's sister, with whom she conspired to learn mathematics 'instead of doing worsted work and practising quadrilles'. Her difficulties were multiplied by the fact that she was evidently a success at the feminine role: 'very gay . . . Her demure exterior concealed wit. She danced beautifully . . .' For this success she reproached herself: 'All I do is done to win admiration' she wrote in a private note. When she was 16, Florence received her first call from God. 'On February 7, 1837, God spoke to me and called me to His service'. The voice reappeared three more times: in 1853, just before she took up her first post at the Hospital for Poor Gentlewomen in Harley Street; before the Crimean War in 1854; and after the death of her friend and 'Master', Lord Sidney Herbert in 1861. Seven years after the first call, and after an intense inner struggle, Florence became certain that her vocation was to nurse the sick. It took nine more years to convince her family that this was what she should be allowed to do. Her mother was 'terrified' and 'angry', her sister 'hysterical'. Her father was disappointed that his education of Florence had led to this unsuitable wilfulness, but he did eventually grant her an allowance of £500 a year, and later bought her a house. In his last years, they were completely reconciled and had 'long talks on metaphysics' together.

Such closeness between father and daughter allows the model of a masculine life-style to filter through the barrier of feminine socialization pressures. A study of women enrolled in the Harvard

Business school in the mid-1960s picked up this theme in the childhood histories of 'managerial' women. Most were first children, and 'All had extremely close relationships with their fathers and had been involved in an unusually wide range of traditionally masculine activities in the company of their fathers, beginning when they were very young' (Hennig and Jardim, 1978, p.99). While the *absence* of a father appears to endanger the learning of masculinity in boys (Tiller, 1967), his presence would therefore seem to encourage androgynous development in girls.

The role played by fathers as powerful and affectionate representatives of non-domestic culture can, of course, be taken by mothers as well. Daughters of working mothers have less rigid conceptions of gender roles than daughters of 'non-working' mothers (Morantz and Mansfield, 1977; Hansson *et al.*, 1977). They tend to have less 'feminine' identities, stressing such masculine qualities as independence and self-reliance (Hoffman and Nye, 1974).

In a very different society, that of the !Kung bush people of the Kalahari desert, the same general importance of women's socially valued productivity is seen. Among the !Kung, women's agricultural work is crucial to everyone's physical survival. Women have a great deal of autonomy and influence over the economic resources of the community as well as its ceremonial and power relations:

A common sight in the late afternoon is clusters of children standing on the edge of camp, scanning the bush with shaded eyes to see if the returning women are visible. When the slow-moving file of women is finally discerned in the distance, the children leap and exclaim. As the women draw closer, the children speculate as to which figure is whose mother and what the women are carrying in their karosses. [Draper, 1975, p.82]

Women's work is part of their childhood games, of female socialization:

We . . played at being hunters and we went out tracking animals and when we saw one we struck it with our make-believe arrows. We took some leaves and hung them over a stick and pretended it was meat. Then we carried it back to our village. When we got back, we stayed there and ate the meat and then the meat was gone. We went out again, found another animal and killed it. We again threw leaves over a stick, put other leaves in our karosses, and brought it back. We played at living in the bush like that. [Interview with !Kung woman, *Spare Rib*, October 1975, pp.15 – 16]

In a society where small children of both sexes are brought up by women but expected to learn to be different genders, it is also true to say that girls have an obvious built-in advantage. There is no room for doubt as to who they are expected to be like — whereas boys have the problem of working out what masculinity is and switching from an early identification with their mothers to a later and more enduring one with their fathers. Two linked findings are consistent products of the research on childhood gender differences: first, girls *are* more androgynous than boys until puberty; and, second, the male 'cissy' is more uniformly feared and denigrated than the female 'tomboy'.

John and Elizabeth Newson (who did not set out to examine the development of gender, but rather the whole upbringing of children) did not come across much gender differentiation in their studies of 1-and 4-year old Nottingham children. But by age 7, the sexes are beginning to draw apart, and by 11 'they have polarised so sharply that a totally biological explanation is tempting' (Newson *et al.*, 1978, p.31; quite why it is tempting they do not say). The core of the polarization is that between the ages of 7 and 11 girls learn to play with girls and boys with boys, and the established pattern is for mothers to share interests with daughters more than with sons. At 11, 72 per cent of mothers (46 per cent of fathers) said they shared an interest with a female child, whereas 46 per cent (65 per cent of fathers) said they shared an interest with a male child. Preferred 'feminine' activities have become shopping, sewing, baking and 'other domestic occupations'; masculine ones are sport, gardening, car-cleaning and masculine home-maintenance jobs. Table 5.2 shows how mothers' expectations of children's behaviour distinguish between boys and girls in this age group (fathers were not interviewed). Both outside jobs and doing errands are boys' jobs. This indoor/outdoor division is striking, preparing the way for a similar division in adult life-styles.

The mothers in the Newsons' survey expressed a great deal of concern with traditional gender-role stereotypes.[4] They were self-conscious or defensive about any deviation from the characterization of boys as

---

[4] In their writing on parental perceptions of children's deviation from gender standards, the Newsons reflect the very cultural concern they are identifying: boys are discussed first and in more detail than girls.

TABLE 5.2 *Eleven year olds' participation in household duties*

Duty	Boys %	Girls %	Both %	Significance Boys v. girls
Washing up	40	63	51	p<.001
Indoor housework (tidying, vacuum cleaning, dusting, bedmaking, etc)	19	44	32	p<.001
Miscellaneous dirty/outside jobs (gardening, sweeping yard, cleaning car or windows, making or mending fires, peeling potatoes, shoecleaning, emptying bin, etc.)	36	8	22	p<.001
Going on errands	39	21	30	p<.001

Source: Newson *et al.*, 1978, p.36.

rough, outdoor types, often grubby and careless of their physical appearance, interested in building, carpentry or mechanical model-making or in pursuing technological hobbies

and of girls as

following indoor pursuits, interested in making and exchanging gifts, writing stories and letters, buying or making clothes, keen on acting, dancing and so on. [Newson *et al.*, 1978, p.32]

The Newsons found a feminine boy much more of an embarrassment to parents than a tomboy girl — tomboyishness was regarded as a merely transitional stage in development: 'she'll grow out of it'.

Around the time of puberty something does undoubtedly happen. Girls lose their capacity for androgyny and become more unquestionably feminine. It is clear that during adolescence parents, educational institutions and society do in general act to bring much greater pressure to bear on girls to fit their feminine destiny. As Maccoby and Jacklin note, for example

Our educational institutions are dedicated to the proposition that these changes [in gender differences from childhood to adolescence] are not entirely (or even primarily) a result of simple maturation . . . [1974, pp.127–8]

The curriculum of formal educational institutions is particularly relevant to the intensification of feminine socialization that occurs with adolescence, as we shall see in the next chapter.

ARTIFACTS OF GENDER

Parental work in the area of teaching gender also takes place within the broad context of cultural artifacts that separate the world of girls from the world of boys.

Gender-appropriate toys are both the cause and the proof of correct gender identification. In the case of the boy whose penis was accidentally removed and who was reassigned as a girl at the age of 17 months (see Chapter 3):

The mother reported: 'I started dressing her not in dresses but, you know, in little pink slacks and frilly blouses . . . and letting her hair grow.' A year and six months later, the mother wrote that she had made a special effort at keeping her girl in dresses, almost exclusively, changing any item of clothes into something that was clearly feminine. 'I even made all her nightwear into granny gowns and she wears bracelets and hair ribbons.' The effects of emphasizing feminine clothing became clearly noticeable in the girl's attitude towards clothes and hairdo another year later, when she was observed to have a clear preference for dresses over slacks . . . . [Money and Erhardt, 1972, p.119]

The girl asked for dolls, a dolls' house and a dolls' pram for Christmas; her brother, a toy garage with cars.

Walum (1977, p.49) did an analysis of the 1972 edition of the Sears Roebuck Christmas toy catalogue. Her base unit was each half page of the catalogue showing a different toy with a picture of the child (female, male, both genders) for whom it was promoted. She found that 84 per cent of the toys portrayed as suitable for girls fell under the heading of 'preparatory for spousehood and parenthood', whereas none of those portrayed for males did so; 75 per cent of male toys were 'manipulatory' in character, and 25 per cent related to male occupational roles. As Alice Rossi once remarked, a girl may spend more time playing with her dolls than a mother will ever spend with her children (Rossi, 1964, p.105), and the message is clearly that girls play house and do not play the kinds of games with the kinds of toys that would prepare them for other occupational roles. Beyond the doll stage, toys such as Palitoy's 'Girl's World', apparently a tremendous commercial success, take over:

It is a near life-size orange – pink plastic bust with a thick brown wig. The face is a pert young teenage Miss, and under the base of the shoulders are large plastic suckers so you can stick it to the table while you brush its hair. Its jaunty face, with a retroussé nose, and full curvy lips, looks not entirely unlike the sort of thing you might find in a porn shop, only it hasn't got a body. [*Guardian*, 17 December 1979]

The child's own space within the home is full of gender signals. In a middle-class area of a university community, 'a locale that would presumably be on the less differentiated end of the sex role socialization spectrum' (Weitz, 1977, p.61), the bedrooms of boys and girls were instantly identifiable. Boys' rooms 'contained more animal furnishings, more educational art materials, more spatial – temporal toys, more sports equipment and more toy animals. The rooms of girls contained more dolls, more floral furnishings and more "ruffles"' (Rheingold and Cook, 1975, p.461). The 48 girls' rooms boasted 17 toy vehicles — the 48 boys', 375; 26 of the girls' rooms had dolls, compared with 3 of the boys'.

Parents often defend themselves by arguing that these different artifacts are requested by children themselves. But the essential point is, of course, that something of such cultural importance as gender differentiation of personality and role cannot be left to the idiosyncracies of parental behaviour alone.

Another potent source of gender messages is children's literature. Comics are read by 98 per cent of children (Braman, 1977, p.83), and some of the fifty or so titles currently on sale in Britain are *Emma, Jinty, Misty, Debbie, Bunty, Tammy, Warlord, Battle, Tiger, Scoop, Short, Roy of the Rovers, Hulk* and *2000 A.D.*: there are no prizes for guessing which are for girls and which for boys. The strategies for female survival in comic fiction are clear: housework, looking after children, marriage, deference to the superior power, bravery, initiative and general value of men. Tales of female initiative usually have a familiar twist at the end. In *Jinty* (28 April 1979) Alice Jones and her friends discover the lost golden city of the Incas and the spring of eternal life, from which Alice is forced to drink. She is transformed into a slave working in the temple kitchens. *Penny* runs a series called 'Blunder Girl', in which Diana Squints (a malevolent looking child with glasses and a spotty face) turns herself into a feminine parody of Superman. In one issue (11 September 1979), she visits her local post office to find a hold-up in progress, changes herself into Blunder Girl, but gets her hand stuck in the posting box. However, everything turns out all right because she grabs a nearby stick and hits the bank robber with it, thereby denting a canister of black paint on his back with which he had been threatening to deface all the mail. It springs a leak and covers him in black paint so that Blunder Girl, in the last frame, is able to congratulate herself 'now he's really a black male' (women's humour is not their strong point).

The femininity formula in girls' comics may be somewhat exaggerated but its outlines are unmistakable in pre-school picture books and in school reading schemes. Weitzman *et al.*'s survey of the former begins by noting the fact that women are barely visible in most of them. In their sample of prizewinning books, the male: female sex ratio in pictures of people was 11:1 (for animals it was 95:1). Most of the plots centred on some form of male adventure and females figured chiefly in their traditional service function or in the more imaginative, but ultimately no less restrictive, roles of fairy, fairy godmother and underwater maiden. In the duo *What Girls Can Be* and *What Boys Can Be* (Walley, n.d.), the pinnacle of achievement for a boy is to be President of the nation and for a girl it is motherhood.

Using some of the same material and examining it over time, Czaplinski (1976) has shown that sexist bias (as judged by the relative representation of female and male characters) decreased during the 1940s and 1950s and increased markedly in the 1960s. During the war and immediately after, women's participation in public life was raised, but the 1950s and early 1960s were the era of the 'happy housewife heroine'. Czaplinski's findings should be seen in the context of another piece of research into the gender imagery of children's literature: McClelland (1961) used children's books as indicators of achievement values in his cross-cultural study of economic development, and found a strong positive relationship between masculine achievement imagery and subsequent economic growth.

Although much of the early analysis of sexism in children's literature was done in the United States, similar studies in Britain have shown no substantive differences, except perhaps that British material lags behind American in revising the stereotypes it presents to children. Glenys Lobban (1976) looked at six popular British reading schemes: *Janet and John, Happy Venture, Ready to Read, Ladybird, Nipper* and *Breakthrough to Literacy*. Table 5.3 gives some of her findings. It shows the same definition of girls and women as relatively passive, indoor creatures, the same glorification of masculine adventurousness as the American research.

Many contemporary heroines of children's fiction follow in respectable fairy tale tradition; indeed, as Belotti observes in her retelling of some traditional fables, the pervasive stupidity of women doesn't change:

'Little Red Riding Hood' is the story of a girl, bordering on mental deficiency, who is sent out by an irresponsible mother through dark wolf-infested woods to take a little basket full to the brim with cakes, to her sick grandmother. Given these circumstances her end is hardly surprising. But such foolishness, which would never have been attributed to a male, depends on the assurance that one will always find at the right moment and in the right place a brave huntsman ready to save grandmother and granddaughter from the wolf. [Belotti, 1975, p.102]

It is sadly true that female figures in fairy tales and in children's fiction generally belong to two alternative categories: the good but useless, and the wicked. It has been calculated that 80 per cent of the negative characters in comics and fairy tales are female (d'Ascia, 1971), and the myth of feminine evil is a pervasive cultural theme with which women still have to contend (see pp.325 – 9).

Lastly, children's television provides no relief from the relentless feminine message. Even such 'liberal' programmes as Sesame Street do not place girls and women in prominent or seriously powerful positions. It is relevant to observe that most of the controversy about the effects of television on children is about the prevalence of male aggression in programmes directed at children. It is also important that children spend more of their lives watching television than they do at school, and that much of what they watch from an early age is adult television: they are thus exposed to the general range and effect of media representations of women.

OUT OF PLACE

All cultures have a division of labour by gender, but some are more divided than others. The need to differentiate children's roles and

TABLE 5.3 *Sex roles occurring in three or more of six British reading schemes**

Sex for which role prescribed	Content of children's roles				Learning new skill	Adult roles presented
	Toys and pets	Activities		Taking lead in both-sex activities		
Girls only	Doll Skipping rope Doll's pram	Preparing tea Playing with dolls Taking care of younger siblings		Hopping Shopping with parents Skipping	Taking care of younger siblings	Mother Aunt Grandmother
Boys only	Car Train Aeroplane Boat Football	Playing with cars Playing with trains Playing football Lifting/pulling heavy objects Playing cricket Watching adult males in occupational roles Heavy gardening		Going exploring alone Climbing trees Building things Taking care of pets Flying kites Washing and polishing Dad's car	Taking care of pets Making/building Saving/rescuing people or pets Playing sport	Father Uncle Grandfather Postman Farmer Fisherman Shop or business owner Policeman Builder Bus driver Bus conductor Train driver Railway porter
Both sexes	Book Ball Paints Bucket & spade Dog Cat Shop	Playing with pets Writing Reading Going to seaside Going on family outing				Teacher Shop assistant

* Janet and John, Happy Venture, Ready to Read, Ladybird, Nipper, Breakthrough to Literacy.

Source: Lobban, (1976), p.40.

girl is also a boy and a boy is also a girl' which reflects their perception of the equivalent position of the two genders in the occupational division of labour. In the inheritance of property, the significant variable is age not sex: the first born, whether boy or girl, is given the family's best rice fields. Their socialization is even, with neither sex awarded particular privileges; when meat, a rare commodity, is available at meals, each child is given a piece of fat and a piece of lean meat, but older people receive larger portions than the young. Parents both participate in the rearing of children, who are initiated at an early age into the chores of agricultural and domestic labour.

The Tanulong and Fedilizan are not unique among pre-literate cultures described by anthropologists (see, for example, the Mbuti pygmies studied by Turnbull, 1965, and the !Kung bushmen of the Kalahari desert — Draper, 1975). In general, the socialization of boys and girls is in step both with the requirements of the economic system and the personality values of a culture (Barry *et al.*, 1959; Whiting, 1963). It is also the case that the bipolar sex and gender categories — either female or male, either feminine or masculine — of Western industrial civilization would puzzle many pre-industrial peoples, whose thought and attitudes are more liberal and allow not only for the irrelevance of biological sex to cultural gender attribution but for the possibility of physical sex states that are neither female nor male (Martin and Voorhies, 1975).

identities by sex is therefore immensely variable. Such variation must
be borne in mind when viewing our own arrangements, which are one,
not the only, way of grouping children in readiness for their adult life.
The Tanulong and Fedilizan peoples of Southeast Asia teach their
female and male children the lesson that gender is not an important
discriminator of personal identity or occupational role. They are a
mountain-dwelling people with a staple diet of rice and sweet
potatoes, supplemented with other vegetables, coffee and the keeping
of a few animals such as chickens and pigs. Kinship is bilateral
(descent through both mother and father is important), and it is
assumed that both man and woman will bring property (e.g. rice
fields) to marriage. The adult division of labour shows a high degree
of interchangeability: an activity that is said to be usually women's is
often done by men, and vice versa; there are also many jobs men and
women habitually do together (see p.140, p.180 lists of these). Albert
Bacdayan, who studied these people, writes:

The ethnographer there cannot miss the predominantly bisexual nature of
most work and activity groups in the fields and the village. In subsistence
production, for instance, one is likely to see men, women and children of both
sexes engaged in the same tasks, harvesting, preparing the soil for planting,
bundling seedlings, and planting. In cases where they are seen performing
different tasks they are still working together: if men are repairing broken
terraces, using a carabao to plow, or hauling the harvested rice home to the
village, the women are likely to be close by smoothing the soil, cutting the
grass around the field, or harvesting the rice to be hauled away.
    This pattern of working together is observable in the domestic scene too.
During the harvest season, one is likely to find the entire family bent over a
huge basket outside their home removing the beans from their pods, spreading
bundles of rice to dry, or carrying the rice inside to store in the granaries. At
other times they may be pounding rice or cooking together. Even childbirth is
a bisexual affair. The husband is likely to deliver his wife, attended or helped
by older children and maybe an older female relative such as his own mother
or the wife's mother. Many of the relatives of both sexes gather around for the
birth process. [Bacdayan, 1977, p.286]

Economic decisions and 'public display of economic power' are
shared, as is participation in village politics. So far as children's
preparation for this society is concerned, the birth of boys and girls is
welcomed, with a slight edge in favour of girls, who are thought to be
more likely to stay in the village as adults. The people have a saying 'a

CHAPTER.SIX

Education for Womanhood

'Educate women like men,' says Rousseau, 'and the more they resemble our sex the less power will they have over us'. This is the very point I aim at. I do not wish them to have power over men; but over themselves. [Wollstonecraft, 1929, p.69]

Mary Wollstonecraft's reply to Rousseau was written at a time when it was rare for females to get any education — in the formal sense — at all. Until the last quarter of the nineteenth century, women's education consisted mainly of a training in feminine accomplishments provided by governesses at home. Girls' schools, where they existed, were geared chiefly to teaching the art of husband-catching with a repertoire of superficial accomplishments: a smattering of foreign languages, singing, dancing, sewing, 'a preparation for a flirtatious courtship' — not, significantly, for practical housewifery (Delamont, 1978a, p.135). If working-class girls went to school at all, which they mostly did not, it was to a charity, dame, Sunday or part-time factory school. Hannah Mitchell, a suffragette, recalled her own experience as a child in a rural area of Northern England in the 1870s in her autobiography *The Hard Way Up* (1977). The nearest school was five miles away; her father and her uncle taught all the children in the family to read, but the prerogative of attending school was reserved for the boys (though Hannah did manage eventually to acquire the grand total of two weeks' schooling). Her feminism was born at the age of 8 when the weekly task allocated to her was that of darning all the stockings for the household. While she darned her brothers' stockings,

they read or played cards or dominoes. Sometimes the boys helped with rugmaking, or in cutting up wool or picking feathers for beds and pillows, but for them this was voluntary work; for the girls it was compulsory, and the fact that the boys could read if they wished filled my cup of bitterness to the brim. [Mitchell, 1977, p.43]

With the quick-witted opportunism that has had to characterize women who have conquered such an oppression, Hannah managed to turn her brothers' schooling to her own advantage:

Finding that the schoolmaster was willing to lend the boys any books they wished to bring home at weekends, I made a bargain with them. I offered to do several small tasks, such as cleaning boots or gathering firewood, which they were expected to perform at weekends, on the understanding that they brought me home a book each Friday; if no book were forthcoming, the work would be found undone the following week, I told them! [Mitchell, 1977, p.43]

Education in institutions outside the home has always had a special place in feminist programmes of reform. Wollstonecraft and Mill hung their hopes on it; the 'Declaration of Sentiments' and 'Resolutions' adopted at the Seneca Falls Convention in America in 1848 named women's lack of education as one of the manifold injustices perpetrated on them by men. Education was the golden door, the automatic escape from second-class citizenship. Twentieth-century feminists cherish a similar vision, and have attached a similar importance to the right of equal education as the necessary strategy for freeing women from the 'ideological prison' of femininity (Northern Women's Education Study Group, 1973, p.149).

The idea seems obvious enough. If education is a prize men have, and it is oriented to such noble (and apparently gender-neutral) ideals as the pursuit and kindling of knowledge, then there are two reasons why women must have it: it is good in itself and it must enable them to claim the same portion of power and fortune that men have. However, the argument as it was put by educational reformers in the nineteenth century, and as it is put by feminists today, suffers from two fatal flaws. One is a consequence of the particular function education has in capitalist society; the other derives from the ideology of women's incapacity to be anything other than slaves to their bodies which has been such a persistent feature of their treatment in Western culture.

CLASSING GIRLS

The capitalist economy not only produces goods; it produces people too. In order to achieve its goals of commodity production, both the forces of production (workers and technology) and its relationships — between employers and employees, between social classes, and between men and women — must be constantly reproduced. The economic system maintains the means of production through the accumulation of profit, but it is the role of other institutions to ensure the continuation of labour power and the social relations of production. The family is one such institution; education is another. They can be said to function as 'ideological state apparatuses', transmitting the ideas and practices intrinsic to the survival of capitalism (Althusser, 1971). Some degree of conflict between workers and owners of capital is a characteristic of capitalism, and the same could be said of the educational system. It is the meeting place of contradictory beliefs and values — about society, human potential and the desirable role of the educational system itself. Employers use schools as suppliers of amenable and profitable workers. On the other hand, students, parents and minorities (including women) see schools as promoting other objectives such as material security for the individual, personal fulfillment, and a more just society.

Tables 6.1, 6.2 and 6.3 should be read together. They show subject divisions by gender in certain school courses, and occupational divisions by gender in a number of important employment categories in Britain in 1977. At school and at work similar demarcation lines between the sexes obtain. Women workers predominate in catering, cleaning, hairdressing and other personal services (75.6 per cent), in clerical work (73.3 per cent) and in education, welfare and health (64.8 per cent). At school girls take English literature and French, while biology is their favourite science (21 per cent take this, as opposed to 9

TABLE 6.1 *Percentage of boys and girls taking particular 'A' level courses, England and Wales, 1973*

Subject	% of girls	% of boys
English literature	53	23
French	24	8
Biology	21	16
Art	15	9
Maths	15	41
Chemistry	13	30
Physics	9	41
Economics	8	22

Source: Department of Education and Science (1975). Crown copyright.

TABLE 6.2 Certificate of Secondary Education (*CSE*) entries, 1972

Subject	Girls	Boys	% Girls
Domestic subjects	66,161	1,901	97
Technical drawing	593	55,356	1
Metalwork and woodwork	213	63,233	0.3

Source: Department of Education and Science *Statistics of Education* (cited in Byrne, 1978, p.124). Crown copyright.

TABLE 6.3 *Employees by selected occupations, Great Britain, 1977*

Occupation	Women	Men	% Women
Catering, cleaning and other personal services	13,692	4,423	75.6
Clerical and related	22,311	8,548	73.3
Professional and related in education, welfare and health	9,843	5,346	64.8
Literary, artistic and sports	252	757	25.0
Professional and related in science, engineering, technology and similar fields	517	6,775	7.1
Processing, making and repairing and related, metal and electrical	1,109	22,041	4.8
Construction, mining and related	13	5,620	0.2

Source: Department of Employment (1977) Part E, Table 135 (1% sample). Crown copyright.

per cent who do physics). Certificate of Secondary Education 'domestic subjects' are a female specialism — with 97 per cent of entries for metalwork and woodwork come from girls. At 'A' level, maths, physics, chemistry and economics are masculine subjects. In the work world, 99.8 per cent of workers in construction and mining are men, as are 92.9 per cent of professional workers in science, engineering and technology. A salient fact never mentioned in employment statistics is that only women are housewives.

Girls' education first became compulsory in Britain in 1880 following the 1870 Education Act, which made schooling available for all children up to the age of 10. Proposals for a system of state education had been introduced in Parliament for some time as the requirements of capitalist industry for an educated, or at least literate, workforce intensified. The extension of the franchise in 1867 increased this pressure. Although the 1870 Act is given pride of place in many history textbooks (e.g. Ensor, 1936; Trevelyan, 1942), it was only a beginning — and, for girls, not much of one. Not until 1891 did elementary education become even partially free. Education was viewed by parents and employers as less of a necessity for girls than boys; children's attendance at school followed the curve of economic recessions and booms: when work was not available, they went to school; when it was, they did not.

However, the nineteenth century did witness some earlier and more solid successes in enlarging middle-class girls' education. In the United States, Oberlin College opened its doors to the first women undergraduates in 1837, although its ostensible purpose was to provide ministers with intelligent and cultivated wives (Graham, 1978). In 1848, Queen's College was founded in London, principally to ameliorate the condition of governesses by providing them with elementary education and certificates of proficiency. (Its stated objective was to teach 'all branches of female knowledge', whatever that meant — Strachey, 1928, p.61.) A year later came Bedford College for Women, which remained a single-sex institution until 1966. About the time Bedford was founded, another pioneer came upon the scene: Emily Davies, 'a small, sweet-faced woman of modest manner and unimpeachable respectability' (Holcombe, 1973, p.21). Emily Davies had watched her brothers go to Cambridge while she was educated at home and expected, as a clergyman's daughter, to busy herself in parish work. Out of this grew the conviction that women should enjoy the same educational opportunities as men. According to a story that may, or may not, be true, her childhood friendship with the Garrett daughters, Elizabeth (later Elizabeth Garrett Anderson, one of the first women doctors) and Millicent (later Millicent Fawcett, the suffragette), included the following encounter:

Emily, the story runs, went to stay with the Garretts at Aldeburgh, and at night the two friends sat talking together by Elizabeth's bedroom fire. Millicent Garrett, then quite a small girl, sat nearby on a stool, listening, but saying nothing. After going over all the great causes they saw about them, and in particular the women's cause, to which they were burning to devote their lives, Emily summed the matter up. 'Well, Elizabeth,' she said, 'it's quite clear what has to be done. I must devote myself to securing higher education, while you open the medical profession to women. After these things are done,' she added, 'we must see about getting the vote'. And then she turned to the little girl who was still sitting quietly on her stool and said, 'You are younger than we are, Millie, so you must attend to that.' [Strachey, 1928, p.100]

The Schools Inquiry Commission, appointed under the chairmanship of Lord Taunton in 1864 to study middle-class schooling, proposed to leave girls' schools out of the survey, but Emily Davies persuaded them to rectify this omission. She and two other feminist educationalists, Frances Buss and Dorothea Beale, were called before the Taunton Commission as the first expert female witnesses to be examined in person before a Royal Commission. (Emily Davies founded Girton College, Cambridge, Dorothea Beale Cheltenham Ladies' College, and Frances Buss took over North London Collegiate School founded by her parents, and reformed it into her ideal of what girls' schools should be: stripped of the superficial feminine accomplishments, geared to serious academic study and mindful, not of the social origins of its pupils, but only of the development of their intellecual potential.)

Pauline Marks (1976) has distinguished three different approaches in the history of girls' education. In the first, educators see no relevant differences between boys and girls. In the second, girls are handicapped or deficient boys who need special help to 'catch up' with boys. In the third, boys and girls are perceived as entirely different and in need of completely different types of education. These solutions have interacted with class-differentiated prescriptions to produce an uneven history.

In the first half of the nineteenth century, educational thinking proposed gender as an important and educationally relevant division — but for middle- and upper-class children only. Middle- and upper-class boys received a schooling that approximated to the notion of a 'good-in-itself' education; girls were trained for marriage. (An interesting implication of this distinction is, as Marks notes, the idea that the learning of femininity is a central task of the school, whereas that of masculinity is not.[1]) But the ideology of working-class schools was one of the 'moral' education thought necessary by the upper classes for the 'civilization' of the poor — and both boys and girls were exposed to this 'vocational' definition of education. As working-class education enlarged, the vocational aspect was elaborated to take account of gender differences. It was thought appropriate for girls and boys to be educated directly for their adult occupational roles — which, so far as girls were concerned, were largely those of wife and domestic servant. By 1876, domestic economy had become one of the subjects that earned grants for schools; in 1882 cookery was added, and in 1890 laundry work (Deem, 1978). Even the achievements of Miss Beale and Miss Buss in the arena of middle-class girls' education were inspired to some extent by a vocational motive — the problem of those women who, because of the population imbalance, would remain unmarried.

In 1927 the Hadow Report directly confronted the issue of curricular differences appropriate to the 'needs' of boys and girls. Academic experts were asked for evidence relating to 'natural' sex differences in mental/physical capacity and educability. The evidence they gave was that such differences were relatively small and probably not relevant to the design of educational curricula; this was largely discounted by the Committee, which set more store by the declarations of teachers to the effect that girls were distinguished from boys by their passivity, emotionality, intuition, lethargy and preference for arts subjects (Board of Education, 1927). Sixteen years later, the Norwood Report subscribed to the same belief: it outlined the destiny of girls as marriage and motherhood and the destiny of boys as a job (for working-class or 'academically less able' boys) or career (for middle-class or 'academically able' boys) (Secondary Schools Examination Council, 1943).[2] Later still, the Crowther Report (1959) observed that the label of 'less able' in the case of girls attracted a particularly feminine school curriculum. Taking the

---

[1] Certain aspects of masculinity, such as physical prowess, are encouraged, but the learning of masculine gender identity and role is not presented as the central *content* of education.

[2] Marks (1976) points out how these class and ability labels have been interchangeable in much educational writing.

'needs' of girls to include the statistical fall in the age of marriage, the Report noted that in the case of 'intellectually abler' girls, not much could be done in school hours to cater for their special needs 'as women', but for 'less able' girls it was sound educational policy to take account of the 'natural' domestic specialization of the adolescent girl: 'her direct interest in dress, personal appearance and in problems of human relations should be given a central place in her education' (Crowther Report, 1959, p.34).

In the 1960s, the debate about girls' education was revitalized by the reactionary announcements of John Newsom, a well-known educationalist, to the effect that girls should not be educated to be like boys but to be better housewives, wives and mothers. His favoured curriculum of housecraft,[3] mothercraft, cooking, needlework and 'social graces' appears in the pages of *Half Our Future* (1963), the report of a committee chaired by Newsom on education in the 13 – 16 age group. Newsom believed that girls must be educated to understand the role of 'real housewives' by playing on their 'natural interest in dress and personal appearance and social behaviour' (p.136). It was most important that girls be led 'to see that there is more to marriage than feeding the family and bathing the baby, and that they will themselves have a key role in establishing the standards of the home and in educating their children'. Not surprisingly, 'Married teachers who have returned to the profession after bringing up their own families can make a specially valuable contribution here' (p.137).

The official ideology of education and gender visible in government reports of the 1950s and 1960s is in direct line of descent from the ideology that emerged in the last quarter of the nineteenth century, along with the beginning of mass education for a capitalist society. Capitalism, by then, had clearly shown itself to require the existence of two classes of labour power: productive and reproductive. Women as the bearers of children seemed naturally fitted for this latter role.

A QUESTION OF FITNESS

The capitalist economy itself provided a powerful metaphor in the debate about women's 'fitness' for education:

---

[3] The transformation of housework into 'housecraft' has ideological implications as part of the mythologization of women's household labour.

Medical men saw the body as a miniature economic system, with the various parts — like classes or interest groups — competing for a limited supply of resources. Each body contained a set quantity of energy which could be directed variously from one function to another. Thus there was inevitably a tension between the different functions, or organs — one could be developed only at the expense of others. Strangely enough, doctors saw no reason to worry about conflicts between the lungs and the spleen, or the liver and the kidneys, or other possible pairs of combatants. The central drama, in bodies male and female, was that great duel between the *brain* and the *reproductive organs*. [Ehrenreich and English, 1979, p.114]

Men had to develop their mental, and conserve their sexual, energies. (Hence the Victorian dread of the evils of masturbation, which directly voided the blood vessels of capitalism.) Women's lives, conversely, had to be spent with the uterus and its requirements always in mind; at puberty, and during menstruation and pregnancy, it was advisable that all activity, and especially *mental* activity, should cease altogether; the rest of the time intellectual stimulation was, at the very least, a threat to women's health and injurious of national well-being.

The theory that biology made women unfit for education was most eloquently put in relation to higher education, since this occupied the period of women's lives when their biology 'ought' to have precedence. One book published in America in 1873 by an 'expert', Dr Edward H. Clarke, went rapidly through seventeen editions and set forth the argument that education directly caused the uterus to atrophy. (Dr Clarke was also concerned about the ill-health of factory women, but he thought factory work less damaging to women than education because in the factory it was the body that was occupied and not the brain.) In support of his contention that educated women were damned, Dr Clarke produced cases from his own practice. One young woman, a student at Vassar, had fainting spells during her menses, which were painful and scanty. When she graduated, it was as an invalid with constant headaches; her reproductive system had its development arrested because of her concentration on education. (She was also flat-chested.) A study in 1902 showed that 42 per cent of women admitted to insane asylums were well-educated compared with only 16 per cent of the men; ergo, education drove women crazy (Bullough and Bullough, 1977, p.130). Even the redoubtable Dr Elizabeth Garrett Anderson conceded that reproductive development taxed girls more than it did boys. However, she drew the conclusion that what women needed was more training in hygiene and physical exercise (such as could be provided in schools and colleges); women could be educated out of their invalidism, which had a social, as well as biological, origin.

But voices such as hers were largely drowned by the axiom that 'science pronounces that the woman who studies is lost' (Coleman, 1889, p.238). Victorian 'scientists' backed up doctors in seeking 'to use the calm, dispassionate truths of science to prove that the demands of feminist "agitators" were founded on unscientific claims about the capabilities of women'. Their object was to establish, in areas as diverse as zoology, embryology, physiology, heredity, anthropology and psychology, 'that the idle middle-class lady was natural, inevitable and progressive; any other model of female conduct was, accordingly, to be deplored and discouraged (Fee, 1976, p.180).

If you considered what the uterus needed for proper functioning, you could see that the brain was dispensable, and the science of phrenology provided further ammunition for the deficiency of the female brain by condemning it to an altogether different class. Phrenologists claimed that, presented with the fresh brains of adult females and males of any species, they would be able to differentiate between the two. Women's brains were, of course, absolutely smaller than men's. (In fact, if the ratio of brain weight to body weight is considered, the advantage lies with women.) The nervous tissue was said to be softer and more slender in females, and the frontal lobes were supposedly less developed, 'the organs of the perceptive faculties being commonly larger than those of the reflective powers' (Spurzheim, cited in Shields, 1975, p.740). At the turn of the century, when the parietal lobes replaced the frontal lobes as the seat of intellect, it was discovered that women's frontal lobes were actually more developed than men's — but were no sign of intelligence after all.

The changing content of medical 'knowledge' of women's anatomy and physiology did not lead to any *volte face* in doctors' views of women's unfitness for any occupation other than motherhood and domesticity. A German doctor, E. F. W. Pflüger, had noted in 1861 that a woman whose ovaries had been removed did not menstruate. From this, he, and many other physicians, concluded that menstruation and ovulation were simultaneous events, both provoked by nervous stimulation. Such a theory could be taken to implicate a powerfully detrimental role for education. More accurate knowledge of hormonal factors has not entirely mitigated this, since, as we saw in Chapter 3, 'scientific' work on the social consequences of women's hormonal make-up has functioned to support the view that women are specially handicapped domestically, educationally and occupationally by their biology.

It is very difficult to realize now just what an impact medical theories in the late nineteenth century had on women who desired higher education. Was it really the right thing to do? Would there really be a dreadful price to pay in terms of loss of femininity, of the respect of men? Martha Carey Thomas, president of Bryn Mawr college (founded in 1889) looked back at her own trepidation in the early days of higher education for women:

> The passionate desire of the women of my generation for higher education was accompanied throughout its course by the awful doubt, felt by women themselves as well as by men, as to whether women as a sex were physically and mentally fit for it . . . . I was terror-struck lest I, and every other woman with me, were doomed to live as pathological invalids in a universe merciless to woman as a sex . . . .

Before she herself went to college she had met only one other woman who had done so, and Martha's own family thought her college career 'as much of a disgrace . . . . as if I had eloped with the coachman' (Thomas, 1908; reprinted in O'Neill, 1969, pp.68 – 70).

The question of women's educability in relation to men is by no means an outmoded issue in the 1970s. 'Experts' continue to debate certain 'sex difference' findings, especially those relating to spatial ability, and how far such imputed natural differences explain general differences in educational and occupational achievement (see, for example, Buffery and Gray, 1972; Maccoby and Jacklin, 1974). A recent issue of the *Educational Review* devoted to the topic of education and sex roles contained a paper entitled 'The impact of innate perceptual differences between the sexes on the socializing process' in which the author states that it is 'of paramount importance' 'to establish differences between the sexes in some psychological process which could in no conceivable way be attributable to the environment' (McGuiness, 1975, p.232). The author draws two somewhat contradictory conclusions from a brief survey of sensory sex differences (women hear better, men see better). Firstly, while boys are trained to overcome the 'natural' associated disadvantage in verbal skills,[4] girls are not so trained in the area of mechanical – spatial ability (which they ought to be in order to cope with labour-saving machines in the home). Secondly, there is no point in using the same teaching techniques on boys and girls since their respective perceptual – cognitive predispositions mean that they *learn* differently. This would seem to be merely a modern and more sophisticated version of the invidious phrenological arguments of the early nineteenth century. Although modern 'experts' may observe that the point is to place equal value on each sex's unique educability (McGuiness, 1975, p.238; Dale, 1975), the flowering of such a naive vision is ruled out by the masculinist social context within which modern educational institutions operate.

MANNISH MAIDENS

Overheard in a staffroom: Female teacher, 'The best physicist in my year is a girl'. Male teacher, 'Yes, but she's got a boy's brain'. [*Guardian*, 8 May 1979]

In the nineteenth century, the combined effect of the domestic ideology of women and the masculinity of the educational world they wished to penetrate meant that educated women were accused of manliness — of being, or wanting to be, men. Charlotte Perkins Gilman recalled that

Under the universal assumption that men alone were humanity, that the world was masculine and for men only, the efforts of the women were met as a deliberate attempt to 'unsex' themselves and become men. To be a woman was to be ignorant, uneducated; to be wise, educated, was to be a man. Women were not men, visibly; therefore they could not be educated, and ought not to want to be. [Gilman, 1911, p.152]

Educated women were 'defeminated', 'hermaphrodite', 'mongrel', 'a species of vermin', 'one of the most intolerable monsters in creation' (Delamont, 1978b, p.180). With some justification, it could be said that the legacy of the feminist educational pioneers was the creation of two new stereotypes: that of the celibate career woman, and that of

---

[4] By means of 'remedial' reading classes, for example. As King (1978) observes, boys predominate in such classes.

the wife who was an intellectual partner in marriage, 'an articulate companion who could swap Greek epigrams or scientific formulae' (Delamont, 1978b, p.184). What they did not succeed in establishing was the idea that education was a good in itself to be shared equally between the sexes and independently of any future occupation (domestic or otherwise) they might pursue.

In 1946 the American sociologist Mirra Komarovsky found women college students aware of the expectation that they should play two sorts of roles: one in which intellectual achievement was recommended; the other in which intellectual under-achievement was ordained. As one of the students said:

When a girl asks me what marks I got last semester, I answer, 'Not so good — only one A', but when a boy asks the same question, I say very brightly, with a note of surprise, 'Imagine, I got an A!' [Komarovsky, 1946, p.187]

In 1976, a study of schoolgirls in West London produced exactly the same finding: the girls 'agreed that boys do not like girls to do better than them in schoolwork. The implication is therefore, if you want to attract boys, don't start by showing how clever you are' (Sharpe, 1976, pp.135 – 6). Most follow-up surveys of the relationship between measured intellectual ability, on the one hand, and educational/occupational achievement, on the other, show a consistently lower association for females than males (e.g. Terman and Oden, 1947). Coleman (1961), working with American high school students, suggested that this is because 'bright' girls do less than their best because of the contradictory expectation of academic achievement, which has remained a masculine standard, and femininity, which prescribes deference rather than personal accomplishment. Matina Horner in America (herself President of Radcliffe) has explored this 'motive to avoid success' (Horner, 1970). Horner asked 18- and 19-year-old female and male students at the University of Michigan to write four-minute stories in response to the following cue: 'At the end of first term finals, Anne/John finds herself/himself at the top of her/his medical school class'. (The women wrote about Anne, the men about John.) The successful woman was described in negative terms by 65 per cent of the women, compared with 10 per cent of the men's accounts of the successful man. A typical story was

Anne is an acne-faced bookworm. She runs to the bulletin board and finds she's at the top. As usual she smarts off. A chorus of groans is the rest of the class's reply . . . She studies twelve hours a day, and lives at home to save money. 'Well, it certainly paid off. All the Friday and Saturday nights without dates, fun — I'll be the best woman doctor alive'. And yet a twinge of sadness comes through — she wonders what she really has . . . [Cited in Sharpe, 1976, p.137]

Horner concluded that 'femininity and individual achievements which reflect intellectual competence or leadership potential are desirable but mutually exclusive goals' (Horner, 1972, p.157).

Goldberg (1968) gave female college students several articles to read in strong 'masculine' (law, town planning), strong 'feminine' (primary school teaching, dietetics) and neutral (linguistics, art history) fields. Three articles had female authors, three male authors; the gender of the author was reversed for half the sample. A general bias against women was found regardless of the field, and even in traditional feminine fields an article was considered more valuable and its author more competent when the author was a man. The bias was strongest in the case of 'masculine' articles with a female author. In another ingenious study, female students were given two versions of a vocational test (designed to help students choose careers), one with ordinary instructions and one with the addendum that they should imagine a male preference for intelligent women and a capacity on the part of women to manage careers and families simultaneously. In this latter case the career interests of women rose in five occupations: physician, lawyer, life insurance agent, psychologist and artist (Farmer and Bohn, 1970).

All this helps to explain a particularly puzzling aspect of girls' educational development: the drop in their achievement (compared with that of boys) at puberty. One study that showed this was Douglas's *The Home and the School*, a follow-up survey of all the children born in Britain in one week in March 1946. Douglas wrote:

There is much evidence from past studies that girls are more successful than boys in the primary schools. In reading, writing, English and spelling, the average eleven-year-old girl beats the average eleven-year-old boy. But although the girls retain their superiority in these basic subjects when they reach the secondary schools, they fall behind the boys in many others, particularly arithmetic, geography and science. [Douglas, 1964, p.70 – 1]

By the age of 15 the sex difference is well established, and boys surpass girls overall in their school performance — though girls continue to do better in verbal intelligence tests. In examination entries and passes, the relative position of the sexes varies — for example, a higher percentage of boys than girls leaves school without having attempted any exams, but a higher proportion of boys sits 'A' level GCE examinations (Deem, 1978, pp.65 – 6). The female disadvantage is, as Byrne (1978, p.130) has pointed out, most marked in the case of those pupils who acquire three 'A' level passes, 'the level of qualification needed for completely free movement in the higher education sector'. In 1973, 6.6 per cent of girls in the relevant age group obtained three 'A' levels compared with 9.2 per cent of boys (Department of Education and Science, 1974).

Throughout their secondary school careers there is a mounting bias against science and mathematics in girls' education (Tables 6.1 and 6.2 showed some evidence of this). In 1976, girls took 37 per cent of 'O' level maths passes and 21 per cent physics; by 'A' level the percentages had fallen to 21 per cent and 18 per cent. Taking examination *entry* rates into account, girls are less successful than boys in passing maths and science examinations, a fact that applies equally to the curious case of biology, widely considered in schools to be a feminine science subject: here there is a higher female entry but a higher male pass rate. That some of this gender gap may be due not to the subject itself but to the way it is taught is suggested by the finding that girls' scores improve if maths problems are reworded to include home-making terms (Bem and Bem, 1970).

The tendency for girls to specialize in arts subjects is a particular handicap for those who wish to enter higher education. There is great pressure for arts places at university and many polytechnic courses have a scientific/technological bias. In further education, some two-thirds of the courses offered require the maths or physics examination passes that girls seldom possess. In 1975, women made up 2 per cent of further education students and 4 per cent of university undergraduates on engineering and technology courses. Only 35 per cent of university undergraduates and 26 per cent of postgraduates are women. This represents a proportional increase over the period from 1969; however, in absolute numbers, the gap between female and male representation has widened (Equal Opportunities Commission, 1978 – 9).

In *All Our Future* (1968), the sequel to *The Home and the School*, Douglas and his colleagues observed that, during the crucial years from 11 to 15 when the school careers of boys and girls diverge, the two sexes increasingly see the future in different terms — his is work,hers is marriage. The career assumptoins shown in Table 6.4 were made by both pupils and staff in a sample of British mixed schools in the early 1970s. The underlying rationale, whether articulated or not, is that education has a function for males that it does not have for females.

TABLE 6.4 *Career assumptions of pupils and staff*

Girls become	Boys become
Nurses	Doctors
Shop assistants	Manágers
Clerical officers	Administrative and executive officers
Typists	Sales managers
Comptometer operators	Accountants
Computer programmers	Computer engineers or salesmen

Source: Byrne (1975), p.187.

The intrinsic masculine values of education are most pronounced in its highest echelons. The indispensable question is: what kinds of institutions are universities? Adrienne Rich describes the university as

. . . a system that prepares men to take up roles of power in a man-centred society, that asks questions and teaches 'facts' generated by a male intellectual tradition, and that both subtly and openly confirms men as the leaders and shapers of human destiny both within and outside ácademia. The exceptional women who have emerged from this system and who hold distinguished positions in it are just that: the required exceptions used by every system to justify and maintain itself . . . .

The university is above all a hierarchy. At the top is a small cluster of highly paid and prestigious persons, chiefly men, whose careers entail the services of a very large base of ill-paid or unpaid persons, chiefly women: wives, research assistants, secretaries, teaching assistants, cleaning women, waitresses in the faculty club, lower-echelon administrators, and women students who are used in various ways to gratify the ego. Each of these groups of women sees itself as distinct from the others, as having different interests and a different destiny. The student may become a research assistant, mistress, or even wife; the wife may act as secretary or personal typist for her husband, or take a job as lecturer or minor administrator; the graduate student may, if she demonstrates unusual brilliance or carefully follows the rules, rise higher into the pyramid, where she loses her identification with teaching fellows as the wife forgets her identification with the student or secretary she may once have been. The waitress or cleaning woman has no such mobility, and it is rare for other women in the university, beyond a few socially aware or feminist students, to support her if she is on strike or unjustly fired. Each woman in the university is defined by her relationships to the men in power instead of her relationship to other women up and down the scale . . . [Rich, 1975, pp.26 – 9]

Like the mental hospital and the psychotherapeutic situation, universities, says Rich, are replicas of the patriarchal family. Without a reversal of these values and the abolition of this gender hierarchy, women come out where they went in: as potential wives, housewives and mothers. At the very least, it will be contended that 'to educate women is to educate the teachers of men', a phrase that was used as propaganda for the first institution devoted to the higher education of women in Britain in the mid-nineteenth century (Wolpe gives examples of more modern uses of this justification — 1977, p.7). It is of course, proof of the continuing relevance of this dictum that women *are* the teachers of men, or at any rate they are so in the mass of poorly paid and low status teaching positions.

HIDDEN AND NOT-SO-HIDDEN CURRICULA

There are two kinds of educational curricula: the public and the private. In the sociology of education the term 'hidden curriculum' has achieved importance in recent years as referring to aspects of educational practice that cannot be deduced from the public agenda of what schools *say* they do. The term refers to 'those aspects of learning in schools that are unofficial, or unintentional, or undeclared consequences of the way teaching and learning are organized and performed' (Meighan, 1979, p.102). It includes school rules, routines and regulations, the expectations of teachers, the knowledge structures implied by teaching techniques and the constraints provided by the architecture of school buildings. The hidden curriculum is important both because of its obvious capacity to shape pupils' attitudes and progress, and because, being implicit and often unconsciously implemented, it is peculiarly resistant to change.

In most respects, official educational ideology in Britain now supports the axiom of sex equality. The Plowden Report, which laid down the guidelines for primary schools, took the view that gender distinctions are 'artificial' and 'unhelpful' (Plowden Report, 1967, p.249) and said that boys and girls should do the same subjects — except for netball and football. The Robbins Report on higher education (1963) bemoaned the shortage of women among university students, particularly those taking applied science, and did not (unlike the Newsom Report) blame this on female biology. The Sex Discrimination Act 1975 outlawed discrimination against females in admission and access to 'benefits, facilities or services' in educational institutions with the exception of educational charities, physical training courses and single-sex establishments, and with special enforcement arrangements for the public sector.

Despite this, even the formal curricula of primary and secondary schools separate the sexes. A survey by the Department of Education and Science found that formal differences in curricula between the sexes began to crystallize at the age of 7, starting with crafts and games. In most mixed-sex secondary schools, boys have been separated from girls in certain areas of the curriculum well before the age of 16; this fact, said the DES, is 'too striking to be accepted without question' (DES, 1975, p.21). It is not only that pupils are pressured (directly or indirectly) to take certain subjects but the teaching and examination of these subjects presupposes the saliency of one gender rather than another. Deem asks how a boy might feel faced with these questions from a CSE 'Housecraft' paper:

Your brother and his friend are arriving home for breakfast after walking all night on a sponsored walk. Iron his shirt that you have previously washed, and press a pair of trousers ready for him to change into. Cook and serve a substantial breakfast for them including toast. Lay the table ready for the meal . . .

Describe how to clean the following (i) a nonstick frying pan (ii) an ovenware glass casserole (iii) a thermoplastic (Marley) tiled floor (iv) a vinyl-covered floor (v) a lavatory pan. [Deem, 1978, p.45]

The stereotyping of educational achievement, particularly in a scientific field, as masculine, is supported by various formal and informal structures within the educational system. These are communicated to schoolgirls as inseparable and cumulative effects, as one among many dimensions of school experience. The following comments were published in *Spare Rib* recently:

There's a history teacher at our school who never stops insulting women. He says we never stop 'gossiping' — he never shuts up himself. Once in a lesson on Nazi Germany he told us how clever Hitler was to stop all married women from working, because it solved unemployment, and the British Government should do the same thing. Recently, he gave us a test and worked out that the average boy's mark was 1.5 higher than the average girl's. He said this proved that men are superior to women.

In an art lesson once the [female] teacher said: 'Today we are going to draw aeroplanes. The ladies [sic] may like to draw birds instead.' I drew an aeroplane. In a geography lesson, the [male] teacher complained about my untidy map, saying, 'I thought girls were supposed to be able to draw neatly'.

Although there are mixed classes for needlework, cookery and woodwork, the work we do is different. In needlework the girls have to make aprons and the boys make ties or cravats. [*Spare Rib*, October 1978]

James Douglas has observed that 'girls excel in subjects that are taught by women and boys in those that are taught by men' (Douglas, 1964, p.71). Since the primary school is a highly feminine teaching environment, this is probably one explanation of girls' success at the primary school stage. Many teachers, even at primary school level, believe in educationally relevant sex differences. 'Nice children' is an epithet more often handed out to girls (King, 1978; Clift and Sexton, 1979), whereas boys are thought to be lazy, rough and hard to discipline (Douglas, 1964). This different typification carries the corollary that nice (girl) pupils are conformist whereas intransigent boys are enterprising and inventive — two of the terms that appear in the list of adjectives describing 'good male students' produced by an American study of junior high school-teachers (Table 6.5). In line with this premium on male assertiveness, Feshback (1969) found that teachers preferred obedient and compliant pupils but that the child's sex mediated their ratings, so that independent girls were the least preferred category.

Observational studies of teacher – pupil interaction reveal a further fruit of the belief on the part of teachers in the difficulty of educating boys: a raised amount of interaction with them. Boys apparently receive both more negative and more positive attention from teachers at both primary and secondary levels (Martin, 1972). In another study, high achievers among boys received more teacher attention than high achievers among girls (Good *et al.*, 1973). Most of the work in this area has been done in the United States. Lobban (1978, p.59) reflects that in British schools exactly the same findings might not emerge; in particular, patterns of teacher – pupil interaction are likely to be affected by the factor of single-sex versus mixed-sex schools, the former being more common in Britain than in America.

TABLE 6.5 *Attributes of 'good' female and male students*

Adjectives describing good female students	Adjectives describing good male students
Appreciative	Active
Calm	Adventurous
Conscientious	Aggressive
Considerate	Assertive
Co-operative	Curious
Mannerly	Energetic
Poised	Enterprising
Sensitive	Frank
Dependable	Independent
Efficient	Inventive
Mature	
Obliging	
Thorough	

Source: Kemener (1965).

Two other aspects of the hidden curriculum are resource allocation and timetabling. School timetables are built around certain taken-for-granted assumptions about girls' and boys' subjects:

Our timetable was worked so that if you did art, you couldn't do technical drawing, or woodwork or anything. No girls done woodwork. I wanted to do art, so I couldn't do technical drawing — I couldn't do both. [student quoted in Sharpe, 1976, p.149]

One survey of 587 mixed comprehensive schools in 1970 found that half had subjects open only to boys or only to girls (Benn and Simon, 1970). Moreover, resources are not equally shared between the two sexes: official standards for boys', girls' and mixed schools prescribe fewer science laboratories and technical rooms in girls' schools (Byrne, 1975).

One reason why the hidden curriculum of educational institutions supports such divisions is because gender is a primary organizational term.

Teacher: 'What must you do before you do any cooking?'
Children: 'Roll up your sleeves and wash your hands.'
Teacher: 'Right, girls go first.'
The boys put on green-striped aprons, the girls flowery ones. The teacher goes through the ingredients. 'We need four ounces of sugar.' She points to 4 on the scales. 'We could use butter but we'll use margarine. It's just as good and it's cheaper than butter.' The mixing stage is reached. 'Now who's going to have first go? We'll have someone who didn't shout out.' [King, 1978, p.67]

Aside from learning how to make a cake, these children are also being taught hygiene, numbers, food economy, politeness, and gender differentiation — as if they didn't know this already. Ronald King, who quoted this example in his study of primary schools, observed that teachers separate boys and girls in a whole variety of ways. Boys hang up their coats separately from girls and are lined up in separate rows at the door. Children are divided for activities — the girls are the horses in Humpty Dumpty and the boys the king's men. Histograms of height or foot length are colour coded for sex. Pupils' official record cards are also colour coded, and the registers list boys and girls separately.

These practices were completely taken for granted by the teachers, who, when I talked with them, generally said they had 'never thought about it', and that to divide the class by sex was 'convenient' and 'natural'. They were sometimes puzzled by what to them were my silly questions like, 'Why do you line boys and girls up separately at the door?' [King, 1978, p.68]

The use of gender as an organizational principle is akin to streaming, which has known cognitive effects. Lacey (1970) has suggested that under-achievement is a product of streaming, a proposal that would seem obviously relevant to the question of gender labelling. Whether or not educational institutions are single-sex or mixed-sex affects the extent to which separatist categorizations are possible. Almost all state primary schools in Britain are co-educational, but about a third of state secondary schools and most independent schools are still single-sex. The DES survey of curricular differences mentioned earlier reported more cross-sex choices (e.g. girls/science, boys/languages) in single-sex than mixed-sex schools. Sport and history were the only subjects that received the same preference rating in single-sex as in co-educational schools. Girls liked science and boys liked languages more in single-sex schools. A study by King (1965) established that in mathematics both boys and girls from single-sex schools did better than those from co-educational ones. There is some evidence that boys may do better academically in mixed-sex schools and girls rather worse because, while boys have girls to compete against, competing with boys deters girls from showing their academic prowess (see Shaw, 1976). Moreover, unless co-educational schools are models of sex equality, they are likely to disadvantage girls in less direct ways. Women teachers will be outnumbered by men, and dramatically so for subjects such as maths and science. The Head will be male, and where the Deputy Head is female, in practice the functions are liable to be sex-typed — he deals with education, she with social welfare. Such a handicapping polarization of attitudes (from the girls' point of view) is not so likely to be found in an all girls' school, where girls and women take the centre of the stage. Men are marginal, as in one British girls' boarding school described by Okely (1978), where contacts with males were limited to the school chaplain, two gardeners, the boilerman, two elderly, retired part-time language teachers, the part-time tennis coach and the headmistress's male dachshund.

The belief that women can escape a feminine destiny by taking education as the golden pathway to uncountable opportunities has been one of the most subversive elements in the hidden educational curriculum during the post-war period — indeed, since women first gained access to education in the nineteenth century. It will be obvious from the evidence presented in later chapters of this book that the vision of emancipation through education has not materialized. Women's formal education mirrors, rather than determines, their position in society.

Labour

What is women's work?

CHAPTER SEVEN

Employment

I once was a dull, narrow housewife
With nothing to talk of at all
But the loves, the frustrations,
The rows, the relations
Of the woman from over the wall.
But now I've a job I'm quite different
I can talk with a sparkle like wine
Of the loves, the frustrations,
The rows, the relations,
Of the girl at the desk next to mine.
[Fremlin, 1959; quoted in Pahl and Pahl, 1971, p.131]

Many feminists have seen a paid job outside the home as an answer to feminine problems. The work-as-liberation argument is essentially the same as the education-as-liberation argument discussed in Chapter 6. In this chapter I want to look at the contradictions of this argument as applied to women's paid labour in capitalist societies. I shall take Britain as a test case, but much of what I have to say applies generally to other European countries and to the USA.

Three important themes in any discussion of women's work are (1) that the work of women is secondary to their family-producing role; (2) that it is uniquely a product of modern industrial civilization; and (3) that women workers are becoming more and more like men, the major remaining problem being that of integrating their reproductive and productive roles. I argue in this chapter that all three of these views are selective misrepresentations of women's labour arising in the particular economic circumstances of twentieth-century industrial capitalism. Their effect, of course, is to characterize women as deficient labourers. Whether it is natural or 'man-made' conditions that prevent equality in employment the point is the same — namely, that women can't quite make it.

WOMAN'S PLACE IS EVERYWHERE

We saw in Chapter 2 how it has been (and indeed remains) the fate of women workers to be drawn into, and ejected from, the labour force in response to the governmentally defined economic needs of the country. One function of women is, thus, that of a 'reserve' labour force.

According to Marxist theory, capitalism neither demands, nor necessarily produces, full employment; on the contrary, it requires an industrial reserve army (1) to provide a flexible population of workers who are 'free' to enter or leave certain branches of production as technical change demands changes in the type or amount of labour needed; and (2) to depress wage levels and increase the extent to which workers can be exploited in the interest of maximizing profits. Women do not form the only industrial reserve, but they are obvious candidates because of the ease with which they can be made, or seem, to 'disappear' back into the family — a structure that rests on the assumption (though often not the reality) of male support (see pp.292 – 5). Wars, economic recessions, major technological change and periods when the birth-rate is seen to be falling more than is nationally desirable, are the main occasions marked by the clarion call of women's retreat from, or advance into, the labour force.

The Marxist view, which allows one to see women as a particular kind of industrial reserve army, has the advantage that the ebb and flow of economic policy on women's work can be tied to the ideological lens through which women are viewed as unimportant people. On the other hand, there is a crucial disadvantage to the determinism of Marxist theory: it tends to represent women as passively meeting the needs of the economic system. Thus, the post-war rise in married women's employment is interpreted as a response to the expansion and diversification of capitalist commodity production, and not as a sign of domestic dissatisfaction on the part of women themselves. This 'overdetermined' and 'oversocialized' view is surprisingly akin to the way sociologists (both left- and right-wing) have seen women's work and the relationship between the economic and family systems. Families are adaptive institutions without an influence of their own, and so are women.

The evidence does not quite support this point of view, however. In her study of women temporary clerical workers (an industrial reserve *par excellence*), Fiona McNally did not find a 'passive orientation'. Instead, she reported that

> The vast majority of female temps are engaged in strategies which enable them to counter or to overcome a wide range of constraints. In some cases, these strategies involve a flight from the oppressive features of domesticity. In other cases, they involve an attempt to establish a sense of control over the work situation. It cannot be denied that these strategies frequently end in frustration or resignation, but they do at least remind us of the lesson learnt from history, that women are capable of resisting structures of oppression [McNally, 1979, pp.186–7]

A quarter of the office 'temps' who answered McNally's questionnaire said they preferred temporary office work because of its more varied routine. One fifth were doing it while looking for a permanent job; a tenth were about to move or go abroad.

In her survey, McNally found a high degree of importance attached by temps to the actual nature of the work they had to do. Similar findings have emerged from other studies: for example, interviews with Punjabi women working in a foundation garment factory in Southall, Middlesex, discovered a high degree of job dissatisfaction among a segment of the workforce that is generally supposed to be glad of any work it can get (Williams, 1972).

Women do not, then, respond passively to their imputed role as a reserve army of workers. One reason is because the notion that women are new to the labour force is one of the 'persistent myths' of our time (Turner, 1964). According to this myth (which is part of the 'progress' model of gender relations in which women today have never had it so good), women have only recently emerged from the dark ages of an exclusive preoccupation with motherhood to a new golden world of economically useful work. Part of the problem is epistemological: what is 'work'? Like everything else, it has different definitions in different times and places (Tilgher, 1931). To the ancient Greeks, for instance, all involvement in the material world was the lowest form of existence: work, '*ponos*', was a curse, with the same root as the Latin '*poena*' meaning 'sorrow' or 'burden'. Early Christianity gave work the sense of atonement for sin and the function of a means to charity; just as life for life's sake was an unacceptable message, so was work for work's sake. It took the rise of Protestantism to establish the moral conditions in which capitalism, as 'the social counterpart of Calvinist theology' (Tawney, 1930, p.2), could emerge and flourish.

In industrial-capitalist societies there are three main forms of productive activity: that geared to goods that will be directly *used*, that which leads to goods for *exchange*, and that which, in less tangible ways, results in the cyclical reproduction of labour power.

The last of these is an important domain of female labour and is examined in Chapters 8 and 9. The production of goods for use or exchange has also been a 'traditional' role for women. In medieval society women's skills of spinning, embroidery, accounting and supervision were a key part of the 'gross national product' and did not have the economically marginal character they have since acquired. Most women were also rural cultivators. 'There was hardly any kind of agricultural work from which women were excluded' (Clark, 1919, p.62) — women made good, if slightly cheaper, [1] sheep-shearers, hay-thatchers, harvesters, accountants and muck-spreaders. Wives were not 'kept' by husbands but paid their own way by helping to support their families. Both husband and wife brought marketable skills and economic resources to their union: a French marriage contract dated 1700 shows that the wife brought to marriage 'a bed, a half dozen sheep, an oak chest, a cow, a year old heifer, a dozen sheep, 20 pounds of linen, two dresses and a half dozen table napkins' (quoted in Tilly and Scott, 1978, p.43).

Added to agricultural and textile work, women's pre-industrial sphere included the skilled trades (tailors, shoemakers, chandlers, etc.), retailing and the provision trades (baker, miller, butcher and the legendary fishwife). Their professional work had begun by the seventeenth century to be limited by ecclesiastical and legal dictate, but in their capacities as nurses, healers and midwives, women controlled the nation's health and reproduction.

All this is very like the picture of women's work that emerges in many anthropological accounts of life in non-industrialized communities in the twentieth century: 'In traditional societies women

---

[1] A difference that seems to have developed some time after the thirteenth century. See Casey (1976), p.228, and also Clark (1919).

begin their working careers early in life and continue working on through old age. Only extreme senility or death itself marks a finish to their working life' (Hammond and Jablow, 1976, p.66). Table 7.1 shows some key 'work' activities and their division by gender among the Tanulong and Fedilizan peoples of Southeast Asia. Of the 50 tasks shown here, 80 per cent are done either by females or males equally or by one sex usually, with the other participating on occasion. Only 18 per cent are said to be the province of men only. Bacdayan describes this as 'mechanistic co-operation' implying 'the performance of the same tasks by men and women in a pattern of work that brings the sexes together in the same working situation' — the residential and economic unit of the nuclear family (Bacdayan, 1977, p.270).

In communities such as that described by Bacdayan, some 60 – 80 per cent of the food supply is generated by women's work. This means that, although today about a third of the officially enumerated world labour force is female (Boulding, 1977), a very important part of women's labour is not visible in official labour statistics because it falls outside the realm of the exchange economy. In modernizing economies, three-quarters of the work is still done by women (Boserup, 1970), although Western male technical 'experts' are biased against women as farmers to the extent that it is the men (many of whom have never farmed before) who are trained in new techniques and the use of new equipment (van Allen, 1974).

A transformation in the nature of the economy radically alters women's relation to their work. The traditional economy of the !Kung bush people of the Kalahari desert allotted an important role to women as agriculturalists providing the staple food supply (Draper, 1975). When Patricia Draper did her fieldwork among the !Kung in the late 1960s, some of them were beginning to adopt a more settled way of life with the men taking up herding and the women agriculture. This change from a nomadic foraging existence was accompanied by marked changes in the social relations of the sexes and definitions of gender roles. In the bush setting, argues Draper, women have a high degree of autonomy and power within the community. When economic conditions alter to a settled way of life centred on animal husbandry and crop planting, relations between the sexes become asymmetrical and women lose their independence. The most important factor accounting for this revision of women's place is their relation to work. In the bush setting they are independent workers and

TABLE 7.1 *Tasks and their performers in Tanulong and Fedilizan*

Task	Performer
Agriculture or subsistence tasks	
Preparation of the soil	B
Planting	B
Weeding the banks of the fields	B
Plowing with animals	M
Weeding in between the rice plants	FM
Watering	B
Erecting scarecrows	MF
Guarding against rice birds	B
Trapping rats and mice	M
Installing magical objects to scare rats	B
Checking to see if rice is ready for harvest	B
Harvesting	B
Sowing seeds	F
Removing seedlings from seedbeds	B
Clearing upland fields	MF
Planting vegetables	B
Clearing the padi dikes	FM
Fertilizing with organic matter	B
Planting beans	FM
Installing bean poles	FM
Gathering beans	FM
Weeding upland sweet potato fields	FM
Fencing	B
Building stone/earth walls	MF
Fixing dikes	B
Fertilizing with mineral soil	B
Planting sweet-potato vines	FM
Digging up sweet potatoes	FM
Preparing upland fields	B
Taking care of animals in the pasture	MF
Cutting grass for animals	MF
Cutting sticks for fencing and poles	B
Preparing bamboo for binding rice bundles	MF
Milling sugar cane	B
Hauling rice from the fields	MF
Digging up new upland fields	B

Task	Performer
Search for food	
Fishing in the river	MF
Trapping birds	M
Gathering mushrooms	M
Snaring rice birds	M
Trapping fish in the rice fields	MF
Gathering edible snails	FM
Gathering beetles	B
Hunting	M
House-building tasks	
Gathering thatch roofing	B
Roofing	M
Gathering vines for binding	M
Preparing wood	M
Preparing the ground for building	B
Hauling the material to building site	B

Note: B = tasks performed equally by females or males; F = tasks performed by females only; M = tasks performed by males only; FM = tasks performed usually by women; MF = tasks performed usually by men.
Source: adapted from Bacdayan (1977), pp.282 – 3.

they retain control over the product of their labour (food). They are just as mobile as men and no more tied to the home: their travels outside the village to get food give them an acquaintance with bush life (the location of animals, water, etc.) that is of enormous political importance, since it makes them the unique possessors of knowledge crucial to the community's survival. When life becomes more settled, the men, through herding and participation in waged work outside the village, develop a pattern of absence, while the women become more bound to the home. Consequently, men come to 'carry an aura of authority and sophistication that sets them apart from the women and children' (Draper, 1975, p.103). At the same time, domestic chores multiply: food preparation becomes more complex, material possessions proliferate, houses become more permanent and private.

The egalitarianism with which children were reared gives way to an emphasis on gender-differentiated responsibilities: boys, expected to help with the herding, regularly move out of the village, whereas the lives of girls are more narrowly defined by the cycle of female domestic activities.

This change in women's work among the !Kung has features in common with the trauma which the introduction of capitalism in the West inflicted on women's lives. In both situations, the transformation of material conditions led to increasing differentiation between the work roles of adult men and women. In both, a chasm between 'family' and 'society' developed: women came to represent the first, men the second.

DANGER: WOMEN AT WORK

The Council of the London Stock Exchange announced yesterday that from March women would be allowed to apply for membership to the Exchange. One elderly stockbroker had to be helped by two clerks to his car when he heard the news. [*Guardian,* 3 May 1972]

In 1750 two out of three people in England worked in agriculture; by 1850, the figure was nearer one in five. Manufacturing and 'service' industries provided the new forms of work. National figures for women's employment are not available before 1850 (it had to be seen as a problem before government statisticians were motivated to collect data on it), but in 1850 about 30 per cent of the market labour force was female, or, to put it another way, 27 per cent of women were employed (Tilly and Scott, 1978).

It was in the 1830s and 1840s that the employed woman in Britain first became a problem — a public nuisance to be defined, regulated and averted: 'Indeed, it is as though the Victorians discovered her, so swiftly and urgently did she become the object of public concern' (Alexander, 1976, p.60). Since, as we have seen, there was nothing new about the phenomenon of the working woman, it is this sudden awakening of consciousness that needs to be explained.

In the first place, working women were a problem because all women were a problem: there were too many of them. Secondly, wrested from the land, from a way of life in which the skills and resources of men and women were equally necessary for their own upkeep and the production of families, people faced the question of what, stripped of their traditional function, women should *do*. To say that 'people' faced this question is, of course, to beg the more important question of who formulated women as the problem and why. Women may have discovered new questions and doubts, but it was men who discovered that women themselves were an issue, a contradiction and an anomaly: creatures of Nature uncomfortably trapped in a market- and profit-oriented world. As Barbara Ehrenreich and Deidre English (1979) observe, it was this attitude to women as out-of-place and the consequent, misdefined, search for women's 'true' place, that provided a blueprint for whole armies of experts who debated and prognisticated on the subject of what women — for their own good, but mostly for other people's — ought to do with themselves.

Apart from the threat of competition with male labour, three themes were prominent in Victorian objections to women's employment: the disturbance of reproductive function, the imminent collapse of family life and the direct moral danger to women and society. '"I had a child born in the pit" said one woman, "and I brought it up the pit shaft in my skirt"' (quoted in Pinchbeck, 1969, p.261). Dead and ill-cared for babies signalled the collapse of family life, with employed women not the victims but the chief protagonists:

A man came into one of these club-rooms, with a child in his arms. 'Come lass', said he, addressing one of the women, 'come home, for I cannot keep this bairn quiet, and the other I have left crying at home.' 'I won't go home, idle devil', she replied, 'I have thee to keep, and the bairns too, and if I can't have a pint of ale quietly, it is tiresome. This is the only second pint that Bess and me have had between us; thou may sup if thou likes, and sit thee down, but I won't go home yet!' [*Hansard*, vol. 73; 1096, quoted in Neff, 1966, p.35]

Middle-class factory inspectors were appalled at the way mill women hired out the family washing and that, of thirteen wives in one mill, only one could make a shirt.

One significant and enduring outcome of the debate about the dangers of women's employment was that they became 'protected' workers. In 1842, the Mines and Collieries Act prevented the underground work of boys under 10 and all women and girls; the 1844

Factory Act excluded women from night work and limited their working hours to 12 a day; further Acts in 1847, 1850 and 1853 reduced them to 10. These provisions governing women's employment are now embodied in the Factories Act, 1961, the Employment of Women, Young Persons and Children Act, 1920, and the Hours of Employment (Conventions) Act, 1936 (see Health and Safety Executive, 1973, for a useful summary). With the addition of various provisions and exceptions, their main effect is still to disallow night work and excessive overtime (unless special exemption orders are granted), a privilege that some women today feel is discriminatory in its effects.

In America, the nineteen protective labour laws that existed by 1968 owed their origins more to feminist agitation than to male protectiveness. Title VII of the 1964 Civil Rights Act has operated to invalidate many such labour laws — for example, the weight-lifting limit that applied to women until a legal challenge in 1969. In America, most feminist organizations argue that protective laws really protect men's jobs, and so ought to be repealed. In Britain, opinion is divided. The National Council for Civil Liberties' Rights for Women Unit holds the view that the repeal of protective labour legislation would not improve women's lives, and so should not be encouraged; they advocate instead the extension of protection against anti-social employment conditions to men (Coussins, 1977). The Equal Opportunities Commission (EOC) says that such laws cause discrimination and inhibit equal opportunities. According to a survey carried out by the EOC, 60 per cent of women are in favour of repealing the shift work and overtime provisions, and 40 per cent say they would favour the removal of the obstacle to night work (EOC, 1979).

Whatever stand is taken, it has historically been an integral part of legal definitions of women that they are regarded as in need of protection by men. A Californian Court put it this way in 1971:

Laws which disable women from full participation in the political, business and economic areas are often characterised as 'protective' and beneficial. Those same laws applied to racial or ethnic minorities would readily be recognized as invidious and impermissible. The pedestal upon which women have been placed has all too often, upon closer inspection, been revealed as a cage . . . [Purcell, 1974, p.149]

WORKING WONDERS

In 1850, 1911 and 1951 alike, 31 per cent of the employed labour force in Britain was female. These figures, strikingly shown as an almost straight line in Figure 7.1, of course hide a variety of demographic changes, but they do not provide much fuel for the contention that anything revolutionary has happened to women's labour force position in the last century.

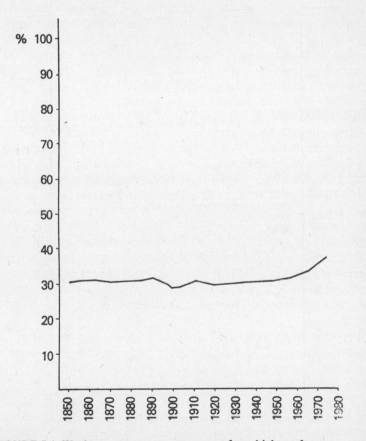

FIGURE 7.1 *Working women as percentage of total labour force, Great Britain, 1851–1976*
Source: Adapted from Tilly and Scott (1978) p.70.

Much the same conclusion can be drawn from Figure 7.2, which shows employed women as a percentage of the total female population. The proportion fell slightly in the later nineteenth century until the outbreak of the First World War, and only began to rise dramatically in the late 1940s. Although it was popularly believed in the 1890s that women's employment was expanding rapidly, this was due chiefly to the influx of women into the new clerical occupations, part of the trend that brought women from 0.1 per cent of clerks in

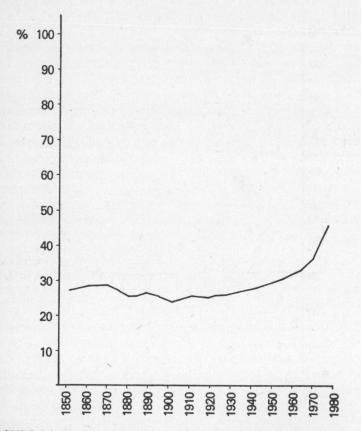

FIGURE 7.2 *Working women as percentage of total female population, Great Britain, 1851 – 1976*
Source: Adapted from Tilly and Scott (1978) p.71.

1851 to 71.9 per cent in 1971. Retailing also grew and the number of shop assistants tripled between 1861 and 1901. In 1861, four-fifths of employed women were either in domestic service or in textile and clothing manufacture; many of the rest worked in laundries or in needlework, millinery and dressmaking. The jobs women took — whether new or old — tended to be those at the bottom of every scale: low paid, low status, unskilled 'women's work'. 'Females', as the 1842 Mines Report knowingly put it, 'submit to labour in places where no man or even lad could be got to work' (quoted in Pinchbeck, 1969, p.181).

The rising curves in both Figures 7.1 and 7.2 from about 1950 on do, however, point to one change in the pattern of women's employment in the twentieth century that applies to most of the industrialized world. For the first time since the disruptive effect of industrialization was felt on men and women's work, marriage is not preventing many women from taking a paid job. In 1911, one in ten married women had a job; in 1951, one in five; in 1976, one in two. Two out of three employed women are now married. This increase in married women workers as a proportion of the labour force has been widely acclaimed as a 'revolution'. Like all revolutions, it has been seen to pose social and political issues of 'magnitude and urgency' (Klein, 1965, p.xi). Introducing one of the first attempts to analyse the industrial phenomenon of married women's work, Pearl Jephcott said:

The married woman who leaves her home each day and goes off to work has become a familiar, if controversial, figure in western society. Some see her as a symbol of freedom, but to others she is the epitome of irresponsibility and neglect. [Jephcott, 1962, p.19]

Jephcott and her colleagues examined the pattern of women's employment in Bermondsey, an area of south London where one of the main demands for female labour was in a biscuit factory. The study attempted to answer the 'who', 'why' and 'how' questions about women's work, with a heavy emphasis on how the families of employed women were affected by their employment. Its conclusions were that the 'typical' married woman worker was not the mother of young children; that women went out to work not to 'meet basic economic needs nor to provide personal pleasures' for themselves, but to raise the family's standard of living; that Bermondsey wives coped with their dual roles by relying on labour-saving aids in the home, doing less cooking and getting more help from relations with childcare; that working mothers did not neglect their children (or their husbands); and there was no evidence that their absence from the home caused juvenile delinquency.

These findings were all picked up enthusiastically by the press reviewing the book. *The Daily Telegraph* called their piece 'Mummy's Gone-A-Hunting' and commented that the study found women to be

good, steady employees. More important, the team could not find that there was any adverse effect on the children: *not overtly anyway* . . . . Many mothers *even* argued that their working helped unify the whole family and created a deeper relationship between them and their husbands and between their husbands and their children. [7 May 1962; italics added]

The Daily Mail's review ended by citing two of the book's conclusions:

The desire of wives to find paid employment is not a passing phase but a permanent feature of modern society. A job outside the home is meeting deep-seated needs which are now felt by women in general. [*Daily Mail*, 17 May 1962]

On both these counts Jephcott was probably right, although *Married Women Working*, as a species of the larger genus of post-war investigations into the 'problem' of married women's work, misconstrued the situation. There was felt to be a need to *explain* why women took paid jobs, whereas, historically speaking, what really needed to be explained was the rise of the ideology, material conditions and gender relations that placed women in the home. The question 'Why do you work?' that the 1950s and 1960s literature on women's employment took as its theme was itself a social product: a response to the pre-existing ideological construction of women as fundamentally incapable of serious activity.

If it was reassuring to find that women took jobs out of altruism (raising the *family* standard of living) rather than selfishness (because they wanted to), it was even more consoling to uncover a financial motive. For, if women took jobs solely for the money they brought in, they could have no other motivation. Most of the research done by social scientists and others since the 1950s in Britain and other countries has been singularly uninformative about women's real motives for taking employment because it has started from this preconception (Beechey, 1978; Roby, 1975; Klein, 1965; Hunt, 1968). 'What was the *main* reason you worked?' women questioned in a recent OPCS *Family Formation* survey were asked of the period after marriage and/or after the birth of the first child; 'was it *because you really needed the money*, because you wanted extra things for yourself and the family, or because you liked it?' (Dunnell, 1979, p.31; italics added). Not surprisingly, half said they needed the money and a quarter that they wanted extra things; only one in five admitted that they liked working. Table 7.2 from the *Family Formation Survey* is interesting because it shows a rise in the percentage saying that work itself is the reason for working — from 16 per cent in 1956 – 60 to 22 per cent in 1971 – 5. The report describes this as a 'very small' change — which it is, statistically speaking — but it does suggest that the public acceptability of selfish and work-centred reasons for employment may be growing. Three-quarters of the employed women interviewed in a National Opinion Poll survey conducted in 1977 said they would work 'even if they did not need the money: they would get bored stuck at home' (*Sunday Times*, 27 February 1977).

TABLE 7.2 *Reason for working between first and second live births in four different time periods*

Worked because:	1956 – 60	1961 – 65	1966 – 70	1971 – 5
Really needed the money	52	51	48	47
Wanted extra things	27	25	27	27
Liked it	16	19	20	22
Other reason	5	5	5	4

Source: Dunnell (1979) Table 6.5, p.31. Crown copyright.

The so-called 'revolution' in married women's employment is perhaps more of a revolution in marriage than in employment. For, if more married women now go out to work, the same is true of married men. Marriage is more popular: more people marry, they marry at younger ages and live longer as married people in 1980 than in 1880. But the impact of marriage on men's employment is not known, because men's work-attitudes are not thought to be dependent on their position in the life-cycle as women's are (and men are not asked the question 'Why do you work?'). If any assumption is made, it is that marriage makes men more dedicated workers because the support of their wives and children is at stake.

'Revolutions' commonly imply a change in ideology, but there has been barely any ideological component in the post-war rise in married women's work. It was not a feminist demand for work as the right of women that produced the change. Demand among employers has clearly been important (Almquist, 1977), but another interpretation, which I shall outline in the next chapter, is that women's behaviour in productive labour can only be explained by their situation as *reproductive* workers. Their changed situation vis-à-vis childbearing, childrearing, housework and husband-care breeds a desire and a need to escape the home. This inappropriate response of women to their allocated role has been veiled by the sexist methodologies of work-attitudes surveys, which have conspired to prove that paid work outside the home is merely an extension of women's responsibilities within it.

A SEX APART

It is, of course. That is, while women do not necessarily take jobs to serve their families, the jobs they take outside the home are very like those they do inside it.

Women's employment has tended to be concentrated in a small number of industries and confined to a range of jobs which might be described as 'women's work'. Even where women work alongside men, they usually hold positions of lower responsibility and perform tasks of a less skilled nature . . . men are the employers, managers, top professionals, foremen and skilled workers in our society. [*Social Trends*, 1974, p.16]

Hakim (1979) has examined this picture of occupational segregation by gender in detail and she concludes that the main change over the period from 1911 to 1971 was in the reduction of exclusive or near-exclusive occupations for men and women. On the other hand, where men and women supposedly are engaged in the same broad categories of work, there is greater separation between the sexes than there used to be (see also Department of Employment, 1977). Table 7.3 is more than suggestive. According to Hakim, change since 1970 has been faster in the United States than in Britain, where (to take just one illustration) in 1977 only 13 per cent of employed women fell into the category of skilled manual, professional and managerial occupations as compared with 62 per cent of employed men, a position virtually unchanged since 1971 (Manley and Sawbridge, 1980). More than half of employed women in Britain work in three service industries: the distributive trades (shops, mail order, warehouses) — 17 per cent; 'professional and scientific' (typists, secretaries, teachers and nurses) — 23 per cent; 'miscellaneous services' (laundries, catering, dry cleaners, launderettes) — 12 per cent. A quarter of employed women work in manufacturing industries. Of these, half are in only four industries: food and drink manufacture, clothing and footwear, textiles, and electrical engineering.

TABLE 7.3 *Occupational concentration in Britain, 1901 – 1971*

	Total number of occupations identified at each census	Proportion(%) of all occupations having:		
		No women workers	70% or more women workers	A higher % of women workers than in labour force	A higher % of men workers than in labour force
1901	380	9	9	26	74
1911	475	13	9	27	73
1921	611	8	8	22	78
1931	591	8	8	23	77
1941	–	–	–	–	–
1951	587	6	11	28	72
1961	201	9	10	26	74
1971	223	2	12	26	74

Note: The number of jobs with no male workers is negligible.
Source: Hakim (1979), p.23, from population census reports 1901 – 1971.

This kind of concentration is not found in male employment: no single industry contains more than 10 per cent of the male workforce. Table 7.4 shows female and male employees by industrial sector in

TABLE 7.4 *Employees by industrial sector, Great Britain, 1977*

Industrial sector	% men	% women
Mining and quarrying	96	4
Shipbuilding and marine engineering	93	7
Construction	93	7
Metal manufacture	89	11
Vehicles	89	11
Mechanical engineering	85	15
Agriculture, forestry, fishing	84	16
Coal and petroleum products	84	16
Transport and communication	82	18
Gas, electricity and water	80	20
Timber, furniture, etc.	80	20
Bricks, pottery, glass, cement, etc.	75	25
Chemicals and allied industries	74	26
Metal goods not elsewhere specified	73	27
Paper, printing and publishing	70	30
Instrument engineering	67	33
Other manufacturing industries	66	34
Electrical engineering	64	36
Public administration	62	38
Food, drink and tobacco	60	40
Leather, leather goods and fur	59	41
Textiles	57	43
Insurance, banking, finance and business services	50	50
Distributive trades	47	53
Miscellaneous services	46	54
Professional and scientific services	32	68
Clothing and footwear	26	74

Source: Department of Employment Part E, Table 135 (1% sample). Crown copyright.

Great Britain according to the 1977 *New Earnings Survey*. The most 'masculine' sectors are mining and quarrying, shipbuilding and marine engineering and construction; the most 'feminine' are professional and scientific services, clothing and footwear, miscellaneous services and the distributive trades. The distribution of men and women in managerial occupations follows this pattern, female managers being non-existent in strongly masculine trades. Table 7.5 gives the picture in a sample of ten occupations. In professional work, women's highest representation is in the occupations of dentist, general practitioner and veterinary surgeon (see Table 7.6).

There is also an essential division of labour *within* occupations. Tables 7.7 and 7.8 show female and male staff in selected occupational groups in the civil service and female and male hospital consultants by subject specialty. In the civil service there is an almost direct correspondence between the status of the job and its gender. The higher the status of the position, the more 'masculine' it becomes. No permanent secretaries are women, whereas more than three-quarters of clerical assistants are. Among hospital consultants, the medical specialties where most women are to be found are those relating to children and mental disorder. They also put people to sleep, chart the behaviour of microbes (microbiology), concern themselves with people's skins (dermatology) and take pictures of people (radiology). None of these areas has high status within the medical profession, whereas the majority of surgical specialities, which men control, command much higher respect. The pattern described by a female medical student is an extreme example of the general difficulties faced by women when they enter gender-inappropriate work:

For a long while I had considered myself neither male nor female, human rather. Now I was sitting in lecture rooms whose words told me outright it was no accident women's brains were smaller than men's [see p.122]. The implicit orthodoxy of the medical faculty allowed them [women] two possibilities only. Either you could be an easy lay and preferably dumb, or you could be miraculously hard-working and reticent. If you were neither you felt lost.

Medicine was only rarely Elizabeth Garrett Anderson, mainly it was Doctor in the House and lascivious mnemonics. A lot of the teachers were men in their fifties and sixties who had gone into academic medicine because they weren't prepared to work in the NHS when it was introduced in 1948. They tended to

TABLE 7.5 *Women as percentage of managers in ten selected occupations, Great Britain, 1971*

Occupation	% managers women
Miners and quarrymen	0
Furnace, forge, foundry and rolling mill workers	0
Woodworkers	2
Leatherworkers	3
Food, drink and tobacco workers	8
Textile workers	12
Clothing workers	13
Clerical workers	15
Sales workers	26
Service, sport and recreation workers*	47

*Includes publicans, housekeepers, stewards, matrons, housemothers, proprietors and managers of boarding houses and hotels, restaurateurs, cooks, hairdressers, beauticians and manicurists, launderers and dry cleaners.

Source: OPCS *Census 1971, Great Britain, Economic Activity Part II*, Table 8 (10% sample). Crown copyright.

TABLE 7.6 *Men and women in ten selected professions, 1977*

Profession	% women	% men
Dentists	15	85
General practitioners	14	86
Veterinary surgeons	10	90
Barristers	6	94
Architects	5	95
University professors	2	98
Chartered surveyors	1	99
Civil engineers	1	99
Bank managers	under 1	over 99
Mechanical engineers	0	100

Source: quoted in Miller (1978) pp. xxv – xxvi.

TABLE 7.7 *Non-industrial Home Civil Service: male and female staff in post in Open Structure and Administrative Group, 1 January 1980*

	Staff in post % men	% women
Open Structure (excl. Parliamentary Counsel)		
Permanent secretary	100	0
Deputy secretary	97.5	2.5
Under secretary	95.6	4.4
Administrative Group		
Assistant secretary	94.3	5.7
Senior principal	97.5	2.5
Principal	92.2	7.8
Senior executive officer	92.5	7.5
Higher executive officer (A)	71.1	28.9
Higher executive officer	83.5	16.5
Executive officer	62.4	37.6
Clerical officer	34.1	65.9
Clerical assistant	20.0	80.0

Source: Civil Service Department *Civil Service Statistics, 1980*, Table 4. Crown copyright.

restrain their sexism until very drunk, then it came out in venomous laughter. 'But of course women are incapable of being doctors'.

Doing anatomy taught me a lot about the extent to which the human body has been defined as male. Women are described only when their anatomy differs from men's. I suggested this to one of the men on the course when we came to study sex organs. His eyes went cold with impatience: 'I suppose you think it's sexist that the instruction sheet for the dissection starts with male genitals'. [*Spare Rib*, 22]

'Women's work' is typically work that requires little training, little in the way of mental initiative, and characteristically consists of interruptible short time-span tasks. It is often also described as 'caring' work — work that promotes the welfare of others, rather than the welfare or development of the worker herself. On these grounds, and especially if they are attractive, women may be tolerated in the public world. Lord Annan, 'peer and columnist', phrased it thus:

TABLE 7.8 *NHS hospital consultants, England and Wales, 1977 — twelve most 'feminine' and twelve most 'masculine' specialties*

Specialty	% women	% men
Child and adolescent psychiatry	32.7	67.3
Mental handicap	19.6	80.4
Neuropathology	17.2	82.8
Anaesthetics	17.2	82.8
Immuno-pathology	17.2	82.8
Paediatric surgery	16.7	83.3
Clinical neurological physiology	16.2	83.8
Medical microbiology	14.8	85.2
Paediatrics	14.4	85.6
Dermatology	12.6	87.4
Gynaecology and obstetrics	12.2	87.8
Radiology	10.9	89.1
Forensic psychiatry	0	100
General pathology	0	100
Urology	0	100
Gastroenterology	0	100
Clinical pharmacology and therapeutics	0	100
Infectious diseases	0	100
General surgery	0.9	99.1
Neurosurgery	1.2	98.8
Plastic surgery	1.3	98.7
Nephrology	2.4	97.6
Cardio-thoracic surgery	2.6	97.4
Clinical physiology	3.9	96.1

Source: Hospital Medical Staff, England and Wales, National Tables, 30 September 1977. DHSS Statistics and Research Division, February 1978, Table 7a. Crown copyright.

All the women in the House of Lords are . . . *particularly* nice . . . . They bring the leaven into the bread, the seasoning into the pot — the salt and pepper, and the sauce as well. Barbara Wootton's my favourite — superb, supreme, magnificent. She's got a fine face, a lot of chin, but that doesn't matter . . . I hope we will go on having life peeresses. I'd like another 50 . . .But we should always have a male majority [*Sunday Times*, 9 November 1975]

Certain work-identities allowed to women follow directly from their domestic roles — that of secretary ('office wife') is a case in point (Benet, 1972). A contest organized by Women Office Workers (WOW) in 1977 asked applicants to submit the most ridiculous chore asked of office workers by their bosses. One secretary said she had to take her boss's toupee to be dry-cleaned and re-styled, another that she had to clean her boss's false teeth. However, the winner of the contest was a secretary who had to pluck out her boss's grey hairs and who had been required by him to shave off his moustache, taking photographs of 'before' and 'after' (McNally, 1979, pp.70 – 1).

Teaching is another example. As Byrne has put it

Women's commitment to teaching is a tradition second only in importance to her domestic role, throughout recorded history and in both East and West, and has acquired an aura of 'inborn gifts' and extended maternality that seems ineradicable. [Byrne, 1978, p.213]

Byrne documents the *fall* in women's share of leadership roles in education over the decade from the mid-1960s to the mid-1970s. By the time the higher echelons of the university sector are reached, women are barely visible at all: 1 per cent of university professors in Britain are women, 5 per cent in America. Women make up 9 per cent and 12 per cent respectively of total university staff in the two countries (Blackstone and Fulton, 1978). At the lower end of the status scale, 99.1 per cent of infant teachers are women, 77 per cent of primary school teachers and 44 per cent of those at secondary level (Deem, 1978, p.113).

In those occupations where women's domestic and maternal capacities are most at a premium, the attributes of the 'good' worker are liable to parallel those of the 'good' women. Florence Nightingale, herself a rebel against the feminine stereotype of the idle lady (see p.102), fell into the trap of another when she wrote in 1881:

To be a good nurse one must be a good woman, here we shall all agree . . . . . What makes a good woman is the better or higher or holier nature: quietness – gentleness – patience – endurance – forbearance, forbearance with patients, her fellow workers, her superiors, her equals . . . . You are here to be trained for *Nurses* — attendants on the Wants of the Sick — *helpers* in carrying out Doctors' orders . . . [Cited in Gamarnikow, 1978, pp.115 – 16]

An ideological shift took place in the definition of a good nurse, so that good woman = good nurse became nurse = mother = housewife.

Even in the top professional jobs the gender formula cannot entirely be avoided. A study by the American sociologist Cynthia Epstein of husband – wife law partnerships demonstrates how the threat of competition with men is averted in the intimate environment of marital relationships: the women did the same types of work as other female lawyers, specializing in family law, matrimonial cases, criminal work and probate; they defined themselves as their husbands' 'helpmates' both in and out of the office, carrying almost all the responsibilities involved in home-maintenance and child-socialization. Moreover, Epstein noted,

When I conducted interviews with women lawyers in their homes, I was commonly offered refreshments and gifts of homemade cakes or jam — gestures of friendliness and hospitality, but also demonstrations of their proficiency in the womanly arts. In the same terms in which they described their need to prove themselves as lawyers . . . these women apparently also wanted to prove themselves as good or better than fulltime housewives. [Epstein, 1971, p.560]

Whatever the origins of the division of labour by gender, one essential mechanism in its maintenance is the presence of discriminatory stereotypes in the heads of those responsible for the hiring and firing of workers. One recent British survey of managers formulating and implementing personnel policy discovered that more than a third of managers (in 223 establishments) believed that women are not career-conscious; half thought women belonged at home and were inferior employees because of their high absenteeism and turnover rates (Hunt, 1975). (In fact, both absenteeism and turnover are related to the type of work done. They are higher in low-grade, low-skill, low-pay work. Since women are concentrated in such work, their absenteeism and turnover rates are slightly higher than those of men, but the attribution of the difference to gender is erroneous — Hunt, 1975; Hulin, 1966; Wild and Hill, 1970.)

The aspect of managers' attitudes the author of the British survey found most striking ('almost shattering') was that men came out top on virtually every attribute managers rated as important in the hiring of workers — from 'personality characteristics' to 'salary required', from 'education' to 'domestic requirements'. 'The lesson to be learned here', she concluded, 'is that a majority of the people who are responsible for the engagement of employees start off with the belief that a woman is likely to be inferior to a man as an employee . . . .' (Hunt, 1975, p.82).

The ideology of managers in relation to women employees does not seem to be quite so reactionary in America as in Britain, judging by one survey reported in 1971 (Bass *et al*.) Whereas the 174 male managers interviewed concurred with British managers in viewing women as unreliable workers bereft of supervisory potential, they were less willing to discriminate against women on grounds of capability, emotionality, life style or level of career-orientation. The norm of female – male *deference* was strongly emphasized, so that women were judged to be unfitted for supervisory positions not because of their inherent capacity, but because it was wrong for men and women to have to defer to a female boss.

In this brief summary of women's employment position I have so far omitted to mention what is possibly its most important aspect — the fact that many women work part time. In 1976, 40 per cent of employed women in Britain worked part time as opposed to 5 per cent of employed men; Table 7.9 shows the significant increase that took place over the period from 1971 to 1976. Part-time work is now a vital feature of the British economy, as it is generally in industrial – capitalist countries, though as Table 7.10 shows the United Kingdom leads the field in this respect.[2]

Part-time work is intimately linked as both cause and effect to the exploitation of women. A 1978 survey by the Low Pay Unit in Britain showed that three-quarters of part-time working women earned hourly rates of less than £1.20 — a figure that would qualify full-time employees for supplementary benefit. Few had any entitlement to sick pay, paid holiday or pension schemes, and 40 per cent were not even allowed any meal or tea breaks during their work stint (Hurstfield,

---

[2] One reason for this is that social security and employment legislation in the UK have drawn a particularly compelling distinction between part- and full-time work. A reflection of this is the recent rise in registered unemployment among women — by 53 per cent from January 1976 to January 1978 (the corresponding male figure was 9 per cent). New National Insurance regulations mean that a married woman's right to pay a lower contribution will be phased out: more women hence register as unemployed because more are entitled to benefit if they do so.

TABLE 7.9 *Employees in part-time employment, Great Britain, 1971 – 6*

Year	Men, % part-time	Women, % part-time
1971	4.4	33.5
1972	4.5	34.5
1973	4.9	36.3
1974	5.2	38.3
1975	5.3	39.6
1976	5.3	40.1

Source: Equal Opportunities Commission (1979) p.44.

TABLE 7.10 *Women's employment, selected countries 1977*

Country	Women as % of workforce			% of employed women who work part time	% of women who work
	Total	Industry	Services		
UK	39	24	51	41	43
Germany	38	24	46	28	35
France	38	25	49	18	41
Netherlands	25	10	36	28	22
Italy	29	23	29	12	25
USA	40	25	50		

Source: Manley and Sawbridge (1980) p.32.

1978). Moreover, promotion opportunities for part-time workers are few (Hunt, 1975). Promotion is aided by taking further education or training courses, but these are not likely to be possible for part-time workers; in any case there is a substantial bias against women here, and three times as many males as females are released by employers for such courses (Blackstone, 1976, p.206).[3]

Many part-time workers are also mothers; motherhood provokes

---

[3] Blackstone points out that this gender division is far more significant than that in higher education because the numbers involved are so much larger.

demotion, with movement into jobs 'which are at a lower level, according to the Registrar-General's classification, than their usual jobs' (Hunt, 1973, p.28). The particular situation of employed mothers underlies two other facets of the occupational division of labour. Firstly, women do less manual work than men (in the ratio of roughly 1:2), but within this field the proportion of women doing unskilled work is increasing: from 15 per cent in 1911 to 27 per cent today (Mackie and Patullo, 1977, p.40). Secondly, women's earnings as a percentage of men's have fallen from the 1977 figure of 75.5 per cent to 73.8 per cent (Equal Opportunities Commission, 1979). Figure 7.3 indicates the effect of the Equal Pay Act (operational in 1975) and shows that even with it the UK has only begun to approach the norm of other EEC countries (and appears now to be going in the opposite direction again). The two most important factors in this financial differential are the greater tendency of men to work overtime and the basic structure of occupational segregation by gender, which, by allocating men and women to different jobs, determines the rewards they are likely to receive in them.

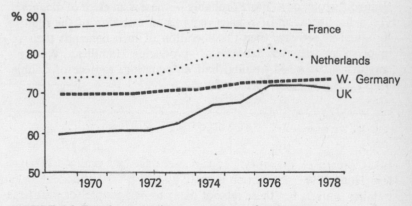

FIGURE 7.3 *Female earnings as a percentage of male earnings (non-agricultural sectors)*
Source: ILO Bulletin of Labour Statistics QI 1979

As Laura Balbo (1979) argues, the idea that women are free to choose whether they should take employment or not is liberal propaganda for a situation that from women's own point of view is experienced very differently. The axiom 'women in the labour force are here to stay' is true — more or less. The new silicon chip technology will enormously cut the number of jobs available to women in female-intensive areas of employment, and the present economic recession will, like all others, lead to pressures on women to give up their jobs to men. But many women must work to live. And aside from the economic constraints, what is offered to women by prevailing values and opportunity structures is a relatively rigid three-stage model: full-time work up to marriage and then afterwards until shortly before the first child is born; more or less full-time domesticity until the youngest child is five years old, then part-time work in a job compatible with home duties.

Simone de Beauvoir proclaimed in *The Second Sex*:

It is through gainful employment that woman has traversed most of the distance that separated her from the male; and nothing else can guarantee her liberty in practice. Once she ceases to be a parasite, the system based on her dependence crumbles . . . [De Beauvoir, 1960, p.372]

Either we are nowhere near this situation, thirty years after De Beauvoir wrote, or — more probably — there is an error of diagnosis. For if the liberation of women requires an assertion of the right to 'productive' activity, then the liberation of men demands their re-involvement in the labour of producing families. Women's employment is a red herring, half an equation, a piece of double-think; it is not a path to paradise.

CHAPTER EIGHT

Domestic Work

You didn't know that domestic work was Britain's largest industry? Well, it is, and it is also the largest consumer of time. We hear a good deal about manhours at present: more are spent on domestic work than anything else . . . It is time that you and I, the women of Britain, took up this matter. Domestic work is our problem . . . [Burton, 1944, p.3]

Calculations of the importance of housework in relation to other industries set the figure at more than a third of the GNP — 39 per cent in Britain, 35 per cent in the USA (Wickham and Young, 1973). These figures are based on time-budget studies of housework and calculate the total market value of the housewife's services in her various capacities as cleaner, cook, laundress, nursemaid, etc. However, the exercise of adding up the hourly rates for these jobs to see what housework is 'worth' is an academic one only. For the first characteristic of women's work as housewives is that it is not paid. All over the world in the late 1960s and early 1970s, feminists rediscovered what earlier feminists knew: that the question of women's equality with men cannot be restricted to the world of paid employment and public power, but resides firstly in their domestic relationships.

WHAT IS HOUSEWORK?
An all-consuming function of production
According to J. K. Galbraith, housework exists to service the consumption function of the economy. The rising standards of consumption made possible by advanced capitalism are only attractive economic goals if they do not mean the loss of labour power. A gourmet meal is enjoyable when not preceded by long hours in the kitchen; a well-furnished house soothes the eye as long as its maintenance has not already worn one out. It is the conversion of women into a 'crypto-servant class' that renders consumption pleasurable to the dominant economic group. 'True' servants are available to only a minority of the population, but

... the servant – wife is available, democratically, to almost the entire present male population ... If it were not for this service [of women as housewives] all forms of household consumption would be limited by the time required to manage such consumption — to select, transport, prepare, repair, maintain, clean, service, store, protect, and otherwise perform the tasks that are associated with the consumption of goods. The servant role of women is critical to the expansion of consumption in the modern economy. [Galbraith, 1974, p.33]

Before the establishment of industrial capitalism, housework had the character of manufacture rather than service. In the southern colonies of America in the seventeenth century, for example, the housewife's duties included the gathering, drying and distilling of herbs for curing the sick, the making of conserves, syrups, jellies, pickles and wines, and the construction of 'Oyles, Oynments and Powders to Adorn and add Loveliness to the Face and Body' (Spruill, 1972, p.210). The eighteenth-century Purefoy family of Shalstone Manor in Buckinghamshire in England recorded their domestic organization in a series of letters (Purefoy, 1931; quoted in Davis, 1966). Mrs Purefoy and her adult son Henry produced the basic food consumed by themselves and their six servants at home. They had several cows, sheep, asses, goats, pigs, poultry, a dovecote and three well-stocked fishponds. They brewed their own ale and made their own bread. Clothes and household extras — tea, fancy spices and herbs, sugar, coffee-berries — had to be purchased, either in London or in the local shops, usually by letter. More of these commodities were bought than a generation before as rising living standards allowed them to be redefined as necessities instead of luxuries.

The majority of British and American homes before and during industrialization were not places where much housework, in the modern sense of cleaning, dusting, tidying and polishing, could be done. Rooms did not have individual uses and were plainly and sparsely furnished as places of work — in the undifferentiated sense of production for use and for exchange:

The labor needs of the household defined the work roles of men, women and children. Their work, in turn, fed the family. The interdependence of work and residence, of household labor needs, subsistence requirements, and family relationships constituted the 'family economy' [Tilly and Scott, 1978, p.12]

The architecture and furnishing of homes reflected this: beds and spinning wheels or other tools of the family's trade shared rooms; cooking, eating, 'working' and relaxing were activities all housed in the same space. The idea of the kitchen as a special room where women prepared food started to emerge among the upper class in the late sixteenth century but was not a general feature of working-class homes until the early twentieth century (Chapman, 1955; Henderson, 1964). Margaret Plant describes the typical eighteenth-century rural home in Scotland as follows:

There was normally one main living-room where the family had their meals, slept, did their work and chatted with the neighbours who dropped in for the evening. Its social centre was the common fireplace, which . . . was large and open and surrounded, beneath the great wide chimney, with seats for family and guests . . . Roughly hewn boughs formed a not unattractive ceiling, and the space between them and the roof proper was floored with brushwood covered with dried moss or grass. The resulting attic made a useful storeroom; or, if the main living-room would hold no more beds, an extra bedroom, the entrance to it being by way of a ladder and a trap-door.

Behind the living room was the 'spence', or parlour, where the housewife put the best furniture and kept the Sunday clothes, and, on great occasions, received company. A passage known as the 'through-gang' joined the living-room to the cow-house and stable (a rather doubtful advantage). [Plant, 1952, pp.24 – 5]

'Carpet' meant a tablecloth and what went on the floor was turf. People tended to eat out of the same wooden dish and share a single glass, and those attending meals elsewhere were well-advised to take their own knife and fork; it was the custom for the diner to wipe and re-use utensils between courses.

Housekeeping is also a simple activity in pre-literate societies where women's (and men's) energies are concentrated on the production of food. The African Nyakyusa, considered among the most well-to-do of all 'primitive' cultures, live in permanent well-built houses, but these are still one-room dwellings made of traditional wattle and daub (Hammond and Jablow, 1976). There is little in the way of household furniture in such cultures, few pots and pans, no complicated recipes to absorb a cook's time.

As the level of material possessions rises and definitions of women and work change, a radical transformation is brought about in women's relationship to their work. Production for family use is converted into consumption for family use. Commodities become available on the market that require little of the housewife even in the way of preparation. At the same time, more energy and hours are needed in home-maintenance activities — dusting, polishing, carpet-shampooing, curtain-washing and so forth. These may be, in Galbraith's terminology, 'the crypto-servant functions of consumption administration', but such language hides the chief significance of the housewife's invisible and unpaid work from the viewpoint of the maintenance of the economy. The housewife's work remains productive, for what she produces is workers for industry: her husband with his clean clothes, well-filled stomach and mind freed from the need to provide daily care for his children; the children fed, clothed, loved and chastized ready for their own adult gender-specific role as workers or worker-producers.

To say that the modern housewife is still a productive worker, despite the changes that have stripped the housework role of its manufacturing aspect, is an important restatement of the position of women. In the early years of the women's liberation movement when feminists began to grapple with the theoretical problem of how women's subordination might be explained, it was the situation of women as unpaid workers in the home that came to be seen as the central enigma. Margaret Benston, in one of the first analyses, stated that housework

is pre-capitalist in a very real sense. This assignment of household work as the function of a special category 'women' means that this group *does* stand in a very different relation to production than the group 'men' . . . The material basis for the inferior status of women is to be found in just this definition of women. In a society in which money determines value, women are a group who work outside the money economy. Their work is not worth money, is therefore valueless, is therefore not even real work. And women themselves, who do this valueless work, can hardly be expected to be worth as much as men, who work for money. In structural terms, the closest thing to the condition of women is the condition of others who are or were also outside of commodity production, i.e. serfs and peasants. [Benston, 1969, pp.15 – 16]

Housework is pre-capitalist according to Benston because it produces only 'use values' — products and services consumed directly by the family. The disadvantage of this argument is that it allows housework to be seen as some kind of incongruous historical relic; its advantage is that it shifts women's labour from a marginal to a central economic position: it thus 'completely changed the terms on which a discussion of women's work had to be carried on' (Malos, 1977, p.7).

Since Benston wrote, a great deal of discussion both in and outside the women's movement has been devoted to the thorny question of the exact meaning of the term 'productive labour' as applied to the housewife's work. Did Marx himself define housework as productive? Apparently not:

In volume one of *Capital* he said that the reproduction of labour power was *productive consumption*, but he did not say it was productive *labour*. [Malos, 1977, p.15]

Domestic labour is unproductive (in the economic sense) and conforms with Marx's description of an unproductive labour 'exchanged not with capital but with revenue, that is wages or profits'. [Secombe, 1974, p.11]

'Production' in capitalism, according to Marxist theory, means the creation of surplus value — the part of labour that enables capitalist profits to be made. (Workers sell their labour power to capitalists who extract profit from their use of this labour power by paying workers less than the amount for which they sell the products of labour on the market.) Housewives create goods through their labour as producers and consumers in the home, but these goods do not enter the commodity market. Wally Secombe maintains that, while housework is productive in the sense of actually transferring and creating value, it is not productive 'in the specific context of capitalist production' because it is not 'conducted in direct relation with capital' and it does not produce surplus value. (Just to complicate matters, others have countered that it does, on the other hand, produce a surplus-value-creating commodity: labour power — Dalla Costa and James, 1972.)

The central point in the Marxist domestic labour debate is 'that the housewife works for the maintenance of capitalism rather than simply being a worker for her family' (Glazer-Malbin, 1976, p.919). Industrial capitalism as an economic system requires *somebody* to buy the food, cook the meals, wash the clothes, clean the home and bear and bring up the children. Without this back-up of domestic labour the economy could not function — or, at least, enormous and profit-handicapping resources would have to be devoted to catering for these personal and reproductive needs. Women as housewives who meet these needs are thus the backbone of the economy, and their contribution, whether viewed as the psychological welfare of children, the stability of marriage or the employer's pocket, is certainly 'productive'; only Marxist purists need concern themselves with any epistemological uncertainty on this point.

The promotion and prevention of housework

Leonore Davidoff (1976) has observed that the Marxist model of domestic labour can interpret the housewife's oppression (by privatized, unpaid and socially trivialized work) but cannot show why this oppression takes the form it does. Early industrial capitalism in England bred a factory system based on female and child labour that was only transformed into one based on male labour through the propagation of a domestic ideology of women.

The relationship between material conditions and gender ideology was (and still is) a complex one, and nowhere better illustrated than in the fate of women's household labour in socialist economies. Following Marx and Engels, the 1917 Revolution in the USSR promised women a new era of equality based on their emancipation from the privatized oppression of household labour. Sixty years later, there have certainly been achievements in the public role of women (not only women's 51 per cent share in employment, but their 40 per cent uptake of engineering posts, 59 per cent of technical jobs and 50 per cent use of places in higher education), but the amount of time demanded by household chores is the same now as it was in the 1930s (Lapidus, 1978, p.128) and most of this work continues to be done by women. In fact, looking at time-budget studies from the 1920s to the 1960s in the USSR, Michael Sachs has shown that the female – male ratio in domestic work has remained unchanged: 'Males continue to have as much free time as females have housework' (Sachs, 1977, p.798). Moreover, while 13 per cent of male housework time in the 1920s was spent on gardening and the care of animals, this figure was 30 per cent in the 1960s.

Soviet women's double burden has been justified since the 1930s by an official conception of femininity that has yoked a glorification of wifely and maternal responsibilities to the national duty of economic productivity:

Our feminine hearts are overflowing with emotions [proselytized a fictional heroine in 1937] and of these love is paramount. Yet a wife should also be a happy mother and create a serene home atmosphere, without, however, abandoning work . . . She should know how to combine all these things while also matching her husband's performance on the job. [Quoted in Lapidus, 1978, p.131]

The story of a young Moscow technical worker published in the Russian magazine *Novy Mir* attracted a flood of sympathetic letters for the familiar strains it documented. Olya, the story's central character, is also the mother of two young children. She is asked to fill in a questionnaire at work aimed at discovering the reasons for the falling birth rate:

how many hours do I spend on '(a) housework, (b) occupation with the children, (c) cultural leisure pursuits'. 'Leisure' is explained: radio and television broadcasts, visits to the cinema, theatre, etc., reading, sport, tourism, etc.

Ah, leisure, leisure . . . The word sounds clumsy, somehow — 'lei-sure'. 'Women, fight for cultural leisure!' What rubbish . . . Lei-sure. Myself, I'm addicted to sport: running. I'm always running: to work, from work, shopping — a shopping basket in each hand . . . upstairs, downstairs, trolley bus — bus, into the underground — out of the underground. There aren't any shops near our new housing estate yet, we have been living there now for more than a year, but they still haven't been built.

She is also asked to provide the total number of workdays lost last year through her own or her children's illness. This she works out later, while doing the ironing — 78. Her husband responds:

'What do you think, Olya darling, maybe it would be better if you didn't go out to work? Just think nearly half the year you're sitting at home anyway.'

'So you want to lock me up for the whole year? Do you think we can live on your salary?'

'If I am freed from these jobs' — Dima glares round the kitchen — 'then I could earn more. I could probably get two hundred to two hundred and twenty. In fact, if you work out the unpaid days, you only earn about 60 roubles a month. It just doesn't pay!'

'Great', I say, 'Just great. You mean all these boring jobs' — I also glance round the kitchen — 'will be for me alone, and you'll have all the interesting work. Just fancy, "doesn't pay" — capitalist!'

'Capitalist indeed', Dima gives a short laugh, 'the money isn't the only point. The children would benefit from it. The nursery school isn't so bad, but the creche . . . Gulka hardly ever goes for a walk in winter. And these endless colds!'

'Dima, do you really think that I wouldn't like to do what's best for the children? Of course I would. But what you suggest is just . . . it would destroy me. And my five years studying? My diploma? My working record? My job? It's easy for you to chuck all that overboard! And what'll I be like, sitting at home? As cross as hell: I'll nag at all of you, the whole time. But what are we talking about? We can't survive on your salary, and you haven't been offered anything else . . .'

'Don't be hurt, darling, you're probably right. I shouldn't have started it. I just had a glimpse of some sort of . . . sensibly organized life. And also that, if I didn't have to rush after the children, I could work differently, not restrict myself . . . maybe that's selfishness, I don't know. Let's stop this though, OK?'

He goes out of the kitchen. I follow him with my eyes, and suddenly I want to call him and say: 'Forgive me, Dima.' But I don't. [*Spare Rib*, December 1976; June 1977]

This situation can be traced directly to the lack of prominence given to household work in Marxist theory. While some Soviet economists in the 1920s propounded the view that all social forms of labour that promote national welfare are productive, the theoretical position that came to predominate in the 1930s was the more orthodox Marxist one, according to which only labour that directly creates national income is productive. The limited economic resources of the Soviet Union were hence directed into the most 'productive' sphere of the economy — heavy industry — and away from public services. Despite a subsequent investment in state childcare (Olya's two children attended a state-run creche and nursery school) and in some communal dining, the inadequate development of the service sector combined with the limited production of consumer durables and general shortage of consumption goods and retail outlets inflated women's domestic burden to a point exceeding that of many women in the West. One ironic consequence is that advanced capitalism has done more *potentially* to lighten the burden of domestic labour than state socialism. There are more semi-processed foods, rationalized shopping facilities, specialized laundry services and mechanized household appliances in the West than the East; for example, in 1970 the USSR boasted 4,400 laundries and dry-cleaners for a population of 244 million, while the UK had 5,593 for a population of 55 million (Heitlinger, 1979).

It is part of the conventional wisdom of family life that, just as 'the' family has historically lost its functions (of production to industry, of reproduction to the hospital, of child socialization to the educational system), so women within families have lost their function to household technology — it is the washing machine, not the vote, that is the true liberator of women. However, it is nearer the truth to see mechanical household aids as rather like the Marxist model of women's emancipation: theoretically, both ought to free women from housework, but in practice neither does so. One factor is that housewives have not benefited to the same extent as other segments of the population from technological advance; it is obvious to anybody who does housework that existing household equipment is not designed with maximum efficiency in mind.

Second, the machines-liberate-housewives view ignores, as Cowan (1974) has pointed out, the possibility that the component activities of housework are merely profoundly transformed when they undergo mechanization. Technological innovation always occurs in a social context, and Leonore Davidoff has described how the hierarchical structure of the household (master versus mistress, mistress versus servant) acted against the 'rational' application of science and technology to household work from the very beginning:

For example, it must have been known by experience that soaking very dirty pans in water overnight made it both much easier and much quicker to clean them, but it was the rule that every single pan had to be scoured and polished and put away before the servants were allowed to go to bed, no matter how late the hour, and young scullery maids could be hauled out of bed to scrub the pans if they had neglected this duty. [Davidoff, 1976, p.144]

(It is still a mark of bad housewifery to leave dirty unscrubbed pans in the sink overnight.) What is 'rational' in household management is what is dictated by prevailing ideas of the kind of activity housework is (and the kind of people houseworkers are).

Thirdly, to assume that domestic technology liberates housewives is to ignore all that is known about the social impact of technology on work. Increasing division of labour and increasing routinization are the almost inevitable products of general technological 'improvements' in the work process, and what *these* lead to for the worker is an intensified sense of powerlessness, not a feeling of freedom from the bondage of work. As Betty Friedan so aptly pointed out in *The Feminine Mystique* (1963), technology cannot in itself mitigate the psychological law that 'housewifery expands to fill the time available'. Touring American suburbs in the 1950s, she confronted the same question again and again: given the same house and the same housewife, the same work could take one or six hours.

The answer to the paradox identified by Friedan was the 'glorification' of women's domestic role. Occurring at the same time as 'barriers to her full participation in society were lowered', this evidenced 'society's reluctance to treat women as complete human beings; for the less real function that [women's] role has, the more it is decorated with meaningless details to conceal its emptiness' (Friedan, 1963, p.239). Against the 'need' to change and wash the sheets once a week is set the 'need' to change them two or three times a week and to get them 'whiter than white'. For this reason, housework hours have actually risen with the invention of new household appliances (Vanek, 1974). In my own interviews with British housewives (Oakley 1974b), there was a strong association between the standards housewives set for themselves and their weekly hours of housework, as shown in Table 8.1. The average working week in this sample of housewives was 77 hours. Other time-budget studies show an increase in housework in urban as opposed to rural conditions, and a definite increase over the last fifty years in the time spent on housework despite the raised level of household mechanization and the rise in housewives' employment

TABLE 8.1 *Housework hours and specification of standards and routines*[1]

| Standards and routines | Weekly housework hours | | Total |
| | 40 – 69 | 70 or more | |
	No. (%)	No. (%)	No. (%)
High	2(10)	19(91)	21(100)
Medium	4(29)	10(71)	14(100)
Low	4(80)	1(20)	5(100)
Total	10(25)	30(75)	40(100)

Source: Oakley (1974b) p.111.

[1] 'Specification' here refers to the detailed rules about the way housework should be done evident in housewives' accounts of their work. These may derive from many sources (feminine socialization, media stereotypes, etc.), but the point is that they are felt as psychologically binding.

outside the home. (In fact, some studies actually suggest that outside employment raises housework hours.) Other studies point to the fact that the employment of wives and the addition of more children to the family only in extreme cases raises the amount of housework done by men (Meissner, 1975; Szalai, 1972).

One mechanism for the decoration of housewifery is the advertising industry, which sells to housewives through the sexist messages of the media not only X brand of carpet shampoo and Y brand of washing powder, but an immensely powerful imagery of virtuous womanhood. The image is constructed and propagated through the use of stereotypes: 'A particular reality is presented as if it were the only reality. A particular idea of what life is like is presented as if it were the only, or at least the best, way of life' (Millum, 1975, pp.51 – 2). Housewives in Millum's analysis of women's magazine advertisements are typically, of course, shown in the home, but the most invidious message is that the hardworking housewife is at one and the same time the calm, satisfied, attractive woman; housework is a labour of love performed with scarcely a hair out of place and a permanently unruffled, cosmetically enriched grin. (It is instructive to compare this with the attitude of the drug companies promoting tranquillizers and anti-depressants as the housewife's necessary aids — p.79 – 80.) The message 'this product takes the hard work out of housework' appeals to the very notion of femininity that got women into their present predicament: the idea that real femininity is incompatible with real work. At the same time, it most sympathetically acknowledges that housework *is* work, hoping to win the hearts of its female customers by taking their side in the sexual politics of marital domesticity.

I always say housework's harder work, but my husband doesn't say that at all. I think he's wrong, because I'm going all the time — when his job is finished, it's finished . . . Sunday he can lie in bed till twelve, get up, get dressed and go for a drink, but my job never changes. [Oakley, 1974b, p.45]

The prison-house of home

The *unendingness* of housework, together with its repetitious character, were the most frequently named 'worst' aspects of being a housewife in my own study of housework carried out in London in 1971. Most (70 per cent) of the housewives in this study were dissatisfied with housework as work — a finding that was not confined to the middle-class women, but applied equally to working-class housewives. While housewives valued the autonomy of their role ('You're your own boss'), the effects of this were described as an intensification of responsibility: since no one else tells the housewife how and when to do her work, she has to be her own supervisor and arbitrate her own standards. Rules — a 'job definition' — are even more necessary because housework is not paid. Apart from the appreciative remarks of husband, children and others, the housewife gets no feedback on her job performance; the only remaining course open to her is to reward herself by laying down standards and routines for housework and then achieving self-satisfaction by meeting them.

Yet the pat on the back is a constant struggle — against the pervasive cultural devaluation of housewifery ('only' or 'just' a housewife) and against those aspects of housework that render it a displeasing activity. The more a housework task (and the tasks that make up housework *are* different) resembles assembly-line factory work, the more it is disliked. Ironing comes top of the 'dislike' list; cooking, a potentially creative act, is the best-liked chore. Overall, three-quarters of the women found housework monotonous; 90 per cent complained about its fragmentation — its character as a series of unconnected tasks, none of which requires the worker's full attention. 'The routine is never quite routine, so the vacuum in one's mind is never vacuous enough to be filled. "Housework is a worm eating away at one's ideas"' (Peckham Rye Women's Liberation Group, 1970, p.5). Table 8.2 compares the experiences of monotony, fragmentation and excessive pace (having too much to do) among

TABLE 8.2 *The experience of monotony, fragmentation and speed in work: housewives and factory workers compared*

Workers	Percentage experiencing:		
	Monotony	Fragmentation	Speed
Housewives	75	90	50
Factory workers*	41	70	31
Assembly line workers*	67	86	36

*These figures are taken from Goldthorpe *et al.*, (1968) p.18.
Source: Oakley (1974b) p.87.

housewives and factory workers. The parallel between housewives'
and assembly-line workers' attitudes is striking.

But perhaps most disturbing of all is the isolation of the housewife
and her work. As Margery Spring Rice said in a unique record of
working-class women's domestic labour in the 1930s:

She eats, sleeps, 'rests', on the scene of her labour and her labour is entirely
solitary . . . . Whatever the emotional consequences, whatever her devotion,
her family creates her labour, and tightens the bonds that tie her to the lonely
and narrow sphere of 'home'. [Spring Rice, 1939, pp.105 – 6]

Over half the women in my own study felt they did not see enough
people during the day, and this feeling was more likely, not
surprisingly, in those who were dissatisfied with housework. Aside
from the question of how many people housewives actually see and
talk to during the day, there is also the general sense of captivity noted
in countless research reports and personal testimonies:

Twenty five per cent of the working class wives had no friends at all . . . Many
middle class wives felt that they were becoming rather isolated . . . [Gavron,
1966, p.142]

The lack of contact with other people coupled with the almost non-existence
of a social life or leisure activities participated in by women outside the home,
presents a depressing picture of the lives of many women. [Hobson, 1978,
p.87]

One woman in Hobson's study looked out of the window of her ninth-
floor flat and counted the cars going by on the road 'just for
something to do'; another talked to her cat until her first baby arrived
to give her 'a bit of company'.

But children, for many women the *reason* for being at home,
necessitate work of a different kind from housework. 'I could never
consider the possibility of staying at home as a housewife, even part-
time', said one housewife 'if I had no child to humanize the work for
me'. Yet

My feelings of satisfaction or happiness are never connected with the
housework, and are often in strict opposition to it, because Carl's vivacity and
lawlessness oppose the reign of order and hygiene . . . It is a waste socially,
psychologically and even economically, to put me in a position where my only
means of expressing loyalty to Carl is by shopping, dishwashing and sweeping
floors. [Gail, 1968, pp.147 – 8]

Of course, not *every* woman perceives contradiction and ambivalence in this situation; not *every* housewife is dissatisfied. But the fact that some are should not be taken as indicating personal disorder. Because housework is private and feminine, attitudes to it are easily and erroneously laced with the moral invective of individualized discontent. Any description of the structure of the housewife's oppression 'assumes querulous and complaining tones, the tones of a private neurosis to express a social fact' (Peckham Rye Women's Liberation Group, 1970, p.6). As we saw in Chapter 4, the private neurosis of housewives is depression, a psychiatric label that most adequately hides the social fact of the housewife's loneliness, low self-esteem and work dissatisfaction.

WHO DOES HOUSEWORK?

Obviously women do, and that is why a chapter on domestic work is of such importance in a book of this kind. Definitionally speaking, a housewife is 'the person wholly or mainly responsible for running the household' (Hunt, 1968, p.25) — 85 per cent of women aged 16 – 64 in this survey were classed as housewives. Through upbringing and the social pressures of various kinds charted in Chapters 5 and 6, it is women's fate to have the description 'housewife' as an inseparable part of their self-images, at least as these can be tapped by social science researchers. Asking women to describe themselves is liable to yield the following kinds of self-portrait:

I am a housewife	I am a good housewife
I am a mother	I am good to my children
I am ordinary	I am good at housework
I am a wife	I am good to my husband
I am happy	I am good at washing
I am reasonably attractive	I am fed up at times
I am a sister	I am bad tempered at times
I am a neighbour	I am very happy with my work
I am a friend	I am happy with my children
I am sociable	I am seldom unhappy [Oakley, 1974b, pp.122, 124]

Of 40 women asked to describe themselves by completing the sentence 'I am . . .' ten times, 25 wrote 'I am a housewife' somewhere in their lists of self-descriptions and 20 of these put it in first or second place;

41 per cent of all the statements concerned housework or domestic roles generally ('I am a cleaner', 'I am a slave', 'I am a good houseworker').

This intense personal involvement in housework poses a considerable problem for women who wish to share it with men or with other women. To do so implies the obligation to examine one's own standards: where did they come from, and how 'rational' are they? Requiring other people to adhere to uncritically reviewed personal standards is hardly liberation — for others or for oneself. From a slightly different but related perspective, anthropologist Mary Douglas, in her analysis of concepts of pollution, acknowledges a debt of inspiration to her husband. 'In matters of cleanliness his threshold of tolerance is so much lower than my own that he more than anyone else has forced me into taking a stand on the relativity of dirt' (Douglas, 1970, p.viii). Dirt is not absolute. Every culture has its own notions of dirt and defilement; these stand in opposition to its notions of the positive structure that must be preserved. For, as Mary Douglas argues, the elimination of dirt is not a negative movement; rather, it is a positive attempt to organize one's environment to conform with some prior notion of order. So it is these cherished classifications we must understand.

Current European and American preconceptions about housework originated in the domestic hygiene movement that developed in the late nineteenth century. In America, Ellen Swallow Richards, a 'firmjawed, heavy-browed, confident' ex-chemist, was an early popularizer of the message of domestic science. This was a direct result of discrimination against women in her chosen profession: at the Massachusetts Institute of Technology she had been forced to study apart from the male students and was commandeered by her professors to sort their papers and mend their suspenders. But not even suspender-mending could qualify her for a graduate degree or for a job in the male world of chemistry. What she did instead was to teach people 'the science of right living', a mixture of chemistry, biology and engineering geared to the practical tasks of housekeeping. The idea was, as a colleague of Richards put it, that

Nature has assigned to her [woman] special duties which man has deemed safe to be trusted to her instincts, yet in reality need for their performance the highest scientific knowledge. [Cotten, 1897, p.280]

Biochemistry could reform cooking and economics would revolutionize shopping. But behind it all was the magnificent Germ Theory of Disease, whose foundations were laid when Pasteur discovered micro-organisms in 1857. Pasteur's discovery had the advantage that disease could be reclassified as in principle under man's control — or, more specifically, as controllable by means of the cleanliness and common sense of women. It had the disadvantage that germs, being invisible to the human eye, might be anywhere. By the 1890s an epidemic of public anxiety about contagion was in full swing. When the typhoid epidemic of the 1870s nearly killed the Prince of Wales, wealthy householders began to confront the problems of indoor sanitation. In America, the case of 'Typhoid Mary', an Irish — American cook who communicated typhoid to 52 people in the homes of her employers, was seen to raise in an especially urgent form the question: who is responsible for the public health?

For various cogent reasons the answer seemed obvious — women. In the first place, women were already defined by their domestic function — if not as housewives in the modern sense, then at least as the moral guardians of the home and as domestic servants. In the second place, the domestic science and sanitary reform movements were seen as relevant to an issue that was of direct biological concern to women: the question of infant mortality. Germs played a large part in the diarrhoeal diseases of infants responsible for a quarter of all infant deaths (1 in 6 babies died in their first year in 1899). Diarrhoea was diagnosed as a 'filth disease' to be prevented only by 'scrupulous domestic cleanliness':

Infant mortality, it became clear, was a matter not so much of environmental hygiene, but of personal hygiene. It was more a social problem . . . The mother was evidently the factor of paramount importance. [McCleary, 1933, p.35]

Mothers were taught not only how to feed babies artificially without giving them gastro-enteritis, but also how to eliminate germs from their homes. The penalty of a dead baby for careless maternal housework provided an immensely powerful moral justification for the zealous housewife: bad housecleaning equals child abuse.

While the intrusion of 'science' into housekeeping was argued as a strategy for *reducing* housework, its overall effect was undoubtedly to *increase* it. Instead of mindless routine, housework became a quest for new knowledge, became white collar work (analysing, planning and consulting with the experts). The education of consumers eventually became their manipulation into the belief that good housewives had to employ a wide range of expensive products to achieve a clean home and a satisfied family. And the moral imputation that proper womanhood is a state of grace only gained when everyone's health and domestic comfort has been cared for, was, of course, presented in such a way as to be quite irresistible.

Yet a third reason why women were seen as guardians of the public health has to be dredged out of the buried subsoil of cultural attitudes. Pollution and purity rituals such as housework are attempts to impose cultural patterns on the natural world, and, in particular, to maintain boundaries between people, activities and places that are felt to be antithetical: the kitchen versus the dining room, poor people versus rich people, urination versus conversation. Because women can more easily be construed as natural creatures than men (only they have the body products of menstrual blood, babies and milk), their social position is more readily defined as marginal than that of men. As Douglas (1970) has shown, it is people at the margins of society — not only women, but little children, ethnic minorities, and lower castes and classes — who are felt to be most potentially dangerous and polluting. The paradoxical consequence of this is that they are required to act as the agents of other people's purity, in order to guarantee their own. Ideas of physical cleanliness as communicated by the nineteenth-century domestic economy movement in Britain and America are mixed with ideas about social and moral purity. A belief in the threatening contamination of femaleness struggled with an intransigent vision of women's inherent goodness to produce a situation in which women can never be just ordinary but must be either angels or devils.

It is not of course the case that only women do housework. In many pre-literate societies, what we call housework is turned over to small children or old people of both sexes who are not able to do other kinds of work. In colonial societies, as Davidoff (1976) points out, native men in preference to native women have provided most of the domestic labour for the foreign dominant group. Table 8.3, which shows the division of domestic and childrearing tasks among the Tanulong and Fedizilan people of the Phillippines, is the other half of Table 7.1, which showed the 'productive' work roles of men and women in the same society. Of the 29 tasks in Table 8.3, 12 are shared

TABLE 8.3 *Tasks and their performers in Tanulong and Fedilizan*

Task	Performer
Domestic household chores	
Cooking	B
Washing dishes	B
Feeding animals	B
Skinning sweet potatoes	FM
Pounding rice	B
Keeping floors clean	FM
Gathering sweet potato leaves for pigs	FM
Waking up to cook in the morning	B
Splitting wood	MF
Cutting wood from the forest	MF
Preparing pig's food for cooking	B
Preparing cotton thread for weaving	FM
Weaving cloth	F
Washing clothes	FM
Sewing/mending clothes	FM
Washing dishes and pans	FM
Dressing and sacrificing chickens	B
Killing pigs	M
Distributing meat	MF
Cutting up meat for meals	MF
Fetching water	B
Babysitting	B
Keeping the child clean	FM
Feeding the child	B
Washing the child	FM
Cutting the child's hair	MF
Seeing the medium when child is sick	B
Taking care of sick child	FM
Counseling children	B

Note: B = tasks performed equally by females or males; F = tasks performed by females only; M = tasks performed by males only; FM = tasks performed usually by women; MF = tasks performed usually by men.
Source: Adapted from Bacdayan (1977), p.282.

equally, 15 are shared, but less equally, and only cloth-weaving (feminine) and pig-killing (masculine) are one-sex activities.

In some cultures men regularly do the cooking (Firth, 1965), or they may participate only on ritual occasions (Little, 1954). In others, who cooks what is determined by the division of labour in procuring food. Among the Tiwi of Northern Australia, foods are divided into men's and women's, with men hunting the products of the sea and air and women those of the land (Goodale, 1971); for the Ilongots of the Philippines, the division is between rice, which is cultivated, cooked and distributed by women, and meat, which is provided, cooked and allocated by men (Rosaldo, 1974). Malinowski, discussing *The Family Among the Australian Aborigines* (1963) noted that Kurnai men's work was confined to hunting opposums and making rugs and weapons, a strange combination from a Western point of view. Among the Tungus of Siberia, men who are too old to hunt share with women their work of caring for reindeer herds, dressing and preparing skins for clothing and managing tents and their belongings (Forde, 1957). Men of the Mbum Kpau tribe in Africa fetch water and sweep the courtyards of houses, weave mats and baskets and dress skins; but they will not pound grain, make beer or oil or render salt (O'Laughlin, 1974).

THE SERVANT PROBLEM

Mrs Wrigley, a plate-layer's wife, was born in a Welsh village in 1858. At the age of 9, she became a servant:

. . . . the doctor's wife came to our house and said a lady and gentleman wanted a little nurse for their child, to go back with them to Hazel Grove, near Stockport. My little bundle of clothes was packed up and I went in full glee with them. Instead of being a nurse I had to be a servant-of-all-work, having to get up at six in the morning, turn a room out and get it ready for breakfast. My biggest trouble was I could not light the fire, and my master was very cross and would tell me to stand away, and give me a good box on my ears. That was my first experience of service life. I fretted very much for my home. Not able to read or write, I could not let my parents know, until a kind old lady in the village wrote to my parents to fetch me home from the hardships I endured. I had no wages at this place, only a few clothes.

Her last job in domestic service, before her marriage to Mr Wrigley, was a happier experience:

Here there was four servants, and I was engaged for the cook. It was a real gentleman's house. They kept coachmen, farmer and gardener, the very best place I had in all my life. We had plenty of freedom, going out in our turn. We were not treated as servants but as all one family, and the children was taught to treat us kindly and with respect. The servants was thought so much of, and when we had a ball the kitchen staff was allowed to have one dance with the guests . . . . I was there five years, and I married from there . . . I was sorry to give up such a good home . . . . [Davies, 1977, pp.58, 60]

Personal accounts such as Mrs Wrigley's are rare, for, as Theresa McBride notes, the most completely ignored social group in European history has been the servant class:

Historians have been content to take servants for granted in the same way that their employers expected them to be always unobtrusively present. [McBride, 1976, p.9]

Servants are the counterparts in the market economy of housewives — ubiquitous and essential, but working in the coerced silence of a double oppression as women and as secret agents maintaining the all-important cultural boundary between personal and public life. It is not coincidental that servants, like women, were defined as the dependants of men (property-owners) and were the last social group to receive enfranchisement as citizens.

The experience of leaving home for domestic service was a fairly typical one in the nineteenth century; in 1871, 12 per cent of female servants were aged less than 15 (McBride, 1976, p.45). At the end of the nineteenth century in Britain, around 20 per cent of households employed servants, and around one-sixth of all English women were domestic servants. The number of 'indoor' female domestic servants exceeded by some 300,000 all the women employed in textiles, nursing, teaching, shop work and the civil service put together (Davidoff and Hawthorn, 1976, p.73). Even the families of skilled working men often had a young living-in servant girl to do the scrubbing and dirty work and babyminding. Roughly two-thirds of all female servants were 'general' domestics of this kind (McBride, 1976, p.14). Conditions of work were poor. In the early 1800s, for instance, servants slept in the kitchen or in cupboards under the stairs. Later, when allocated the attics, employers often forbad their servants to display pictures or any personal objects, and considered it their right to look through servants' belongings. Servants were not allowed to sing or laugh at work, were expected to do their work noiselessly, never to speak unless spoken to, to stand in the presence of their employer and to walk out of the room backwards (Davidoff and Hawthorn, 1976).

Until about 1840, domestic service continued to be the major occupier of women throughout Western Europe and in the United States, but a decline set in the late nineteenth century as more women took jobs as clerks, shop assistants and factory workers in preference to domestic service. There was also a trend away from living-in servants and towards daily 'charring' as the ideology of family privacy intensified to exclude strangers — even those who would lighten the rapidly mounting burden of married women's domestic work. Magazines for women such as *Housewife* (1886), *The Mother's Companion* (1887), *The Ladies' Home Journal* (1890), *Woman at Home* (1893), *Home Notes* (1894), *Home Chat* (1895) and *Home Companion* (1897) arrived to bemoan 'the servant problem' and provide manuals of advice on 'the conduct and management of the home'.

Because research into domestic work is almost non-existent, the current position of paid domestic workers in industrial societies is not well-documented. One survey of the home help service in England and Wales carried out in 1967 found that the women who worked for it tended to be older and have more domestic responsibilities themselves than the average employed woman. (Home helps are paid by local authorities to do housework and generally look after people either temporarily or permanently unable to look after themselves.) Half had children under 16; one in six had to look after at least one elderly or infirm person in their family. Pay was between 23p and 28p an hour; only one in four were paid travelling expenses, and one in six were not paid for their travelling time between jobs. Many received no sick pay. One in five were issued with no protective clothing, and only one in ten were provided with equipment. Many of the women worked in homes where equipment and amenities were poor: a quarter had no hot water supply, half did not possess a vacuum cleaner; a third of the home helps used their own equipment or bought items with their own money for use in the homes they worked in. Not surprisingly, 85 per cent wanted improvements in their working conditions (Hunt, 1970).

Nightcleaning is another form of paid domestic work:

Q: Why do you actually do night work?

A: Because of my children, you see, I cannot manage to work in a hospital fulltime, I had to see about one [daytime job] this morning: 7.30 to 1.00 for £10, which is a good salary for me, but 7.30 to 1.00 I can't manage because of my youngest child. The others are alright, they can look after themselves to go to school, but she, I cannot leave her here on her own . . .

Q: What else do you have to do during the day besides get the children off to school?

A: Well, I have to take them to school, I have to come home and prepare something for them to eat because I cannot afford a full dinner money for four of them at school. I have to take them back to school and go collect them in the afternoon, do my housework, cook and wash.

Q: How much sleep do you get?

A: Well, two hours, when my husband is in, he's working in the afternoon, he helps me do a bit of cooking when he's in, but when he's not in, I'm not getting no rest.

Q: Can you get along like that or does it make you feel irritable and nervous?

A: If I don't get any rest I always feel nervous, because my doctor has stopped me from my night job once, he told me I'm not getting enough rest with all these children . . . [*Shrew*, December 1971, p.5]

Nightcleaning is 'contract' labour: large offices contract their cleaning to cleaning companies who contract to provide a certain number of women to clean so many feet of office space. Since no one checks how the work is actually done (those who might do so are asleep in bed), there is a golden opportunity to make huge profits out of employing fewer women to do more work than the contract states. Nightcleaners are women who are too old, too untrained or too burdened with childcare to get other work. They often put in a full working week, but they do so at a time, in a place and for the kind of rates that lead their jobs to be dismissed as 'casual' part-time work.

ALL IN A DAY'S WORK

Factories at night mimic the invisibility of the home:

Jean works in her bedroom. She machines pillow ticks while watching the clock. She is pleased because she can make 21 in 1 hour and soon she hopes to be quick enough to make 24. She finds it difficult to build up speed, though, because she is always being interrupted by the demands of her family. Jean has four children of school age. Her husband, John, works in a shoe factory and with 5 hours overtime he brings home £27 a week, not enough to support a family. [Hope *et al.*, 1976, pp.91 – 3]

Jean and her family live in two rooms plus a kitchen and they share a lavatory with fifteen people that is cleaned by Jean 'because no-one else will do it'. Jean earns 2p for each pillow tick she makes and she averages 48p an hour.

Thousands of women in Britain are in paid employment as homeworkers, although it is hard to get national figures because the opinion of those who organize the work of the government statistical service has been for half a century that homework doesn't exist in any significant sense. Jean was one of those interviewed for a small North London survey — one of the few attempts to find out about homeworkers' conditions. It uncovered atrocious conditions (low pay, no allowance for overheads such as heating and lighting, no training and no expenditure by the firms on capital equipment such as sewing machines). Another investigation of homeworkers in the toy industry showed that over four-fifths of homeworkers were paid less than the legal minimum for piecework. Two of the 178 women surveyed got holiday pay; none got sick pay. All said that the money they earned was not just pin money, but was a large part of the family income (Advisory Conciliation and Arbitration Service, 1978).

However one approaches the subject of domestic labour, one is thus returned constantly to the same theme: the benign refusal to call housework proper labour. I shall end this chapter by mentioning two further consequences of this.

One is that the conditions of family life do more than mark the prosperity or poverty of families: they are work conditions. According to the *General Household Survey*, in Britain one in twenty homes still do not have baths, or inside lavatories, half lack central heating, a third have no washing machine and one in ten no refrigerator (*General Household Survey*, 1978, Table 2.20, p.36). Similarly, occupational hazards of housework as work are not recognized. One — depression, or 'housewife's disease' — has already been mentioned. Another is accidental injury or death. 'Twenty people die each day from accidents in the home, and the kitchen is the single most dangerous place' (Politics of Health Group, 1979, p.26). Whereas men are more likely to die in violent accidents and from suicide, women predominate in deaths from accidental falls and in deaths caused by fire (Office of Population Censuses and Surveys, 1977), many of these occurring at home. More than a third of all fatal accidents in the UK are domestic. The double-think of assigning childcare to housewives is exposed by the stark fact that more young children die accidentally at home than anywhere else; fires, the inhalation of food and suffocation are the commonest causes (Macfarlane, 1979a).

Secondly, housework has prevented women from pursuing many avenues of self-development open to those who do not do it.

The house seems to take up so much time [wrote Katherine Mansfield to John Middleton Murry], I get frightfully impatient and want to be working [writing]. So often this week you and Gordon have been talking while I washed dishes. Well, someone's got to wash dishes and get food . . . And after you have gone I walk about with a mind full of ghosts of saucepans and primus stoves . . . [Cited in Olsen, 1972, p.108]

The reason why women do not produce works of art is that they are perpetually involved in an unrecognized and unremitting labour of love (which must be considered a work of art of equal value, if of another kind).

The psychological effect of housework combines with women's economic dependence to mould a certain opportunity structure. Housework remains an incredibly important limit on what women are able to do and become. But one aspect of housework only briefly mentioned in this chapter is its intermingling with the work of bringing up children. 'Generational reproduction' is discussed in Chapter 10; first we must look at a type of creative labour at which women not only excel, but in which they are the sole performers: the biological bearing of children.

CHAPTER NINE

Reproduction

At present, reproduction in our society is often a kind of sad mimicry of production. Work in a capitalist society is an alienation of labour in the making of a social product which is confiscated by capital. But it can still sometimes be a real act of creation, purposive and responsible, even in conditions of the worst exploitation. Maternity is often a caricature of this. [Mitchell, 1966]

In 1914, a time when the spotlight shone particularly brightly on women as breeders of Britain's future, the campaigning 32,000-strong Women's Co-operative Guild fought a battle for the improvement of the maternity and infant welfare services available to poor women. During this campaign, the Guild asked its members for their personal experiences of childbirth:

I do not know that my experience of childbearing has differed much from the women of my class [wrote one]. I was a factory girl, and an only child. I was married at twenty, and the mother of three children by the time I was twenty-three . . . .

I was weak and ill, could not suckle my second baby . . . and to crown my misfortune my husband fell out of work, and I had to do shirt work at home in order to keep a roof over our heads. My third baby was very tiny and thin when born. I put this down to the worry and the shortness of food which I had to put up with, and though he lived till he was three years old he died from diphtheria . . .

I do not think I was very different in my pregnancies to others. I always prepared myself to die, and I think this awful depression is common to most at this time . . .

After the first three living children, I had three stillborn children. I was six months advanced when I fell downstairs over a stair-rod, which killed the child, which was born after forty-eight hours' labour, and perhaps it seems wicked to you, but I was glad, because it left my hands free for a time to look after the other two, for I was fearfully weak and ill. After a lapse of two years I had another seven months baby born dead, and again, after another two years, a five months stillborn child, all three stillborn children being boys. I had a miscarriage after this of two months, and when I was thirty-five years old had my last baby, who is now living, nine years old.

I do hope you will not feel that this letter is morbid, and that I delight in writing horrors, for I do not, and had you not asked for information I should never have written this all down . . . please do not think I am miserable, for I am not, for I believe — in fact, I know — that there is a brighter day dawning for the mother and child of the future. [Davies, 1978, pp.165 – 7]

She was right. A brighter day did dawn, and the situation has changed radically in the last half century — though most of the change has taken place relatively recently. In 1915, when the Guild published their collection of letters, one British mother died for every 250 live babies born. This figure remained more or less constant until the 1930s, and had not improved much since the 1840s, when national figures first began to be collected. William Farr, pioneer statistician to Britain's first Registrar-General, called it, memorably, 'a deep, dark and continuous stream of mortality' (Farr, 1885, p.279). The stream included the humble and the famous alike — two of the many who succumbed to 'the terrors of childbed' were Mary Wollstonecraft and Mrs Beeton of household management fame.

Today, in Britain, one mother dies for about every 7000 live babies born, and death in childbirth is no longer the major fear of mothers or the common experience of most doctors; a large maternity hospital doing 3000 – 4000 deliveries a year, for instance, will only lose a mother every two years on average. Since 1952 maternal deaths have been sufficiently small in number for each to become the subject of a special investigation in England and Wales. The results of these enquiries are published; the latest report (Department of Health and Social Security, 1979) analysed 387 deaths representing 94 per cent of maternal deaths in England and Wales during the years 1973 – 5. Of these, 235 were considered to be 'true' maternal deaths, the rest due to deaths associated with maternity (if a pregnant woman dies of lung cancer, the death is coded as caused by cancer, not pregnancy). The biggest groups of deaths were due to 'hypertensive diseases of pregnancy' (17 per cent), to pulmonary embolism (15 per cent) and to abortion (12 per cent — this figure includes both spontaneous and induced abortions); 9 per cent of women died of haemorrhage, 9 per cent of ectopic pregnancy and 9 per cent of 'sepsis'. In addition, 6 per cent of the mothers died from amniotic fluid embolism, 5 per cent from ruptured uterus and 19 per cent from 'miscellaneous causes'. These causes of mothers' deaths represent a considerable change from 1937 when the (then) Ministry of Health published a *Report on*

an Investigation into Maternal Mortality (Ministry of Health, 1937).
At that time most mothers died from sepsis (34 per cent), followed by
hypertensive diseases (22 per cent) and abortion (16 per cent); 11 per
cent died from haemorrhage, 4 per cent from embolism and 2 per cent
from ectopic pregnancy. The control of septic infection, haemorrhage
and the direst effects of pregnancy toxaemia, and the reduction of
deaths from abortion are the main ways in which the outlook for
mothers has improved; as deaths from these causes have fallen, so
deaths from others have become proportionately more important.

If a British woman having a baby today need not entertain the
possibility of her own death, the outlook for her baby is not so good.
The perinatal mortality rate (baby deaths from 28 weeks of pregnancy
until one week after birth) in 1978 was 15.5: for every 65 live babies
born, one is stillborn or dies soon after birth. Yet this figure is vastly
lower than it was; in 1931 — the first year that perinatal mortality as
such was calculated (only then did national data on stillbirths begin to
be collected) — the rate was 62.1: for every 16 live babies born, one
died. Comparison with the situation before that has to take the
somewhat different but related index of infant mortality, defined as
deaths between the age of one week and one year. In 1915, the infant
mortality rate in England and Wales was 108.7: death claimed more
than one in ten of all young babies. Today, one baby in 76 dies before
its first birthday (1978 figure).

Looking at the risks of death faced by mothers and babies is one
way to answer the question of how women are, and have been, defined
by their function of reproduction. But hidden behind crude statistics
of maternal and baby deaths are other potent determinants of
women's role as mothers: how many babies women have, whether
they are able to choose through the use of contraception to have them,
and whether operations for the termination of unwanted or otherwise
fated pregnancies are available. According to Juliet Mitchell (1966),
reproduction is one of the four structures that combine to form the
'unity' of women's condition — the others are production, sexuality
and child socialization. It is thus one of the areas in which women are
either liberated or oppressed, either free to determine their own
destiny or compelled to have it chosen by others. Which of these two
alternatives obtains will depend not only on the success with which
childbirth is managed, but on the elimination of involuntary
reproduction and, equally (a more problematic statement), on the cure

of involuntary infertility, so that all those women who want babies are able to have them. *Limiting* reproduction as a female power has had priority in liberationist manifestos: 'Without the full capacity to limit her own reproduction, a woman's other "freedoms" are tantalizing mockeries' (Cisler, 1970, p.246). Yet limitation is only one aspect of control, and, as I shall argue later in this chapter, such control will not be achieved until women envisage reproduction as more than simply a burden to be dropped, a problem to be excised by preventive medicine.

IMPORTANT MISCONCEPTIONS

A woman who gave birth to a healthy baby boy after an unsuccessful abortion was yesterday awarded nearly £20,000 damages against the Harley Street doctor who carried out the operation . . .

[The Judge] awarded her £3,500 for diminution of marriage prospects, £7,000 for loss of past earnings, and £7,500 for loss of future earnings in her job as an audio secretary.

He also made an award of £750 for 'pain and suffering' in childbearing, and for the 'anxiety, distress and mental suffering' she had experienced. But, he argued, these matters had to be weighed against 'the happiness motherhood has obviously brought' . . .

Mr Justice Watkins said he rejected an argument by the defence that it was 'wholly repugnant' and against public policy to regard the birth of a perfectly healthy child as a loss. [*Guardian*, 19 May 1979]

It is unusual for a 'perfectly healthy child' to be the unintended consequence of abortion, and this case neatly isolates the paradox of motherhood's double status as handicap and prize. But abortion as a strategy for controlling reproduction does have various unintended side-effects, of which the most severe is, as we have noted, death. (Other important side-effects of induced abortion are infection, sterility and an enhanced risk of bearing a premature or stillborn child — Potts *et al.*, 1977.)

Figure 9.1 shows the marked effect the 1967 Abortion Act in Britain has had on deaths from illegal abortion, and hence on abortion deaths generally. This Act, which was the culmination of thirty years' campaigning by the Abortion Law Reform Association, redefined termination of pregnancy as a non-criminal offence when it is carried out before 28 weeks of pregnancy with the certification of two medical practitioners to the effect that *either* the pregnancy is likely to end in the birth of an abnormal child, *or* it is a danger to the health of the mother. The important criterion is that the danger of continuing with

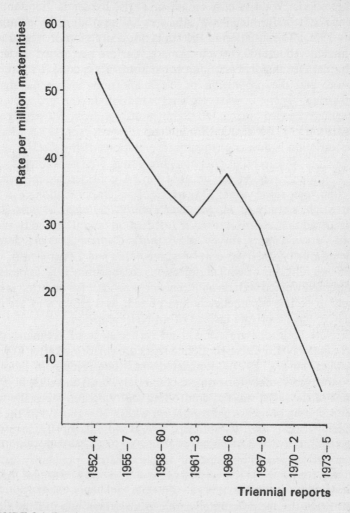

FIGURE 9.1 *Death rate per million maternities from illegal abortion, 1952 – 75.*

Source: Department of Health and Social Security (1979) p.49. Crown copyright.

the pregnancy is greater than the danger of ending it. (Since childbirth is now more dangerous than abortion, this is always true, literally speaking.)

Question: 'What is easy to get in Paris, harder in London, and harder still in Birmingham?' Answer: 'A legal abortion' (*Times*, 9 July 1975). The situation in Britain is not a situation of 'abortion on demand'. About 100,000 abortions a year are performed under the National Health Service, but an equal number are done in the private sector, and the proportion of NHS abortions shows no sign of increasing. There is wide regional variation in the proportion of abortions carried out in NHS hospitals — from 90 per cent in Newcastle to 23 per cent in Birmingham (Fowkes *et al*, 1979). Much of this variation is due to unequal interpretations of the Act.

Doctors who feel that abortions are wrong are less willing to agree to a woman's request for an abortion. A considerable minority of doctors voice these views: 37 per cent of general practitioners in Ann Cartwright's study of *Parents and Family Planning Services* (1970) considered that abortion is never justified on 'social' grounds, and in Jean Aitken-Swan's survey of *Fertility Control and the Medical Profession* (1977) 30 per cent of women GPs and 22 per cent of male GPs had religious or ethical objections to abortion. It is, apparently, unmarried women with no children whose request for abortion is most likely to be unsympathetically interpreted; as a group they are most likely to have a private instead of an NHS abortion.

Private abortions are done at an earlier stage of pregnancy than those in the NHS, where about one in six are performed after 13 weeks (Fowkes *et al.*, 1979). Restricted and late access to abortion jeopardizes its safety for women; conversely, open and early abortion is one of the safest ways of controlling reproduction, especially when the technique of menstrual aspiration within 10 – 18 days of the first missed period is used (Goldthorp, 1977). Most illogically, menstrual aspiration is avoided by doctors because of its dubious legal status as an abortion procedure, since it is done before pregnancy can be reliably confirmed — its very advantage to women, who are thereby spared the knowledge that an embryo has been destroyed. But worldwide the most common induced abortions are still the illegal ones. Peter Diggory and John McEwan (1976) estimate that in the early 1970s 130 million births across the world were matched by about 40 million induced abortions; probably 25 million of these were illegal. Only in the United States, Russia, China, Japan and Eastern Europe is abortion freely available as an accepted right of the pregnant woman (Potts *et al.*, 1977).

If conventional wisdom has it that women are liberated by being able to interrupt unwanted pregnancies, the chief instrument of this reproductive liberation is seen as being the contraceptive pill. Family life and 'working women' are characterized as instantly emancipated from the unprogressive evil of an endless row of mouths to feed: women can do what they want and the living standards of families rise — more food, more consumer durables, fewer babies. Nothing, it seems, could be simpler.

Suitably, the pill was originally the brainchild of a feminist — Margaret Sanger, founder of the American organization Planned Parenthood and protagonist of women's rights. At the age of 88, Margaret Sanger was introduced to Gregory Pincus, a reproductive scientist; she subsequently raised $150,000 to fund Pincus to carry out research on a 'simple, cheap, safe contraceptive to be used in poverty-stricken slums and jungles and among the most ignorant people' (quoted in Seaman and Seaman, 1978, p.79). Pincus's product was first tested on mental patients in the mid-1950s (men and women — it worked on both), and then on women in Puerto Rico, although tests only included 132 women who had taken the pill continuously for a year or more. In 1961 the pill was approved for general use by the Federal Drug Administration in the United States and the Committee on the safety of Medicines in Britain.

A leader in the *Lancet* (2 June 1962) soon after, cautiously observed that 'twenty years may go by before we can be sure about the safety of oral contraceptives'. Its author advocated restricting its use to the treatment of menstrual irregularities and the control of fertility in women who could not use other methods. In 1974 the British Royal College of General Practitioners (RCGP) released the results of a five-year study of its side-effects. Entitled, optimistically, *Oral Contraceptives and Health*, it reported a 17 per cent increase in illness among pill-users compared with non-users; this included a raised incidence of chickenpox, urinary infection, depression (up 30 per cent in pill-users), high blood pressure, deep vein thrombosis and 'cerebrovascular accidents' (stroke). Its authors concluded

While it is evident that there are disadvantages associated with the use of oral contraceptives, the risk of serious effects is small . . . . the estimated risk . . . of using the Pill is one that a properly informed woman would be happy to take . . . [RCGP, 1974, p.85]

Reactions to the RCGP report included many who did not think that 'properly informed' women would be ready to take the risk of using the pill. Valerie Beral, a doctor at the London School of Hygiene and Tropical Medicine, observed that the study showed a mortality from combined causes 39 per cent higher in users and ex-users of the pill than among non-users (Beral, 1974). By late 1977, with a further three years' experience of the benefits and hazards of pill use, official medical opinion revised its policy of pill-promotion to one of pill-prevention in certain 'high risk' groups: women over 35, women who smoke, women on the pill for five or more years (RCGP, 1977). More than half a million women subsequently stopped taking the pill (*Guardian*, 5 October 1978). This was the beginning of the end of the pill's heyday: in July 1978, the *Guardian* reported 'The Pill Boom is Over'.

The pill is a hormonal preparation with systemic effects, that is, it affects every cell in the body. It is because the pill's action affects the whole body that so many diverse problems have been reported with its use. This fact, as feminist health care groups have noted, hardly makes it the ideal contraceptive. However, because it requires no knowledge of anatomy, no physical contact with the genitals on the part of its user, and its ingestion is separate from the unpredictability of sexual intercourse, it is still recommended to, and taken by, many women — 6 – 7 million American women and 3½ million in Britain. At the peak of its use in America, it was estimated that one in five women aged 15 – 44 were under the influence of the pill's artificial hormones (Stewart *et al.*, 1979, p.167).

Figure 9.2 shows the relative popularity of the main contraceptive methods among American married women in 1973 and British married women in 1976. The pill was used by more than a third of contraceptive-users and in both countries similar percentages chose the IUCD or sterilization. In Britain, withdrawal was more popular than in the United States, and so was the condom, a 'traditional' method of contraception which first appeared (made from the intestines of sheep) in England in the eighteenth century. Condoms protect against venereal disease, and the statutory tales of ruptures in

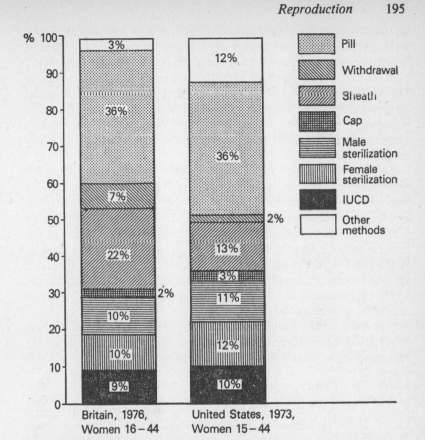

FIGURE 9.2 *Percentage of currently married women using contraceptives, by method.*
Sources: Dunnell (1979), p.42; National Center for Health Statistics (1978) p.4.

use or of holes made by manufacturers in league with governments artificially to raise the birth rate underestimate their effectiveness at around seven pregnancies per 100 woman years of exposure. Condoms have no side-effects, but some couples dislike them and they have the devastating disadvantage for women that they place the control of fertility (literally) in the hands of men. This cannot be said of the condom's female partner, the diaphragm or cervical cap,[1] used by a mere 2 per cent of British couples, and with a track record of effectiveness when used with a spermicidal cream of more than 90 per cent. In Britain and America, feminists are recommending a return to the cap because it is a female-controlled contraceptive method and because, after nearly a century of use, it has no known side-effects. In America, the cap and condom are attracting more followers among ex-pill-users than the IUCD, which has come under particularly heavy attack.

The IUCD, although discovered[2] in 1909 by a German physician who recommended the insertion of several strands of silkworm gut into the womb, really took off in the early 1960s. With an effectiveness in preventing pregnancy of 95 per cent IUCDs can cause a miscellany of problems, from spontaneous expulsion in 5 – 10 per cent of users, to heavier menstruation, pelvic inflammatory disease, perforation of the womb, ectopic pregnancy, septic abortion and limb-reduction deformities in infants gestated alongside them (Barrie, 1976; Guillebaud *et al.*, 1976; Seaman and Seaman, 1978; Vessey *et al.*, 1974; Williams *et al.*, 1975).

It is difficult adequately to summarize the full social and medical implications of intrauterine contraception, but perhaps the following 'announcement' does some justice to this task:

I.P.D. Being Fitted

The newest development in male contraception was unveiled recently at the American Women's Surgical Symposium held at the Ann Arbor Medical Center. Dr Sophie Merkin of the Merkin Clinic announced the preliminary findings of a study conducted on 763 unsuspecting male undergraduates at a large Midwestern university. In her report, Dr Merkin stated that the new contraceptive — the IPD — was a breakthrough in male contraception. It will be marketed under the trade name 'Umbrelly'.

---

[1] The cervical cap is smaller than the diaphragm and is made to fit over the cervix. It pre-dates the diaphragm and, although still available in Britain and useful to women whose vaginal muscles cannot keep the diaphragm in place, is considered by many to be a defunct method of birth control (the British edition of *Our Bodies Ourselves* — Phillips and Rakusen, 1978 — omits it).

[2] The idea that a foreign body in the womb prevents conception is a very ancient one. See Himes, 1963; *Family Planning*, 13, 4 (January 1965) pp. 95 – 6.

The IPD (intrapenile device) resembles a tiny rolled umbrella which is inserted through the head of the penis and pushed into the scrotum with a plunger-like device. Occasionally there is perforation of the scrotum, but this is disregarded as the male has few nerve endings in this area of his body. The underside of the umbrella contains a spermicidal jelly, hence the name 'Umbrelly'.

Experiments on 1000 white whales from the continental shelf (whose sexual apparatus is said to be closest to man's) proved the IPD to be 100% effective in preventing the production of sperm, and eminently satisfactory to the female whale since it does not interfere with her rutting pleasure.

Dr Merkin declared the umbrelly to be statistically safe for the human male. She reported that of the 763 undergraduates tested with the device only two died of scrotal infection, only 20 developed swelling of the testicles, and 13 were too depressed to have an erection. She stated that common complaints ranged from cramping and bleeding to acute abdominal pains. She emphasized that these symptoms were merely indications that the man's body had not yet adjusted to the device. Hopefully the symptoms would disappear within a year.

One complication caused by the IPD and briefly mentioned by Dr Merkin was the incidence of massive scrotal infection necessitating the surgical removal of the testicles. 'But this is a rare case,' said Dr Merkin, 'too rare to be statistically important'. She and other distinguished members of the Women's College of Surgeons agreed that the benefits far outweighed the risk to any individual man. [From *Outcome* magazine, the East Bay Men's Center Newsletter, and *The Periodical Lunch*, Andrew Rock publisher, Ann Arbor, Michigan, USA]

The safest and most reliable method of contraception is, as the standard medical joke puts it, an aspirin — between the knees. More realistically, Christopher Tietze (1976) has shown that the safest method of birth control is the diaphragm plus spermicidal cream backed up by early abortion in the event of method failure.

Use of artefacts to prevent or interrupt conception may free women from the burdens of childbirth, but overall it adds to their risks of mortality. Valerie Beral has suggested that a new term, 'reproductive mortality', be introduced to measure all the reproduction-associated deaths women undergo. The new term includes deaths due to abortion (spontaneous and induced), complications of pregnancy, delivery and the postnatal period, and adverse effects of contraception (including the pill, the IUCD and operations for female sterilization).[3] According

---

[3] There are no recorded deaths of men caused by vasectomy.

to Beral's calculations, for British women in the two age groups 25 – 34 and 35 – 44 mortality from pregnancy alone has declined by more than 85 per cent since 1950. General reproductive mortality has also declined in the younger age group. However, in the older age group 85 per cent of reproductive deaths were due to the pill, and these outweighed the fall in pregnancy mortality, so that overall reproductive mortality increased (Beral, 1979).[4]

The control women are able to exercise in any society over their fertility and the different types of risk they face in so doing are one clear demonstration of gender inequality. Men simply do not have to grapple with the same problems (though they may be variously involved in their partners' attempts to do so). Yet this is also an area in which considerable social class differences confound the picture and illustrate the truth of the dictum that gender and class are interlocking axes of discrimination (see pp.285 – 9).

WHOSE BABY?

The quotation at the beginning of the chapter describes childbirth in our society as alienated labour, as creative, purposive and responsible *despite* the social and medical context in which it happens. This is certainly the picture given by a large number of studies done in the last twenty years of women's attitudes to the maternity services (Arms, 1977; Breen, 1975; Cartwright, 1979; Fleury, 1967; Graham and McKee, 1978; Oakley, 1979, 1980; Shaw, 1974; see also Riley, 1977). Janet Streeter had her first baby in a London hospital in 1975:

My waters broke at eleven o'clock on Sunday evening. My husband phoned the hospital, and they told me to come in. When I was in, they gave me an examination, and she said, oh, no, you're not in labour at all . . .

On the Monday morning the pains started . . . five minutes, half an hour, twenty minutes. And then they stopped. And then they induced me, because of infection really. Some consultant came to see me and decided that. I'd

---

[4] Beral's argument makes a number of assumptions (for instance about the quantification of contraceptive risks) that, as Potts and Edelman (letter, *British Medical Journal*, 24 November 1979, p. 1362) point out, are country-specific and probably group-specific as well. In third world countries the measurement of reproductive mortality would have to include the risks of genital mutilation, still performed on millions of girls in Africa and the near East (Garcia, 1979).

never seen him before. The thing that happened was that apparently my stomach [uterus] went into spasms, so they had to keep turning the whole inducing thing [machine regulating the dose of oxytocin] off, and that presumably was why it took so long — seventeen hours.

I had an epidural before I was induced, because one of the midwives said I must have one: she said, I had one, it was really fantastic. By that time the whole environment of the hospital was making me very nervous, so I said yes. I had it before I needed it, but presumably that was because it was a suitable time for them to do it. I did feel the epidural going in — it was an extraordinary feeling. Jolly uncomfortable . . . She [the anaesthetist] kept saying, look, will you keep still? And I kept saying, it's really uncomfortable. Where? It can't be. She actually said that. It didn't work very well either, the pain was quite excruciating. I found the fact that I couldn't feel my legs a most horrifying feeling . . .

I had a monitoring machine as well as the epidural: I don't know how many wires and tubes I had. The monitoring machine kept stopping and the heartbeat kept stopping — the machine kept breaking down, so I didn't enjoy watching the heartbeat at all . . . also, I felt if I watched the contractions [on the machine] it made it far worse, psychologically; I couldn't control the pain.

Some doctor I didn't know and couldn't possibly recognize again did the delivery. When I pushed, I wasn't having any effect at all. They kept telling me I wasn't doing it properly, which maybe I wasn't. I think I tried about six times. And then the midwives went out, presumably to get the doctor. The baby's head was at the wrong angle. It was quite extraordinary — they kept on trying to make me push . . . . and then they suddenly decided that anyway the head was twisted. [Her hospital notes record 'delay' in the second stage of labour as the reason for the forceps delivery.] The doctor came in and didn't say anything at all, except that he was going to use forceps.

They held a big sheet up: I wasn't allowed to watch the delivery. And anyway, I was in no state to: I was in absolute agony for the whole time he did the forceps . . I'm quite sure a lot of people don't believe me when I say it was like that. I really do feel I don't want another baby: I really do feel that. [Four years later, she has not changed her mind.]

I remember feeling disappointed when I heard it was a boy. [She wanted a girl.] Quite honestly, I wasn't interested in him at all. When they put him in my arms, I said, very nice, thank you very much — take him away. It was like something you didn't feel part of, perhaps because I hadn't been through it naturally. It was just that I'd been through that pain and this was just something that may have come from next door, you know. I couldn't sort of get the two together. I really didn't feel he was anything to do with me.[5]

---

[5] This account comes from the research project on the Transition to Motherhood described in Oakley (1979, 1980).

This is not a horror story, in the sense that the baby survived and was healthy and his mother did establish a bond with him gradually in the few weeks after his birth. But it is not an unrepresentative tale. In the study from which this account was taken, 41 per cent of the women had their labours either induced or 'accelerated' with syntocinon; 52 per cent had an instrumental delivery and 69 per cent said they didn't feel in control of themselves and what was going on during the labour.[6] Experiences of pregnancy and childbirth in Britain in the 1970s documented by other researchers have drawn attention to the same pervasive problems: mothers' feelings of being a passive object rather than active agent in the process of childbearing; lack of information about obstetric techniques employed; the high level of not-altogether necessary technology used in pregnancy, labour and delivery; a clash between what mothers feel and what staff tell them they ought to be feeling; the inability to develop a relationship with particular medical care providers; and a failure to give social/emotional aspects of childbearing as much attention as physiological ones.

This is not to say that Britain is devoid of women who find childbearing joyful and free from these stresses; it is, however, to say that because of developments in the management of childbirth over the last fifteen years, it is becoming increasingly difficult to avoid an experience such as Janet Streeter's. Bemoaning this fact is not, as Dana Breen notes, a question of 'idealising the body processes and the body's ability to give birth naturally without help, but of pointing out the deep sense of violation many women feel when their body is taken over' (Breen, 1978, p.25). I am also not arguing that Britain should be singled out as the only place where the management of reproduction has acquired this unfortunate tone; in the United States, for instance, some of the difficulties listed above are reported to occur much more frequently than in Britain (Arms, 1977; Shaw, 1974).

There is an intimate association between perinatal mortality statistics and the medical manipulation of birth as an alienated, technological process. A British obstetrician has described the

---

[6] The first two figures are raised because these women were having their first babies: induction is a slightly more common procedure and instrumental delivery a considerably more common procedure in first births. The figures for this sample are representative of practice in the particular hospital from which the sample was drawn in 1975.

connection as akin to what happens when a football team finds itself doing rather badly. In this situation there is a flurry of activity: managers are sacked and large sums of money are spent to buy in new and expensive talent. In maternity care the reaction is the same; it is assumed that more expensive facilities will necessarily improve league standings — the dangerous argument that more means better (Kerr, 1978).

Many of the techniques used in modern obstetrics have doubtfully beneficial and possibly hazardous effects. For example, Iain Chalmers and his colleagues (1976) showed that a trebling of the number of inductions done in a Welsh population in 1966 – 72 was not associated with any change in perinatal mortality. On the other hand, comparing the proportion of firstborn babies weighing less than 2,500 grams over the period 1965 – 74, an increase in the proportion of low birthweight babies in the later years was noted as probably associated with the increased use of induction (Newcombe and Chalmers, 1977). Other hazards of induction are the baby's death from premature separation of the placenta, ruptured uterus with a high risk of both maternal and fetal death, and a rise in the probability of jaundice in the newborn (Chalmers and Richards, 1977; Chalmers *et al.*, 1975). Mechanical fetal monitoring, another procedure endured by Janet Streeter, is a technique that has been shown to have only one unequivocal result, and that is an increase in the caesarean section rate (Wood and Renon, 1976). Such techniques as caesarean section and instrumental delivery rates have been on the increase — the latter from 4 per cent in 1968 (Chalmers and Richards, 1977) to 13 per cent in 1976 (Chalmers, 1979) — without any clear clinical indication of the 'need' they are meeting and with a long list of documented ill-effects. As Chalmers and Richards comment, the very big international differences in the use of these techniques (for example, 35 per cent of all deliveries were instrumental in the USA in 1975, compared with 5 per cent in Norway) suggest that they are a response not to biological population differences but rather to 'fashions' among obstetricians for preferring one mode of delivery to another.

The trouble with fashions is that they catch on. Treating high-risk women with high-risk procedures is a risk because women (and their babies) who do not need these procedures receive them and may suffer damage as a result. But, as one leading obstetrician has aptly observed, there is a premium in modern obstetrics on intervention 'as a form of personal insurance for the doctor', which means that the doctor who interrupts a normal pregnancy is absolved from blame, where one who does not is censured if anything goes wrong — whether or not he or she could have acted to prevent it (O'Driscoll, 1975). As a matter of fact, there is hardly any component of modern obstetric practice that is free from this problem. Most have been introduced without systematic evaluation, contrary to the widespread belief that innovation in medical practice is accompanied by 'quality control'. Peer review in professional meetings and the medical press, and clinical experience and discussion with colleagues, are the only type of assessment procedures applied to most innovations in obstetrics with the exception of new drugs, which are usually tested reasonably thoroughly prior to their wide-scale introduction. The clinical freedom to determine treatment is hotly defended, but is 'irrational' and certainly not 'scientific' according to any accepted meaning of that term (Richards, 1975a).[7]

THE KINGDOM OF THE MEDICAL MAN

It is often a matter of pride that we know what is best for our patients; how closely this is allied to benign paternalism or even savage despotism I must ask you to examine in your consciences. [Lennox, 1969, p.19]

Sally Macintyre quoted this invitation in her discussion of medical attitudes to the 1967 Abortion Act in Britain. Looking at public statements made by doctors prior to the Act's introduction, she commented that

'Benign paternalism' appeared to underlie the arguments both for and against the Bill. Where it was argued that the doctor was a servant to his patients, the analogy was with a nanny — who, though an employee, always knows best . . . . One continued theme was the desire to maintain the consultative decision-making aspect of professionalism and the fear of status degradation to that of technician. [Macintyre, 1973, pp.129 – 31]

Doctors want to be more than technicians. The 'frame of reference'

---

[7]The same must, however, be said about some recent non-clinical innovations in obstetrics. For instance, a randomized controlled trial of the Leboyer approach to childbirth showed that the only discernible benefit was a shortened first stage of labour (Nelson *et al.*, 1980).

they apply to childbearing does not entertain the possibility of a symmetrical relationship between the providers and users of reproductive care. It takes as axiomatic the status of reproduction as a specialist medical subject, the status of pregnant women as patients and the measurement of successful outcome in terms of biological mortality rates. For mothers, conversely, childbearing is more likely to be seen as a natural biological process; an event that is an integral part of their whole lives and development; an experience to be evaluated in terms of its contribution to happiness in a more general way than mere survival; and a process that women as the possessors of wombs know something about (Graham and Oakley, in press).

The medical frame of reference evolved with the development of obstetrics and gynaecology as a medical specialism. In 1522, the only way a man could witness childbirth was the strategy adopted by a German physician — dressing up as a woman (Donegan, 1978). In 1979, 88 per cent of British consultant obstetricians are men. Doctors took over the control of childbirth from female midwives in a process spanning more than three centuries marked by periods of intense professional rivalry in which doctors' (or earlier men-midwives') claims were couched in a language of moral superiority. The superiority was that of 'scientific' knowledge as opposed to the benefits of experience, the advantages of intervention in the processes of pregnancy, labour and delivery as opposed to allowing events to take their natural course; it was also shaped by a belief that men know more about women than women do.

From the beginning of their ascendancy as managers of childbirth, male midwives were identified with the use of instruments (they were members of the Barber-Surgeons company, the ancestors of the modern Royal College of Surgeons). It was very largely the possession of forceps by a group of men-midwives that enabled them to gain the upper hand, not because forceps had a high success rate — though there must have been some mothers and babies whose lives were saved by them — but because of the very considerable mystique they engendered. This mystique both facilitated and was fed by the men-midwives' contention that unproblematic childbearing is exceptional, and that pregnancy and parturition are not normal physiological conditions (Kobrin, 1966; see also Oakley, 1976). In the early lying-in hospitals, this belief was put to the test. For example, William Goodell, physician in charge of a Philadelphia hospital, developed the following regime to tackle the possibility of puerperal fever in the 1870s (its exact cause was not known at the time):

When the patient came to the hospital, some days or weeks before delivery, she was put on a regular dosage of quinine, then a kind of all-purpose preventative. Each woman received drugs for constipation, headaches, and sleeplessness. When labor began, each received a cathartic and a bath. The staff then ruptured the amniotic sac, used forceps to expedite delivery, gave ergot when the head appeared, and hurried the expulsion of the placenta by pressing on the stomach. After cutting the cord and bathing the woman again, they gave her morphine each hour until she felt no more afterpains and gave her quinine 'until her ears rang'. [Wertz and Wertz, 1977, p.137]

Goodell thought his procedures made hospital delivery safer than home delivery. This rather central contention of modern obstetrics is still unproved. In Britain, the 1958 national perinatal mortality survey showed that having a baby in an NHS consultant unit carried the least risk of the baby dying. The safety of delivery in a GP unit, at home or privately outside the NHS was the same (Fedrick and Butler, 1978). But these figures are out of date and there are ways in which hospital is not a place of safety for normal childbirth either in Britain (M. Richards, 1978) or in the United States (Stewart and Stewart, 1976). What is striking about the hospital versus home debate (and it is one about which some women feel very strongly) is that in Britain today it has become impossible for many women to choose to have a baby at home, and 97 per cent of births now take place in hospital — an increase of 30 per cent since 1964 (Tew, 1978). Perhaps more important, few obstetricians concede the right of women to make the decision about place of delivery for themselves. Whether home or hospital turns out in the end to be safer, we do not arbitrate people's rights to select health hazards for themselves in other areas of life. They drive cars, fly in aeroplanes, smoke cigarettes and encourage their dogs to defaecate in places where their children play; there is no official policy to ban these activities on the grounds that experts say they are injurious to health (which, of course, they undoubtedly are).

Disease is a socio-political rather than bio-medical concept: 'when doctors or other people label something as a disease all they are really saying is that they regard medical intervention as appropriate' (*British Medical Journal*, 29 September 1979). In the nineteenth century, as we saw in Chapter 6, the scope of this definition of disease came to include the reproductive organs of women; it is a twentieth-century extension of this to regard pregnancy and birth as diseases too. The terminology of obstetrics and gynaecology alike is impregnated with male names — from the Fallopian tubes and Graafian follicles to Braxton-Hicks contractions and the forceps of Christian Kielland (Speert, 1958). In their very alliance (childbearing *and* women's diseases), obstetrics and gynaecology suggest the abnormal.

Midwifery on the other hand, in modern Britain defined as the profession that cares for women 'throughout the normal childbearing process' (Walker, 1972, p.130), does not. Midwives are still very important as providers of maternity care in Britain and many other countries, and they are experiencing a revival in the United States. Although the 1975 Sex Discrimination Act opened the door to male midwives (once again), most midwives are women with a disposition to stress the potential normality of the childbearing process. Jean Walker (1976) asked doctors and midwives what they thought midwifery was, and found that most midwives distinguished between midwifery and obstetrics, with 'midwifery' describing normal maternity care and involving greater contact with mothers. Most doctors, on the other hand, just thought obstetrics was the modern word for midwifery and saw midwives as 'obstetric assistants', carrying out routine aspects of maternity care under the direction of a doctor.

Mothers, too, are seen by the medical profession as passive recipients of doctors' instructions. The idea that it is *women* who cause the deaths of babies — by not going to antenatal clinics (or not going early enough), by smoking, eating the wrong food, having sexual intercourse, not being married, or reading the *Sunday Times*[8] — implicitly acknowledges women's disobedience in doing what *they* think is best for themselves and their babies. The notion of maternal culpability emerges very clearly in a series of official documents emphasizing preventive health and health education (Department of Health and Social Security, 1976a, b, 1977c). It is an answer, as Hilary Graham (1978) has argued, to the current crisis of confidence about the abilty of medicine to reduce deaths and disabilities among babies

---

[8] Two articles published in the *Sunday Times* in 1974 (13 and 20 October) by Louise and Oliver Gillie contained a powerful critique of modern obstetrics. In a series of doctor — patient consultations I observed in a London hospital in 1974 – 5, doctors confronted by women who queried their treatment often referred to these articles as improper sources of information.

(or, a bad workman blames his tools?). Responding indirectly to the critique of modern medicine posed by Illich (1975), official views are popularizing the notion that *people* carry some responsibility for their own health, but when it comes down to it, what is meant is that *mothers* are blameworthy — a new version of the old dogma that blaming the victim is not only conscience-salving but cheaper. For example, encouraging women to attend earlier and more often for antenatal care in the hope that this will reduce perinatal mortality (and even paying them a pittance to do this — a popular suggestion) is cheaper and a good deal easier than either redesigning the maternity services in accordance with women's declared wishes or tackling the social and economic causes of death and illness in mothers and babies (Chalmers, Oakley and Macfarlane, 1980).

THE NATURAL SPHERE OF WOMEN

Biological reproduction is 'the most essentially female function of all' (Calloway, 1978, p.164). In other words, how reproduction is managed and controlled is inseparable from how women are managed and controlled. Hilary Graham has illustrated this in her discussion of images of pregnancy. Pregnancy, in the medical literature,

epitomizes femininity: it offers woman her ultimate social and psychic fulfillment. But it is also a time of emotional and physical vulnerability: the expectant mother is in need of protection. [Graham, 1976, pp.195 – 6]

She has to be protected from the consequences of the invasion of her body by the alien foetus, but, also crucially, society has to be protected from the dangers of the indeterminate state represented by the pregnant woman and her unborn child. In this sense, pregnancy is a form of spirit possession requiring elaborate rituals for its taming into a non-disruptive element of the social order. Such rituals may be carried out by spiritual healers whose function is the domestication of wayward spirits, or by medical professionals working with a physicalist model of reproduction and a feminine construction of women within the orbit of medical 'science'.

   Women are the polluters *par excellence*, a role that has already been discussed (see p.179). Their marginal social status is one reason for this, but their reproductive function is its foundation. In producing babies, women seem to cause, or at least represent, an untidy and dangerous blurring of the boundaries between bodies and the social spaces they occupy.

I have been able to discuss only some aspects of reproduction in this chapter; some others come under the heading 'children' (Chapter 10). Sexuality, its still necessary precursor, is discussed chiefly in Chapter 11. Some of the facets of reproduction covered in this chapter are important concerns of the contemporary women's liberation movement, as part of its demand that women should be given the means to take charge of their own bodies. Easily available abortion, sterilization and contraception fall into this category. Other matters, such as the extent to which necessary technology is used in birth, are not so obviously the material of feminist agitation. This raises the problem of how far feminists in general have seen childbearing as an important arena of women's activity. On the whole the answer is that they have not, and it is reasonable to suppose that the immense satisfaction many women experience in having children is one reason why feminist sympathies are not more widely embraced among women. But for feminists and non-feminists alike, the issue is not one of how the female ability to bear children determines the social position of women. Rather, it is a question of *whose* definition of biology has become part of the cultural lens through which women's function as mothers is seen. As Hastrup (1978, p.58) comments: 'It must be the woman's conception of female biology that sets the frame if biology is to act as a central theme in our self-identification.'

Relationships
Who are Women's friends?

CHAPTER TEN

Children

That the child is the supreme aim of woman is a statement having precisely the value of an advertising slogan.

But the fact remains that unless the circumstances are positively unfavourable the mother will find her life enriched by her child. [De Beauvoir, 1960, pp.232, 222]

Women contain wombs, and the failure of medical technologists to develop artificial reproduction means that, for the present at least, bearing children is a biological capacity whose implications women are unable to avoid. [1] But the ability to gestate children is often given a social meaning incalculably more profound than a mere biological occupation. It is as the social rearers of children, rather than as their biological bearers, that women's identities and activities have been chiefly constrained.

As Margaret Mead (1962) said, the biological division of labour between the sexes lays down a certain groundplan for their social differentiation. Because women 'have' children, a process in which the male contribution is both cursory and private, elaborate social mechanisms have to be developed to enable children to be seen as the property of men. Also, the presence of a biological model for sex differentiation suggests the appropriateness of other 'rules' for dividing the sexes. Primary among these is the idea that the physical and emotional work of bringing up children is a woman's job. Not all societies advocate this (Kardiner, 1955; Mead, 1935), and the fact that

---

[1] Fertilization of the ovum has been achieved in the laboratory, but there is, as yet, no substitute for the womb as a place of gestation.

many do cannot be divorced from the sexist solipsism of those anthropologists who have studied them (see pp.331 – 2).

In non-industrialized societies, the need for women to be involved continually in productive work competes with the responsibility for childcare. Men's reactions to children are rarely those of a detached onlooker. Among the African Nuer

> . . . the father also takes an interest in his infant children and one often sees a man nursing his child . . . Nuer fathers are proud of their children and give much time to them, petting and spoiling them, giving them titbits, playing with them, and teaching them to talk; and the children are often in the [cattle] byres with the men. [Evans-Pritchard, 1951, p.137]

In such cultures, the tie of lactation, still of immense importance world-wide in guaranteeing the survival of children, may extend the biological rationale for women's mothering into and beyond the immediate post-natal period, thereby putting some limits on male participation. It is, in fact, after weaning that fathers in many cultures play a central role in childrearing, particularly in the rearing of boys.

A further essential fact is that in such societies children are not classified as incapable of economically productive work:

> The care of a child is not regarded as a net liability from the economic point of view [wrote Rosemary Firth of Malay peasant society]. Many people have said to me, what would they do without a child to help in the house, carrying water, gutting fish and a host of minor duties. [Firth, 1966, p.15]

Of the many paradoxes surrounding the position of women in industrialized societies, the restriction of lengthy, dependent childrearing to the nuclear family of two parents is certainly one. Another, which I shall be discussing at length in this chapter, is the idea that mothering derives its necessity from the absolute need of children for absolute care and attention. This policy — for the idea has been enshrined as the policy of central government in many countries — evolved out of a prior preoccupation with the causes and consequences of population decline. If women are the ones with wombs, it follows that they are responsible for the quality and quantity of the population. Women's situation is the key that unlocks the conundrum of the survival of the British nation — or any other, for it has been the fate of women in most capitalist and socialist countries to have been the target of both pro-natalist and anti-natalist policies.

WHO WANTS BABIES?

. . . Napoleon was right when, after being beaten on a celebrated field of battle by soldiers who mostly came from country districts, and who did not know what a comforter was, and who did not know what canned meat was, who played in the open air, and were breastfed in the only decent and proper way by their mothers, he on the morrow of his defeat said, 'Oh, those English mothers!' [Burns, 1906, p.15]

The birth rate in Britain began to decline in the 1870s, some thirty years before the rate at which babies died showed any tendency to lessen. Added to this, the Boer War in 1899 uncovered a large amount of illness and disability in volunteers for army service, which suggested that the stock of British manhood left much to be desired (flat feet, bad teeth, weak lungs, rheumatic tendencies and inferior size were frequently mentioned). Major General Sir Frederick Maurice KCG wrote an influential article in which he said

Whatever the primary cause . . . we are always brought back to the fact that . . . the young man of 16 to 18 years of age is what he is because of the training through which he has passed during his infancy and childhood. 'Just as the twig is bent the tree's inclined'. Therefore it is to the condition, mental, moral and physical, of the women and children that we must look if we have regard to the future of our land. [Maurice, 1903, p.50]

He went on to mention a study of Jews in Whitechapel that found that Jews were healthier and lived longer because Jewish mothers, unlike their Christian counterparts, did not go out to work.

Children thus became in the early years of the twentieth century a prized 'national asset', a matter of 'imperial importance', not only as the citizens of tomorrow who would be virile enough to win wars, but as agents who would turn the British Commonwealth into 'a Commonwealth of the British' (McCleary, 1933, p.3). 'Physical' or 'race' 'degeneration' and 'deterioration' became the slogans of the day. The Right Honourable John Burns, MP, the expert who alluded to Napoleon's comment on mothers as makers of good English soldiers, himself thought alcohol was to blame, along with improper feeding and 'vanity, fashion and capricious dress'.[2] Underlying all of

---

[2] Alcohol as a cause of malformations and ill-health in babies is re-occupying the limelight today ('Social drinking can harm unborn babies' *Observer*, 19 November 1979).

these was the evil of married women's paid work. 'What are we to expect of the children,' he asked, 'whilst the mother is nine or ten hours a day, even sometimes twelve hours, away from her home in a factory?' The breeding of 'anaemic, saucy, vulgar, ignorant, cigarette smoking hooligans' was his answer.

The debate about the physical deterioration of the population lead to the practice of sterilizing 'degenerates' (the physically or mentally abnormal or unfit, alcoholics and TB patients), a school medical service, the feeding of children in elementary schools, the founding of maternity and child welfare clinics, the development of state instruction in mothercraft and domestic economy — and indeed, as Richard Titmuss (1950) has noted, eventually to the whole superstructure of the National Health Service in Britain. Of enormous importance in prompting these developments were the two world wars: as Titmuss (1958) has argued, war has a general tendency to focus the attention of the state on the biological characteristics of its people. If the Boer War revealed the inferior quality of British military manhood, what the Second World War, in particular, revealed was the deplorable condition of children's health. The evacuation of women and children in 1939 produced reports that 'aroused the conscience of the nation':

There were children who did not know how to use a knife and fork, children who had never slept in a bed and were too frightened to do so, and children who not only were not provided with nightclothes, but were sewn into their underwear. Worse still were slum mothers who smoked, went to the pub, and used obscene language. [Wilson, 1977, p.136]

In the subsequent five years the government assumed a remarkable degree of concern for the health and well-being of children and their mothers. Free school meals for all children, a national milk scheme providing half price milk for all expectant and nursing mothers and children under 5 and the mass immunization of seven million children against diphtheria were some of these measures. A dramatic improvement in stillbirth, infant and maternal mortality rates during the war years seemed to suggest that this state intervention was of direct physiological benefit to women and children.[3]

---

[3] Other factors may be involved: the 'better physical stock' of mothers in the 1940s versus their counterparts in the 1920s and 1930s, and the declining birth rate among high-risk mothers (Titmuss, 1950, pp.535−7).

Renewed consciousness of the national asset children represented was, however, accompanied by a regeneration of interest in the subject of 'race suicide' — the title of a book published the year the war ended (McCleary, 1945). Contraceptives were compared with high explosives (as powerful and far-reaching in their effects), and there were some who wanted them banned altogether. Women were accused of being more interested in a career than motherhood, and men of choosing inappropriately between 'the baby Austin in the garage and the baby in the nursery' (Reddaway, n.d., p.28).

Many practical proposals for making the rearing of children easier were put forward in this debate. The report of the Royal College of Physicians, published in 1949, came down in favour of a multi-faceted approach to the problem — which they saw as raising the birth rate from 2.2 to 2.4 children per family, a figure that would secure replacement of the population. They proposed an increase and extension of family allowances (introduced in 1946 and payable for each child after the first); a system of rent subsidies; income tax reform; housing schemes; family welfare services (home helps, sitters-in, nurseries, nursery schools, laundry facilities, cheap family holidays and holidays for mothers); education for parenthood; medical help for infertile couples; and general attention to the 'medical, nutritional and social care of mothers and children' (Royal College of Physicians, 1949).

Underlying these and similar recommendations was a mechanistic view of women as baby-producers, according to which various financial and other material inducements would bring about the desired change in reproductive behaviour. However, a survey of working-class couples published in 1951 showed that women were not prepared to have babies for five shillings a week (the current family allowance rate); what they wanted were day nurseries to lessen the 'drudgery' of childrearing (Slater and Woodside, 1951).

A focus on women as guardians of population quality and quantity has not, of course, been unique to Britain — though the combination of laissez-faire capitalism and welfare statism has given it a singular interpretation in Britain. Falling birth rates have been a cause for concern in most industrialized countries from the mid-1950s on, and many of these have also exhibited a eugenicist interest in those sub-groups within the population with persisting high fertility rates (Chapman, 1955).

Policies for controlling the population are 'family' policies, because promoting the idea of a normal family serves the double purpose of providing a logic for women's place and of marking, unmistakably, the contours of that place. As Kamerman (1977) has pointed out in relation to the United States, and Land (1978) for Britain, family policies are rarely explicitly identified as such by governments. Since a crucially central ethic of family life is that families are private places, the extent of state intervention in family life must be veiled; families are to be frail sanctuaries from, not examples of, the intrusiveness of the state — not only transmitters of culture on behalf of the nation, but the providers of a counter-culture, just as John Ruskin put it a century ago (see p.7).

The most important development in family policy over the last thirty years, and the one that has affected women as social childrearers the most has been the idea that families should be agents acting in the best interests of children's psychological health. Both childbearing and childrearing have decisively entered the realm of the medical, and the state, acting on the advice of obstetric and paediatric experts, has dictated both how children should be born and reared and what the structure of a 'proper' family life should be. The value of the family as an insurance scheme not only for sound bodies but for sound minds marks a departure from the ideology of the early 1940s and before. Its central assertion is that women must put their children first, if irreparable damage is not to be done to the mental health of the nation.

'A NEW AND SUBTLE FORM OF ANTI-FEMINISM'

In 1948 the World Health Organization asked an ex-army psychiatrist by the name of John Bowlby to produce a report on the psychological effects of separating young children from their homes. The result, 'Maternal Care and Mental Health', appeared in 1951 and has been compared to a bomb for its impact on both professional and lay child-carers; its popular version, *Child Care and the Growth of Love*, published by Penguin two years later, became a bestseller.

Building on the psychoanalytic insight that early experience can have lasting effects on adult behaviour and personality (a surely reasonable proposition), Bowlby took the particular case of children separated from their mothers and argued that evidence on this

collected by psychiatrists and others justified the claim that mothers'
more or less continual presence was essential to their children's mental
health. As Bowlby phrased it in his original report,

What is . . . essential for mental health is that the infant and young child
should experience a warm, intimate and continuous relationship with his [*sic*]
mother.

. . . the evidence is now such that it leaves no room for doubt . . . that the
prolonged deprivation of the young child of maternal care may have grave and
far-reaching effects on his character and so on the whole of his future life.
[Bowlby, 1951, pp.361, 396]

Bowlby held that the relationship was analogous to the effect of
rubella on the fetus or of a shortage of vitamin D in infancy.
Separation from the mother had a simple causal status in explaining
an inability to form affectionate relationships in later life, just as
rubella caused fetal malformations and vitamin D inadequacy led to
rickets.

Bowlby identified three categories of maternal deprivation:
(1) living with a mother who has an 'unfavourable' attitude to her
child;
(2) losing one's mother through death, illness or desertion;
(3) being removed from one's mother to strangers by medical or
social agencies.
Failure of a child's 'natural home group' was identified as a main
cause of maternal deprivation, and under this heading Bowlby
included illegitimacy, divorce, chronic parental illness or
psychopathy, poverty, parental imprisonment, and maternal
employment: 'Any family suffering from one or more of these
conditions must be regarded as a potential source of deprived
children' (p.423). *Preventing* maternal deprivation, thought Bowlby,
thus required both what he termed 'direct aid' to families (family
allowances, assistance for one-parent families, medical care, marriage
guidance counselling, etc.) and 'long term community programmes'
aimed at tackling the problems of social fragmentation and family
break-up. So far as these were concerned, he said, an essential
component was that mothers of young children 'should not be free to
earn' (p.441).

Some of the sentiments attributed to Bowlby in the years following
the publication of the WHO report are undoubtedly the result of

misreading and misquotation. Moreover, his work has been beneficial to women in the sense of alerting people to the unhappiness caused to many mothers and children by unwarranted separations — for example, when small children are hospitalized or in the labour ward, directly after birth, a practice Bowlby referred to in 1951 as 'an astonishing practice', an 'aberration' of Western society unlikely to promote a close mother – child relationship (Bowlby, 1951, p.499). [4]

However, there is also no doubt that Bowlby based his conclusions on inadequate evidence, much of which failed to distinguish the multiple variables involved. (What was the cause of the separation? Who (else) was the child separated from? What was the child's relationship with her/his caretaker before and after the separation? What do 'normal' mothers do for their children in the way of play, stimulation, etc.? How is the child's distress (if any) at separation measured? and so on.) This led to the invidious and certainly untrue proposition that bad homes must always be better than good institutions. The concept of 'maternal deprivation' is itself vague and confused (Rutter, 1972), and fathers are omitted from Bowlby's picture because no one had studied them and because the mother – child relationship was regarded as 'without doubt' the most important.

Comprehensive critiques of Bowlby's work now abound (see, for example, Andry, 1966; Mead, 1966; Wootton, 1966; Rutter, 1972; P. Morgan, 1975; Clarke and Clarke, 1976) amplifying these and other points. Margaret Mead noted the important consideration that, far from being the natural arrangement, ' . . an exclusive and continuous relationship between mother and infant is only possible under highly artificial urban conditions' (Mead, 1966, p.248). Some years earlier, she had diagnosed theories of maternal deprivation as

a new and subtle form of antifeminism in which men . . . — under the guise of exalting the importance of maternity — are tying women more tightly to their children than has been thought necessary since the invention of bottlefeeding and baby carriages.

She went on to say that

---

[4] It is an interesting question why this observation, now currently extremely fashionable among paediatricians (see Klaus and Kennell, 1976; Brimblecombe *et al.*, 1978), did not receive much attention at the time.

It may well be, of course, that limiting a child's contact to its biological mother may be the most efficient way to produce a character suited to lifelong monogamous marriage, but if so then we should be clear that that is what we are doing . . . . [Mead, 1954, p.477]

As Elizabeth Wilson (1977) has observed, what really needs to be explained is *not* why a child's separation under stressful conditions from a loving and familiar environment is hurtful — both to the child and to those who care for it — but why so many people should have been so impressed by Bowlby's views in the last thirty years that they have become the single most influential theory of child development, despite considerable scientifically respectable evidence that the theory doesn't fit the facts either of how children in 'normal' families are reared or of what happens to those who are not reared in 'normal' families (Rutter, 1972; Clarke and Clarke, 1976; P. Morgan, 1975; Schaffer, 1977; Schaffer and Emerson, 1964; P. Smith, 1979).[5]

The reason why Bowlbyism caught on was that his message fitted the spirit of the times: the 1950s were a reactionary era for women, and were already child-centred. Childhood is a modern invention. Until the eighteenth century in Britain, only very young children were recognized as dependent non-adults. When they came out of their swaddling bands, they were dressed in adult clothes and expected to participate in adult work and play. (There were no toyshops in London until the mid-eighteenth century, and until about that time the only books for children were the Bible and religious tracts.) As in non-industrialized cultures today, the child was an intrinsic part of the agricultural economy — and of the early industrial economy too (Thompson, 1963). From the late seventeenth century onwards, when the state began to assume some minimal responsibility for the poor and propertyless, unsupported children were put to work, not educated.

Under these earlier conditions of childrearing, parental affection

---

[5] Bowlby has revised and developed his theories since 1951, chiefly in the direction of placing the analysis of mother–child relationships within the framework of 'attachment behaviour', a concept that owes a great deal to Konrad Lorenz's work on 'imprinting' among animals. Yet what one reviewer of Bowlby's penultimate book (*The Making and Breaking of Affectional Bonds*, 1979) referred to as Bowlby's 'ideological preoccupation with mother-love' (*New Society*, 27 September 1979), shows no signs of having abated in these reconsiderations.

was not necessarily lacking,⁶ but children had a more prosaic value than they do now, being seen as units of labour and mouths to feed, rather than as packages of individual potential to be cherished. This failure to differentiate children's personalities is reflected in naming habits: in the Middle Ages, identical names were often given to siblings, who were then distinguished by birth order labels. By the early modern period this practice had stopped, but a dead child's name could be given to a sibling born later. Today, no two siblings are given the same name, and a name is seen as an intrinsic part of the irreplaceable individual. But it is not until the twentieth century, dubbed by historian Arthur Calhoun (1919, p.131) 'the century of the child', that we encounter the full blossoming of the notion of childhood, the *idea* that society should have a commitment to uncovering and satisfying the needs of its most junior citizens. The child also took its place as 'father of the man', and the thought that the experiences of infancy and early childhood might determine adult behaviour and happiness became the most cogent reason imaginable for attaching importance to the needs of children (Clarke and Clarke, 1976). With minds like 'soft wax', an image that is 'the most popular metaphor for the psychology of the young child' (Kagan, 1978, p.13), children came to be seen as both infinitely malleable and profoundly vulnerable.

The rise of child psychology combined with women's role as targets for population policies and as the lynchpins of families to produce a situation in which the new experts on childrearing addressed themselves to an all-female audience; for, as President Roosevelt aptly said, 'you cannot really be a good mother if you are not a wise mother' (quoted in Ehrenreich and English, 1979, p.171) — which means that mothers who are not wise, cannot be good.

Janet Edwards took her 2 year old to the health visitor's clinic for a check-up in 1974. The conversation reproduced below between mother and health visitor illustrates the close surveillance given to all aspects of childrearing by experts who have taken it upon themselves to pronounce on the moral and physical rectitude of everything that parents (mothers) do in the name of loving and caring for their children.

---

⁶ There is dispute about this. See Aries (1962) and the contributions in de Mause (1974).

Health visitor: How are we doing?
Janet Edwards: She's fine, except for her sleep.
HV: Feeding alright?
JE: Oh, marvellous, yes. No trouble.
HV: Talking?
JE: Yes. Never stops.
HV: How about the potty? Out of the question, is it?
JE: A couple of times, that's all.
HV: You're not worrying her too much about it?
JE: Oh no, I don't. If she doesn't want to go, I just leave her.
HV: She's out of nappies during the day?
JE: No.
HV: Well, why not turn round and have a bit of a concentrated effort? Not to worry her. But take her in with you, before meals or after meals, regularly, and sitting her on the pot — or does she use the toilet?
JE: No, she uses a pot.
HV: If she uses the toilet, I think you'll have to put a trainer seat on it.
JE: She's not too keen on that at all.
HV: You see at this age they get so excited and so worked up that they go before they realize it. Because they're busy, so busy, doing other things — when they've done it they'll tell you quite often. So if you can get her into the habit of going at regular times, it does help quite a bit.
JE: Yes.
HV: What's this business about sleeping, then?
JE: Well, she just doesn't seem to . . . last night was a good night, she woke four times. And on a bad night . . .
HV: Is she sleeping in her own room?
JE: No, we've only the one bedroom.
HV: So she shares your room?
JE: Yes.
HV:There's no way of turfing her bed out into another room?
JE: Well, we've tried quite a few times, but to get the cot out you have to get it over our bed — we've really only got a very small bedroom.
HV: Because I think this has an awful lot to do with it — you disturb her, and then she wakes up and she knows you're there.
JE: Yes. And she just won't go back to sleep until you pick her up.
HV: Will she go back in bed? She doesn't come into your bed?
JE: No, I won't have her in our bed.
HV: Don't start that, will you, because it's easily done.
JE: No, I never did like that.
HV: It's very difficult, you see, because she wakes up, she sees you there and she's going to keep on until you're awake, but if you possibly could turf it out

into the sitting-room, I think I'd be inclined to have a go at it . . .

JE: And just let her cry if she wakes up?

HV: Well, the thing is, if you know very well she is alright, she doesn't want to be changed and she's not coming into any danger, then leave her alone . . . Immunizations — she's had them all, has she?

JE: Yes, yes, yes.

HV: Now, she's only just two. Do you take her into any of the one o'clock clubs round here?

JE: Actually, I'm just going up now.

HV: Which one do you go to?

JE: The one in the park . . .

HV: Have you thought about schooling?

JE: Yes. You mean nursery school? Yes, I'd like to get her into nursery school.

HV: You've got her down for full-time school?

JE: I have her down for full-time school, yes.

HV: What, a Catholic school?

JE: Yes.

HV: Yes, well, then, in Saint James road there's a little school and they take them in at three, but they have got a waiting list. So when they get back in September I'd pop along there and see if you can't get her in there. It's a lovely little nursery school . . .

JE: Yes, yes. There seem to be little rashes on her face she's had since she was born.

HV: Yes, leave it alone. You're not putting anything on it? You do find that they get this and quite often when they're teething it comes up even worse. Not that I'm saying teething gives them a rash. But leave it alone, and see the doctor at the clinic when she comes for a check. Alright?

JE: Thank you. [Oakley, unpublished data, 'Transition to Motherhood' study]

In this encounter, which is typical of many, the health visitor conveys to the mother that the whole of the child's development is her concern: physical development; feeding and sleeping patterns; 'habit-training'; psychological welfare; and educational future. However, it is more than a friendly interest; certain methods of socializing children are quite definitely right and others are wrong.

Hugh Jolly puts the case for consulting experts in his *Book of Child Care: the Complete Guide for Today's Parents*:

I am often asked whether I think it is a good idea for parents to read books on child care and for there to be radio and television programmes on the subject.

As the author of this book I have obviously answered in the affirmative — but why?

Before answering the question it is relevant first to ask why it comes to be asked. We accept that training and advice are required for every job a man or woman undertakes. The job of bringing up our children, the most important we undertake, is no exception . . . Since these early years are so vital is there any need to argue the need for child upbringing to be a subject of study, in books and other media, for all parents?

The modern mother takes for granted that she will have the advice of experts and will not have to rely on the advice of her mother. The previous generation of mothers may not necessarily be the best advisers of the present generation . . . . Today's parents are probably better at bringing up their children than any previous generation. They are more aware of the importance of the early years and, knowing this, they are more concerned not to make mistakes. [Jolly, 1975, p.17]

In order to avoid mistakes, rules for normal development must be learned:

A six month old baby is a chubby little fellow . . . He can sit propped up in his pram with the support of pillows, and he eagerly turns his head from side to side to look about him, particularly when taking his daily outings.

At nine months a baby has graduated to hard foods and can hold, bite and chew a biscuit by himself . . . He enjoys games with Mummy and Daddy. Simple games, like peek-a-boo, and pat-a-cake, cause great excitement.[Family Doctor publication, *First Baby*, 1976, pp.10, 13]

And reasons for deviation must be appreciated, along with their correct remedies:

Nail-biting is a sign of tenseness . . . Is she[7] being urged or corrected or warned or scolded too much? Are the parents expecting too much in the way of lessons? Consult the teacher about her school adjustment . . . A child beyond the age of three may be helped by a manicure set . . . [Spock, 1979, pp.396 – 7]

But just what is a mistake? One incurable dilemma for mothers is that following expert advice must be balanced against the advice that they, through instinct, are their own experts. 'The trouble is that one can't

---

[7] In the 1979 edition of his *Baby and Childcare*, Spock tried 'to get away from the implied assumption in previous editions that the child is always a boy' (p.xvi).

teach love' (Schaffer, 1977, p.97), or, as Spock in both his 1957 and 1979 editions so appropriately put it, 'trust your own instincts, and follow the directions that your doctor gives you' (1957, p.3; 1979, p.1). This double expectation that childrearing comes naturally and must be learnt from experts is one of the greatest problems women face in becoming mothers today. Suffused with guilt because they do not naturally know how to help a baby take the breast, how to make a 7 year old go to bed or how to counsel a rebellious teenager through her first love affair, mothers receive from experts the clear message that there is a scientifically correct way to bring up children and that whatever vices their children have as adults are to be attributed, one way or another, to faulty mothering. Catch 22 is that the experts themselves are in a quandary about what the 'right' way is, and it is, of course, a strange and false notion that the same rearing techniques have the same effect on all children:

'Wind' is . . . air, swallowed with the milk and solid foods, or gulped down when the baby is hungry or crying . . . Distension with wind is common, and is indicated by a miserable crying after feeds when he wants to go to sleep. [Vosper, 1974, p.95]

. . . many babies, while feeding happily, have their meal interrupted in order to be winded. This in itself is enough to make a baby cry . . . The other more serious mistake is to ascribe a baby's crying to wind. [Jolly, 1975, pp.79 – 80]

AREN'T CHILDREN WONDERFUL?

Studying the behaviour of doctors and patients in development assessment clinics, Davis and Strong recorded a prominent appeal made by doctors to children's essential nature as 'wonderful'.

Children as a class are commonly seen as wonderful. All children it would seem can be described as 'wonderful', 'gorgeous' and a source of 'joy'. In contrast, we feel that to apply such epithets to *all adults* seems a strange claim to make. 'Aren't adults wonderful?' seems an odd statement. [Davis and Strong, 1976, pp.160 – 1]

Holding up children as wonderful has a special function in such clinics where some children are obviously not normal. However, it is also a core value of the way childhood and motherhood are defined in the industrialized West that children are *sacred*. They can do no wrong — or rather any wrong that they do is a consequence of faulty care.

Moreover, children properly elicit positive not negative emotions.

Again, there is much evidence to show that this embargo on negative feelings is a particular problem for mothers today. The prevailing image of mother – child relations, being that of a 'natural' unit, allows no room for irritation or anger or mere disinterest. Three-quarters of mothers interviewed in my own study of first-time motherhood did not feel love for their babies immediately after birth: the common feeling was one of detachment, a selfish feeling of wanting to be left alone to recover from the ordeal and triumph of giving birth. Three-quarters said that they sometimes felt angry with their babies in the early months and might give in to the occasional shake or mild slap or simply handle them more roughly than usual (Oakley, 1979). These are more than transitional problems in adjusting to parenthood. In the Newsons' valuable follow-up study of attitudes to bringing up children, 75 per cent of mothers smacked 4 year olds and 41 per cent smacked 7 year olds at least once a week (Newson and Newson, 1970, 1976).

Smacking is one index of the fact that childrearing does not usually — even in 'normal' families — go smoothly and that parents as well as children are prone to temper tantrums (although parents are not conceded the same right to spells of anger as children are). It was in the 1950s that the medical profession 'discovered' child abuse. 'Non-accidental injury', the now fashionable term, is thought seriously to affect several thousand children a year in Britain. Searching for the cause of non-accidental injury to children has been a notably fruitless exercise — because there is no single cause. In the USA, David Gil asked 1,520 people for their attitudes to child abuse: more than half believed that 'almost anybody could at some time injure a child in his care'; a quarter thought *they* could injure a child; one in nine said they had come close to it; 0.4 per cent admitted they had actually done it (Gil, 1970).

One English mother wrote to the *Sunday Times* with an account of how close she had come to harming her second baby:

When I read a story of a baby battering I can't help thinking 'There but for the grace of God go I' .... If all the mothers who have ever shaken a screaming baby, or slapped it, or thrown it roughly into its cot, stood up to be counted, we would make a startling total.

I am not speaking of uncaring mothers, but those who love their babies dearly .... The accumulated weariness of days and nights of coping alone with a 'difficult' baby or young child can lead even the most placid or resilient mother into behaviour she immediately regrets.

I recall the seemingly endless period when my second baby screamed every night for anything from four to six hours with so-called 'three month colic'. The screaming would keep my one-year old daughter awake and she would scream too unless I nursed her.

But the baby's screaming reached fever pitch if I sat down and could only be reduced to a whimper if I paced the floor with him. So I would alternately sit and pace, always with one or the other crying and usually with tears streaming down my own face.

I was given medicine for the baby and assurances that the phase would pass, but not a word of advice on how to survive such a time without succumbing to an impulse to knock their heads together. [*Sunday Times*, 30 May 1976]

She weathered the storm, but some parents in less fortunate circumstances do not.[8] Most parents who injure children are poor. Many are very young. The children are concentrated in the under-5 age group; most vulnerable are the under-1s and toddlers of 2½ − 3. Children particularly at risk are those who had difficult deliveries, were of low birth weight and/or were separated from their mothers postnatally (Lynch and Roberts, 1977). As Martin Richards has put it, some children

are much easier to love than others. Some children behave in ways that any parent will find upsetting, difficult or frustrating . . . . Frequent crying, piercing cries, regular waking at night, feeding problems, vomiting after feeds and non-cuddliness are all often mentioned in case histories. It is fairly easy to see how any of these characteristics could push a parent who otherwise might cope, over the edge so that the whole situation breaks down and the child is injured. [Richards, 1975b, p.8]

Richards points out how little knowledge many parents have of children before they have their own, how geographical mobility and reduced family size have removed much valuable family support for parents, and how the ethic of reliance on experts militates against maternal self-confidence. It could be said that in no other occupation is it the case that total responsibility combines with the imputation of

---

[8] Estimates of the percentage of child batterers who are women vary from 50 per cent to 88 per cent (Freeman, 1979, p.28). The preponderance of women (if there is one) must surely reflect the greater amount of time women spend with their children.

professional incompetence, lack of social supports and economic rewards to render the worker a victim of her/his own promotion to 'the most important job' in the world.

Why, then, do women want babies? This is not an easy question to answer, for the simple reason that it has usually not been asked. 'Family intentions' surveys have concentrated on how many children of what sex couples want, on the extent to which families are truly planned and on whether so-called 'family planning' services help or hinder them to match precept and practice. Much attention has been given to which personal, social and economic factors are important determinants of family size, with the aim of understanding and predicting reproductive behaviour and of interpreting changes in the birth rate. Hence, to take one example from an extensive literature, Ann Cartwright's *How Many Children?* (1976) was addressed to the question of why the British birth rate had fallen from 93.0 live births per 1000 women aged 15 – 44 in 1964 to 71.7 in 1973. She compared data from two family intentions surveys done in 1967/8 and 1973, concluding that the reduction was due to a fall in ideal family size among mothers who had already had two or three children. This may seem a rather obvious conclusion, but it is perhaps interesting that there does not seem to be a rising preference for the one-child family: the 'cereal packet' norm of two (boy and girl, in that order) still prevails, or prevails more uniformly than it used to. Like others who have studied what people say about their plans for having children, Cartwright observed that economic factors are often mentioned as a constraint. Since the idea that wealth makes more children possible works for the middle classes, but applies inversely to those with manual occupations (the poorest families are the largest), the whole question of identifying how economic considerations affect childbearing is extremely complicated.[9]

Sally Macintyre (1976a, p.151) has pointed out that one approach to the topic of reproductive behaviour is to look at the taken-for-granted assumptions that make the question 'Why did/do you want a baby?' not only one that does not occur to researchers, but one that

---

[9] There may be a parallel here with motives for maternal employment in which money is identified as a reason by researchers not necessarily because it is the primary motivating factor for mothers' employment, but because it is a simple and socially acceptable reason.

prospective parents, by and large, do not ask themselves. John Peel and Griselda Carr (1975) asked people 'Do you think it's important for a man and wife to have children?' Of the women asked, 80 per cent said yes, the majority observing that children make a marriage. Thus, having children cannot be separated from getting married: both are credentials of 'ordinary' adulthood, especially for women (Payne, 1978). Childless marriages are to be pitied:

I am thirty one, married and childless. For 3½ years, we have been trying to start a family. We have done the rounds of infertility clinics, doctors and hospitals, and suffered the indignities of cold showers, temperature charts and endless examinations. It now seems most unlikely that we shall succeed in our desire. As I attempt to face this fact I am beginning to look back on a period marked solely by an obsessive drive towards motherhood and to question my own and society's attitude to infertility . . .

I can now see that what has made the last few years so difficult is that I accepted, along with society, that childlessness within marriage is not only abnormal but socially unacceptable . .

During the last 3 years I have sometimes longed to be told that I could never have a child. Not because this is what I want, but because accepting the fact would allow me to live again. Yet hospital, family and friends conspire to protect me against this. They see my attempts at acceptance as 'giving up'. Whereas I see it as the only possible step towards the future. [Juliet Miller, 'The misery of an infertile marriage', *Sunday Times*, 28 January 1978]

The idea that women want babies is, as Macintyre says, propagated especially by the medical profession. Women who don't want babies tend to be seen as abnormal and it is their motives that need to be explained. However, there are two versions of reality: one for married women and one for single women. In the former, childbearing is to be promoted (within limits); in the latter, it is to be prevented, as in the classic joke:

Doctor: I've got good news for you, Mrs. Brown.
Patient: It's Miss Brown, actually.
Doctor: I've got bad news for you, Miss Brown. [Macintyre, 1976b, p.160]

The prevalence of the paradigm of normal women as naturally maternal[10] has obstructed research on motherhood as it is actually experienced by women themselves. The American feminist Charlotte

---

[10] I have discussed this elsewhere. See Oakley (1979, 1980).

Perkins Gilman achieved notoriety in the early years of this century by identifying the family, the home and mothers as damaging instead of safeguarding the health of children. Home-making, she said, took precedence over child-training:

The ideal which instantly obtrudes itself is this: A beautiful, comfortable house meeting all physical needs; a happy family, profoundly enjoying each other's society; a father, devotedly spending his life in obtaining the wherewithal to maintain this little heaven; a mother, completely wrapped up in her children and devotedly spending her life in their service, working miracles of advantage to them in so doing; children, happy in the home and growing up beautifully under its benign influence . . .

But the reality is different:

In our homes today the child grows up . . . not at all in that state of riotous happiness we are so eager to assume as the condition of childhood. The mother loves the child, always and always; she does what she can, what she knows how; but the principal work of her day is the care of the house, not of the child. [Gilman, 1903; reprinted in Salper, 1972, pp.111 – 2]

Gilman's own experience as a mother was not happy. After her daughter's birth a prolonged depression was not cured by the advice of the best-known American specialist in women's diseases, S. Weir Mitchell, who told her that if she gave up reading and writing altogether she would adjust to parenthood.

In 1972, Alice Rossi found that full-time mothers who don't work outside the home spend relatively little time interacting with their children. For many mothers, the obligation to get housework done cannot simply be assigned a low priority when the needs of children intrude, for being a good housewife is as central to the image of how women ought to be as is being a good mother. Birnbaum's (1971) study comparing employed and non-employed mothers in America showed that those without jobs had a lower sense of personal competence even with respect to childcare skills and expressed more concern over identity issues than employed mothers. Full-time mothers stressed the *sacrifice* motherhood entailed more often than employed mothers, who talked more about how children had enriched their lives.

The effect of children on women (another unstudied subject) is not uniform; here, as elsewhere, the habit of generalizing about women as a category can be deeply misleading. However, and as the second quotation from Simone de Beauvoir at the beginning of this chapter indicates, children have a lot to offer. Whatever the deprivations entailed in having them, to see a child of one's own flourishing through the care and love one has given it is a quite uniquely satisfying human experience. Mary Wollstonecraft, two centuries ago, put it like this:

I once told you, that the sensations before she was born, and when she is sucking, were pleasant; but they do not deserve to be compared to the emotions I feel, when she stops to smile upon me, or laughs outright on meeting me . . . after a short absence. [Wollstonecraft, 1796, p.124]

The symbolic value of children is not only, or even principally, their capacity to transform a marriage into a family and ensure the passage of a genetic inheritance into the future — though both these elements are stressed in family intentions surveys. For women as a minority group children represent an achievement over and beyond this. They are the inalienable property of women, who otherwise are placed by society in a propertyless condition: 'I look at her and think you're *mine*, you're nobody else's' (Oakley, 1979, p.264). They symbolize achievement in a world where under-achievement is the rule:

It's given me something in life; I feel that I've *achieved* something now. Whereas before, I mean work and everything, maybe it was the jobs I had, but I always felt like I was in a rut and was never *achieving* anything. But I feel as though I've done something *useful*, and if I can turn her into a nice person and put her into the world I'll feel that I've really *achieved* something.

And they make a woman feel genuinely wanted:

A few weeks ago I was just feeding her and I suddenly was sort of overwhelmed with love for her and I thought this is good, this is great, this is what life is all about. It's so rewarding, the feeling of her dependence on you and the way she's growing and the way you're bringing her up, the way she responds to you. I've always wanted to be a mother: I wanted a family and I wanted to be a mother to fulfil my life. [Oakley, 1979, pp.263, 265]

PROVIDING FOR CHILDREN

Finally in this chapter I want to discuss briefly the question of what facilities are provided for looking after children outside the orbit of the nuclear family, and what factors help to determine the level of this provision.

The American sociologist Jessie Bernard (1974, p.268) has remarked that American policy on motherhood has been ambiguous: suggesting that women stay at home to care for the childi en on the one hand, while pursuing the anti-natalist policy of making room for them in the labour force on the other. In fact, the majority of developed nations have submitted women to this contradiction. The state itself is unclear whether being a producer or a reproducer is or should be women's primary role. One measure of the value governments have attached to reproduction is the level at which maternity grants have been paid. Table 10.1 shows how Britain fares in this respect. However, state policy in many countries aims, often implicitly, to

TABLE 10.1 *The level of maternity grants in Britain and some other countries, 1977*

Austria	£283
East Germany	£279
Luxembourg	£278
France	£218
Czechoslovakia	£106
Iceland	£ 94
Norway	£ 93
Hungary	£ 72
West Germany	£ 64
Portugal	£ 29
United Kingdom	£ 25
Australia	£ 20
Cyprus	£ 7.80

Source: Kendall (1979) p.14.

distinguish between two situations. Where there are grave social and economic problems — maternal illness, paternal unemployment, a fatherless family, gross poverty — it is regarded as reasonable for the state to step in and fill the gap by looking after the children (some mothers have to work). Where there is no 'reason' why mother cannot look after the children herself, she is expected to do so (mothers shouldn't work). The fact that she doesn't wish to do so, or is unhappy if she does, are not morally acceptable justifications for handing over her maternal responsibilities to other people. Policies towards mothers in both these categories are determined by the varying needs of differently aged children (as interpreted by paediatric experts) and by labour force requirements. Time lag complicates the simple supply and demand model; thus Hungary continues to provide a childcare allowance for mothers of under-3s to stay at home, although there is an economic need now to have these women in employment (Kamerman, 1979).

Undoubtedly the most striking aspect of out-of-home provision for children in most industrial capitalist countries is that whenever the demand among mothers for such provision is measured it is very much greater than the actual supply of these facilities. Audrey Hunt, in her 1968 survey of women's employment in Britain, reported that a quarter of the mothers of under-5s in her survey said they would work if childcare facilities existed. One in five employed mothers of 0 − 2 year olds and one in six employed mothers of 3 − 4 year olds wanted, but did not have, nursery places; one in six employed mothers of schoolchildren wanted after-school facilities, and one in four mentioned the need for alternative care for their children during school holidays. Hunt's estimate was that between 3 and 3½ *million* places were needed in nurseries, nursery schools, after-school and holidaycare facilities. The actual number of places officially provided at that time in England, Wales and Scotland was 497,886 (this includes local authority day nurseries and legislations under the Nurseries and Childminders' Regulation Act, 1948). The then Ministry of Health found this estimate of demand greatly alarming, and inserted a comment into the official report of the study:

The Ministry of Health state that, as far as day nurseries are concerned, they have been provided by local health authorities since 1945 primarily to meet the needs of certain children for day care on health and welfare grounds. The service is not intended to meet a demand from working women generally for subsidized day care facilities. [Hunt, 1968, p.107]

Almost a decade later, Margaret Bone's study of *Preschool Children and Their Need for Day Care* (1977) found that nearly two-thirds of mothers of under-5s would like to share the task of childrearing with someone else. The Central Policy Review Staff's examination of *Services for Young Children with Working Mothers* (1978) opened with a diagrammatic representation of the size of the problem (Figure 10.1). This shows that in 1976 two-fifths of all children under 11 and a

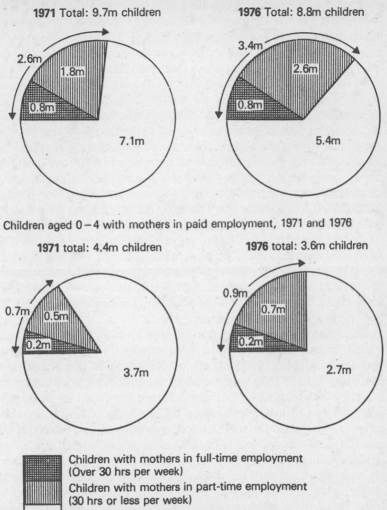

Children aged 0 – 10 with mothers in paid employment, 1971 and 1976

1971 Total: 9.7m children   **1976** Total: 8.8m children

2.6m
1.8m
0.8m
7.1m

3.4m
2.6m
0.8m
5.4m

Children aged 0 – 4 with mothers in paid employment, 1971 and 1976

1971 total: 4.4m children   **1976** total: 3.6m children

0.7m
0.5m
0.2m
3.7m

0.9m
0.7m
0.2m
2.7m

Children with mothers in full-time employment
(Over 30 hrs per week)

Children with mothers in part-time employment
(30 hrs or less per week)

Children with mothers not in employment.

FIGURE 10.1 *Children aged 0 – 10 and children aged 0 – 4 with mothers in paid employment, 1971 and 1976, Britain.*

Source: Central Policy. Review Staff (1978). Crown copyright.

quarter of children under 5 had mothers in paid employment compared with a quarter and a sixth only five years before (which was five years *after* Hunt assessed the level of demand for childcare facilities at between 3 and 3½ million places). The report observes the existence of some 900,000 under-5s whose mothers have a job, for only 120,000 of whom the government provides either full- or part-time day care, and of 2½ million 5 – 10 year olds with employed mothers, for whom virtually no provision is made outside school hours. Only 3 per cent of the public money spent on health, education and social services in Britain in 1976 was devoted to 0 – 4 year olds, of which less than a third (1 per cent of the grand total) was used for educational and related provisions of some help to employed mothers.

Not surprisingly, many mothers place their children with childminders (a word only recently included in the *Oxford English Dictionary*). It is possible that 1,200,000 British children are left daily with unregistered minders (Jackson, 1979). In 1977 there were also 31,398 registered minders catering for 70,288 children on a full-time basis and a further 2,635 with part-time places for 17,949 children (Hughes *et al.*, 1980, p.105). Britain's uncoordinated and laggardly effort in the area of childcare provision is not unusual; indeed, as Kamerman (1979) shows, it is the prevailing governmental response to the rise in mothers' employment.

Countries where more attention has been given to this question have varied in the policies adopted. For example, Hungary's income maintenance policy for mothers of the under-3s includes a cash maternity benefit paid to the mother on childbirth, paid maternity leave for 20 weeks; and a flat rate childcare allowance for 31 months after the end of maternity leave if the mother looks after the child herself. This 'wage for motherhood' guarantees job protection and pension entitlements, but is only equal to about 40 per cent of an unskilled worker's wage. In Sweden, where 58 per cent of all mothers of under-3s work, only about 14 per cent of their children are cared for in high quality day care facilities, and the main emphasis in recent years has been on children of working mothers being the children of working fathers as well. The Parent Insurance Scheme allows for either parent to stay at home for the first eight months of the child's life and to receive a wage-related taxable cash benefit. The Swedes are also pressing for a shorter working day (six hours) for parents of young children, regarding them collectively as in need of special provision, not exclusively because of the children's needs but also because of parents' desires to be with their children.

Pro-natalist and anti-natalist policies are, as I have already noted in this book, often structured on the assumption that women are such unenterprising creatures that they will change their behaviour when confronted with simple material inducements. If you pay them to go to the antenatal clinic, they will go; if you give them some money to stay at home, they will give up their jobs.

Adequate provision for out-of-home childcare is not increasing in countries such as Britain and the United States — but the proportion of employed mothers is. In both countries the employment rate for mothers of pre-school children more than doubled between 1961 and 1977 (it rose from 12 per cent to 27 per cent in Britain — Hughes *et al.*, 1980, p.27; Adams and Winston, 1980, p.1). There is an international trend for the employment patterns of mothers of pre-school children to become like those of mothers of older children (see Table 10.2), and the availability of state-funded day care is only one determinant of this trend, though, equally, it must be said that it is one reason why employed mothers find themselves in what Peter Moss (1976, p.11) has termed 'a job ghetto within a job ghetto'. In the 1974 British Family Expenditure Survey, 21 per cent of employed married childless women were in semi-skilled or unskilled manual work, compared to 47 per cent of those with a child aged 5 – 10 and 54 per cent of those with

TABLE 10.2 *Labour force participation rates of women by age of child, 1976*

Country	Age of child		
	0 – 3 years (%)	3 – 6 years (%)	School age (%)
France	43	44	48
Federal Republic of Germany	32	34	41
German Democratic Republic	80	80	80
Hungary	82	75	75
Sweden	58	64	69
United States	35	48	56

Source: Kamerman (1979) p.636.

a child under 4 (unpublished analysis of FES data cited in Moss, 1976, p.8).

A young mother, who was hoping to become a motor mechanic, may have to choose between her career and her 2-year old child. Lord McDonald, sitting in the Court of Session on 18th January said of Fiona McDermid of Broomwalk, Livingstone, 'Even if she got custody of Kevin, she intends to pursue a fulltime career which would involve him in being in the care of a registered childminder during her working hours'. The judge granted her a divorce, but awarded custody to the child's father . . . Ms McDermid was told that the question of custody could be reviewed . . . if she can offer more personal daily care than she at present contemplated. [*Scotsman*, 19 January 1979]

After more than two decades of research on the social problem of working mothers, two messages stand out. Firstly, researchers find that maternal employment per se is not detrimental to children's health and is, in many ways, beneficial (Hoffman and Nye, 1974; Tizard *et al.*, 1976). (It would be interesting to compare these findings with their equivalents in the field of paternal employment. However, no such study has been done.) But, secondly, it really is of no consequence what researchers find. The pronouncement that employment is not equivalent to maternal deprivation incorporates the highly political language of women's natural relation to their children, by subscribing to the idea that children are women's responsibility whatever women (or men) do.

I end this chapter with one mother describing how she experiences the mother – child bond both as a biological and social tie and as ever-resilient ideology.

The bad and the good moments are inseparable for me. I recall the times when, suckling each of my children, I saw his eyes open full to mine, and realized each of us was fastened to the other, not only by mouth and breast, but through our mutual gaze: the depth, calm, passion, of that dark blue, maturely focused look . . . . I remember early the sense of conflict, of a battleground none of us had chosen, of being an observer who, like it or not, was also an actor in an endless contest of wills. This was what it meant to me to have three children under the age of seven. But I recall too each child's individual body, his slenderness, wiriness, softness, grace . . . I remember moments of peace when for some reason it was possible to go to the bathroom alone. I remember being uprooted from already meager sleep to answer a childish nightmare, pull up a blanket, warm a consoling bottle, lead a half-asleep child to the toilet. I remember going back to bed starkly awake, brittle with anger, knowing that my broken sleep would make next day a hell, that there would be more nightmares, more need for consolation, because out of my weariness I would rage at those children for no reason they could understand.

This was looking back. At the time she wrote in her diary:

My children cause me the most exquisite suffering of which I have any experience. It is the suffering of ambivalence: the murderous alternation between bitter resentment and raw-edged nerves, and blissful gratification and tenderness. Sometimes I seem to myself, in my feelings toward these tiny guiltless beings, a monster of selfishness and intolerance. Their voices wear away at my nerves, their constant needs, above all their need for simplicity and patience, fill me with despair at my own failures, despair too at my fate, which is to serve a function for which I was not fitted. And I am weak sometimes from held-in rage. There are times when I feel only death will free us from one another . . . [Rich, 1977, pp.31 – 2, 21]

CHAPTER ELEVEN

Men

Feminists have only brought into the open a view of men that women have shared secretly all along. The truth is that we expect them to be frail creatures, rather than the reverse. And we excuse behaviour in our men we would never permit ourselves or pardon in others of our kind. That is our peculiar double standard. We think of this as love. [Johnson, 1978, p.30]

Women in modern industrialized societies are, on their own, imperfect creatures. It is only through their relationships with men that their womanhood, and thus their normal, respectable humanity, can be proved. Spinsters, divorcees and lesbians are suspect because they appear to deny the truth of the cultural dogma that men and women unite to form a whole; happy spinsters, divorcees and lesbians are even more suspect, for they must surely be operating with some kind of false consciousness. The imputation of contentment goes against nature — that is, against the attributed nature of women, which is to be heterosexual, monogamous and 'complementary' to the role and character of men.

In this chapter I look at female — male relations as a defining feature of femininity in the modern world. Because the (ideal) locus of such relations is marriage and the family, this chapter may be considered the equivalent of the chapter on 'the family' that appears in most sociology textbooks as the place where the position of women is discussed.

WHAT ARE HUSBANDS FOR?

Most girls in the last decades of the twentieth century are still brought up to envisage their destinies in the cloudless, confetti-bedecked land of Mr Right, the tall, dark, handsome stranger who will colonize their lives and make them happy ever after. Interviewing London schoolgirls in 1976, Sue Sharpe found that 82 per cent of 15-year-old girls wanted to marry, a third by the time they were twenty. Very few girls did not see their lives as centred on married bliss; few saw any conflict between their future as wives and mothers and their future as workers (or as divorcees or as mothers of adult and absent children).

When girls describe their future projected lives, men — as husbands and fathers — are important, but they have a strangely insubstantial existence. Joyce Joseph, analysing girls' written accounts of their projected lives, said:

One of the interesting facts which emerged when the life stories were examined was that large numbers of girls reported the deaths of their husbands when their husbands had performed the limited function of providing them with children. In some the husband died and the woman went back to her job, or more commonly went to live with, or near, her children. Some married again, or lived alone as a romantic widow enlivened by visits of their grandchildren, or even replaced their husband by a dog. [Joseph, 1961, p.182]

A third of Joseph's 'husband killers' dispensed with their husbands when the children became self-supporting. Men, thus, have a symbolic significance. They are recognized to be economic providers, bestowers of status and marks of respectability. What, after all, are husbands for? This question, whose answer comes so easily to 15-year-old schoolgirls, has preoccupied anthropologists for decades. The quandary is usually put in these terms: the relation of women to children is biological — through gestation and lactation the tie is visible to everyone; but the relation of men to children and of men to the mothers of children is hidden or may (in the former case) be strictly unknowable (see, for example, the discussions in Fox, 1967, and Mair, 1977). So what accounts for the personal and publicly legitimized connections between men, on the one hand, and women and children, on the other, in most, if not all human societies? What about this slippage between 'most' and 'all' — is it sensible or warranted to claim the universality of the family as the achievement that makes us different from ('better than') apes?

The early anthropologists saw the Victorian patriarchal family as the last and most civilized form of human relations (Morgan, 1877; Taylor, 1865). 'Primitive' societies, they thought, were just that: riddled with promiscuity and with such morally disreputable arrangements as group marriage and communal childrearing, which attached no value to the singular, lifelong, family-creating union of one man and one woman. (Of course such arrangements gave greater recognition to the sexuality and independence of women, but that was one reason why nineteenth- and early twentieth-century anthropologists disliked them.)

By the 1950s, this belief in 'primitive communism' had died out, and it was speedily becoming 'an article of faith with most students of society that one can find everywhere the individual or "nuclear" family of a man and woman with their children' (Mair, 1977, p.7). This article of faith persists. Most sociologists today find a way of interpreting other cultures' arrangements for licensing heterosexual unions and legitimizing and 'rearing children so that they are essentially no different from Mr and Mrs Jones in their suburban home in Birmingham (England or Alabama) with their wedding photographs in the drawer, their mortgage and their 2.4 children. (See, for example, Fletcher, 1966; Harris, 1969.)

According to George Murdock, whose *Social Structure* (1949) prompted the post-war revival of interest in the universality of the family debate,

The family is a social group characterized by common residence, economic cooperation, and reproduction. It includes adults of both sexes, at least two of whom maintain a socially approved sexual relationship, and one or more children . . of the sexually cohabiting adults . . . The nuclear family is a universal human social grouping. [Murdock, 1968, pp.37 – 8]

It depends, of course, on what you mean by the family. Among the Nuer it is possible for a woman to marry a woman. She pays bridewealth for her 'wife', her wife and children are under her authority, she has the right to damages in the event of her wife's adultery, and the children belong to her lineage in exactly the same way as holds for male husbands (Evans-Pritchard, 1951). The Nayars of Malabar allowed their women as many lovers as they liked; however, every girl before puberty went through a marriage ceremony in which a certain man, who might have no further contact with her, became her 'husband'. A woman's brothers were responsible for supporting her, and although her lovers might acknowledge their biological responsibility to her children by paying the midwife's fee, these children were the responsibility entirely of the mother and her kin (Gough, 1968). In Israeli kibbutzim, mothers, fathers and children do not share a common domicile and do not constitute an economic unit; children are not reared by parents. Yet the sexual exclusivity of married female – male pairs is honoured (Spiro, 1968). To make matters even more complicated, the French anthropologist Claude Levi-Strauss, studying the Tupi-Kawahib of central Brazil, personally observed a mother and daughter married to the same man together sharing the care of children who were 'at the same time, stepchildren to one woman and, according to case, either grandchild or stepbrother to the other'. This conundrum resulted from the fact that chiefs could marry several related women, and the women 'do not seem to mind very much whether they nurse their own children or not' (Levi-Strauss, 1969, p.265).

What is the point of reducing these arrangements to the common denominator of the universal nuclear family? Clearly, women must bear children if societies are to survive; thus, men must impregnate women. But how and in what context this happens (and how the actors view the happening) are not determined by some functional need of human beings or societies for 'the' family. The licensing of sexual relations, the legitimizing of children, their socialization, the inheritance of property between generations, the provision of food, clothes, shelter and other material resources — these are conditions of social life that every human culture must meet, but not necessarily in the same way.

However, it has to be said that men have a problem. As Mead (1962, p.158) has put it: 'The recurrent problem of civilization is to define the male role satisfactorily enough — for men, that is'. Women's achievements are listed by nature: childbearing is their authentic accomplishment *as women*. By comparison, the achievements of men have no ready-made definition, but have to be wrestled out of a strictly cultural mould. Husbands, cross-culturally,

are important mainly as fathers; that is to say, as men who give their name, their status in so far as this is inherited, and the right to inherit their property, to the children of a woman with whom they have made a particular kind of contract. [Mair, 1977, p.17]

It is important for men to claim 'the family' as their property (*pace* the term 'a family man') for three reasons: firstly, it subjects the realm of the natural to the reign of the social; secondly, it gives them control over women and children; thirdly, where families are basic units of social organization, there are political advantages to be had in being their managing directors.

HAPPY FAMILIES

If the satisfactoriness of marriage and family life is to be gauged from the extent to which people enter these institutions, then pledging oneself to *one* man (or one woman) must make people very happy indeed. 'Marriage', it is said, 'has never been more popular' (*The Times*, 17 August 1976). Since the mid-1940s in Europe and the USA marriage rates have increased enormously and the age of marriage has fallen.[1] In Britain, by the mid-1960s, 95 per cent of men and 96 per cent of women were, or had been, married by the age of 45 compared with 88 per cent and 83 per cent in 1921 (Ryder and Silver, 1970, p.250). Since the mid-1960s, there has also been a growth in the popularity of re-marriage among both widowed and divorced persons; one index of this change is that chances of remarriage by the age of 35 doubled for British women born in 1940 as compared with those born in 1930 (Leete, 1979, p.9). International trends in marriage and remarriage are very similar, though there are differences in detail from one country to another; for example, a post-1970s fall in first marriage rates has been particularly pronounced in Scandinavia, where larger numbers of couples cohabit than in the less sexually libertarian countries.

Twenty years ago Margaret Mead noted a paradox behind the growing popularity of marriage. Almost every human need, she said,

that has historically been met in the home can now be met outside it: restaurants serve food; comics, movies and radio provide amusement, news and gossip; there are laundries and dry-cleaners and places that mend one's socks and store one's winter coat, wash one's hair and manicure one's nails and shine one's shoes. For sex satisfaction it is no longer necessary to choose between marriage and prostitution; for most of those without religious scruples sex is available on a friendly and amateur basis and without responsibility. The automobile has made it even unnecessary for one of a pair of temporary sex partners to have an apartment. Entertaining can be done in a hotel or at a club. When one is sick, one goes to a hospital, and when one dies, one can be buried quite professionally from an undertaking establishment. A telephone service will answer one's telephone, and a shopping service do one's

---

[1] In Britain, the 1970 Family Law Reform Act lowered the age at which parental consent for marriage was not needed from 21 to 18, and helped to account for a drop in the average age of first marriage immediately after. Since the early 1970s the decline in the age of first marriage has halted somewhat.

shopping. The old needs of food, shelter, sex, and recreation are all efficiently met outside the home — and yet more people are married today than ever before in the country's recorded history. [Mead, 1962, pp.298–9]

Why? Replacing some of the functions of the family with purchased services outside it obviously calls for money that some people do not have. Extracting labour from the unpaid duty of wives is cheaper than paying its market price. But, aside from this, it is not a general rule in other areas of life that as something becomes increasingly archaic and useless it becomes more popular. Horses are not purchased in large numbers as cars become assets within the reach of more and more people; pianos move out of people's front rooms and into junk shops as radios, television, records and cassettes spread music to places it never went before. A reservation has to be added to this general rule: the tendency for useless items of social life to drop out of fashion can be reversed by a well-mounted advertising campaign. Hence white sugar, cigarettes, instant puddings, unreliable cars, immediately breakable toys — things that are not only useless but positively dangerous to human health and happiness — can be kept in circulation if enough money is spent on telling people they cannot live without them. It is not too far-fetched to see marriage and the family in these terms. Thus, one answer to the question, 'why is marriage so popular?' is that people are constantly told it is good for them. The second answer is that statistics of marriage's popularity hide its failures, which are many. Rephrasing these answers from the point of view of women, we can say that women are encouraged to believe that they will find lifelong happiness in monogamous unions with men, but what they are in fact likely to find is that it is precisely marriage that oppresses, suppresses and depresses them.

The convention of conventional families

The nuclear family is a state of mind rather than a particular kind of structure or set of household arrangements. It has little to do with whether the generations live together or whether Aunt Mary stays in the spare bedroom. Nor can it be understood with kinship diagrams and figures on family size. [Shorter, 1977, p.204]

It can, in fact, only be understood as ideology. 'The' family or 'the family' is the major paradigm of social relations in which the inhabitants of modern technologically complex societies are encouraged to believe. 'The family' in its attenuated, conventionalized form (two parents, 2.4 children, father breadwinning and mother housekeeping, each family in a home of its own) is held out to be both the normal way of living and the happiest place to be. But 'the family' is also 'mapped on' to the cartography of other social institutions. As the radical psychiatrists Laing (1969) and Cooper (1972) have observed, its gender and generation hierarchies provide a powerful model for the social relations of factories, schools, universities, business corporations, religious organizations, political parties, governments, armies and hospitals. It is because the character and function of women is so typed by the convention of their place in the family, and especially by their relation to men as husbands and fathers, that the politics of female – male relationships are echoed throughout society.

Some origins of the idealized image of the conventional family have been explored earlier in this book. So far as present-day society is concerned, this imagery is ubiquitous — informing the socialization of children (Maccoby and Jacklin, 1974, pp.303 – 48), the educational system (King, 1978), employment opportunities (Mackie and Patullo, 1977), health and welfare provision (Leeson and Gray, 1978; Land, 1978), language (Miller and Swift, 1979), advertising (Goffman, 1979) and the media generally (Dixon, 1977; White, 1970; Karet, 1977; and Koerber, 1977). The paradigm of the conventional family is part of the ideological apparatus of the state. Thus, official morality has mushroomed to lay down the rules for non-marital heterosexual relationships:

Where a husband and wife are members of the same household their requirements and resources shall be aggregated and shall be treated as the husband's, and similarly, unless there are exceptional circumstances, as regards two persons cohabiting as man and wife. [Second Schedule to the Ministry of Social Security Act, 1966, para.3(1)]

This provision of the Ministry of Social Security Act, 1966 — the infamous 'cohabitation' rule — enabled the British exchequer to save £887,000 in 1971 by cutting supplementary benefits to unsupported women and children (Lister, n.d., p.1). The women involved were those who could be construed by social security officers to be having a relationship with a man upon whose shoulders the financial burden of fatherhood and/or husbandhood could be said (by the state) to fall.

Since what (according to the Supplementary Benefits handbook) has to be established is that a man and woman are living together 'as man and wife', the strategies adopted are most revealing of official definitions of marriage. Sharing a home, sharing a bed and swapping housekeeping and income-providing services, so that the woman provides the first for the man and the man provides the second for the woman, are the necessary criteria. Examination of actual cases, however, shows that social security officers attach 'undue attention . . . to the question of sexual relations.'

> A typical case was that of Mrs Brown. Her boyfriend had been a friend of her husband's from whom she was separated. He had continued seeing her after the separation out of sympathy and had started staying the night. He usually slept at Mrs Brown's four or five times a week, but considered his home to be at his mother's. He kept all his clothes in his bedroom at his mother's house and contributed to her household expenses. He went home each morning to collect his sandwiches and ate his evening meal with his mother. He made no contribution to Mrs Brown's household other than to provide the Sunday lunch which he ate with them. He had no intention of supporting Mrs Brown and the question of marriage had never been discussed. Mrs Brown tried to make clear to the officer that it was purely a sexual relationship, that 'Mr X does not live here, he just shares my bed'. However, neither the Commission nor the appeal tribunal were able to grasp the distinction that she made between a man staying with her and his living with her. [Lister, n.d., p.11]

Sexual services are something a man is supposed to pay for — inside and outside marriage. Or, to put it another way, if women are allowed to draw supplementary benefits regardless of the income of any man with whom they happen to be associated, the Supplementary Benefits Commission will be involved in paying women who are unable to take a job because they are looking after children. The cohabitation rule is 'logic's last bulwark against the spectre of wages for housework' (Fairbairns, 1979, p.321), a distinctly anti-conventional-family demand.

In view of the all-pervasiveness of the conventional family ideal, it is hardly surprising that the two questions 'should I marry?' and 'should we have children?' apparently do not occur to most people.

> Parenthood, like marriage, was taken for granted [says Lyn Richards of Australian couples she interviewed]. 'Why not stay single?' and 'Why not stay

childless?' had been equally non-questions. Virtually none of the men or women had asked either question of themselves or their partners . . . Almost everyone interviewed remembered people expecting them to have children. Having children . . . had been expected from childhood . . . ; marriage and children were part of the same unquestioned assumption about growing up. [Richards, 1978, pp.87, 92 – 3]

Marriage establishes the credentials of maturity, of personal and sexual competence. For women the idea of a 'proper' marriage with all its romantic trimmings is also a cover for economic realism — the only way to improve on the economic standing of their family of origin and to combat their disadvantaged labour market position.

Doing right but feeling bad
Like white sugar and cars, marriage may be popular but it is definitely hazardous. Of British marriages made in the 1970s, more than a quarter will end in divorce at some point in the next thirty years; for American couples, the figure is nearer 40 per cent (Leete, 1979). Some guide to the accelerated growth in the divorce industry is provided by the British *Family Formation* survey (Dunnell, 1979). In this, information about marriage-related behaviour was obtained from 6,589 women in England, Wales and Scotland in 1976. A tenth of women first married in 1966 – 70 were separated from their husbands within five years of marriage, a figure similar to the proportion separating after ten years of marriage among women married in 1961 – 5, and to the proportion separating after fifteen years of marriage among the cohort married in 1956 – 60.

It can be, and has been, argued that more divorce does not mean less happiness; men and women are simply freer to discard unsatisfactory marriages than they used to be. The reasoning is that romantic love and the emancipation of women have improved marriage but made it inherently unstable;[2] however, this instability is no bad thing since it indicates 'an enlarged degree of opportunity and happiness' (Fletcher, 1966, p.148). Furthermore, 75 per cent of divorcees remarry, which hardly suggests that marriage is a decaying institution (Ryder and Silver, 1970, p.253).

---

[2] Shorter (1977) argues that the inherent instability of the couple combined with the loss by parents of control over their adolescent children are distinguishing features of the modern family.

It seems a little strange to argue that the fact that something breaks down a lot proves that it is really working very well. A more convincing argument is that, for one reason or another, people want to retain their faith in marriage's successful functioning in the face of considerable evidence to the contrary. Problems with marriage are not new. Julia Spruill's commentary on *Women's Life and Work in the Southern Colonies* notes that

Those who point to the colonial period as a golden age of family relationships can hardly be acquainted with the eighteenth century discussions lamenting the decadence of the domestic virtues, with the suspicion and distrust reflected in private papers, with the large number of public notices of absconding wives and voluntary separations, and with the many complaints by husbands and wives in court records.[Spruill, 1972, p.167]

'Reflections on unhappy marriages', a favourite journalistic subject then, paralleled the 'Is the family a dying institution?' articles today. In both cases the cause of the trouble is seen to lie in individuals (emancipated undomesticated wives, broken homes, adulterous husbands) or in particular social circumstances (changes in divorce laws, more contraception and choice in childbearing). Unsuccessful marriages are interpreted as problems, not solutions to problems; yet, as Wright Mills (1959, p.9) observed, the imaginative enterprise of connecting personal troubles and public issues must suggest that divorce statistics indicate, not a proliferation of unique personal difficulties, but 'a structural issue having to do with the institutions of marriage and the family'.

There are two sides to this structural issue. One is that the cultural expectation of great intimacy between men and women clashes with the very different and, in some ways, contradictory, socializations of the sexes. Men and women are reared primarily as masculine and feminine individuals, the one to notions of potency, public-mindedness and emotional invulnerability, the other to standards of fragility, domesticity and emotional hypersensitivity. While individuals with such dissimilar preparations for adulthood might be expected to find some way of cooperating with one another residentially and economically, it is hard to see how they can hope to be one another's greatest friends. And, as for the idea of complementarity — another fashionable idiom in which the marital relations of the sexes are discussed (Zelditch, 1956) — surely this is just a euphemism for uncomfortable division and difference?

The second structural consideration is that discussed earlier in this book and by Christopher Lasch in his suggestively named *Haven in a Heartless World*. Lasch's contention is that the family is conventionally regarded as a haven, but that the realities of present-day society have stripped it of even this mystification. Capitalist industry profits from the concentration of psychological welfare work in the family. Indeed, it promotes this work under the guise of the family being a free and sacred retreat from the exigencies of paid labour. Yet in fact

the modern world intrudes at every point and obliterates its privacy. The sanctity of the home is a sham in a world dominated by giant corporations and by the apparatus of mass promotion . . . . The same historical developments that have made it necessary to set up private life — the family in particular — as a refuge from the cruel world of politics and work, an emotional sanctuary, have invaded this sanctuary and subjected it to outside control. A retreat into 'privatism' no longer serves to shore up values elsewhere threatened with extinction. [Lasch, 1978, pp.xvii – xviii]

Thus, the family is not what it is held out to be — for men, women or children. It is not an easy answer to the drudgery of work or to the heartlessness of the outside world.

Some signs of strain inherent in marriage and family relationships for women have already been mentioned in earlier chapters. In the rest of this chapter, I shall discuss four areas of conflict between men and women in their attempt to make the fairy story of marriage come true: (1) the division of labour; (2) communication; (3) power; and (4) sexuality.

HIS WORK AND HERS

Peter G . . . was 23 years old, very inhibited, and socially inept. Raised in a strict, religious home, he had had very little contact with girls and virtually no dating experience until his second year of college. He was sure that no woman would find him attractive unless he was making good money . . . He needed expensive clothes, a big sporty car, and a thick wallet; all these were extensions of his penis. Money would show women he could give them what they needed, and thereby get him what he thought he needed, 'a beautiful girl with big boobs.' His idea that women were essentially passive and looking to be taken care of by a big, strong male demanded that he 'make' good money before he could 'make' the woman of his dreams. [Gould, 1974, pp.96 – 7]

Peter G has not got it all wrong. Personal relations between men and women are infiltrated by the logic of their social relativity: men are people who put work first, women are those whose work must be called by another name — making a home, loving children, performing wage labour for 'pin money'. According to sociologists whose theory of gender roles and the occupational system hinges on how all combine to make capitalism prosper, this division between his and her work is an excellent arrangement. The values necessary for raising and maintaining families are different from those required to drive a bus or run a large corporation. Conflict is avoided if activities implying different values are assigned to different individuals whose motivations and characters have already been selectively moulded to match the requirements of each role (Parsons and Bales, 1956). Hence masculinity has to be equated with occupational achievement: men must feel they are not proper men unless they are successful in their work and bring home enough money to prove it. Women, on the other hand, should specialize in occupational under-achievement. [3]

Functionalist sociology provides a neat academic justification for the oppression of women (see D. Morgan, 1975; Beechey, 1978); but it does, for this reason, describe a set of real pressures. So far as men are concerned, a desire to spend more time caring and less time providing runs counter to masculine ideology. (That there are many men who express no such desire is, of course, another problem.) Robert Fein, the author of several accounts of the male role problem in the United States, cites one man, 'Mark Z., a PhD chemist in his mid-30s', who works 60 + hours a week in a responsible laboratory position:

Realizing that his two children, ages 7 and 4, were growing up, and that he found much satisfaction in being with his family, he attempted to change his schedule so that he would spend 40 – 45 hours a week at work. These efforts were greeted with concern by his supervisors who felt that he was not 'committed' enough to his work. 'I feel that I am being given two choices' (he said). 'Either I can continue to take on all the special projects and extra work that is asked of me at a pressured, 60-hour-a-week pace, or I can drop out and

---

[3] This is the prevailing conceptualization of the 'problem' of women's public role-asymmetry with men (as offered, for example, by research-funding agencies).

try to find another job . . . I don't want to do either. I want to work reasonably hard and be able to spend a lot of time with my family. Right now I'm being told that my "ambivalence" about my work is jeopardizing my chances of advancement in the lab.' [Fein, 1974, p.32]

The incidence of such dissatisfactions with the masculine role nationally and cross-nationally is not known. A small survey conducted by Peter Willmott in England found that 41 per cent of senior male staff and 32 per cent of male works people in two industrial plants felt that the demands of work interfered with home and family. Significantly, 59 per cent and 29 per cent also felt that home and family interfered with other leisure: 'I'd like to play golf all Saturday and Sunday. I don't like shopping or decorating' (Willmott, 1971, p.583).

Men who make ardent attempts to break through the his/her work barrier will often find what they already, perhaps, suspected: women who recite the frustrations of motherhood and housewifery are not simply giving vent to the feminine character, but are describing something real, and real in its effects — the housewife's disease is catching. Paul Morrison, writing in *Achilles' Heel*, a magazine written by men in men's consciousness-raising groups, describes a form of fatherhood indistinguishable in its social configuration from motherhood:

A situation: I am in the park with Corey, aged eighteen months. Familiar social-democratic greensward, surrounded by traffic. The sun is shining. I would prefer to be here with a friend. Or better still, a friend and a child . . . Corey and I play with a ball on the grass. I have brought a book with me and some toys and books for Corey. I try to look at mine, hoping she will go exploring, but she doesn't. She still wants my attention . . .

I am lonely. I am just trying to get through. I feel bad about this . . . But I do feel underutilized . . . 'What have you been doing today, Paul?' 'Not a lot. I just had a quiet day with Corey' . . .

When anyone tells me that it is an important and difficult thing that I am doing, that I am doing something good and right, I curl up with delight.

Paul would be the first to admit that he is learning a lesson all mothers know. It is the experience that counts:

In Corey's first year, I had a part-time teaching job at a college in South London. Two days a week, or sometimes three, I was expected to be tough, effective, together, capable, knowing, imaginative, efficient, abrasive and dynamic. This was the ideal way of being a male teacher on this particular course, which was partly a technical and practical one.

Yet after my days and nights with Corey I found myself going to work feeling tired, frail, sensitive, sometimes peaceful but as often emotionally unbalanced — particularly if Corey had been crying at night, at all — and certainly often emotionally open and tender.

Putting together these two different ways of being in one life was incredibly difficult. [*Achilles' Heel*, no 3, pp.12 – 14]

— and remains so, of course, for many women whose men see only the disadvantage inherent in what is commonly, but unimaginatively, called 'role-reversal'.

In the 1970s and 1980s, women are doing more of 'his' work than they used to, but men have made few inroads on 'hers'. This applies both to 'feminine' types of paid work and to feminine work in the home. Table 11.1 compares the time-budgets of employed women and employed men in France, Poland, the USA and the USSR. In no country do employed men spend more than half an hour a day on housework. As Elise Boulding points out, the relatively short amount of time shown in Table 11.1 for childcare is misleading, since childcare runs concurrently with housework, use of media and what is curiously called 'leisure'. (Many of the methodological difficulties inherent in time-budget studies derive from the vacuity of the concept of free time as applied to most women.) A study by Martin Meissner and his colleagues of Canadian dual-worker couples produced more detailed information about the domestic labour category. A summary of this is given in Table 11.2. The message of this table is clearly that men treat their homes as havens from work, not as workplaces. The Canadian data show what other investigators have found, namely that the amount of work done by men in the home is relatively insensitive to how much work (outside or inside the home) wives have to do, although a wife's change of status from being employed to not being employed can act as an excuse for men to withdraw even a minimal level of help (Bahr, 1974; Oakley, 1979).

One obstacle for researchers probing the domestic division of labour is that men often say they do more in the home than they actually do (MGM Marketing Research and Surveys, 1978; Hunt, 1975). 'Overall, husbands emerge as strikingly progressive in their *attitudes* to women's rights and roles . . . but husbands are far less willing in their *actions* to share home and family obligations equally'

TABLE 11.1 Workday time-budgets of employed men and employed women (time spent in primary activities, in average minutes per day)

	Six cities, France		Torun, Poland		Jackson, USA		Pakov, USSR	
	Women	Men	Women	Men	Women	Men	Women	Men
Total work (job)	492	583	490	563	482	570	478	506
Total housework	156	26	180	31	133	21	170	28
Other household obligations*	17	32	20	29	31	29	27	39
Total childcare	24	8	27	20	16	8	30	30
Total personal needs (includes sleep)	621	621	543	560	590	572	546	573
Study and participation	7	9	23	25	17	27	27	52
Total mass media	47	76	70	117	65	114	73	125
Total leisure	60	70	56	71	63	59	48	55
Total travel	57	75	86	91	73	85	81	20
Total minutes	1440	1440	1440	1440	1440	1440	1440	1440

* Includes garden, animal care, errands, shopping.

Source: Szalai (1972); cited in Boulding (1977) p.70.

TABLE 11.2 *Per cent* and hours of wives and husbands in housework activities*

Activities	Workday		Weekly hours	
	Wives%	Husbands%	Wives	Husbands
Cooking	86	13	8.0	0.7
Cleaning	74	8	7.8	1.1
Washing up	47	4	2.1	0.2
Shopping	54	15	3.9	1.2
Laundry	36	1	2.9	0
Childcare	36	7	3.3	0.9
All regular housework	97	39	28.0	4.1
Irregular food/ clothes work †	25	0	3.3	0
Irregular purchases	8	4	0.7	0.2
Sundry services‡	31	22	1.4	1.1
Repair & maintenance	5	11	0.2	2.2
Building	0	3	0	0.4
All irregular housework	54	36	5.6	3.9

*Of all wives or all husbands reporting having engaged in each activity.
†Eg. canning, mending.
‡Eg. household accounting.
Source: Meissner *et al.*, (n.d.) p.7.

commented *The Sunday Times* (27 February 1977) on a National Opinion Poll survey of British husbands. 'Helping the wife' is an acceptable, even expected, masculine attitude these days; but to regard this as synonymous with equal task division in the home (a favourite trick of sociologists and others — e.g. Young and Willmott, 1973) represents the *reductio ad absurdum* of this line of reasoning. As Beechey (1978) has observed, such an article of faith is a close cousin of the Victorian evolutionists' naively supremacist belief that history must mean progress. It doesn't, and it depends on whose vantage point the scene is surveyed from whether the change is good or bad.

KEEPING THE PEACE AND FINDING A VOICE

Jacqui Sarsby (1972) asked British teenagers what they looked for as desirable characteristics in the 'opposite' sex. The boys answered in terms of girls' physical appearance, especially the shapeliness of their figures. The girls mentioned factors such as boys' height and hair colour, but were most concerned with finding someone who would understand them, treat them with sensitivity and be kind to them if they were depressed. In America, Mirra Komarovsky, studying working-class marriages some years ago, wrote:

One of every three marriages in this study falls short of the prevailing American ideal of psychological intimacy between married partners . . . . The emphasis upon barriers [to intimacy] unfortunately reinforces the common assumption that high rapport in marriage is natural and requires no explanation. The ability of two individuals to share fully their inner lives is no more natural, however, than their failure to do so. [Komarovsky, 1967, p.148]

Failure to achieve psychological intimacy, says Komarovsky, stems from three aspects of men and women's lives. Firstly, the sexes are divided in their interests; they simply do not occupy the same social worlds. As one husband put it: 'Women talk about the silliest details that don't matter, and they don't want to talk about interesting things'; and, as one wife responded, 'Men are different, they don't feel the same as us — that's one reason men are friends with men and women have women friends' (Komarovsky, 1967, pp.150 – 1). Secondly, the families Komarovsky surveyed did not have many social relationships with other individuals or families, and were relatively isolated: their social lives were not rich, and did not provide much to talk about. Thirdly, the men suffered from what Komarovsky called a 'trained incapacity to share'. Expressing feelings and talking about worries and personal problems are types of communication identified from early childhood on with *women*.

Komarovsky's findings are far from unique, and the picture of marriage she uncovered has been found elsewhere (see Klein, 1965). Lilian Rubin in a more up-to-date study comments that, before and after marriage,

an interesting switch occurs. Before the marriage and in the first years, it is the wife who seems more eager to be married, the husband, more reluctant . . . [But] with time, he finds ways to live with some constraints, to circumvent others. For him, marriage becomes a comfortable haven — a place of retreat from the pressures and annoyances of the day, a place where his needs and comforts are attended to by his wife, the only place perhaps where he can exercise his authority. He begins to feel that he's made a good bargain: 'I like being married now. I don't even feel tied down anymore. I'm out all day and if I want to have a drink with the boys after work, I just call her up and tell her I'll be home later. When I get home, there's a meal — she's a real good cook — and I can just relax and take it easy. The kids — they're the apples of my eyes — they're taken care of; she brings them up right, keeps them clean, teaches them respect. I can't ask for any more. It's a good life.' (38-year old plumber, father of 3, married 17 yrs)

For his wife, time works the other way. She finds herself facing increasing constraints, or, at least, experiencing them as more oppressive. For her, there are few ways to circumvent them — no regular work hours:

'When I was a kid and used to wish I was a boy I never knew why I thought that. Now I know . . .' [Rubin, 1976, p.95]

Marital communication patterns vary with social class; more education, better job security and more money may iron out some of the problems, but they do not touch the masculine embargo on expressing feelings, on revealing the unmasculine but human malaise of weakness and vulnerability. 'I must show no emotion and not kiss my mother in public' is one of ten commandments recited by British public schoolboys (Tolson, 1977, p.35); in adulthood, reserve and self-constraint are the rule. John Money and Patricia Tucker in their *Sexual Signatures* quote an example of a man who broke down and cried in front of an office colleague. The news of his crying was all over the office in an hour; jibes at his masculinity followed, but

What really hurt was that two years later, when I was doing very well and being considered for a promotion, it was brought up again . . . . my manager . . . . said, 'What do you think about that crying incident?' You can bet that was the last time I let myself cry. [Money and Tucker, 1977, p.150]

WHO HAS THE POWER?

In the romantic idyll of marriage, it is a free mutual exchange of love that joins men and women together. Companionship — along with the perpetuation of their own genes into the next generation — is what they are after. But the realities of marriage and family life, as we have seen, often turn the dream on its head.

One reason for this is that marriage is a property relationship. It is a device whereby men are enabled to 'extort gratuitous work from a particular category of the population, women – wives' (Delphy, 1976, p.77). It is an institution that ensures women's continued subordination — economically, fiscally, legally, politically, emotionally — not only within the pseudo-haven of the home but paradigmatically as 'wife' and 'husband' signify gender identities whose mark is to be found throughout society. As Colin Bell and Howard Newby argue:

At best an explanation of inequality in terms of attributes is tautologous — women are subordinate because they are women — at worst it is false. We need instead to concentrate our investigations on male – female relationships, for an individual is only powerful or powerless in relation to another individual or individuals. [Bell and Newby, 1976, p.152]

Most men and women today subscribe to the idea that men are more powerful than women and should remain so (*Sunday Times*, 27 February 1977).

There are two main sorts of power men exercise over women. The first is economic. Blood and Wolfe found in their study of *Husbands and Wives* (1960) that husbands with prestigious occupations had a greater say in marital decisions, but income was the most sensitive predictor of power. Men are expected to support women financially, which means (amongst other things) that the law says the standard of living of married couples must be selected by the husband, that he may decide how much of his income she may use, and that she may leave him and require maintenance if he defaults on this obligation. 'A wife is classified as a dependant, even if she is a wage-earner' (O'Donovan, 1979, p.141). However, even if the male breadwinner – female dependant formula is enshrined in law, the law does not regulate the conditions of domestic production. The only relevant provision is that (in Britain) of the *Married Women's Property Act* (1964), which decrees that prudent wives who save a portion of their housekeeping money must give half of it to their husbands.

Family-budget enquiries, especially among working-class couples, persistently show that many wives are kept in ignorance of their husbands' earnings (Young and Willmott, 1973, pp.80 – 4; Gorer, 1971); British husbands are notably less generous in this respect than others: 70 per cent of British husbands in one study did not tell their wives what they earned, compared with 40 per cent in West Germany and 1 per cent in the United States (Feandel, 1975). Moreover, a wife's housekeeping money tends to be a fixed sum, not a percentage of earnings. Young and Syson, researching the effects of inflation on family budgets, found that half one sample of working wives had received no increase in their housekeeping money even though their husbands were earning more (Young and Syson, 1974, p.15). In other words, 'mothers and children can be in poverty while husbands are not' (Young, 1975, p.15). Surveys of middle-class marriages concur in finding that less than half the pay rises men get are passed on to wives (Land, 1977, p.168). Jeremy Tunstall's description of a fishing community (1962) shows how these norms of income distribution within the family may be institutionalized in trade union practice; overtime earnings, not regarded by the men as part of the wage packet to be shared with their wives, were a popular item for negotiation. It is important to note that the system used by some (usually working-class) families whereby the husband hands over his entire wage packet to his wife (see, for instance, Kerr, 1958) is not necessarily liberation from the dogma of male financial control. Indeed, it may represent a simple additional domestic chore for the wife (she has no control over the size of the wage packet). 'Sharing' one's income (via a joint bank account and joint cheque books) may fit the middle-class ethic of companionate marriage, but it, too, renders wives crucially dependent on husbands' economic resources.

Along with the power of the purse goes the power of the hand:

Foul Play. Whenever West Berlin football clubs lose their home matches, the city's shelters for battered wives prepare for a flood of new applicants. For Berlin's soccer-mad husbands take their teams' defeats out on their womenfolk. After one particularly humiliating match, 60 bruised wives asked for shelter. [*Sunday Mirror*, 4 March 1979]

Knowing how many men actually batter the women they live with is not possible, because much wife battering is an unrevealed affair. In any case, many official statistics do not divide victims by sex, except for homicide: here McClintock (1963) and others (e.g. McCarthy *et al.*, 1974; Wolfgang, 1969) have calculated that around a third of homicides are domestic disputes. Most reports of violence involving family members received by police departments are complaints of assaults on wives by husbands. Physical abuse of women also figures prominently in divorce petitions. A community survey by Steinmetz and Straus (1974) of a nationally representative sample of American families suggests that approximately 1.8 million wives are beaten by their husbands in any one year in the USA (4 per cent of all married women); applied to Britain, this would yield about half a million husband-assaulted wives. Yet other statistics (Sachs and Wilson, 1978, p.132) put the figure at half the married female population.

It is, of course, absolutely essential to see the experience of male domestic violence from the victim's point of view:

My face was so swollen from being punched that I was not recognizable. I lost a front tooth. He stripped me naked. He banged my head against a brick wall for an hour . . . six ribs were broken from being kicked. I was black all down one side from being punched and kicked. I was dragged downstairs by my hair. He repeatedly stamped on my bare toes with cuban heel shoes . . . He then fetched a knife and said he was going to kill me . . . He tried to stab me but I managed to stop the blow by raising my arm and received a long gash under the armpit. All this took place in front of my daughters aged 5 and 9. Eventually the police arrived after a neighbour had called them eight times. They would not enter the house although the front door was open. He went out and told them that he was beating me up because I had left the children alone. I pleaded with them to take me to the hospital but they would only do so if I charged him. They left telling him to keep the noise down as the neighbours were complaining. [Hanmer, 1978, p.226]

This woman eventually got herself to hospital, but the hospital staff were, like the police, on her husband's side, and they returned her almost immediately to her husband. In the end, she entered a Women's Aid Refuge.

Men's right to keep their wives in order by any means they choose is another item on the covert agenda of sexual relations behind the tempting fantasy of the romantic idyll. In marriage, men must do what they want with an authority that is very improperly usurped by a wife. After listening to conversations in the masculine institution of English rural pubs, Ann Whitehead reported that

The men acted as if a married man should be able to do just what he liked after marriage. He should be able to come to the pub every day; to stay all evening after 'calling in' on the way home from work, and to stay out as long as he liked. He could and must row with his wife, hit her or lay down the law. Rows and quarrels in which he had the upper hand brought a·man esteem, but if his wife rowed with him, locked him out of the house or refused to cook for him, he lost esteem. [Whitehead, 1976, p.193]

Many theories have been put forward to account for wife beating: the machismo validation of violence in men, individual male psychopathology and stress all carry some weight (see Freeman, 1979, pp.136 – 41). But, like other problems of, and with, marriage discussed in this chapter, it is false to see the problem in individualistic terms. It is not individual men whose psychic structure turns them against individual women in a moment of temporary and understandable aberration. Physical force and its threat used against women by men in marriage is a form of collective social control, 'the structural underpinning of hierarchical relations, the ultimate sanction' (Hanmer, 1978, p.229) of a dominant group keeping its subordinates in line. Male – female relations are the prototype of dominant – subordinate relations, but black – white relations provide a most chastening analogy (Dollard, 1937).

Having learnt to seek the 'protection' of a man in marriage, a woman is exposed to his untrammelled physical fiat. From the point of view of women's relations with men, it is ironically true that they have more to fear from the men they 'love' than from the strangers in dark alleys and worn raincoats they are taught from girlhood to avoid. One reason for this is that the family is a cradle of violence. Child abuse, wife beating, 'granny bashing', and husband assault all take place within its supposedly safe haven — though the first two are the predominant forms.[4] Violence in the home, as Erin Pizzey (1974) and others running battered wives' refuges have shown, is the shadowy, uninvestigated underworld of crime, because husbands and wives and parents and children ought to love each other and if they don't it is nobody's business but their own.

Another reason is that the state both supports the asymmetry of husband – wife relationships (husbands have a legal duty to maintain wives; wives must provide sexual relief for husbands, and so forth) and ultimately condones male domestic violence by taking less notice

---

[4] Freeman's book on *Violence in the Home* (1979) has 4 pages on 'husband beating', 3 on violence by children and 2 on 'granny bashing', compared with 87 on violence to children and 74 on violence to wives.

of a man beating his wife behind even an open front door than of almost any other violent crime.

DOUBLE BEDS

'In recent writing on domestic violence, the connection between sexuality and violence has received less emphasis than it deserves . . . the link is a close one', said the British Working Party on marriage guidance (Home Office, 1979, p.87). Here, too, there are inequities in the distribution of rights, responsibilities, resources and rewards.

Females and males do not differ with respect to the physiology of sexual response, and their apparently contrasting anatomies conceal the same basic format, noted Alfred Kinsey and his colleagues in 1953 — a conclusion subsequently confirmed by sex researchers William Masters and Virginia Johnson. However, problems of 'human sexual inadequacy' are 'widespread' (Masters and Johnson, 1966, p.8), or, as Kinsey *et al.* (1953, p.11) put it, 'there is the problem of sexual adjustment in marriage'. It has been apparent for a long time in Euro-American culture that men and women have a difficult time getting on with one another in bed, a conclusion that would surprise members of many not so advanced societies where sex is fun and sexuality is an enjoyed and expected attribute of both males and females (Ford and Beach, 1965). While the Victorian medical profession could confidently assert that women 'are not very much troubled with sexual feelings of any kind' (Acton, 1871, p.163), this condemnation of women to an asexual existence was a reversal of eighteenth- and seventeenth-century attitudes; John Hunter (1728 – 93) 'discovered' the clitoris as an analogue of the penis, and popular love manuals took it for granted that women enjoyed sexual intercourse as much as men, and even needed to in order to conceive. (Is this the origin of the contemporary belief that female orgasm is needed for conception?) Acton's renowned statement derived from the Victorian dogma that sexuality was not only bad for women but bad altogether, 'a curse and torture, and the only hope of salvation for men lies in marriage to a woman who has no sexual desires' (Marcus, 1966, p.32). Women had to save men. So did prostitutes. Their services relieved men too unattractive, too bored or too fearful to find relief in the marital bed.

Unfortunately Victorianism is not dead and sexual encounters between men and women today are still beset with outdated notions of woman's lesser sexual urge and man's naturally aggressive need for sexual release. Like every other aspect of femininity and masculinity, sexuality fits into the wider pattern. It was at the same time as women's sexual vigour declined (according to the experts) that a new stereotype arose — that of her essential *motherliness*: the conjunction is no accident. It is a curious fact that in our culture it is unmarried women ('girls') who are regarded as sexy, while married women — in most non-industrial cultures seen as the only fully fledged sexual females — sink into the domesticated oblivion of the housewife. The 'desexualization' of the housewife is, as Slater (1975, p.78) notes, certainly one of her major defining characteristics.

Housewives have no room of their own, no private space either as a ticket to creativity as Virginia Woolf said, or as a condition for experiencing the self as (at least temporarily) autonomous:

. . . even the possibility of sleeping alone is denied her. [After a day as a public servant] to then have to touch, caress, console yet another person is too much. The hatred of man and sex begins — it is the beginning of such sayings as 'Oh God, he wants his rights again' or the husband saying 'you can't have a headache every night'. [Peckham Rye Women's Liberation Group, 1970, p.6]

As a matter of fact you can, just as in the old music hall joke. The history of the double bed is an unstudied aspect of the development of modern family life.

The ideal, rarely attained but no less powerful for its rarity, is of Mr and Mrs Right, wedded forever to the same bed, achieving simultaneous orgasm three times a week till one of them dies. Even in pregnancy, a time when most women have other things on their mind, there is no respite; indeed, at this time especially, 'A woman should not always wait for the initiation of sex play, but should study how best she can seduce her husband' (Kitzinger, 1962, p.66). The recent discovery that antenatal intercourse somewhat increases the risks of infecting babies (*The Sunday Times*, 9 December 1979) is deeply disturbing to childbirth educators, but is, of course, the only possible justification women can have for refusing intercourse. Women's interests must be couched in the language of maternity: what else are women for?

The idea of an 'open marriage' (O'Neill and O'Neill, 1975)

involving multiple extra-marital relationships seems original, even possibly indicative of changing norms of marriage. But is it? Gilbert Bartell, investigating 'swinging' in the Chicago area in the late 1960s, revealed its most prominent form to involve a foursome of two married couples. For the men, swinging was the acting out of adolescent fantasies; for the women, it represented the fulfilment of the romantic ideal. Married swingers are pursuing the cult of youth and the 'in scene', says Bartell, and the most common reason for taking up swinging is boredom with marriage:

The men are occupied with their work all day, the women with their households; they seek community, but find none . . . They sit in silence and look at television. The woman, who feels restricted to the household environment, believes she should be out doing things, perhaps be a career woman. But she has her obligations . . . [Bartell, 1971, p.279]

Economics, sexuality, childrearing: these functions of the family can be considered compatible only in unusual cases. As I said earlier, it is curious that the contrasting socializations of the sexes should be their apprenticeship for a lifetime of sexual compatibility. For it is true of this area, as it is of all others with which we are concerned in this book, that the social arrangements of men and women are decided by cultural politics and not by natural dictate; sexuality as a personality attribute (for that is what it is) is learnt. Hence the abeyant sexuality of the housewife as the rearer of children — children in Euro-American culture are not supposed to be sexual (again, an anomalous tradition cross-culturally [see Malinowski, 1932, for one 'exception']). Psychoanalysis has a scientific name for this: latency. The concept is constructed on the basis of equating physical pleasure with sexual pleasure, and the whole is further confused by a mystique of synonymity between 'gender', 'sex' and 'sexuality'. In fact (by which I mean considering the anthropological evidence), erotic excitement, the pleasure of an affectionate caress, conformity with social expectations of womanhood, manhood and childhood, and biological state as female or male are not the same thing at all.

However, the modern methodology of the family induces a contrary belief. Sons and daughters are both subjected to a system of maternal rearing out of which adult sexuality must be born. This is a very much harder task for men than for women. Just as women have to be mothers, wives, charladies, mistresses, etc. at the same time, so little boys locked in nuclear families have to take their mothers as the model for all women. From an infant sense of oneness with the mother, they must move to a sense of their own separate masculinity, often with the most imperfect example of the work-absent father to emulate. Later, they must imbibe the idea that as mothers women are to be respected while as sexual objects manipulation is in order.

Mother was warm and loving, always doing a lot for the kids. She always saw to our material welfare and kept us clean. But there was a gap. As long as she had girls to raise, she was okay. She found it harder to communicate with boys. At the same time, I rejected her. I felt that, being a woman, she wouldn't understand boys' things, what boys have to go through. [West *et al.*, 1978, p.22]

This man, who talks quite fondly of his mother, is a rapist. Rape is popularly believed to be the natural outcome of men's aggressive sexual instinct, indeed even a not wholly reprehensible outcome: rapists, like men with an extra Y chromosome (see p.55), are somehow supermen. Rape is, in this way, an essentially 'normal' masculine enterprise (Brownmiller, 1975), and apparently becoming more normal, as it is reported more and more often — a 100 per cent increase in London from the first quarter of 1977 to the first quarter of 1978 (*Guardian*, 23 October 1978), a steady rise in America from the early 1930s on, to a rate of one every nine minutes in 1976 (Bowker, 1978). These apparently rising rates may mean that more rape is declared by victims and not that more is occurring (Soothill and Jack, 1975). But rape and the social attitudes that surround it illustrate the extreme outcome of a system of gender divisions in which the aggressive is set against the passive, the predator against the prey and the powerful against the defenceless. Ultimately, rapists are let off the hook because women have failed to guard them against the consequences of the 'curse' of sexuality, just as Sir William Acton said. A raped woman is always somehow to blame for her assault: her skirt is too short, she was alone in the pub, has had two abortions, or really wanted it in the first place (Coote and Gill, 1975). 'Attractive' women (that is those who match male standards of feminine attractiveness) are especially guilty. An interesting study by Lawrence Calhoun and his colleagues (1978) asked men and women to rate the extent to which a group of mythical rape victims invited attack. Men who were shown a picture of an 'attractive' victim were much more likely than those shown a picture of an 'unattractive' victim to say she asked for it. (Women raters did not show this bias.)

The reality of rapists' psychology is that they are men of insecure masculinity who feel at a disadvantage with women. Abusing women creates 'an illusion of masculinity regained' (West *et al.*, 1978, p.81). Yet this information is powerless to affect the enormous fear women have of being raped. The experience of being controlled by rape and, even more, by its ever-present possibility can be regarded as the ultimate and essential complaint that women have to make against men.

A female-oriented legal system would take rape more seriously than most currently do, which is another way of saying that rape is an extreme expression of a personal relation between men and women that is basically condoned by law. Since women cannot be raped by their husbands, husbands are allowed to rape wives. Marriage is 'licensed prostitution'; or, as Kate Millett expresses it in *The Prostitution Papers*:

.. prostitution is . . . the very core of the female's social condition. It not only declares her subjection right in the open, with the cash nexus between the sexes announced in currency, rather than through the subtlety of a marriage contract (which still recognizes the principle of sex in return for commodities and historically has insisted upon it), but the very act of prostitution is itself a declaration of our value, our reification. [Millett, 1976, p.93]

Prostitution is women selling their souls as well as their bodies. As one prostitute interviewed by Millett said:

It involves a type of contempt, a kind of disdain, and a kind of triumph over another human being. Guys who can't get it up with their wives can do it with whores. They have to pay for it. For some of them, *paying* for it is very important. [Millett, 1976, p.64]

The double dilemma of prostitute-users is a combination of madonna-worship and the capitalist ethic: good women can't be sexual and only money buys happiness.

Prostitution and rape are, through the medium of the feminist movement, now receiving more attention as part of a general questioning of accepted attitudes towards female sexuality. This questioning takes many forms, from seeing prostitutes as the vanguard of the gender revolution, to launching a 'Why be a wife?'

campaign; from researching the history of the nude male (Walters, 1979), to asking women to recount how *they* think about sex. This last mission is undertaken in an attempt to select out female versions of sexuality from the mystifying obfuscation of masculine attitudes (Friday, 1976; Hite, 1977). It seems that, for a start, women are tired 'of the old mechanical pattern of sexual relations, which revolves around male erection, male penetration and male orgasm' (Hite, 1977, p.529). The missionary position is not popular; being on top is more likely to result in female orgasm, but its political associations make it repugnant to some women (and men). In Hite's sample, 53 per cent of the women faked orgasm in intercourse. This, says Hite, is a lamentable consequence of the 'glorification' of intercourse (and, one might add, of wifely deference):

. . . intercourse has been defined as the basic form of sexuality, and the only natural, healthy, and moral form of physical contact . . . The corollary of this institutionalization of heterosexual intercourse is the villainization and suppression of all other forms of sexuality and pleasurable intimate contact — which explain the historic horror of our culture for masturbation and lesbianism/homosexuality, or even kissing and intimate physical contact or caressing between friends. [Hite, 1977, p.244]

Just so.

The fact that relating to men in bed and in marriage is the conventional passport to normal femininity for women need not be taken to mean that all women are unhappy with this state of affairs. They are clearly not. But overall the evidence supports the idea that women lose more and gain less from marital relationships than do men. Jessie Bernard, collater of much of this evidence, argues that 'there are two marriages . . . in every marital union, his and hers' (Bernard, 1973, p.14). One way to interpret this is to say that the popularity of marriage has meant an imbalance between supply and demand in persons fitted for marriage:

. . given what is known about such factors as the distribution of homosexuality and chronic ill-health, psychological as well as physical, among the population at large, it is obvious that the present popularity of marriage must be drawing into the institution large numbers who lack any evident vocation for it. [Finer Report, 1974, para.3.9]

Another is to say that

Insofar as the family as an institution turns women into darling little slaves and men into their chief providers and unweaned dependants, the problem of a satisfactory marriage remains incapable of purely private solution. [Mills, 1959, p.10]

Subversion is an alternative to revolution, and no doubt many conjugal relations have historically been maintained by deceit. Between 15 and 30 per cent of British babies, for example, are not the products of their mothers' husbands (Goss, 1975; Phillipp, 1973).

CHAPTER TWELVE

Sisterhood

Female solidarity is one of the best-kept secrets of patriarchy. It is to the advantage of patriarchy to deny that emotional support, understanding of our lives and needs, skills and knowledge, and love can be had from women (and at a better price than from men). [Laws, 1979, p.377]

There appears to be very much less to say about women's relationships with women than about their relationships with men or children. In the Western cultural tradition, wifehood and motherhood are women's essential identities. By comparison, sisterhood — women's relationships with women — does not count, not even in the sense in which 'the brotherhood of Man' sums up a unifying humanity superimposed on social divisions.

COMPETITION

In her novel *Small Changes*, Marge Piercy describes a woman looking for a woman friend, now married. The only way to find her is to locate her under a new name in the telephone book: 'She had to find out that strange name before she could find her — Miriam Berg was no more. Abolished. Women must often lose a friend that way and never be able to find each other again' (Piercy, 1973, p.344). When Marge Piercy's heroine lost her friend to marriage, she stumbled on the chief barrier obstructing relations between women. It is not so much men, as women's induced belief in men's superiority, that robs them of the capacity to love each other.

Disallowed, according to canons of femininity, the right to compete with men, women in male-dominated societies are driven to engage in a special kind of competition. They are at war with one another, and the object of the war is to gain or hold onto the favours of men. After a lifetime of dealing with men, Praxis, the heroine of a novel by Fay Weldon, reflects thus:

We betray each other. We manipulate, through sex: we fight each other for possession of the male — snap, catch, swallow, gone! Where's the next? We prefer the company of men to women. We will quite deliberately make our sisters jealous and wretched . . . . And all in the pursuit of our self-esteem and so as not to end up old and alone. [Weldon, 1978, pp.218–9]

The student who forms an alliance with her university professor, the aspiring actress who becomes the film director's mistress, the secretary who is the boss's 'office wife': these women are outwitting their sisters in finding a pathway to success. But the most basic form of competition between women relates to the institution of marriage. Husbands must be sought, found and, most importantly, kept. Sexual stereotyping portrays husbands as beings who must be constantly seduced, placated, understood. The husband's fidelity is the wife's work. It is, of course, highly paradoxical that placement in a structure of subordination (marriage) should be regarded as an achievement worth fighting one's sisters for. But marriage is not only subordination; it stands for women's advancement and security in an uncertain world.

Competition between women takes its character from their status as a minority group. A minority group is

any group of people who, because of their physical or cultural characteristics, are singled out from the others in the society in which they live for differential and unequal treatment, and who therefore regard themselves as objects of collective discrimination [Louis Wirth, quoted in Hacker, 1969, pp.131–2]

— or can be so regarded, for it is a central problem of the contemporary women's liberation movement that many women do not see themselves in this light. The observation was first made in relation to ethnic minorities that 'group self-hatred' is a 'frequent reaction of the minority group member to his [sic] affiliation' (Lewin, 1941). One of the aspects of women's behaviour noted by Helen Hacker in her analysis of 'Women as a Minority Group' was the denigration by women of co-members of the caste. This, said Hacker, had three main origins:
(1) women's social 'marginality' and need for affiliation with men as the dominant group;
(2) the psychological effect on women of widespread social and economic discrimination;
(3) the socialization of women among men and to masculine formulations of women's character. Hacker observes:

From those, to us, deluded creatures who confessed to witchcraft [see pp.325 – 9] to modern sophisticates who speak disparagingly of the cattiness and disloyalty of women, women reveal their introjection of prevailing attitudes towards them. Like those minority groups whose self-castigation outdoes dominant group derision of them, women frequently exceed men in the violence of their vituperations of their sex. [Hacker, 1969, p.134]

Hence the 'preference' of women for mixed sex company, for male bosses, for the continuation or elevation of sexual inequality in marriage — viz. the Pussycat league founded by an attorney, an advertising consultant and a rich housewife who believe that 'looking, cooking, and smelling good for men are our major responsibilities and result in more than equal rights for us' (quoted in Hacker, 1974, p.129).

Women who emancipate themselves from such definitions let themselves in for a heightened conflict with their sisters. Career women and housewives mutually berate each other for the opposed sins of despising women as accredited domestics and betraying women's natural and self-chosen duty. It is because women understand each other's psychology and motives so well that they are so ineluctably locked in antagonism — a point made by de Beauvoir (1960, p.252): 'the theme of woman betrayed by her best friend is not a mere literary convention; the more friendly two women are, the more dangerous their duality becomes'.

Janet Lever and Pepper Schwartz went to look at Vassar, a previously all-female college to which a small number of men had recently been admitted: ' . . . being in the minority *did* change the men' they reported. Some men acquired signs of femininity; they sat around talking about each other 'in a petty way'. As one said, 'They get bitchy . . . They came because of the girls and then they become emasculated' (Lever and Schwartz, 1971, p.198). Such 'emasculation' into the feminine mode points to the influence on intra-gender relations of competition for the interest of the other gender. In the world outside Vassar, structural antagonism thus breeds 'bitchiness' as the predominant behavioural repertoire of female – female relations.

Men believe that women are bitchy to each other, and women act accordingly; but is this how women themselves think of each other? This question poses an important dilemma to be discussed in Chapter 15 — that of the contrast between male and female perceptions of 'reality'. There is no doubt that the doctrine of women's unsisterly conduct coexists with various subterranean forms of female collusion. In the next three sections I discuss briefly some of these hidden realities: cooperation between women, the bonds between mothers and daughters, and the taking by some women of their 'sisters' as sexual partners. A closing sections adds to these the important concept of sisterhood in feminist politics.

COOPERATION

I am very close to the gal next door, almost like sisters now. We have lots of coffee get-togethers. Last night she came over at 9.45 for potatoes. You have to be good friends to do that. She almost had her baby in my kitchen last year. [Lopata, 1971, p.243]

This woman, interviewed in Helen Lopata's study of Chicago housewives, went on to say that she cooperated with other wives in her block in looking after each other's children, supplying children with clothes, shopping and planning all-female parties (baby 'showers' and 'koffee-klatsching'). Lopata found that 53 per cent of the women exchanged such services frequently: suburban housewives did so most; urban housewives and 'apartment-occupying working women' the least.

A decade earlier, Peter Willmott and Michael Young surveyed a middle-class London suburb and uncovered a common pattern of 'a small, intimate network of "friends", mostly coming from the surrounding twenty or thirty houses . . . largely organized by the women' (Willmott and Young, 1960, p.102). This sort of network may also be built up in working-class communities:

I've got two very good friends [said Mrs Jarvis, a resident on a council housing estate], Mrs Barker, who lives opposite, has got a spin drier and I've got a sewing machine. I put my washing in her spin drier and she uses my sewing machine when she wants to. [Willmott, 1963, p.62]

Domestic mutual aid between women gets incidental mentions in community studies but has not itself formed the subject of a separate enquiry.[1] In the same way, organizations such as the National

---

[1] Cohen (1978) compares childcare cooperation between English women living on a housing estate and forms of cooperation among Creole women in Sierra Leone.

Housewives' Register (in Britain) and Women's Institutes have performed a probably important but completely undocumented mutual support function (see, for example, Macmillan, 1979).

The most usual pattern in cultures across the world is for women's cooperative relationships with one another to be highly valued psychologically and economically by both men and women, and to be an accepted part of the social system. Some of these cultures have recently been described by contributors to an anthropological volume on the theme of female solidarity (Caplan and Bujra, 1978; see also Hammond and Jablow, 1976, Chapter 8). Pamela Constantinides describes how Sudanese women in an urban situation organize themselves into Islamic cult groups devoted to the treatment of women's illnesses. These groups provide resources for friendship, drama and entertainment, as well as providing a forum for economic transactions, the arrangement of marriages and the finding of employment for husbands and sons. The cult groups are imported from the rural to the urban context, and have, says Constantinides, the crucial latent function of preventing the isolation of individual women that may accompany urbanization and of facilitating the exchange of personal services (hairdressing, body massage, etc.) between women.

In another example, Melissa Llewelyn-Davies reveals how Maasai women of south west Kenya collude to cover up each other's acts of adultery:

No woman would ever give information about the 'adultery' of another woman to any man: women's solidarity on this issue is absolute. It pits all women against all elders, even cutting across the ties between a mother and her son because a mother would never betray her daughter-in-law to her husband. [Llewelyn-Davies, 1978, p.233]

Llewelyn-Davies believes that adultery is the rule for Maasai women and comments that a woman's adultery constitutes an especially firm basis for friendship.

A third example of female solidarity (many more are to be found) is that of the Mundurucu Indians of Brazil studied by Yolanda and Robert Murphy in the early 1950s. When the Murphys left the Mundurucu after a year spent living among them and recording their lives, the men took their parting from Robert with some regret for the departure of a bearer of gifts and an object of interest, but they were accustomed to men leaving their midst; that is what men do. But the women began wailing . . . for Yolanda, telling her that she should stay among them forever. Women remain in place, and together. [Murphy and Murphy, 1974, p.122]

Most of their days among the Mundurucu, the Murphys recalled,

were spent by Yolanda among the women and by Robert among the men. She sat with the women in their houses, worked with them in making manioc flour, went with them to the gardens, bathed with them, and helped them take care of the children. When she was not off with them, one or more women were usually in our house. Mundurucu women are eminently gregarious, and she soon became included in most of their activities. [Murphy and Murphy, 1974, p.ix]

Mundurucu houses have 20 – 25 inhabitants; these are families joined by kin relationships between women, since the custom is for men to join the households of their wives in marriage (though much of the men's time is spent in a separate men's house in the village). The houses have no separate rooms and domestic work is an activity performed jointly and visibly. In their main food-providing work — harvesting and processing manioc flour — women also work together. The senior female of the house directs the work of the other women in it. If individual households are not large enough, women from a group of households collaborate, and since farinha production is such an important part of the domestic economy, cooperation between the women is 'an almost daily affair'.

Exhortations for women in modern industrialized societies to bond together like the Mundurucu and solve their problems this way (Leach, 1979) ignore powerful structural and psychological constraints. For Mundurucu women, the family is neither a production nor a consumption unit. Men's and women's tasks are divided ideologically just as they are in places like Britain and the United States, but

the family is not even the point where the division of labor between the sexes meets . . . . Rather, the division of labor poses all the women of the household and the village in complementarity to the productive efforts of the men. [Murphy and Murphy, 1974, p.130]

In fact, it seems to be particularly those societies that institutionalize the nuclear family that create barriers against female solidarity (Naish, 1978). Before this hardened into an ideal in Western culture, female friendships were able to prosper: 'Gratitude is a word I should never use toward you', wrote 26-year-old Sarah Butler Wister to 28-year-old Jeannie Field Musgrove in 1861. 'It is perhaps a misfortune of such intimacy and love that it makes one regard all kindness as a matter of course, as one has always found it, as natural as the embrace in meeting' (cited in Smith-Rosenberg, 1975, p.4). Marriage and motherhood did not alter the intense emotional relationships of these two women, a relationship that was typical of many. Practical help and advice and a total absence of hostility were marks of this 'female world of love and ritual', a terrain of 'supportive networks . . . institutionalized in social conventions or rituals which accompanied virtually every important event in a woman's life' (p.9). Large families, a prolonged embargo in adolescence and early adulthood on female – male relations, and acceptance of physical intimacy between women and a rigid gender role differentiation in the family and society promoted the existence of such a world. As Rich (1977) suggests, the paradoxical conclusion that can be drawn from this is that birth control and more gender symmetry (in theory, if not in practice) in the twentieth century has been, from the point of view of female solidarity, quite counter to women's interests.

MOTHERS AND DAUGHTERS

In Britain in the late 1950s Margaret Stacey documented a pattern reminiscent of the Mundurucu custom according to which men move into their wives' households on marriage. She found that in an Oxfordshire town 75 per cent of married men who were not householders lived with their wives' parents. Stacey commented that this was a consequence partly 'of the particular nature of the mother – daughter relationship' as expressed in the old saying

A son's a son till he gets a wife
A daughter's a daughter all her life. [Stacey, 1960, p.124]

British post-war sociology has acquired for itself a place in history by 'discovering' the loyalty of mothers and daughters.[2] A 'mother's union' of mothers and daughters was found in Bethnal Green, a working-class district of London, in the 1950s by researchers from the Institute of Community Studies. Mothers and daughters operated a mutual aid system, helping one another out in a multitude of ways. Over half the married women in one sample had seen their mothers within the previous 24 hours, and 80 per cent in the previous week[3] (Young and Willmott, 1957).

Before and after Young and Willmott wrote, other accounts of working-class family life (e.g. Rees, 1950; Dennis *et al.*, 1956; Kerr, 1958) suggested that mother – daughter relations might be important beyond the years and for other reasons than John Bowlby stressed. The preservation of bonds between adult daughters and their mothers gives women in their economically dependent position the protection of a valuable 'trade union': a source of help in troubled times, financial protection in the event of marital breakdown and, perhaps most importantly, a common basis for self-esteem.

This female – female bond is expressed in a very long agenda of 'mother-in-law' jokes. In such jokes, husbands have the company of their wives' mothers (usually large, forceful ladies) forced upon them, but it is the men's antagonism to the mother-in-law's symbolic presence that is the principal point made. According to Komarovsky's (1967) study of American working-class marriage, husband – mother-in-law tension flourishes where the social bond between the wife and her mother is most strongly developed. In middle-class marriages, observes Komarovsky, it is the wife's relationship with her in-laws, not the husband's with his, that is most likely to be a strain — though, one supposes, for different reasons. (So far as I know, this is not discussed in the sociological literature. One reason is the segregation between studies of working-class and middle-class life.)

Three-quarters of a group of London women having their first

---

[2] This seems to have been a particularly British exercise. In America, family sociology has concentrated more on the development of theoretical approaches.

[3] The figures cited by Young and Willmott (1957, pp.28 and 218) also show that kin contacts are maintained by a sizeable proportion of men (66 per cent of whom saw their mothers in the previous week). However, this aspect of family relationships gets little attention in Young and Willmott's analysis.

babies in 1975 – 6 had their mothers' help in learning how to care for the baby, and in coping with domestic work after the birth:

Honestly, I don't know how I would have got through that first week if my mother hadn't been here [said one]. I really did need someone . . . . She did all the washing and ironing and nursing the baby inbetween feeds and calming me down and gradually getting me back into normal life. [Oakley, 1979, p.147]

Childbirth is an occasion that especially unites mothers and daughters, as many investigators of family life have noted (see Rich, 1977, for example). This cannot be because intimate confidences are passed from mother to daughter concerning the 'facts' of sexuality and reproduction: Farrell's (1978) study of how young people learn about sex and reproduction replicates the findings of others (Gagnon and Simon, 1974 ; Schofield, 1968) in showing that more than two-thirds of girls acquire this knowledge outside the family. Despite the medicalization of childbirth, there are still strong vestiges of the belief that childbirth is 'women's business'.

But to seek the exact reason for a specific form of help given by mothers to their adult daughters obscures a basic feature of women's lives in male-dominated culture: emotional ties between mothers and daughters are never really broken, and remain a magnetic focus of attachment for all women throughout their adult careers of alliancing with men. Nancy Chodorow has called this the tendency for men to occupy a position of *emotional secondariness* in women's lives. The bare outlines of Chodorow's argument, stated most fully in *The Reproduction of Mothering* (1978) are as follows. The social divisions between female and male parents allocate childrearing to mothers, not fathers. Therefore both daughters' and sons' personalities are formed initially through the process of an attachment to the mother. But since sons must become 'masculine', they have to break this attachment, repudiate their mothers as models for themselves and learn to identify with fathers (men), so that a 'normal' masculine psychology is developed and women can be reinstated in this psychology as a quite 'other' class of persons. But, so far as mothers and daughters are concerned, the learning of femininity requires no break in a girl's identification with her mother. She must add her father 'to her world of primary objects', but need not 'turn absolutely from her mother to her father'. This gender asymmetry in childhood learning means that girls emerge from childhood

with a stronger basis for experiencing another's needs or feelings as one's own (or of thinking that one is so experiencing another's needs and feelings) . . . From very early, then, because they are parented by a person of the same gender . . . girls come to experience themselves as less differentiated than boys, as more continuous with and related to the external object-world. [Chodorow, 1978, p.167]

This difference may be summed up as

The basic feminine sense of self is connected to the world, the basic masculine sense of self is separate. [p.169]

— a conclusion that has great potential in explaining many of the findings on gender differences presented in this book. For, if the boundaries of the feminine self are more permeable, and women as a group are blessed (or burdened, depending on how you see it) with a heightened sensitivity to other people, their behaviour is never likely to be the same as men's.

The basic gender difference in childhood experience and adult personality also goes a long way towards explaining the sexual politics of motherhood. The traditional gender-divided family does not meet the relational needs women have as a consequence of their own mothering and unbroken female identification. Moreover, women need to have children to complete the triangle they experienced in their own childhoods.[4] In Chapter 5 we saw how mothers tend to identify more with female than male children. This fact and its consequences are, of course, highly problematic. Simone de Beauvoir recalled her own mother thus:

My earliest memories of her are of a laughing, lively young woman. She also had about her something wilful and imperious which was given a free rein after her marriage. My father enjoyed the greatest prestige in her eyes, and she believed that the wife should obey the husband in everything. But with Louise, my sister, and myself she showed herself to be dictatorial and overbearing, sometimes passionately so . . . . I did not look upon her as a saint, because I knew her too well and because she lost her temper far too easily; but her

---

[4] It is interesting that Chodorow sees the desire for a child as competing with female – female relationships as a source of gratification (completing the relational triangle) for women.

example seemed to me all the more unassailable because of that . . . If she had been more impeccable in her conduct, she would also have been more remote, and would not have had such a profound effect upon me . . .

And that is how we lived, the two of us, in a kind of symbiosis. Without striving to imitate her, I was conditioned by her. [De Beauvoir, 1963, pp.39 – 41]

Later on, in adolescence, the picture changed. Simone felt resentful of the close affection between her father and her sister,

But my real rival was my mother. I dreamed of having a more intimate relationship with my father; but even on the rare occasions when we found ourselves alone together we talked as if she was there with us. When there was an argument, if I had appealed to my father, he would have said: 'Do what your mother tells you!' I only tried once to get him on my side. He had taken us to the races at Auteuil; the course was black with people, it was hot, there was nothing happening, and I was bored; finally the horses were off; the people rushed towards the barriers, and their backs hid the track from my view. My father had hired folding chairs for us and I wanted to stand on mine to get a better view. 'No!' said my mother, who detested crowds and had been irritated by all the pushing and shoving. I insisted that I should be allowed to stand on my folding chair. 'When I say no, I *mean* no!' my mother declared. As she was looking after my sister, I turned to my father and cried furiously: 'Mama is being ridiculous! Why can't I stand on my folding chair?' He simply lifted his shoulders in an embarrassed silence, and refused to take part in the argument.

At least this ambiguous gesture allowed me to assume that as far as he was concerned my father sometimes found my mother too domineering; I persuaded myself that there was a silent conspiracy between us. But I soon lost this illusion. [De Beauvoir, 1963, pp.107 – 8]

Daughters are mothers' doubles and turn out to be sexual rivals. In this way a competitive spirit is built into the bond. Ambivalence persists; contrary to the idea that men marry women like their mothers and women marry men like their fathers, Arthur Aron (1974) found in a study of Toronto couples, that both men and women seek to repeat in marriage the early relationship they had with their mothers by choosing a mate who, like a mother, will combine loving care and considerate control. It is important, also, to realize that even a daughter who consciously rejects her mother's influence in adulthood is defining herself in relation to her. Thus, for example in the study of housework attitudes (Oakley, 1974b), rebellion against the mother's point of view is, equally with imitation, a sign of the mother's power (see, also, Friday, 1979).

LESBIANISM

One way to diagnose the cause of lesbianism is to describe it as 'undying fidelity to the mother'. One daughter interviewed by Signe Hammer for her book *Daughters and Mothers: Mothers and Daughters*, said

I knew quite early in life [said one daughter interviewed by Hammer], before I really knew what it meant, that my mother's sexual relationship with my father was not satisfying to her. She found sex very disturbing, and she found her own body disturbing. At the same time, she needed and loved me much more than I was willing to accept. I had this emotional intimacy with her that I didn't really understand. [Hammer, 1976, p.55]

After marriage and two children this daughter declared herself to be a lesbian.

Not surprisingly, the reasons for homosexuality among women have not been so exhaustively sought as those for male homosexuality. Simple uninterest among male investigators is one reason for this omission; but lesbianism can be concealed behind the overt normality of marriage and motherhood in a way that male homosexuality cannot; women who prefer sex with women do not thereby lose their desire or capacity for motherhood. However, female sexuality, always potentially subversive, is more so when it excludes men altogether. This attitude neatly brings out the Janus-faced nature of Madonna-worship in our culture: it is not *mothers* who are revered, but women desexualized through divine impregnation or housewifery.

Kinsey *et al.* (1953) found that 30 per cent of 13-year-old girls had homosexual contacts involving genital exhibitions and examinations; for two-thirds some manual manipulation of the genitals was also involved (which adds up to more pre-adolescent genital play between girls than between girls and boys). By the age of 30, a quarter of all the females in Kinsey's sample recognized erotic responses to other females, and one-sixth had enjoyed specifically sexual contacts with other women. Overall, some 30 – 40 per cent of single women and some 10 per cent of married women were not entirely heterosexual. Female homosexual experience was less common among Protestants,

Catholics and Jews than among non-believers, and more common among college graduates than among non-college graduates. It was particularly pronounced among women who had done postgraduate work (33 per cent of whom felt aroused by other women).

Shere Hite, several decades later, reported that 8 per cent of women who answered an American questionnaire on female sexuality preferred sex with women; 4 per cent were bisexual, 3 per cent preferred to have sex with themselves, and 1 per cent would rather have no sex at all. The rest preferred men 'although many stressed that they did not prefer "men" but rather an *individual* man' (Hite, 1977, p.396). One lesbian who answered Hite's questionnaire compared sex with a woman to sex with a man:

Most of the men in my heterosexual career (when I was twenty until I was twenty-eight), wanted oral stimulation from me of their penis, after which they would mount me and reach their climax. After their ejaculation they would ask, 'Didja come?' In general, my female lovers have taken far more creative and varied approaches to lovemaking. All of them, however, began by being incredibly gentle and aware of my needs, as well as theirs. The women did not act as though I was a 'masturbation machine' for them, nor did they fall asleep when it was over. No woman ever asked me, 'Didja come?' They knew. [Hite, 1977, p.412]

While lesbian encounters encompass a wider range of physical stimulation and emotional experience than heterosexual ones, they are also more productive of orgasms. Comparing women married for five years and lebians with five years' lesbian experience, Kinsey *et al.* (1953, p.457) found that most sexual contacts culminated in orgasm for 70 per cent of the lesbian women as against only 40 per cent of the married women (17 per cent of whom never had any orgasms at all).

In her chapter on lesbianism, Hite makes the observation that

One of the most striking points about the answers received to the questionnaire was how frequently, *even though it was not specifically asked*, women brought up the fact that they might be interested in having sexual relations with another woman, or at least were curious.

Nancy Friday's investigation of women's fantasies led to the same conclusion that, secretly, women express a 'natural warmth and tenderness' towards one another that they do not act out in ordinary life. In their sexual fantasies they are not competitive and ungenerous towards other women. Friday is anxious to point out that this does not mean women want lesbian relationships, although

> What is repeatedly made clear in what so many of the women themselves call their 'lesbian-type' fantasies is that they are seeking from other women in their fantasies what they aren't getting from their lovers in reality . . .
>
> It's the most natural thing in the world that, for the same reason men do, women should turn to women for tenderness . . Woman, the great giver of tenderness, has always been on the short end of the tit . . . The female breast, symbol of tenderness, is there for men to cry on, suck on, lie on for life. But how about women? We all begin on the breast, but little girls are soon turned from their mothers' breasts into their mothers' 'little sisters', and sent into a comfortless world . . . [Friday, 1976, pp.173 – 5]

In other words, lesbianism can satisfy women's deepest needs. (Chester, 1972, discusses this; see also Wolff, 1971). A search for its 'causes', motivated by the overriding assumption that what is unusual must be both unnatural and abnormal, veils the naturalness of the link between the ascription to women of social mothering and the discovery that women can really only love one another when they put each other first.

SISTERS UNITE!

Female solidarity does not automatically mean a feminist consciousness. Women who cooperate with one another in Bethnal Green, in Chicago, among the Mundurucu of Brazil or the Maasai of south west Kenya, are not necessarily aware that the covert bond indexes a common oppression. In fact, women embedded in such all-female connections are probably less likely than others to recognize their subordination, since their bonds with one another protect them from the harsher consequences of gender divisions articulated according to the dogma of the nuclear family.

Equally, you cannot have a feminist consciousness without female solidarity. Dismissing members of the women's liberation movement as 'a bunch of dykes' was (is) a common response to the challenge it represents. Such a response, by reducing feminism to the small change of an unfashionable sexual 'deviation', reveals the lack of any model of an independent woman other than a negative one. As the radical lesbian paper 'The woman-identified woman' expressed it, for a woman to be independent means she can't be a woman — she must be a dyke. That in itself should tell us where women are at. It says clearly: woman and person are contradictory terms. For a lesbian is not considered a 'real woman'. And yet, in popular thinking, there is only one essential difference between a lesbian and other women: that of sexual orientation, which is to say, when you strip off all the packaging, you must finally realize that the essence of being a 'woman' is to get laid by men. [Quoted in Salper, 1972, p.182]

Understanding the dismissal of feminism as the creation of a 'bunch of old dykes' is important for three reasons. Firstly, some lesbians are feminists and, indeed, lesbians were among the first in the late 1960s to seize on re-emergent feminism as a personal and cultural salvation. Feminist theory and practice as a whole must make sense of any divisions there are between lesbians and non-lesbians in the movement. This has been a quite considerable problem for movement members in many countries (see Deckard, 1979, pp. 374 – 8). Secondly, feminist theory has given rise to the belief among some that lesbianism should be deliberately espoused for political purposes: 'Lesbianism is one road to freedom — freedom from oppression by men' (Shelley, 1970, p.601). The argument goes: all heterosexual relationships are contaminated by a female – male imbalance of power; women's continuing participation in them therefore reinforces their second-class citizenship; therefore a political decision to become a lesbian is the only guarantee of personal liberation and is, furthermore, a vital step towards the liberation of *all* women. Thirdly, 'sisterhood', a self-conscious female solidarity, has been a central organizing idea of the modern feminist movement since its inception:

The concept of sisterhood is of great importance in the movement. If women are to cease living their lives through men, male friends and husbands should not play an exclusive role in a woman's life. If women consider their whole sex inferior, they are unwilling to establish friendships with each other. Those who believe in sexual equality must also believe that it is worthwhile 'really relating to' other women. [Carden, 1974, pp.14 – 15]

Feminist sisterhood, like other forms of female cooperation, is a mutual support system providing a sense of 'belonging' in a male-oriented world. By openly sharing their life histories, crises, anxieties, resentments, pleasures, hopes and fantasies with one another, women in a feminist group come to acknowledge the community of their emotions and experiences; it's not *us* who are maladjusted, but society that imposes impossible expectations on us. Such a collective vision bestows confidence and strength (and rage) where timidity and weakness existed before. In the process women begin to feel that other women are truly sisters, though the development of this insight has to be worked at or an insidiously competitive spirit creeps back in. Joan Cassell describes this enterprise in her study of *A Group Called Women* (and what she has to say bears out some of the points made earlier about the psychology of mother – daughter relationships):

Novices frequently express negative perceptions of their mothers in consciousness raising: mothers are described as boring housewives, dependent wives, manipulative parents. The mother is depicted as less independent, less interesting, less *human* than the father, who is envied, even resented . . . . Women . . . often discuss the limits between mother and daughter in hazy and indefinite terms, as though the narrator had difficulty knowing where her mother left off and she herself began. The mother appears to be perceived as part of the daughter, or the daughter seems to feel she is part of the mother. The mother is also described as the daughter's fate, an inferior fate . . . . As women's consciousness is raised, 'society' or 'the system' is gradually defined as the enemy, with both mother and daughter as victims. The mother's childrearing practices, her clinging and manipulative behaviour, are perceived as reactions to a feeling of personal powerlessness, a feeling shared by the daughter. When the daughter redefines herself as a victim of society and redefines her goals to include challenging this victimization, her relationship with her mother is also redefined. She no longer percevies herself as her mother's victim. Instead, the daughter, who in her search for independence frequently identified with the father as an embodiment of autonomy, now identifies with the mother; mother and daughter are deprived of independence by the father and by society. [Cassell, 1977, pp.58 – 9]

Whatever the global achievements of the women's liberation movement in restructuring women's place in society, the quiet revolution that has gone on in many women's heads should not be undervalued. Nor should the fact be overlooked that in redefining the political as the personal women have produced an alternative and more humane version of politics. Whether it is men who are 'really' the cause of women's oppression, and just what the meaning of 'society' as the subject of a sentence is, there is no doubt that dissipating the hostility of women towards women is a crucial first move in any positive transformation of women's world.

SECTION V

Power
What is Womanpower?

CHAPTER THIRTEEN

Class Categories

Given that women still have to await their liberation from the family, it remains the case in the capitalist societies that female workers are largely peripheral to the class system . . . [Giddens, 1973, p.288]

Social stratification on bases other than sex is real, but so is sex stratification. We can no longer pretend that sex stratification does not exist, nor that it exists but is unimportant. [Eichler, 1980, p.102]

Power is unequally distributed in most societies, and depends not only on personal qualities of the individual but on social position. Different people occupy different social positions and men occupy a different position in society from women: class inequality and gender inequality coexist. In this chapter I look briefly at two important interrelated issues. [1] Firstly, in what sense can men and women be said to belong to different 'classes'? What meaning does the conventionally used term 'social class' have for women? Secondly, why is poverty a special trap for women?

WHERE HAVE ALL THE YOUNG GIRLS GONE? GONE TO YOUNG MEN, EVERY ONE

Nichols (1979) has distinguished three definitions of social class: the official, the sociological and the Marxist. Each of these has difficulty with the case of women.

The official definition of social class is that operated by government

---

[1] I apologize for such a cursory look at a subject that has received a lot of hard thought from many feminists.

statisticians, and it is an entirely pragmatic and atheoretical way of describing the population and of analysing social/economic correlates of a range of data. Beginning in 1801 with the first ten-yearly census of the population, the whole historical development of official statistics in Britain has served to ignore the question of 'women and class'. Census enumerators in that year had to answer the question 'what number of persons in your parish, township or place are directly employed in agriculture, how many in trade manufactures or handicraft, and how many are not comprised in any of the preceding classes?' (Nichols, 1979, p.156). The question in this form was not very successful and various revisions were made until, in 1851, a predominantly industrial classification of seventeen classes and sub-classes was arrived at. Around the turn of the century government statisticians began to turn their attention to the question of differential mortality rates. In 1911 T.H.C. Stevenson proposed the idea that the division of the population into social classes should be carried out in such a way that the largest possible differences in mortality rates would be revealed. This, he argued, would prove both the correctness of the social grading system used and the truth of the dictum that mortality is highest in the lowest status groups, although it had to be recognized that 'the lower mortality of the wealthier classes depends less upon wealth itself than upon the culture . . . associated with it' (Stevenson, 1928, p.209).

Stevenson's 'social grades' were very similar to the five social classes used by the Registrar-General today, viz: I. Professional occupations; II Intermediate occupations; III Skilled occupations (divided since 1971 into non-manual and manual); IV Partly skilled occupations; V Unskilled occupations. Table 13.1 shows what percentages of the British population in 1971 fell into these groups. It is obvious from this table that the social class composition of the population varies with its sex composition. In fact, the table tells us that (taking the individual's own occupation) 34.9 per cent of the classified male population is middle class, 52.5 per cent of the classified married female and 61.6 per cent of the classified unmarried female population is middle class and, of the total classified population of men and women over 15, 42.5 per cent is middle class.

Table 13.2 illustrates the problem in another way. According to this table, the percentage of husbands who do not have the same occupationally based social class as their wives runs from 44.7 per cent

TABLE 13.1 Social class composition of people* with classified occupations aged 15 and over in Great Britain, 1971

% in each social class	Men only	Women only			Men + Women	
		Married		Single, widowed & divorced		
		Husband's class	Own class	Own class	Own occupation	Head of family
I	5.0	5.3	0.9	1.2	3.6	5.1
II	18.0	19.8	16.2	19.2	17.8	20.1
IIINM	11.9	11.3	35.4	41.2	21.1	11.9
IIIM	38.5	39.0	10.0	10.8	28.4	37.9
IV	18.1	17.5	28.2	22.7	20.9	18.0
V	8.6	7.1	9.4	4.9	8.2	7.3
Total	100.0	100.0	100.0	100.0	100.0	100.0

*Economically active and retired.

Source: Social Trends, 1975, p.6; cited in Nichols (1979) pp.154–5. Crown copyright.

TABLE 13.2 *Social class classification of wives and husbands in England and Wales*

Social class classification of wives	Husbands whose social class classification is different from their wives %
I – II	44.7
III	75.2
IV – V	90.2

Source: Census, 1971, *Household Composition Tables*, Table 52. Crown copyright.

to 90.2 per cent according to wife's occupation. In fact more than half of all couples have discrepant social classes.

In this sense, social class has a different 'meaning' for women that it has for men: their relations to the class structure are unequal. Yet it is only in the last ten years, with the eruption of feminism inside academic disciplines and government departments that the question of women's relationship to social classes has come to be seen by statistics-users and others as a political issue, technical problem and considerable theoretical puzzle.[2]

Because official statistics are produced to serve government interests and government interests are sexist, if not directly anti-feminist, the official statistical publications of government departments are hardly even defensive about the patriarchal concepts that inform the operationalization of the notion of class. According to government statisticians, all families must have a head and this head is

---

[2] T.H.C. Stevenson and his predecessors were aware of the possible relevance of female occupations to mortality data, but proposals routinely to code married women's occupations did not get off the ground. The 1911 Census (published in 1923) contained an analysis of childhood mortality by mother's occupation from which the conclusion was drawn (with appropriate methodological reservations) that the children of mothers who held a job outside the home were more at risk of dying than those whose mothers did work for pay at home. However, no analysis of such data by married women's own occupations subsequently appeared in Census publications (Macfarlane, 1980).

usually a man. [3] The role of a 'chief economic provider' is deduced from the following set of rules:

(1) those in fulltime employment or not employed at all take precedence over part-time or retired workers;
(2) married men or 'widowed and divorced persons in families' are preferred over other members of families or 'persons not in families';
(3) males are preferred over females;
(4) older persons are selected before younger. [Census, 1971, *Summary Tables*, p.xxii]

Strangely, 'a chief economic provider' is not the person in a household who contributes most income to it.

Most official statistical analyses using the concept of social class take a straight male, occupationally based, criterion. Sociological definitions of social class used in survey research have come increasingly to coincide with the official statistical one in that, as Osborn and Morris (1979, pp.39 – 40) have observed, 'Social class is probably the most commonly used analytic variable and the index of class is almost invariably occupation classified on a hierarchically ordered scale'. Indeed, 'The use of occupation classifications is so taken for granted in many research contexts that "occupational status" has become for many synonymous with "social class".' [4] One reason why this is so is that male occupationally based social class proves to be a powerful discriminator of life chances in many fields. A highly relevant area (from the viewpoint of women) is that of mortality among babies.

In 1911, when Stevenson first addressed the question of infant mortality and social class, he found that mortality among the babies of unskilled men was twice that among the babies of upper-class men (Macfarlane, 1979b). In 1977 there was a similar gap: the perinatal mortality rate of social class V (classified on the basis of father's

---

[3] A rewording of the crucial question B5 just announced for the 1981 Census will make it clear that women can be family heads as well (the possibility that some families do not have 'heads' is not entertained). See Oakley and Oakley (1979) on sexism in official statistics.

[4] While in one sense sociological practice has converged with official statistical practice in taking occupation as equivalent to social class, it could also be said that in another sense it has diverged, and some sociologists have sought to develop a more complex approach.

occupation) families was 22 per 1000 live births and in social class I it was 11 (Office of Health Economics, 1979). These social class differences in perinatal mortality fit into a general pattern of social inequalities in health and illness (Morris, 1979), and in the light of international data (e.g. World Health Organization, 1978) suggest that Britain is an especially class-divided country.

The idea that an association between perinatal mortality and husband's occupation explains why some women's babies die doesn't, of course, make a great deal of sense. The abstract notion of social class (however defined) can't explain anything; it is factors associated with social class membership capable of affecting health that must account for the association. Although there are some direct links between occupation and mortality, it is probable that at least four-fifths of the association is social and environmental in character (Fox and Adelstein, 1978). Once again, this can be illustrated by looking at perinatal mortality rates. Two major causes of baby deaths are congenital malformations and premature births (these accounted for 22 per cent and 70 per cent respectively of perinatal deaths in Britain in 1977). The incidence of both of these is inversely related to husband's occupation: the lower his social class the more likely it is that her baby will be malformed or premature (World Health Organization, 1978; Wynn and Wynn, 1979). Both also vary between different populations as Figures 13.1 and 13.2 indicate. Figure 13.1 takes the particular case of anencephaly (a malformation of the central nervous system in which the brain fails to develop) and shows that some countries, including England and Wales, Scotland and Ireland have particularly high rates whereas others (e.g. Finland and Japan) have low ones. Figure 13.2 performs the same exercise for the proportion of all babies born weighing less than 2,500 grams. Again, England and Wales do rather badly, whereas the Scandinavian countries do rather well. Such international differences are currently taken as proof of the superiority of some countries' medical care systems over others (Chalmers *et al.*, 1980), but they also, as the Wynns contend in their book *Prevention of Handicap and the Health of Women*, point to a relationship between the fate of babies and the health of mothers. Generally speaking, those countries with the highest malformation and prematurity rates are those with the highest death rates of women aged 45 – 54. The Wynns cite an array of evidence implicating nutrition (both during pregnancy and before) as

FIGURE 13.1 *Incidence of anencephaly in various countries*
Source: Chalmers & Macfarlane (1980)

FIGURE 13.2 *Proportion of live births weighing less than 2500g*
Source: Chalmers & Macfarlane (1980)

the single most important determinant of these inequalities between women.

From this example (and others like it) a critical paradox can be deduced — that women's 'second-hand status' in conventional class analysis is both a reality and a lie. The reality is that women in advanced capitalist nations lack economic autonomy and are highly dependent on the uncertain male-determined fortunes of their functions as wives, mothers and housekeepers. The lie is that men's occupations are any index of women's occupations. As a matter of fact none of the three definitions of social class — official, sociological or Marxist — can really accommodate within their frameworks the historical specificity of women's position.

In Marxist theory social classes are defined by their relation to the means of production. The number, nature and relations of social classes then depend on the mode of production. Until recently, Marxist theory has managed to ignore the relations of reproduction that obtain within the family, the domain in which much of women's labour is carried out. Consequently, women have been seen as having only one kind of attachment to the class structure, and that is through the mediation of the male head of the family — the family, as well as the individual man (but not the individual woman), being the unit of stratification. The basic dilemma of feminists wanting to revitalize Marxist class analysis to embrace the autonomous relations of women to the means of production is, as Delphy (1980, p.86) observes, that 'the concepts used to account for exploitation by wages — and it is this which is the subject of *Capital* — cannot account for the exploitation of the unwaged'. Hence the various struggles, outlined in Chapter 8, to impose some orthodox materialist interpretation onto the complexities of the housewife's labour. Delphy's opinion is that Marxism cannot be remoulded so as to overcome the apparently anomalous case of women's membership of social classes. Apart from the consideration that the analysis of capital rules out those primarily embedded in a domestic economy, it is evident that the struggle between workers and capitalists is not the only struggle. The interests of men and women at all levels of society are potentially in conflict, and unity cannot be assumed, especially within the family. The wife's work and the man's wage may complement each other from a theoretical point of view, yet pragmatically this lack of symmetry causes division and difference. It is in fact the very source of gender inequality that Marxist class analysis, with its audacious assumption of family harmony, is wishfully banishing from the scene.

There is no escaping the fact that the Marxist approach to women's situation under capitalism is fatally weakened by androcentrism. Are women, then, a class on their own? Like relations between different ethnic groups, those between men and women are characterized by a permanent caste-like status; neither one's 'race' nor one's sex are categories that can be disowned. Some propositions in favour of seeing women as a separate class are stated by Margrit Eichler (1980, pp.103 – 4) as follows:

(1) ' . . women and men are in a hierarchically ordered relationship in which men are superior with respect to a definite system of privileges and discriminations . . '

(2) ' . . . the distinction is relatively permanent . . . '

(3) ' . . . sex identity [is] a form of class consciousness . . . '

(4) Marriage is 'not a good indicator for social proximity'.

These considerations suggest that it would be reasonable to see women as a separate class. Yet this situation has a problematic of its own. If women are a separate class from the point of view of the gender structure, then there must be some similarity (either manifest or latent) in the way all women relate to all men — that is, to men in the different classes that express men's relationships to the means of production. However, it is a somewhat crucial aspect of women's position that the relations of different women in different social groups to men are rather different. This fact, of course, breeds the anti-feminist argument that not all women are oppressed, whereas the truth is that the oppression of women can be said to consist in this dependence on the way individual men treat them (whether or not this is a material difference, or merely a difference in levels of awareness among women of their oppression).

Another difficulty with the argument that women are a class is that it disputes the centrality of their own relations to the means of production. Unless two different concepts of class are distinguished — that of 'gender' class and that of 'economic' class — the problem is insoluble. For most, if not all, women, have such a relationship at some time in their lives. Why should it be ignored? The most common reason why it is ignored in Marxist, sociological and official statistical definitions of social class is evident in Tables 13.1 and 13.2, and was discussed at length in Chapter 7. Women simply don't have the *same* relationship to the means of production as men. They are concentrated in specific occupations, particularly low-paid white collar work. Table 13.2 hides the biggest difference between female and male occupations by not dividing social class III into manual and non-manual segments. In fact, two-thirds of women in social class III non-manual have husbands in social class III manual (Osborn and Morris, 1979, p.42). Indeed, the concentration of women in this sector was what enabled Anthony Giddens, one of the few theorists to confront the issue of women, to dismiss their role in the class system as peripheral (quotation at the beginning of the chapter). The economic expansion of the white collar sector in recent years has proved quite a problem to Marxists who have wanted to say that it doesn't mean the arrival of a middle-class society — as it might appear to on the surface. Giddens himself adopts this line, and it is part of his 'evidence' that, since women predominate in white collar jobs, society can't be becoming middle class *because women have their class defined by the family*. It is because their primary role is in the family that they constitute the 'underclass' of the white collar sector, monopolizing badly paid occupations in which chances of security and promotion are small.

Such logical absurdities are not the exclusive property of Marxists. Thus, Osborn and Morris reflect on the problem of white collar women married to manual workers: it 'suggests that women in social class III non-manual have a similar socio-economic position to men in social class III manual even though male workers in social class III non-manual are usually accorded higher status than males in social class III manual' (Osborn and Morris, 1979, p.42). For if marriage is the haven of equality that middle-class Marxists and sociologists like to believe it is, it is quite impossible for women to have higher status than their husbands.

Women are a class; women's class is defined by the family; class, for women as for men, depends on individual occupation — none of these options is satisfactory. Since each of them is suggested by existing stratification analysis with its androcentric occupationally based logic, it is not surprising that they don't solve the problem. However, it is likely that each has some applicability and the problem posed is one of their relative salience and interrelation. What is required is a long drawn out attempt 'to reconceptualize our entire stratification model' (Eichler, 1980, p.115), and such an enterprise must begin, not merely end, with the subtleties of women's situation. It must be prepared to acknowledge the dispensability of the notion of class — or at least the importance of the revised notion of 'gender class' — in making sense of women's labour and relationships.

POOR WOMEN

Unfortunately theoreticians' maps of social class are in the heads of policy-makers too. There are a number of ways in which women are disadvantaged economically and socially by a naive adherence to the view that families under the aegis of the male breadwinner protect women from the harsh realities of the market economy. These very concrete disadvantages are even more hidden than the usual hidden injuries of class.

Women constitute a majority of the poor (Young, 1975; Townsend, 1979). Peter Townsend's *The Poverty Report* (based on a national random sample of British households) said:

More than half of the poor were women and girls . . . Women were at a disadvantage at most . . . ages. The proportion of women in poverty was higher than of men at all ages except under fifteen; and on the margins of poverty, higher at all ages except 30 – 44. [Townsend, 1979, p.285]

Women predominate among the elderly, and this is a group especially prone to fall into poverty. Much of women's poverty is also accounted for by a sex difference in the fates of single-parent families. In Britain the 1971 Family Expenditure Survey showed that the region of the country where a family lived had a much weaker effect on the chances of a household being in poverty than whether the 'head' of the household was male or female (Fiegehen *et al*, 1977). Three years later one of the findings reported by the Finer Committee on One-Parent Families was that 31 per cent of fatherless families in London lived in furnished accommodation in 'stress' areas of the city compared with 1 per cent of motherless families. The Committee observed that 50 per cent of fatherless families depended on supplementary benefits as against 10 per cent of motherless families, and in their section on employment they concentrated on the problems of women's employment because

Many of the disadvantages from which working lone mothers suffer are part of the larger problem of the position of women workers as a whole . . . It is for this reason that . . . we are conscious . . . of the special needs of lone mothers. These were summarized for us by the National Council for the Unmarried Mother and Her Child in the following apt words:

'They are dependent upon one wage in a society in which is is becoming more and more common for both parents to work. Where the lone parent is a woman the situation is particularly difficult because of the low level of women's wages and the lack of opportunity for women to participate in skilled and remunerative employment. The position in the labour market of widows, or divorced and separated wives may have deteriorated because of some years of absence from paid employment. Unmarried mothers tend to be younger than other lone mothers and may not even have completed their training or education'. [Finer Report, 1974, p.409]

The Finer Committee's estimate was that in April 1971 a tenth of all families with children were of the single-parent variety. These totalled 620,000, of which 520,000 were fatherless: 37 per cent by separation, 23 per cent by divorce, 23 per cent by widowhood, and 17 per cent were just 'single'. In both Britain and the United States women living on their own with children have emerged as an important group of families in poverty over the period since the early 1950s, replacing in importance other categories of poor families such as those with unemployed male heads or many children (Fiegehen *et al.*, 1977; Ross, 1976). Figure 13.3 gives the picture for the United States from 1960 to 1972; it shows a dramatic shift in female-headed poor families from 29 per cent in 1960 to 43 per cent in 1972.

Such figures prove that family breakdown (or non-initiation) leaves women and their children vulnerable economically, and in this sense the family can never cushion women from economic reality. Indeed, it can be argued that the situation of women in single-parent families reveals particularly sharply the basic contours of the position of women in general. For the forces propelling female-headed single-parent families into poverty are the reasons why women in society as a whole do not have economic autonomy or equality with men. They can't earn enough to support themselves and their children — or they can't get jobs compatible with childrearing. Their longer dependence on inadequate state benefits penalizes them financially for motherhood, in contradiction to the prevailing ideology, which singles out motherhood as the very proper pinnacle of women's achievement in the field of labour.

As in traditional models of statification, employers, government

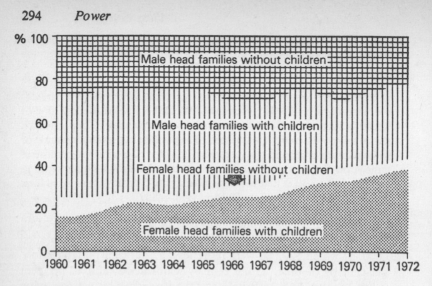

FIGURE 13.3 *Families in poverty, United States, 1960-72*

Source: US Bureau of the Census, *Current Population Reports.* Consumer Income Series P-60, No. 86: 'Characteristics of the Low-Income Population: 1971,' Table 4; cited in Ross (1976) p. 139.

planners and social policy-makers envisage women's employment as the last resort of a bored or impoverished deserted wife and not as something that might constitute a central, authentic relation of women to the social world. Martha Griffiths notes that in the United States, two-thirds of all women workers are either single, divorced, widowed or separated, or have husbands earning less than $7000 a year. Full-time employed wives contribute two-fifths of the family's total income and 'in many cases these earnings make the difference between a middle- and a low-income standard of living' (Griffiths, 1976, p.9). For 2 per cent of British married couples the woman is the 'chief economic supporter' (Lister and Wilson, 1976), and in 5 per cent of dual-earning marriages the wife earns more than the husband (Hewitt, 1980, p.164). On average a wife's earnings represent 25 per cent of the family income (Hamill, 1978). A report on *Low Pay and Family Poverty* in Britain points out that

To achieve the same relative living standards which might have been afforded in the 1950s through the efforts of the breadwinner, families of the 1970s increasingly require the employment of two wage-earners. In many cases the employment of married women represents the dividing line between poverty and adequate living standards. [McNay and Pond, 1980, pp.1 – 2]

Lynne Hamill's (1978) analysis of data from the 1974 Family Expenditure Survey calculated that the number of families with an income below the official (supplementary benefits) poverty line would have been multiplied three times without women's earnings. The low pay of women can thus be seen both as the lever that takes women and their children out of poverty and as the anchor that keeps them there.

Governmental failure to tackle the issue of women's low pay is obviously part-and-parcel of the ideology that views women's employment as a secondary commitment. It also proceeds from the logic of the male breadwinner argument: in its tax, insurance and social security policies the state makes certain assumptions about 'normal' family life, and in Britain at least these remain stubbornly tied to the male breadwinner – female housekeeper formula. The personal income tax system, for example, is based on the assumption that the man is the family's main wage-earner and thus the person responsible to the Inland Revenue for the payment of tax due. Unbelievably, a married man living with his wife owns her income for tax purposes. The man gets a higher personal allowance on marriage whereas the woman loses hers, because it is assumed that 'a man with a wife to support has clearly a lower capacity to pay tax than a single man' (Select Committee on Tax-Credit, 1973, p.360). (The husband can claim a wife's earned income allowance at the same level to be offset against her earnings.) A couple may choose to have the wife's earned (but not unearned) income taxed separately, but this benefits only higher rate taxpayers. Separate assessment, another possibility, enables the tax bill to be divided in proportion to the couple's income and outgoings, but gives no financial privacy to either partner.

So far as social security policy is concerned, Hilary Land summarizes the situation in these words:

The British social security system does not recognize that most married couples share the economic support of their families and that some may wish to share responsibilities for domestic work: breadwinners are male. Only women care for children, the sick and the old and if they have paid employment this must take second place to their domestic duties. [Land, 1979, p.149]

While Britain may be somewhat behind the United States in

legislators' willingness to equalize the rights and responsibilities of men and women, there is no doubt that both the welfare and social security systems continue to discriminate against women (Griffiths, 1976). Essentially the same mythology of women's 'disappearance' into the family is espoused.

There is, then, a certain homogeneity about ideologies of social class and the operationalization of state policies towards the family. Personal sexual relations chart the place of women but men rise above this archaic definition (see p.242 on the cohabitation 'rule'). For that is undoubtedly the main problem: the family, from the viewpoint of the capitalist logic, is an archaic institution. Its structure and functioning obey different rules. Families are impenetrably private and different from one another. The task of the state is to impose pattern and bureaucratic order, casting all families into the same mould. This makes women as a class victims of an ethic of individuality (it's how we differ from each other not what we have in common that matters) while ensuring their superficial conformity to a basic and basically sexist formula.

CHAPTER FOURTEEN

Politics in a Man's World

Since the war, it has become the rule to have a woman in every Cabinet, like those advertisements for chiming doorbells which said that every home should have one. [ex-MP Shirley Williams, *Guardian*, 30 October 1979]

Our politics begin with our feelings . . . The political unit in which we can discover, share and explore our feelings is the small group. Raising our collective consciousness is not a process that begins and ends, but is continuous and necessary given the enormous pressure placed on us everywhere to deny our own perceptions . . . . [San Francisco Redstockings, 1969, pp.285 – 6]

What is significant for our understanding of women and politics is the emphasis given to the importance of administrative actions, whereas modes of political action involving expressions of power, such as manipulation, bluff, influence, gossip, possession, threats of ritual pollution, witchcraft, sorcery, or suicide, have been considered less important and therefore relegated to secondary concerns in the study of politics. [Tiffany, 1978, p.45]

Politics, as traditionally defined, is 'the science and art of government, the science dealing with the form, organization and administration of a state . . . and with the regulation of its relations with other states' (OED). It is derived from the Latin *'politicus'*, meaning civic or civil. As this derivation suggests, whoever participates in politics must first be recognized as a citizen of the state. Women, as earlier chapters of this book demonstrated, have had a long struggle to acquire the rights and duties of citizens. The battle is not yet won, for women's status in society remains defined by their family functions (both actual and supposed) in a way that does not hold for men. Hence, it is somewhat silly to ask the commonly recurring question why women's share in the political process — as defined above — is not yet equal to men's in Britain, North America and other modern political states. Why should it be?

In this chapter I shall look at where women have got to as voters and other wielders of political power in government. The second half of the chapter considers the wider definition of politics mentioned in the second quotation at the beginning of this chapter: the idea that the personal experiences of oppressed groups are of more political importance than the question of who votes which way and which set of genitals the Prime Minister possesses. As a matter of fact, this alternative definition of politics enables us to see that women, in most societies, are tremendously powerful (quotation 3). The context and ways in which most of the power exercised by women throughout history has been deployed not only help us to understand why politics in its narrow definition is not a popular female domain, but also throw light on two central themes of this book: firstly, what is the 'oppression' of women, and is it universal? Secondly, how do women themselves actually experience their confinement to the 'non-political' private and male-dominated sphere of the family?

MASCULINE POLITICS

Canada's relations with Britain will soon be in the hands of two women. Mrs Jean Wadds takes over in January as High Commissioner in London, reporting to the External Affairs Minister, Flora MacDonald, in Ottawa . . .

Mrs Wadds, now 59 . . . comes of rich and thoroughbred Tory stock. Her father, W. Earl Rowe, was leader of the Ontario Conservative Party and a Federal Cabinet Minister in the 1930s. Her first husband was an MP for 33 years, and after his death she represented the same rural Ontario seat for ten years until the liberal landslide in 1968.

But she is no feminist. She said this weekend: 'I have found the so-called women's movement a little foreign to me'. [*Guardian*, 15 October 1979]

This passage illustrates three characteristics of women politicians today. Firstly, they are not likely to be feminist in motivation. Secondly, they tend to enter politics in the footsteps of a father or husband (*pace* Emmeline Pankhurst, Indira Gandhi, etc.; see Chamberlain, 1973, for the equivalent situation in the United States). Thirdly, they are not especially prone to be left-wing in orientation.

All three of these characteristics would come as a great surprise to those gentlemen (and ladies) who opposed the granting of the franchise to women more than half a century ago. A sterling theme in the speeches of anti-suffragists on both sides of the Atlantic was that to give the vote to women would bring about a radical transformation of the entire political system: indeed, fear of the power of a female bloc vote was the main reason why the 1918 Act did not give the vote to women on the same terms as men (Harrison, 1978).

In fact, when women began to vote it made very little difference. Studies of voting patterns in the United States, Britain and many other countries show that women are rather less likely to vote than men (Jacquette, 1974). Although Egyptian women got the vote in 1956, in the 1971 elections only 10 per cent of the voters were women. This is an extreme sex differential; in Sweden in 1970 there was only a 1 per cent difference in the proportions of men and women voting. In British and North American studies, married women vote more than single women but 'husband and wife have a tendency to behave in the same manner — either they vote together or not at all. The husband may vote, and the wife abstain frequently, but the wife rarely votes without the husband's doing likewise' (Jacquette, 1974, p.xv). (As Goot and Reid (1975) observe, from the fact of husband and wife voting alike is usually assumed the husband's leadership of the wife, rather than vice versa.)

Definitions of women as non-voters are embedded in the structure of families and the sociology of women. Thus Kenneth Langton (1969, p.167) has noted that in Jamaican families women tend to be the transmitters of political identification and males are not so interested in politics. Education and employment are both important factors. The University of Michigan's Survey Research Center analysed data from the 1950, 1960 and 1964 presidential elections and found that employed women voted more than housewives (Lansing, 1974, p.14). In the 1968 election, 71 per cent of employed women voted, compared with 63 per cent of housewives.

It is a common assertion about women's role in politics that they are more conservative, with both a big and a little 'c', than men. For France, Maurice Duverger (1955) observed that women do not support the communist and socialist parties despite the fact that these parties have done the most to increase the number of women in Parliament and other kinds of public office. Tingsten (1975) found that women in the Weimar Republic supported centre parties until 1933 when their allegiance shifted to the Nazi party. In Spain, women got the vote after the left-wing republican – socialist coalition won in 1931, and in the 1933 election the right and right – centre parties won important gains: 'the leaders of the revolution discovered that more Spanish women were against them than for them' (Gosnell, 1948, p.68). In countries such as the United States and Britain, where the ideological differences between the parties can be argued to be relatively small, the idea that women favour the right wing has less support. Studies of Banbury, a town in Oxfordshire, showed minor differences in voting behaviour in the direction of women more often voting Conservative than men (Stacey *et al.*, 1975; Stacey, 1960). An analysis by Stan Taylor (1978) of the voting patterns of manual workers' wives in the 1970 British general election revealed an association between employment and direction of voting. Wives with manual jobs were as likely to vote Labour as their husbands, but wives without jobs were more conservative. However, wives with non-manual jobs were even more conservative, suggesting that (amazingly, just as for men) placement in the occupational structure is linked with political attitudes. As Goot and Reid (1975) observe, the doctrine of women's inherent conservatism ignores the specificity of women's political interests to their unique class position.

In any case, what really has to be explained is the very large discrepancy between the possession and use of the vote and the exercise of political power at higher levels in the system: the fact that only 3 per cent of current British MPs are women (a 1.5 per cent drop from 1964); the fact that only 5 per cent of members of state legislatures in the United States, 2 per cent of members of national legislatures in France and 5 per cent in New Zealand are women; the fact that even in the Soviet Union and Eastern European countries, where women have been cajoled and pressured into the public-political world, 'women are virtually absent from the top political decision-making organs' (Jancar, 1974, p.218). (In 1975, 35 per cent of the Supreme Soviet membership was female, 2 per cent of the Central Committee, and 0 per cent of the Politburo — Hough, 1978.) Where women *are* present at the top, things may not be altogether what they seem. In 1966, the President of the Dominican Republic appointed women to the governorships of all the 26 provinces in that country. His motive was that this move would deflect a wave of violence against him and his deputies; the opposition would simply be less likely to shoot women.

It is not only at the executive and legislative levels of government that political power is exercised; much decision-making also goes on in the many branches of the civil service. Table 7.7 (p.155) gave some data on the relative positions of men and women in the British civil service. In America in 1961, when President Kennedy established the first Commission on the Status of Women, approximately 1 per cent of people in high-grade positions were women. In 1967, the percentage was 3.7, and in 1972, it was 4.0 — which is evidence of women's persisting political powerlessness.

A popular interpretation of women's absence from the higher levels of political power has been termed by Jane Jacquette 'insufficient masculinization': 'If only women were more like men (were more informed, had greater feelings of efficacy, were more involved in the real world) so the argument runs, the problem of female deviance from male norms of participation would be solved' (Jacquette, 1974, p.xviii).[1] According to this view, discrimination against women lies with women themselves.

But women do not get where they are or fail to get where they want to be in a vacuum. An alternative theory is that discrimination against women operates at every level of the political process to realize the general rule that 'where the power is, there women are not' (Stacey and Price, 1980, p.2). One case study that supports this theory is provided by Jill Hills' (1978) account of women in the British Labour and Conservative parties. Using the three indices of the number of women at each level in party hierarchies, the number of women candidates at both local and national elections, and the number of 'unwinnable' seats fought by women, Hills shows that considerable biases against women operate to exclude them from the higher echelons of political power.

About 40 per cent of Labour Party members and 50 per cent of Conservative Party members are women. However, women are not represented in these proportions cn the Labour Party General Management Committee or on Conservative Party Constituency Executive Councils. As delegates to party Annual Conferences, women have not been more than 11 per cent (Labour) and 24 per cent (Conservative).[2] On the policy-making and administrative bodies of

---

[1] Greenstein (1973) is an example of how this theoretical assumption structures studies of political behaviour. Greenstein compares the interests of a sample of 9 – 14-year-old girls in New Haven with those of a sample of 9 – 14-year-old boys, and finds girls deficient in politically relevant 'public' interests. He concludes that the adult political differences of men and women emerge early in life.

[2] It look as though a woman should be a Conservative if she wants to enter politics. One reason is, of course, that richer women are more likely to have the resources necessary to enter politics.

the two parties, the proportion of women ranges from 18 per cent (the Conservative Party Advisory Committee on Policy) to 24 per cent (the Conservative Party's National Executive Committee). As candidates in local government elections, Conservative Party women generally do better than Labour Party women, but for either the proportion rarely rises above 20 per cent and both parties show a predisposition for women candidates wherever the chances of election are rather small.

But it is at the level of candidates in national elections that women disappear *en masse*. Between 9 and 10 per cent of nominations are women. Having been nominated, women have a relatively good chance of being selected, but again most are chosen to fight where they have no chance of winning (62 per cent of Labour candidates in the February 1977 elections). One consequence of this is that the few women MPs who are elected tend to gain parliamentary seats in marginal constituencies so that (as the 1979 general election showed) a relatively small swing is sufficient to unseat a disproportionately large number of women. What this means is that until the parties are prepared to select women for safe seats, there is unlikely to be a rise in the number of women in Parliament.

The 'insufficient masculinization' hypothesis, then, does not take account of direct prejudice against women as political actors. Yet the idea that women are exactly the same as men ('it's all a question of personality') is not unpopular among successful women candidates. This is combined with a (somewhat contradictory) appeal to the innate pragmatism of women. In a conversation published in *The Observer* before the 1979 general election, Margaret Thatcher was asked by Kenneth Harris what she thought of the view that through her leadership the Conservative Party would lose votes that it would retain if led by a man:

It depends who the woman is, it depends on who the man is . . . . Of course, some people may be prejudiced. What I think they fail to observe is that a woman might collect a whole lot of votes the party wouldn't otherwise get. Why? Because many people, men as well as women, think a woman can have qualities a man may not have. I *do* my own shopping. I *do* know what women have to put up with . . .

A woman's approach to problems is much more practical, I can tell you. You know, if you are a woman, you sometimes say after there's been a long discussion: 'All right, let's cut the cackle; what does it mean in practical terms?'

Mrs Thatcher was, of course, asked — as all such women are — whether she had had to sacrifice her family in order to get to the top.

I didn't come into the House until the children were six. We could always start the day together and I used to make a point of trying to get home when they came back from school, so I saw them before they went to bed . . . . And I've been very lucky. If the children were ill, they were always ill on a Saturday. [*Observer*, 18 February 1979]

Seventy years after the militancy of the suffragettes, the situation of women in politics is, to put it mildly, disappointing. Women's activism is perhaps less conspicuous now, in Britain at least, than it has ever been. And it has been very conspicuous during most of our history. 'All public disturbances generally commence with the clamour of women' said the *Leicester Journal* in 1800 (cited in Stevenson, 1974, p.49). Many of these were centred on the issue of rising prices and unfair dealing in food. For example, in the same year as the *Leicester Journal*'s complaint:

A number of women . . . proceeded to Gosden wind-mill where, abusing the miller for serving them with brown flour, they seized on the cloth which he was then dressing . . . and cut it into a thousand pieces, threatening at the same time to serve all similar utensils he might in future attempt to use in the same manner. The Amazonian leader of this petticoated cavalcade afterwards regaled her associates with a guinea's worth of liquor at the Crab-Tree public house. [Thompson, 1971, p.82]

But in the eighteenth and early nineteenth century the political activity of women extended far beyond food riots. Lawrence Stone (1977, p.337) identifies 31 January 1642 as the first occasion in English history on which women 'took independent political action on the national level as women'.[3] Four hundred working women, artisans, shopgirls and labourers suffering from hardship as a result of the trade decline, petitioned the Houses of Lords and Commons for a change in economic policy. When the outraged Duke of Richmond cried 'Away with these women, we were best have a Parliament of women', the petitioners attacked him physically and broke his staff of

---

[3] Stone discounts women's recurrent role in economic protests as associated with their 'shopping' function. Since this is a particular viewpoint, his claim that 1642 was the first year in which women acted collectively on a national level may be similarly selective.

office (Stone, 1977, p.338). The next year, hundreds of women held the members of the House of Commons prisoner for several hours and in the end became so obstreperous that the guards attacked them.

The tradition of women's immersion in national and domestic political issues continued in the nineteenth century. As we saw in Chapter 1, it was on the foundation of working-class women's trade union agitation, particularly in the cotton towns of Lancashire, that the suffragettes built the force of their demand for the vote. If the Labour Party is today especially harsh to aspiring women politicians, it is negating its own history in so doing, for women's participation in trade union and radical politics in the nineteenth and early twentieth centuries was absolutely crucial to the development of the modern Labour Party. There were women supporters of the Labour movement more than twenty years before the modern Labour Party was born in 1900, from Helen Taylor (stepdaughter of John Stuart Mill), to Eleanor Marx (daughter of Karl Marx),[4] to Annie Besant, organizer of the striking London match girls in 1888 and many others. From 1906 to 1918, there was a special organization of Labour women, the Women's Labour League, initiated by Mrs Cawthorne, the wife of a dock labourer in Hull, who wrote to the secretary of the National Labour Representation Committee, Ramsay MacDonald, complaining that since women were affected by men's trade unionism they had a right to know more about it. The Women's Labour League devoted itself to enrolling all women in the fight for improvements in the social and economic conditions of the wage-earning class, but the range of issues it embraced was very wide — from conditions of work in the sweated industries to women jurors and magistrates, from the abolition of capital punishment to educational reforms, from pit-head baths to infant welfare clinics (Middleton, 1977). In the light of all this activity, it seems paradoxical that the reason why women in the Labour Party do not reach the top today is largely because of the strength of the trade union vote.[5]

The situation of women in the trade unions in many countries, Britain and the United States included, nowhere near represents their importance in production. Table 14.1 shows that, in the eleven years

---

[4] Male political activists do not, of course, have the names of their fathers (or mothers) tagged on to them in this way, despite the fact that politics runs in families for both men and women.

TABLE 14.1 *Women as a percentage of trade union membership, United Kingdom, 1966 – 1976*

| Year | Men | | Membership Women | | |
	No. (000s)	%	No. (000s)	%	Total (000s)
1966	8,003	78.0	2,256	22.0	10,259
1967	7,903	77.6	2,286	22.4	10,188
1968	7,829	76.8	2,362	23.2	10,191
1969	7,965	76.1	2,505	23.9	10,470
1970	8,437	75.5	2,741	24.5	11,178
1971	8,374	75.3	2,752	24.7	11,126
1972	8,445	74.4	2,905	25.6	11,351
1973	8,443	73.7	3,005	26.3	11,447
1974	8,579	73.0	3,176	27.0	11,755
1975	8,592	71.5	3,425	28.5	12,017
1976	8,816	71.2	3,560	28.8	12,376

Source: Equal Opportunities Commission (1978 – 9) Table 6.8, p.69.

from 1966 to 1976, the proportion of women in the membership of British trade unions rose from 22 per cent to 28.8 per cent, while in 1976 women were 39 per cent of the labour force. It is still true that far fewer women than men become shop stewards or full-time union officials (McCarthy, 1977). In the United States, some 12 per cent of employed women belong to trade unions and a quarter of all unions have no women members (Baxandall, 1976). The view prevails that women are difficult to organize because they are apathetic and/or concerned only with the next wage packet. But the male-dominated trade unions have done little to accommodate their organization and timetabling to the needs of women workers, whose work also includes running homes and servicing husbands and children.

In a sense, as Duverger (1955) pointed out, conventional forms of

[5] Labour women's poor participation at the Annual Party Conference is due chiefly to the fact that most trade union representatives are male. When women want to stand as candidates, there is the obstacle of the two lists held by Transport House. List A contains the names of those nominated by trade unions, and list B those nominated by the constituency parties. There are virtually no women on list A.

political organization such as trade unions have little to offer women, given the belief induced in them that men can be trusted to look after their interests. But in fact these bodies have not promoted issues of direct relevance to women. Their record on this score is poor compared with that of the women's trade union leagues that flourished in Britain and America between 1890 and 1925. Legislation for women workers, English classes for immigrant women, the education of both middle- and working-class women to a shared awareness of their situation, the support of women strikers — all these were prominent themes. Indeed, it seems that the American organizations went some way towards eroding class divisions between women, which is in anyone's eyes a truly revolutionary achievement (Jacoby, 1976).

As Rosalyn Baxandall says in her survey of American trade unions,

Individual contacts and confrontations with industrial management and indeed with male workers on the one hand, and governmental regulation on the other, are clearly no substitute for the sustained, massed power of the (female) working class. [Baxandall, 1976, p.267]

Or: militancy is not the same as militant trade unionism, and in view of the male hegemony of trade unions, women workers' refusal to join may add up to a militant, rational and politically conscious decision (Purcell, 1979). But does this suggest that separatist political organizations for women are the answer?

FEMINIST POLITICS

In 1970 the British women's liberation movement held its first national conference in Oxford. *Shrew*, the magazine of the women's liberation workshop, analysed media reports of the conference. *The Observer*'s reporter described its participants as 'young, violent, radical and very attractive with their long hair and maxi-coats', and mentioned that the bookstall sold the *Thoughts of Chairman Mao*. 'Militancy in the kitchen' was the heading of the *Times* report; the *Guardian*, which devoted only 4½ inches to their report, included one sentence describing the content of the conference. In the *Daily Telegraph* prominence was given to the heckling and call for order ('Squabbling as women talk of liberation'). The fact that 'one group of fathers ran a creche for 40 children left temporarily motherless' was noted. *New Society* conceded that the women were not only 'angry' but 'thoughtful'. The *Spectator* began 'To anyone interested in the suffragettes the news that a "women's weekend" was happening in 1970 was like the discovery of the coelacanth to a zoologist'. Incompetence was stressed (' . . . fighting by stacks of literature which could not be sold because the change was lost') and the conference participants were said to include 'the usual mud-coloured student crowd . . . a sprinkling of nostalgia, student anarchists, communist girls, clothes out of Dr Zhivago' (*Shrew*, April 1970). It hardly sounds like a highly organized and significant political movement. The concentration on details of appearance, on unrepresentative themes and moments of disorganization, conveys a scene of silly schoolgirls thoughtlessly engaging in an act of mild sabotage. No one would guess from this report that ten years later the women's movement would still be going strong. (Although one could perhaps guess that the same attitude of patronizing trivialization would still govern media responses to feminism.)

Feminist politics are self-consciously different from masculine politics. Organized feminism grew, on both its historically important occasions, out of women's dissatisfaction with masculine political organizations as representative bodies and strategies for change. Feminist political organizations have always, by their very existence, challenged the idea that women's interests are best served by participation in the conventional politics of party organization, election procedures and government by elected representatives of the people. But the modern women's liberation movement also challenges the basic framework of conventional political organization: its hierarchy, its impersonality, its pretended altruism.

The small group excluding men and devoted to consciousness-raising exhibits the two hallmarks of the modern women's liberation movement. The emphasis on the small group follows from the dissatisfaction with masculine politics, especially the deceits of participatory democracy in left-wing organizations, and the difficulty of mass communications communicating anything but what is, in the most reactionary sense, newsworthy. Certain precepts apply to the leaderless, structureless groups that are the main organizational form of the women's movement: no one must select herself or allow herself to be selected, even covertly, as the group's leader; representatives needed for external communication are chosen on a rotational basis;

no one's speech, experience or problems should dominate the group's internal communication; women should participate as equally as possible in all the group's activities. The lot system and the disc system are two strategies devised by American feminists for dealing with the way in which class and personality differences intrude into the group's experience. The lot system consist of two sets of lots (for creative tasks like writing papers and work tasks like dealing with the mail) and each person draws for each task. The disc system is designed to stop the monopolization of meetings by individuals:

Each member begins the meeting with a certain number of discs (say, twenty), and every time she speaks, other than to answer a simple 'Yes' or 'No', she must spend one disc. The first time this system was tried, the apocryphal story goes, no one in the room had any discs left after fifteen minutes. The second meeting was slow almost to silence because everyone was hoarding her discs. [Morgan, 1970, p.xxviii]

The idea of consciousness-raising as *the* political activity of feminist groups emerged hand-in-hand with the realization that the difficulties of women are a structural problem rather than a matter of individual neurosis. (This idea, gestated in the 1960s, but hardly mentioned before that, has still not caught on in many circles, as we have seen throughout this book.) Hence the necessity of raising consciousness: 'It is a huge emotional leap for an individual when a psychological situation in which he or she suffers the sense of failure to meet a social norm changes to a condition in which there is dignity as a fellow combatant' (McWilliams, 1974, p.160). Such a leap, on a mass basis, requires three preconditions: a widespread discordance between subjective reality and social norm; the opportunity for its victims to compare experiences; and some feeling of personal or collective efficacy in bringing about the kind of social change that can transform the material and psychological basis of oppression. Robin Morgan, in her introduction to the first collection of writings emerging out of the women's movement in America, thus said:

. . . *you* are women's liberation. This is not a movement one 'joins'. There are no rigid structures or membership cards. The Women's Liberation Movement exists where three or four friends or neighbours decide to meet regularly over coffee and talk about their personal lives. It also exists in the cells of women's jails, on the welfare lines, in the supermarket, the factory, the convent, the farm, the maternity ward, the streetcorner, the old ladies' home, the kitchen, the steno pool, the bed. It exists in your mind, and in the political and personal insights that you can contribute to change and shape and help its growth. It is frightening. It is very exhilirating. It is creating history . . . . [Morgan, 1970, p.xxxvi]

Several histories of the contemporary women's movement now exist. Joan Cassell had the idea suggested to her by her male thesis advisor (voyeurism is one way in which men have traditionally related to women). In her book *A Group Called Women* she offers the following description, based on her own observations, of a typical women's movement group meeting in the United States:

Four to fifteen women may arrive at a prospective member's home. The women usually form a rough circle: consciousness-raising guidelines recommend this . . . At the first meeting an introductory topic is selected. Whether the first discussion is intensely personal or comparatively reserved probably depends less on the temperaments of participants than on previous movement experience. Women with previous experience, or those desperate because of a personal crisis, can talk with devastating openness to a group of strangers.

Members frequently confess that the first meeting was unnerving. Problems of self-presentation arise. Those with previous movement experience have mastered the confessional mode, ritual phraseology, expected behaviours . . . Some groups have a nucleus of experienced women whose verbal militancy may dismay a novice. Many women drop out or are in effect ejected from groups when they cannot accept the ideological assertion of the 'oppression' of women.

After two or three meetings, members have some sense of each other; faces acquire names, personalities, and brief histories. Every group has its own atmosphere, its own implied assumptions, its own modus operandi. After two to three months, an extraordinary feeling of intimacy and trust can develop . . . .

Eating together becomes significant; members may dine together before meetings or take turns bringing refreshments. Women traditionally provide food for men and children, and sharing food among a group of women seems to have great symbolic meaning for members . . .

Confidences are shared at a deeper level than the first outpourings. Members learn one another's histories, and life crises are lived through by the group. The concern and support of the group extend to tangible measures: babysitting, co-signing a lease, legal aid. Members frequently start to meet outside the group: they will go to the movies or theater, initiate projects, borrow cars, share apartments, to experience closeness and intimacy. [Cassell, 1977, pp.35 – 7]

Consciousness-raising is not therapy, since the proper aim of therapy is to breed adjustment (with a leader and the led), while the idea of consciousness-raising is the questioning of the need for the therapeutic treatment of individuals altogether. Nevertheless, a contradiction obtains in that an interest group whose function it is to maximize power is organizing itself in terms of a rejection of power. There is a tendency, as Sheila Rowbotham (1979, p.41) has put it, towards preoccupation 'with living a liberated life rather than becoming a movement for the liberation of women'.

Whatever else feminist politics have done in the last decade, they have broadened the concept of the political. In saying 'our politics begin with our feelings' — rather than with our exercise of the franchise — feminists are drawing attention to the fact that the field of what is usually considered political is a created one. Politics, in any and every sense, is about power, and it is as much about the power that men, wittingly or unwittingly, exercise over women as it is about the power that presidents and prime ministers wield over nations.

MATRIARCHY: FACT OR FANTASY?

Did matriarchal societies ever exist? No question in the history of ancient women has generated more controversy. No topic has been approached by both traditional scholars and feminists with less objectivity. How gratifying it would be for a feminist scholar to discover that in pre-history, a period far longer than recorded history, women were not the second sex at all. Then we could rebuff all the scholars since Aristotle who have complacently been stating that women are by nature inferior. [Pomeroy, 1976, p.217]

Feminist movements give rise to a quest for origins — of women's subordination and a golden age before that when things were not as they are and thus can offer the promise of a different future. It is an idea clung to with tenacity by some feminists in the contemporary women's liberation movement, for example Evelyn Reed, who in an early pamphlet (1969) invoked the work of the Victorian anthropologists to construct a portrait of pre-class society in which women, 'neither sanctified nor degraded', ruled over men.

This mirror-image of the usual emancipation story is entrancing and clearly important as a motif in the search for a more comfortable history of women. However, its importance lies 'not in its historical veracity, which is doubtful, but in its vision of a domain of women's power' (Webster, 1975, p.151) — a type of power that in its non-possessiveness and non-violence differs from that typically exercised by men.

The first thing to be said is that matriarchy, defined as the class rule of women, is a situation that does not preclude, but on the other hand does not equal, individual women assuming political leadership roles in any society. No one would claim that Britain today is a matriarchy simply because it has a female monarch and a female prime minister. In considering what kind of power women actually have, a distinction between power and authority is helpful. Power is 'the ability to act effectively on persons or things, to take or secure favourable decisions which are not of right allocated to the individuals or their roles'; authority is 'the right to make a particular decision and to command obedience' (Smith, 1960, pp.18 – 9). The important difference between the two is that authority is recognized and legitimized power. Authority implies power; power does not imply authority, and indeed may exist in a society totally unrecognized (or at least not validated) by anybody.

What women have most of is power rather than authority. The following two examples are disparate in nature but make the same point. The first relates to the experience of an all-female group teaching English to immigrants in a British local education authority area; the seond to the use of sexual insults by female militants in the West Cameroon.

(1) In the British local education authority of Hutton (the name is fictitious to preserve anonymity) all the decision-makers (the director and the six assistant controllers) are male. The Language Training Group (LTG) is an all-female voluntary group, whose self-appointed function is the teaching of English to immigrants and a general concern with the local needs of ethnic minority groups. Its director and executive committee members are all female. The LTG set up classes (6 in 1974, 22 in 1978) jointly with the local college of further education; it also appointed a language scheme coordinator and set up an office with clerical assistance and equipment. (The money for these activities came mainly from an urban aid grant.) As the group's activities expanded, so did its awareness that the problems of ethnic minorities in Hutton extended far beyond the obvious linguistic needs. This brought them into contact with other local authority services:

health, careers advice and so on. Eventually, the appointment of a new male education advisor to the Education Department with a special brief to consider the teaching of English as a second language led the experience of the LTG to be widely tapped as the basis for a policy directive about the wide-ranging and largely unmet needs of ethnic minority groups in Hutton (Cohen, 1979).

(2) The Bakweri live on the slopes of the Cameroon mountain, a volcano lying on the West coast of Africa. The term 'titi ikoli'

comprehends the following associations: 'a woman's underparts' (the genitals, anus, and buttocks), and the insult of these; and 'women's secrets', and the revealing of these. At the same time it is associated with certain types of mandatory female sanctions which follow upon such insult.

The insult is typically envisaged in the form of an accusation that the sexual parts of women smell. If such an insult has been uttered to a Bakweri woman before a witness, she is supposed immediately to call out all the other women of the village. The circumstances having been recounted, the women then run and pluck vegetation from the surrounding bush, which they tie around their waists. Converging again upon the offender, they demand immediate recantation and a recompense. If their demands are not met they all proceed to the house of the village head. The culprit will be brought forward, and the charges laid. If the insult is proved to have been made, he will be fined a pig of a certain size for distribution to the group of women, or its money equivalent, plus something extra, possibly salt, a fowl, or money, for the woman who has been directly insulted. The women then surround him and sing songs accompanied by obscene gestures. All the other men beat a hasty retreat, since it is expected that they will be ashamed to stay and watch while their wives, sisters, sisters-in-law and old women join the dance. The culprit must stay, but he will try to hide his eyes. Finally, the women retire victoriously to divide the pig among them. [Ardener, 1975, pp.29−30]

Similar sanctions were in force among neighbouring communities relating not only to sexual insults thrown at women by men but to such offences as the beating of a pregnant woman, incest, the pregnancy of a nursing mother in the two years after the birth of a child, and the maltreatment of old women. Among the Bakweri during the late colonial period, formal court procedures replaced the traditional direct sanctions. For example, in 1957 a dispute was taken before the Bonjongo court by Mary Ekumbe and other women of Mafanja against Efende Mwendeley of Mafanja:

The plaintiff claims jointly for self and other women of Mafanja Bakweri Native Town the sum of £20, being damages for defamation of character and slander on about the 14th February 1956 at about 2 p.m. In that Defendant did on 14th February 1956 at about 2 p.m. meet with Madam Therisia Ese at Mafanja town and used the following words in Bakweri language: 'Ngwete ja varana isasosa imbondo jawu. Eveli ndi varana vase. Ese nyi? Ema linga ema na mende o vewa. Ndi na suu mwango.' The above speech in Bakweri language means that the women in this village have smelling bottoms and are not washing their bottoms. [Ardener, 1975, p.31]

After some deliberation, the court ruled in favour of the women, awarding them £10 damages and costs of £4.0.6d.

Example (1) demonstrates the weakness of any concept of a 'political system' that ignores the wider political community — in this case that of an all-female pressure/support group that has influence on decision-making without any direct access to it. Example (2) is doubly meaningful: what is at issue is not purely the ability of the women collectively to repudiate the sexual insults of men, but the imputed masculine devaluation of independent womanhood. The women react *as a group*: to abuse one is to abuse all. Female genitals are a marker of women's collective identity in opposition to men, a biological symbol of their self-esteem accepted by them rather than designated as an overarching role constraint by men.

The effective use of power by women in Hutton and Bakweri points to the fact that juridical – political authority is only one measure of women's political status. It is for this reason that, during epochs that have denied them political 'rights', women have actually been able to make a fairly forceful impression on society. This is true, for example, of the early Middle Ages in Europe, where such customs as identifying people by their mothers' names and the holding of significant portions of land by women are clues to the key economic roles of women in a family-based property system (Herlihy, 1976). Power — of every kind — does have to do with control of resources. The development of private property and the rising importance of production for exchange do tend, as Engels (1891) said, to result in women's domestication and juridical subordination to men. Alternatively, they can be seen to produce an intensification of women's family-based power.

The opposition between the public world of men and the private world of women (a theme mentioned earlier in this book) does not mean that women's power is confined to the nuclear family, the home or the kinship system. Cynthia Nelson (1973), analysing the two social worlds of the tent and the camp in nomadic societies of the Middle East today, concludes that, although disparagingly treated by male ethnographers, women's so-called 'domestic power' has profound ramifications. Women arrange marriages, and marriage ties are of great political significance. They influence the political careers of men by making and breaking their reputations; policy decisions taken by men publicly take account of women's reactions. Thus, the women lack public power but are not powerless; they are inferior, according to men's judgements of them, but not necessarily according to their own.

Although the public – private distinction works for some societies, it is important to note that it does not work for all. Sarah Skar (1979) found that it did not fit the egalitarian social organization of the Quechua Indians of highland Peru. If the private domain is the house, a family's home, the Quechua household is anomalous. It consists of two structures, one of which is a kitchen and a pen for small domestic animals, the other of which is the household's warehouse and contains maize, dried meat, agricultural tools, festive clothing, etc. 'Living' is done mostly in the courtyard or under the overhanging eaves of the buildings. All household members have rights over the contents of the warehouse, which are guarded by night and day. However, the concept of ownership is not communal but individual. At the same time, production and consumption are carried out by the household as a unit: men and women share most work (productive and childrearing) equally. What is produced is consumed; any excess is bartered with another household. In other words, the household is a corporation, and in no way the world of the female sex exclusively.

Matriarchy, then, is no mere shibboleth. But to posit a past in which women controlled everyone and everything is as falsifying a claim as the doctrine that women are universally powerless. The truth lies inbetween, and beyond the constraints of the model that says politics is only about the officially recognized right to have and hold power. Many cultures have matriarchies in their mythology, but it is revealing to look at the uses to which they are put. Take the tale of the Mundurucu Indians, whose men own the village's highly valued and highly symbolic sacred musical instruments. These originated, according to legend, when three women heard music coming from a lagoon in the forest:

They investigated but saw nothing except fish swimming in the waters. Each woman caught one of these fish, and it immediately turned into a karoko [sacred musical instrument] giving a set of three. The women played these instruments daily until discovered by one of the men, who induced them to bring their find to the village. They did so, but the power contained within the karoko enabled them to seize the men's roles and prerogatives. The women occupied the men's house, and the men lived in the dwellings. While the females did little but play the instruments, the men had to make manioc flour, fetch water and firewood and care for the children. Their ignominy was complete when the women visited the dwellings at night to force their attentions upon them. ('Just as we do to them today' added one informant.) But the women did not hunt, and therefore could not make the ceremonial offerings of meat to the karoko spirits. The men, as the hunters, threatened to withhold the offerings of game, and thereby incur the displeasure of the spirits, unless the women yielded the instruments. The women were forced to submit and sex roles became as they are today. But the men must still guard the karoko from the women if they are to keep their dominance. [Murphy, 1959, pp.92–3]

In other words, the purpose of the matriarchal vision is to confirm patriarchy: women didn't only rule, their rule was defeated (Bamberger, 1974). It is highly significant that many such myths regard the holding of power by men as contingent on women's continued and forced acquiescence. Moreover, the mythical justification for gender role divisions is, interestingly, not that these are set by nature. There is no apology for the fact that they are arranged by men.

An important point is that matriarchy is not the same thing as matrilineality. The fact that inheritance operates through women is no guarantee of female power in any sense. Analysing the 'puzzle' of matrilineal systems has been a favourite preoccupation of ethnographers, who regard the central problem as 'how to combine continuity and recruitment through females with control by the *men* of the lineage' (Fox, 1967, p.113). This is a particularly apt illustration of the shortcomings of conventional ethnography. For is kinship a power game? Why should societies be seen as power structures? Whose point of view prevails in this interpretation? There are good grounds, as we shall see in the next chapter, for regarding patriarchy itself as a myth.

A Subject Gender
What are women's studies?

CHAPTER FIFTEEN

Studying Women

Clearly, the bee crushed by the passing elephant is at a relative, indeed a fatal, disadvantage compared to the larger beast, but merely to say that it has been 'oppressed' by the elephant seems to be missing some essential points. The same would, of course, be true of similar statements made about a bee which fatally stung an elephant. [Ardener, 1975, p.xxi]

What is women's studies? What is its relationship to gender inequality, to organized feminism and to the academic establishment? What are its unique problems and perspectives? Is it 'really' a subject?

A GROWING INDUSTRY

The editors of the first British reader on the subject say

. . . we ourselves are not able to offer a neat definition. What we can say is that women's studies is both a growing subject in its own right and an approach to traditional subjects. It is attracting attention in a number of disciplines from sociology to biology, and this growth is a result of a demand which has come primarily from women as part of their desire to understand more fully the past and present position of their sex . . .[Thus] Women's studies, however defined, depends upon a concept of female inequality. [Bristol Women's Studies Group, 1979, pp.3, 5]

Women's studies is the academic offshoot of the women's liberation movement. Those who joined it in the late 1960s and early 1970s reflected that they did not know much about women — about female sexuality and psychology, about women's history, literature and sociology. In the States, black studies set a precedent and educational administrators did not resist the introduction of women's studies as much as they might otherwise have done (Deckard, 1979). But women's studies were not only a way of rediscovering the position of women; of decisive importance in their growth

> was the recognition that mere formal rights in education would have little effect on women's lives in terms of guaranteeing them equal opportunities, as long as they were accompanied by educational contents which continued to display . . . traditional role stereotypes and . . . stubborn superstitions. [Schöpp-Schilling, 1979, p.105]

In this sense, women's studies aims to change the content of education, teaching methods and the structure of educational institutions as a prelude to ridding society of its divisive gender role stereotypes.

There are, however, problems. In Britain, the Manchester conference on women's studies in December 1976 identified the main one as the fact that women's studies is both academic and non-academic: originating *outside* the educational structure, it has radical implications for this structure that cannot be accommodated within it. A second problem derives from the first. Is women's studies a mode of academic consciousness-raising designed to produce feminists out of non-feminists? If so, should it exclude men? What is the relationship between academic work and feminist political work? Yet a third dilemma of women's studies derives from the fact that it is not a subject in its own right. It is interdisciplinary, or, rather, anti-disciplinary.

In the United States, there are now about 275 women's studies programmes, and over 4000 courses in colleges and universities; 90 of these grant degrees and 3 give doctorates (Pastine, 1979). Eloise Snyder (1979) describes three phases in the development of women's studies in the United States. In the first, women's studies concentrated on gaining acceptance for 'credited' courses (courses offered for academic credit) dealing with sex discrimination. In the second phase, women's studies involved a general reassessment of academic literature as a resource for learning about women's situation. Phase three followed from this, for feminists appreciated that fresh theoretical and methodological approaches were needed to eradicate the sexism of women's academic invisibility and/or marginal status.

In Britain the women's studies movement has had a short, less militant and somewhat telescoped history. At the present time there are at least 30 universities with women's studies courses. Mostly these take the form of options in undergraduate courses or MSc courses. There are many women's studies courses as well in adult education, WEA courses and extramural studies: 25 such courses were advertised in the London area alone in the October issue of *Spare Rib* (Murgatroyd, 1979). Most existing women's studies courses operate within conventional disciplinary boundaries for the pragmatic reason that it is easier to introduce new courses into the disciplinary status quo than to change it. (Adult education, WEA and extramural courses are inclined towards greater radicalism because of their non-establishment base.)

Surveys of university-based women's studies in Germany (Schöpp-Schilling, 1979) and Australia (Walker and Smith, 1979) show a similar pattern. Almost every German university has a women's studies course, the majority offered in the social sciences. However, contrary to the situation in the United States, there are not many accredited courses, and most women's studies courses are taught by untenured women faculty members on short, part-time contracts. Most Australian universities offer women's studies courses, chiefly within arts or social science degrees. Lack of tenure is a general problem. At the Australian National University, women constituted 19.3 per cent of total academic staff in 1975, but only 5.7 per cent were tenured. Women's studies courses tend to be taught by young, untenured women with a stronger feminist than academic identification. Combined with the current economic recession, this means that the situation is highly unstable and many courses disappear when the untenured staff leave. In other words, the position and fate of women's studies courses is inseparable from the social destiny of women.

KEEPING QUIET

I think it's a legend that half the population of the world is female; where on earth are they keeping them all? [Russ, 1977, p.204]

Women's studies begins in the places where women are absent, for 'it is never safe to argue from silence'. (Petersen and Wilson, 1976, p.7)

Just as organized feminism breaks the silence and opens women's mouths on the matter of their supposed contentment, so women's studies asks, repetitively, where are the women and why are their voices not heard? Women are not absent from history, or art, or society or whatever; they are present in distorted and distorting images, and mammoth archeological expeditions are required to bring the reality of their existence to our attention. To give some examples: in detective fiction, there are many female counterparts of Sherlock Holmes (what I mean, of course, is that Sherlock Holmes is the male counterpart of many wise and courageous female sleuths) (Slung, 1976). The culture of youth is not without its female half, but the space negotiated by girls has effectively excluded boys, adults, teachers and researchers (McRobbie and Garber, 1975). Although Judaism, Christianity and Islam are in striking contrast to the world's other religious traditions in having a male God, it is worth noting that there was a considerable female imagery for God in the gospels, revelations and teachings rejected for inclusion in the New Testament (Pagels, 1976). The seven lines of military advice spoken by Andromache to Hector in the Iliad were said by early critics to be inauthentic because military advice is not a feminine function, and sexist scholarship is also responsible for a denudation of female power: the Greek verb 'basileuo' is translated as 'to rule' when applied to males and 'to be the wife of a king' when applied to females (Pomeroy, 1976).

What Sheila Rowbotham has to say about 'Women's Liberation and the New Politics' is applicable both to feminism and its academic counterpart, the study of women:

Thinking is difficult when the words are not your own. Borrowed concepts are like passed-down clothes: they fit badly and do not give confidence; we lumber awkwardly about in them . . . .

First there is the paralysis. Their words stick in your throat . . . There is not only the paralysis, there is the labour of making connections. Theory . . . . makes reality intelligible. But this theory is constructed from the experience of the dominators and consequently reflects the world from their point of view. They, however, present it as the summation of the world as it is . . . . [Rowbotham, 1973c, pp.4 – 6]

An anthropologist, studying the legal system of a Mexican community, followed (masculine) ethnographical tradition in regarding marital disputes as unimportant, but came to see the error in this viewpoint:

Like others, I focused my attention on the 'big' cases . . . But as I worked with my field data, I began to realize that an appalling amount of legal time and energy was being spent on domestic quarrels. In simple economic terms, more working time was lost and more bottles of liquor were bought to calm women's angry hearts than for all other kinds of disputes combined. It might have been easy to overlook the wider social consequences of any single marital dispute, but the cumulative result of all marital disputes could hardly be ignored. [Collier, 1974, pp.93 – 4]

To make visible the invisible is not a simple additive formula: traditional history/sociology/economics/psychology/philosophy/ anthropology/literature + women's studies = the whole story. As Joanna Russ, the science fiction writer, has observed (1972), familiar plots do not come from thin air. 'Heroine' is not just another name for 'hero'; heroines are modest maidens, wicked temptresses, beautiful bitches, faithful wives, possessive mothers; what they are not are plain women pursuing their own desires unencumbered by relations with men. Nevertheless, in some fields women's achievements are not hard to find — once one looks for them. For example, against the habitual complaint that art has not been a female domain can be set the fact that throughout the history of the Western world (not to mention others) the tradition of female art has been strong; from fifth-century nuns who engaged in exquisite illustrated calligraphy to Lavinia Fontana (1552 – 1614), official painter to the Papal court (and mother of eleven); from Marie-Anne Collot (1748 – 1821), sculptor of the famous equestrian statue of Peter the Great in Leningard to Mary Cassatt (1845 – 1926), gifted protégée (later enemy) of Degas; from Dora Carrington (1893 – 1932), painter, illustrator, furniture-designer and member of the renowned Bloomsbury group to Kathe Kollwitz (1867 – 1945), sculptor of war, hunger, poverty and motherhood. As Karen Petersen and J.J. Wilson (1976, p.6) comment in their recent attempt at restoring women to art history, 'The only places we have not found women artists are where we have not looked'. Moreover, a concentration on portable painting as *the* art form belittles women's excellence in other artistic fields — ceramics, embroidery, lacemaking, jewellery, metalworking, woodcarving, interior design — fields that only by a perverted twist of logic may be dismissed as unimportant 'domestic industries' (Davis and Goodall, 1979; Callen, 1979). In accordance with this 'perverted' logic, however, recent moves by feminist artists to usher forward a more woman-centred art have met with heavy resistance. Mary Kelly's

'Postpartum Document', an exhibition that displayed used nappy liners as statements of motherhood, appalled art critics in Britain in 1976. A painting of a mother looking at her naked baby is one thing (*pace* a million Madonnas), infant shit on the wall something else indeed.

Similarly, sociology and anthropology have operated with a selective eye which has cast an omnipresent shadow over the structure and content of this book.[1]

Although sociology is defined as the scientific study of society . . . sociology in many respects is the male science of male society . . . Not only are the majority of sociologists men and not only would a ranking based on professional status . . . tend to be male-heavy, but, more important, the concentration of efforts tends to be weighted largely toward content areas representing male interests and values.

With regard to the content areas, emphasis tends to be put on such concerns as analyses of competition and strategies of status aggressiveness, including preoccupations with power, men's work, and conflict, all of which typify society only if women . . . are excluded. [Snyder, 1979b, p.40]

Among the many consequences of this elliptic vision, is the fact that

There is . . no sociological theory of feelings and emotions. This is not because the people we study do not take as real the 'fact' that they feel. Nor is it because a person's job, sex, age, ethnic background or religion is known to be unrelated to how he or she feels in certain situations. It is not, in other words, because the data are not there or are not potentially sociological.

It is because masculine values define 'cognitive, intellectual, or rational dimensions of experience as superior to being emotional or sentimental' (Hochschild, 1975, pp.280 – 1).

So far as anthropology is concerned,

We are, for practical purposes, in a male world. The study of women is on a level a little higher than the study of ducks and fowls they commonly own — a mere bird-watching indeed. [Ardener, 1972, p.136]

The path to the top of the profession for female anthropologists is not ideally a feminist one, and

to survive, women have had to learn to ignore the patronising hostility of male

---

[1] See Oakley (1974b, Chapter 1) on sexism in sociology. Two recent contributions to this critique are D. Smith (1979) and Eichler (1980).

anthropologists; jokes about 'blue stockings' or suggestions that women have succeeded in their profession only by seducing or being seduced by famous male anthropologists. The jokes in fact highlight the two roles generally open to women with careers — i.e. the role of 'pseudo man', or the role of the woman who plays on her femininity in order to get on. Most of us, I suspect, adopt a 'pseudo male' approach . . . [Bujra, 1973, p.2]

Pseudo-masculinity ensures the continued silence of most women. It may also be the case that the voices are there but speak disruptively of female achievements in a male world. Two examples from psychoanalysis and science follow to illustrate this point, an important theme of women's studies in its effort to undo the myth of women's passivity.

Karen Horney

Freud's theory of feminine sexual development (see pp.71 – 2) did not, as one is sometimes led to believe, develop in a vacuum. It was actually worked out in relation to an alternative set of propositions put forward principally by the female analyst, Karen Horney. Born in Hamburg, Germany, in 1885, Horney was founder of the American Institute for Psychoanalysis, the American Association for the Advancement of Psychoanalysis and the American Journal of Psychoanalysis. She published six books, including *The Neurotic Personality of Our Time* (1937) and *New Ways in Psychoanalysis* (1939).

The essence of Horney's position on feminine development was that vaginal awareness in little girls existed early, rather than, as Freud said, only from puberty, and was a separate phenomenon from a later defensive penis envy. She made a distinction between pre- and post-oedipal penis envy, which, since it also appeared in a paper by Ernest Jones, was subsequently credited to him. Freud was quite nasty about Horney and her views. In 1931, in a paper on female sexuality, he appended a footnote:

It is to be anticipated that male analysts with feminist sympathies and our women analysts will disagree with what I have said here. They will hardly fail to object that such notions (as the idea that female sexuality is 'normal' and primary) have their origins in man's 'masculinity complex' and are meant to justify his innate propensity to disparage and suppress women. The opponents of those who reason thus will think it quite comprehensible that members of the female sex should refuse to accept what appears to gainsay their eagerly coveted equality with men. [cited in Rubins, 1978, pp.37 – 8]

This broadside was followed in his last book with

We shall not be very surprised if a woman analyst who has not been sufficiently convinced of her own desire for a penis also fails to assign adequate importance to that factor in her patients. [cited in Rubins, 1978, p.142]

No, indeed, we shall not. Many of Horney's ideas have crept into modern psychoanalytic knowledge, being subsequently 'discovered' by other analysts. Her biographer, Jack Rubins, remarks that 'It was as if her name had been expunged and history rewritten in the best party line tradition' (Rubins, 1978, p.xii)[2]

Rosalind Franklin[3]

Rosalind Franklin was a talented physical chemist who, after several years in Paris working on the X-ray analysis of three-dimensional forms of carbon moved in 1951 to King's College, London, to build up the X-ray diffraction Unit there. Franklin understood that she was to develop a method for studying the structure of DNA. Another member of the Unit's staff, Maurice Wilkins, also had an interest in DNA. Franklin and Wilkins did not see eye to eye at all.

In the autumn of the same year, James Dewey Watson arrived from Chicago to work on the structure of DNA at the Cavendish laboratory in Cambridge. There he met Francis Crick, and the two men both agreed that the structure of DNA was the most important subject to work on. DNA not only held the secret of the gene, the unit of heredity of living organisms: it was the golden molecule that promised a Nobel Prize.

In April 1953 Watson and Crick announced the structure of DNA in the magazine *Nature*. In 1958 Rosalind Franklin died, at the age of 37. In 1962 the Nobel Prize was awarded to Watson, Crick and Wilkins

---

[2] Rubins makes an interesting observation when he says (p.xiii) that he received very contrasting pictures of Horney from the people he spoke to: 'frail and strong, open and reticent, aloof and "with you", distant and close, caring, mothering and uncaring, unsympathetic, loving and unloving, dominating and self-effacing, manipulative and compliant, a leader and a follower, fair and mean'.

[3] The material in this section is taken from Hubbard (1976, 1979)

for their work. Neither the *Nature* account nor Watson's subsequent bestseller *The Double Helix* (1968) acknowledged the importance of Franklin's work, though a more detailed technical account in the *Proceedings of the Royal Society* (Crick and Watson, 1954) makes it clear that both the X-ray data provided by Franklin and her co-workers and Franklin's own interpretation of this were absolutely crucial to the conclusions about the structure of DNA arrived at by Watson and Crick. *The Double Helix* describes the process whereby Wilkins kept Watson and Crick informed of the progress of Franklin's work; this included showing them her X-ray pictures. Franklin is portrayed in *The Double Helix* as Wilkins' uppity assistant who had to be put in her place so that Wilkins could 'maintain a dominant position that would allow him to think unhindered about DNA' (Watson, 1968, p.20); in fact she and Watson occupied equivalent positions. (Watson also discusses her lack of femininity and her 'unattractive' hair, clothes and grooming.)

THE PHALLACY OF PATRIARCHY?

The significance of Copernican innovations was less that the sun rather than the earth was declared to be the center of the solar system than that the position of the observer was no longer fixed and could no longer be disattended in interpreting observations. [Smith, 1979, p.183]

Studying women means asking how patriarchy as a system of thought has effectively concealed women's presence and power. My examples here are witchcraft, and the idea that human society grew out of a primal epoch in which men hunted and women sat in caves minding babies.

Wicked Women[4]

In 1486 Pope Innocent VIII asked Heinrich Kramer and James Sprenger to route out witchcraft in Northern Germany. Kramer and Sprenger wrote *Malleus Maleficarum* (literally 'Hammer of Witches')

---

[4] I am indebted to Elyse Dodgson and the girls of Vauxhall Manor School, London, for this title which they created for a dramatic production on the theme of witchcraft.

which, with Papal blessing, became the accepted legal authority and practical manual on witchcraft for the whole of Europe over many centuries. It went through thirteen editions before 1520, and was printed in a size suitable for carrying in pockets. It is not known how many women were killed for witchcraft, but a number of estimates put the figure at several million in the three centuries following the *Malleus*'s first appearance (the estimates vary from 30,000 to 9 million or more — see Daly, 1979, p.183). Kramer and Sprenger said that witchcraft is a wickedness inherent in women through a natural weakness that makes them creatures of lust. More childlike and impressionable than men, they are, said Kramer and Sprenger, peculiarly open to the persuasions of the devil, and their 'slippery tongues' make them easy communicators of the art of evil (gossip, an activity seen as ineluctably feminine, makes women powerful).

However, according to Barbara Ehrenreich and Deidre English (1973) writing some five centuries later, witches were scientists and healers of the people. Ehrenreich and English argue a hidden connection between women accused of witchcraft, the traditional management by women of birth as untrained midwives and the historical importance of women physicians and nurses before health and illness became the province of a predominantly male medical 'profession'.

It is clear from historical records that trying to cure the sick was an important criterion for witchcraft. In the Church's view, sickness was divinely induced and could only be divinely relieved: therefore every other treatment must be sinful magic — whether it worked or not. Witches were 'wise-women' (the two words have a common root) and 'old wives' (Chamberlain, in press). Bridget Bostock, of Church Coppenhall in Cheshire, was described in the *Gentleman's Magazine* in 1748 thus:

She cures the blind, the deaf, the lame of all sorts, the rheumatic, King's evil, histeric fits, falling fits, shortness of breath, dropsy, palsy, leprosy, cancers, and, in short, almost every thing, except the French disease [syphilis] which she will not meddle with . . . People come three score miles around. In our lane, where there has not been two coaches seen before these 12 years, now three or four pass in a day; and the poor come in cartloads . . . So many people of fashion now come to her, that several of the poor country people make a comfortable subsistence by holding their horses. In short, the poor, the rich, the lame, the blind and the deaf, all pray for her and bless her, but [significantly] the doctors curse her. [Quoted in Hole, 1977, pp.135 – 6]

Midwifery as a witch's occupation has as long a history as healing. Kramer and Sprenger declared 'No one does more harm to the Catholic faith than midwives'. Henry Boguet's 1590 manual of witches observed that

those midwives and wise women who are witches are in the habit of offering to Satan the little children which they deliver, and then of killing them, before they have been baptised, by thrusting a large pin into their brains. There have been those who have confessed to having killed more than 40 children in this way. They do even worse; for they kill them while they are in their mothers' wombs [Quoted in Parinder, 1958, p.51]

Thus, when the Church and the emerging medical profession clamped down on witches, they were at the same time appealing against the female control of childbirth by opposing the power of midwives as autonomous managers of birth (see Oakley, 1976, for a fuller discussion of this).

Witchcraft is also important in non-European cultures, especially in Africa. Both in Africa and Europe, the old, the impoverished and otherwise socially marginal are most likely to be accused of witchcraft, and witchcraft accusations can be seen as a means of accommodating change and of sustaining certain central moral values and institutions (Macfarlane, 1970). Witches are both insiders and outsiders and are therefore prone to flourish in an atmosphere of ambiguous social relations (Douglas, 1970). A further common aspect is that it is particularly *groups* of women who are liable to be suspected of witchcraft, as in the idea of the Witches' Sabbat. Indeed in Europe, it was assumed that in order to be a witch a woman would have to be in communion with other witches. [5]

For this reason modern feminists have been irresistibly drawn to the study of witchcraft. WITCH was an eponym adopted by some of the early American feminist groups: Women's Independent Taxpayers, Consumers and Homemakers; Women Infuriated at Taking Care of Hoodlums; Women Inspired to Commit Herstory, etc. The first of these sang, appropriately,

---

[5] African witchcraft is somewhat different in this respect. See the contributions in Marwick (1970).

Double, bubble, war and rubble,
When you mess with women, you'll be in trouble.
We're convicted of murder if abortion is planned.
Convicted of shame if we don't have a man,
Convicted of conspiracy if we fight for our rights,
And burned at the stake when we stand up to fight.
Double, bubble, war and rubble,
When you mess with women, you'll be in trouble.
We curse your empire to make it fall —
When you take on one of us, you take on us all! [Morgan, 1970, p.551]

Mary Daly (1979) in *Gyn/Ecology* takes a similar line, seeing the massacre of female witches as an attempt to eliminate all those women who lived 'outside the control of the patriarchal family' and who, by so doing, presented the eccentric and challenging option of a self-centred existence.

The phenomenon of witchcraft is allied to mysticism, heretical religions, spirit possession and 'hysteria' as manifestations of women's inability either to acquiesce in, or openly to subvert, a masculine version of society. When Margery Kempe (1373 – 1438), an illiterate brewer married to a Norfolk tax collector, nearly died in her fourteenth childbirth and saw a vision of 'devils opening their mouths all inflamed with burning waves of fire' (Mahl and Koon, 1979, p.25), she concluded, not unreasonably, that God had asked her to abandon her husband and the world. Jane Lead (1624 – 1704), not unlike Florence Nightingale (see p.102), found the life of an upper-middle-class daughter unbearably restricting; and, at the age of 15 when dancing, heard a voice that said 'Cease from this, I have another Dance to lead thee in; for this is Vanity'. Years later, after an unsatisfactory marriage, she had a vision of

'an overshadowing bright Cloud and in the midst of it the Figure of a Woman'. Three days later the luminous figure reappeared, saying 'Behold me as thy Mother'. Six days later the Woman promised to 'transfigure my self in thy mind; and there open the Spring of Wisdom and Understanding'

and went on to prophesy that

'This is the great Wonder to come forth, a Woman Cloathed with the Sun . . . with the Globe of this world under her feet . . . with a Crown beset with stars, plainly declaring that to her is given the Command and

Power . . . to create and generate spirits in her own express likeness . . . '
[Smith, 1979, pp.3, 4]

Being possessed by spirits can, as anthropologist I.M. Lewis (1966)
shows in a discussion of rebellious women among the Somali pastoral
nomads of North East Africa, be an underhand strategy for gaining
the redress of wrongs not publicly accepted as legitimate. But, to come
full circle, we may also say that to see female spirit possession purely
in social – functional terms is to ignore the importance of spirit
possession rituals as counterparts of the witch's healing role. Among
the Luvale of Zambia,

Mothers undergo spirit possession rituals for their own illnesses and on behalf
of their sick children . . .
Traditional spirit possession cults are multipurpose: performances take
place for a woman's illness or her natality problems, for her ailing children, or
prophylactically to prevent miscarriage, stillbirths, and illness or death of a
child. For those who would consider that female possession cults reflect social
tensions alone rather than physiological ailments, the . . . data concerning
Luvale women's ailments show that this is not so.

What this means is that

A Luvale woman's reproductive power is ritually and physically channeled
and transformed through membership in possession cults, to prepare her to
become specialist, expert, and priestess serving and preserving the wider
community. [Spring, 1978, pp.172 – 4, 188]

Man the Hunter
My second example of how women's studies have disturbed
conventional scholarship concerns what we may take to be the origin
myth of Western culture. After Adam's rib became Eve and Eve
managed to turn herself into a wicked woman, human society, so the
myth goes, was made up of archetypal outgoing male heroes and
submissive home(cave)-loving women: men hunted while women
endlessly gestated, lactated and kept the home fires burning.

I have described elsewhere (Oakley, 1974a, Chapter 7), some of the
main historical and logical falsities contained in this myth, not the
least of which is the fact that it is used to justify present patterns of
discrimination against women (see Tiger, 1969; Goldberg, 1977, for
two examples). However, recent work by Nancy Tanner and Adrienne
Zihlman (1978), and Sally Slocum (1975), among others, has shown

how the Man the Hunter myth owes its own origins to the androcentrism of archeology and anthropology confronting the available evidence of hominid evolution.

Humans and apes share a common ancestor; indeed, the divergence is relatively recent (some 4 – 6 million years ago); the crucial moment in human adaptation occurred when populations of apes moved from the forests to the savannas, where a more plentiful food supply existed. In the new ecology, it was not hunting and meat-eating that enabled humans-to-be to survive, but the consumption of plant foods acquired through gathering. By means of a dietary specialization, in which less meat and more plant food (fruit, vegetables, seeds, nuts, roots) were eaten, humans-to-be carved out a special niche for themselves that guaranteed evolutionary success by removing them from competition with the other meat-eating savanna-dwellers. The real question is not 'What were the women and children doing while the males were out hunting?' but 'How did human males evolve so as to complement the female food-providing role?' (Tanner and Zihlman, 1976).

At a later stage of evolution, that of so-called Homo Erectus, which had spread throughout most of the Old World by half a million years ago, it is probable that plant foods continued to be crucial.[6] Among today's remaining gathering – hunting peoples, meat may be a highly valued item, but women's gathering activities provide 60 – 80 per cent of the total diet, and the knowledge and techniques necessary for successful gathering possessed by women as a group constitute the key survival technology.

Digging tools and containers for collected food were particularly necessary in the first gathering – hunting societies, and there is evidence of their use in early hominid culture, that of Australopithecus, some 2 – 4 million years ago.[7] By the time Australopithecus generated Homo Erectus, tools for both plant-gathering and game-hunting exist, but recent evidence shows that many tools that were assumed to be part of a hunting technology were

---

[6] Fossil evidence shows that, although some groups ate large or small game, others did not. On Old World sites such as Latamne in Syria and Olorgesailie in East Africa, animal bones are few or absent.

[7] Slocum (1975) points out that one of the earliest cultural inventions must have been some kind of sling to carry babies in.

actually used for cutting plant material (Keeley, 1977). There are no data to support the existence of a large-scale hunting technology in this period of evolution. It is in the last 300,000 years that hunting became at all important in Europe (as judged by such artifacts as cave-painting and animal carvings), and it is only one of many subsistence patterns when areas other than Western Europe are considered.

Finally, we may ask, was it only men who hunted? Dorothy Hammond and Alta Jablow, discussing the taken-for-granted assumption that the answer to this question is 'yes', comment that, so far as contemporary cross-cultural data are concerned,

while hunting is an occupation usually ascribed to men, there are numerous exceptions (notably among the American Indians). Occupational lines are rarely as clearly maintained in reality as they are drawn in theory. Women on gathering expeditions automatically kill small game to bring back to the campsite along with the wild plant foods they collect. Aranda women even wield their digging sticks to bring down the large animals they encounter. Are they then still gathering, or are they hunting? And what kind of game distinguishes gathering from hunting? [Hammond and Jablow, 1976, p.70]

The Tiwi who live on islands off the northern coast of Australia, divide work — hunting *and* gathering — according to the realms of land, sea and sky. 'Women's foods' are mostly those found on the land — such as the cabbage palm, the cycad nut, yams, lizards, snakes, opposums and tree rats — in the hunting of which they use axes and 'well-trained hunting dogs'. Men collect fish, flying foxes, turtles and crocodiles (Goodale, 1971). Contrary to popular belief, gathering – hunting societies are not the most sexist, but can exhibit a highly egalitarian division of labour (Goodale, 1971; Draper, 1975).

The World turned upside down
Although studies of other cultures are a promising field for feminists, they begin with precepts formed in the investigator's own. Ruby Rohrlich Leavitt and her colleagues (1975) demonstrate this by showing that aboriginal societies are differently described by male and female ethnographers. Male ethnographers portray the economic role of aboriginal women as inferior, emphasize the importance of public political power, stress the culturally dangerous biological limitations of women, decry the importance of reproduction, and show women as wives and mothers subordinate to brutal and domineering males. For the female ethnographers, aboriginal society is an equal partnership of

the sexes in which political institutions are not highly developed and in which women have a large measure of economic control, are not regarded as biologically polluting and are not subservient to uncaring men in anyone's eyes. However, it is not just that the gender of the anthropologist affects the questions he or she asks and the processing of the information he or she receives. The members of the investigated culture may themselves differ on sex lines as to what they 'know' about themselves and their world.

In Middle Eastern Muslim societies women are 'traditionally' highly inferior to men, in actual imprisonment behind the symbolic containment of the veil. From the male point of view women are (must be) excluded from the male world. But this can be restated from the female point of view as the exclusion of men from the world of women. This world is not automatically marked by any individual or collective sense on the part of women of their inferiority or powerlessness.

In San'a, the capital city of the Yemen Arab Republic, the daily ritual of *tafrita* is an occasion on which the women of the community come together to share their involvement in topics of common interest.

Guests arrive all veiled in black, remove their cloaks and shoes at the door, and appear in the majlis (sitting room) dressed in various colours of rich brocades and velvets or the cheaper cloths and synthetics which mark the lower status groups. The women wear their best clothes and display their jewellery . . . . Upon entering a women's majlis, one is taken by the glimmer of all the colours and brocades, by the chatter and music, the pungent smell of tobacco, the heady scent of incense, the sweet fragrance of perfume, and the hot damp atmosphere of the room.

The space in the middle of the majlis is taken up by several tall brass mada (waterpipe or hookah) whose long hoses sinuate across the room and are passed among the guests. Tea and qishr, spicy, hot and sweet, are passed around as well as nuts, raisins, candy . . . . Women enjoy smoking the mada and about one third chew qat [a stimulant shrub] which, they say, cools the body and relaxes it after the fatigues of the day. There may be some riddle-guessing, story-telling and joking at a tafrita. Always there is music . . . [Makhlouf, 1979, pp.22 – 3]

No veils are worn during the *tafrita*, which reveals it as an autonomous female world. Two observations in particular support this interpretation. Firstly, the language spoken at the tafrita is the language of women: 'there is a marked difference in speech patterns of men and women which makes it difficult for a man to understand when women speak among themselves'. Secondly, an 'early warning system' operates to make sure no man intrudes on the gathering. Any man entering a house when a *tafrita* is in progress 'is required to say "Allah! Allah!" loudly a number of times while climbing the stairs of his house, so that the women, hearing him, are able to change their comportment and cover their faces before he sees them' (Makhlouf, 1979, pp.28 – 9).

This exclusion ritual contrasts with the simpler and more common entry of a veiled female into an all-male social group. While serving meals, for instance, women are able to learn a great deal about male society, whereas men are not allowed silently to witness female society in the same way. Such inequalities are paralleled by unequal interpretations of the veil's function: to men it is a mark of women's inferiority but for women it serves as a valuable distancing mechanism from men and male society (a veiled woman could be any women: the veil protects the virtue of all; and the free mixing of the sexes is not synonymous with women's equality). If men see the *tafrita* as a 'part' society, there is no evidence that the women do. More than their retaliation against their exclusion from male society, it represents, as Makhlouf (p.47) puts it, 'a blatant refutation of the ideology of the patriarchal system'.

One could say that there are two ways to approach an account of the position of women. According to the first, the constituent material comes from indices of women's participation in those spheres of society that have a prior identification as men's business: employment, the law, religious organization, electoral politics, the judiciary, etc. The basic premise is that women are deficient carbon copies of men. The second approach begins with the view of culture and gender identity generated by women. Here one asks how women see the position of women, men and society in general. That these two approaches will manufacture a different cartography of women's position follows only if women and men do to some extent live and operate within gender-secluded spheres. It is an item on the agenda of conventional wisdom about the relations of men and women in modern Euro-American culture that companionship and intimacy flourish. Substantial evidence exists (in the form of epidemic divorce rates, difficulties with heterosexual intercourse, etc.) that this is a matter of obstinate belief rather than actual practice. In practice, men and women do not share the same value system. In fact you could say that patriarchy is a myth in the minds of men. It is what men believe about the world they inhabit. Women may not believe in it or they may believe in matriarchy instead.

One way to summarize this is to say that there is, as well as considerable *behavioural* differentiation between the sexes, a mode of *ideological* differentiation in which men and women hold different images of themselves and their social relations. Ideological differentiation does not have to imply hierarchy. If men and women see themselves as different species there is no automatically invidious comparison of importance. Yet, paradoxically, where an idolatry of sex equality arises (men and women are essentially the same, have the same rights and responsibilities, etc.), an imbalance of power may occur because the group with the male model at its centre may come to be the primary reference point for all. Women, in consequence, develop a sense of lost self-esteem. This may, in turn, give rise to a perception of active discrimination and an aggrieved feminism that seeks to give women what are seen as new and essential rights in a male world. But can women be recognized as human only by transforming themselves into male citizens?

CHAPTER SIXTEEN

The Rise of the Second Sex

But where, women wailing above your station, is it you want to go, get to, accomplish, communicate? . . .

Above the laughter, above the miseries, above the clatter of glasses and the cries of children, I hear a voice saying: Isn't there some statement you'd like to make? Anything noted while alive? Anything felt, seen, heard, done? You are here. You're having your turn. Isn't there something you know and nobody else does? What if nobody listens? . . . . What about all the words that were said and all the words that were never said? [Smart, 1978, p.63]

Certain recurrent questions greet the outpourings of feminist academics. 'But what is feminism?' 'Why are women universally oppressed?' (By this question is really meant, it can't all be a male conspiracy; and, your argument is biased since you are a woman yourself.)

Feminism can be defined in many ways and just how to define it is one task of the women's movement at the moment (In Theory Press, 1979). Ultimately any feminism is about putting women first; it is about judging women's interests (however defined) to be important and to be insufficiently represented and accommodated within mainstream politics/academia. However, this position allows a very wide range of stances, theories, practices and recommendations to be selected. Table 16.1 is adapted from Amanda Sebastyen's 'Tendencies in the Movement: Then and Now' (1979). It doesn't claim to be an authoritative or altogether serious statement of contemporary feminist politics, but it does successfully sum up some of the important alignments. [1]

The main division is between socialist feminists and radical feminists. While the former implicate capitalism as the perpetrator of women's oppression, the latter accuse men of being its prime movers

---

[1] Sebastyen is relatively modest about her claims for it, but doesn't discuss to what extent the chart applies to American feminism. My adaptation of the chart chiefly consists in omitting three brands of feminism (the 'Euro Communist', 'Firestone's' and the 'Matriarchist' which could be argued to fall under one or other of the remaining headings.

TABLE 16.1 Tendencies in the women's liberation movement

Positions	What's wrong?	Who benefits?	Questions			What is your relation to men?
			How do we fight?	How did our oppression begin?		

Positions	What's wrong?	Who benefits?	How do we fight?	How did our oppression begin?	What is your relation to men?
Socialist Feminists ('The system's the problem')					
Equal Rights	Women are held back by lack of education and self-confidence; and by prejudice	Nobody except a few hard reactionaries and corporate Big Business	By changing public attitudes	In old-fashioned ideas. (*Discrimination*, not *oppression*, please).	Women must be integrated at all levels of society
Traditional Marxist	The division of labour defines women by their home responsibilities and excludes them from productive labour	Capital — because women are a reserve army of cheap labour	Fighting within the Labour movement for full unionisation, equal pay, maternity leave etc.	With private property and women's exclusion from production	Women must fight with men, although some short-term separation may be necessary
Althusserian	The category of 'the feminine' assumes and perpetuates women's subordination	Capitalism operating through patriarchal ideology	By understanding our oppression 'scientifically' (via psychoanalysis, Marxism, linguistics) — theorizing *is* political practice	In ideology and cultural expectation internalized as femininity	'Theory is . . . not male or female'
Humanist	Men and women are both alienated from their human potential by being forced into masculine and feminine roles	'The system'	By educating people to want equality; living in communal groups; shortening work hours so men can share childcare	With industrialization and work/home split	Men are people too
Unaligned socialist – feminist	Oppression at work and generally limited 'feminine' role-expectations	Capitalism — by women's cheap labour and unpaid family-producing work: men — as 'bosses' in the family	By focusing on 7 demands of women's movement* and allying with other socialists where possible	It's different in different societies but women are everywhere oppressed	Organize separately from men, but our political insights important for rest of revolutionary movement

				Does it matter?	
Wages for Housework	Not 'oppression' — exploitation in housework	Capital — from women's free labour and a divided working class	Autonomously — 'Power to the sisters is power to the class'		Separately because housework puts us in a different class. (Male supporters at the back.)
Radical Feminists ('Men are the problem')					
Feministes Revolutionnaires	Oppression *and* exploitation through housework/childcare	Men — from women's free labour, and subordination in the world at large	Attack marriage and patriarchy generally	The question is suspicious because it is looking for a 'natural' explanation	Alliances with other workers can only be made if they are willing to overthrow patriarchy
Redstockings	Society is male-supremacist as well as capitalist and imperialist	Men as a class	By finding out in consciousness-raising that our personal experiences are shared and can be fought	Women have always been oppressed	There is no place for men in women's liberation movement; but personal engagement with men is the only way forward
Cultural Feminist	Women have been separated from each other and convinced of their inferiority	Men	By living as though men didn't exist (The Future is Female)	Millennia of peaceful matriarchal rule broken up by roving hordes of men	Women are the only alternative society; the lesbian is the only woman who can realize her full potential
Female Supremacist	Women are biologically and morally superior, but men hold power by force of arms	Men, Phallocrats	Take power by any means necessary	Women's biology has always made them vulnerable to male aggression	It's a war — no fraternizing with the other side

*Equal pay; equal education and job opportunities; free 24-hour nurseries; free contraception and abortion-on demand; financial and legal independence; an end to discrimination against lesbians and a woman's right to define her own sexuality; freedom from intimidation by threat or use of violence/an end to male aggression and dominance.

Source: Adapted from Sebastyen (1979).

and beneficiaries. Within both categories of feminism there is a spectrum of opinion. The mildest brand of socialist feminism is the equal rights variety: here there is no talk of oppression, merely of discrimination, which, being seen as a vestige of outdated attitudes, is analysed as amenable to correction by the law, education, etc.[2] The most extreme group is that of the Wages for Housework campaign. Feminists here, although continuing to implicate capital as the chief beneficiary of women's oppression, see women's responsibility for housework as putting them in a separate 'class' from men. Moving to the second half of Table 16.1, considerable differences among radical feminists are evident too. For 'feministes revolutionnaires', political alliances with other workers must be predicated on the goal of overcoming patriarchy, but are nevertheless possible. For 'female supremacists', on the other hand, there is no escape from the sex war.

These varieties of feminism are distinguished from each other on the basis of different theories about why women constitute the second sex. The question 'what are the origins of women's oppression?' cannot, then, be separated from the question, 'what is feminism?' We are, however, in some difficulty because of this assumed need to understand the conditions that brought women's universal oppression about. Not the smallest of our difficulties is that there is no way of directly examining the evidence. In addition, the universality of the situation must first be proved. To do this, an unhelpfully circular logic is needed: such-and-such constitutes the oppression of women, such-and-such can be assumed to exist everywhere; therefore women are universally oppressed. All kinds of factors may be taken as indicators of oppression, but are they? For example, the idea that women's oppression consists in their assignment to a domain of 'nature' opposed to that of 'culture' (Ortner, 1974) is specious because of the hidden generalization that all societies perceive a similar distinction between the biological body and the social space occupied by it (Rogers, 1978).[3] We have only to look at how childbearing is dichotomized differently as qualification and as disqualification. In modern Euro-American society, having children is women's unique

---

[2] It seems just possible that a woman (man?) with a non-socialist party affiliation could be an equal rights 'feminist'.

[3] The interpretation of women and their body products as potentially polluting because of their ambiguity in the nature/culture division (see p.179, 206) doesn't depend on this generalization.

liability and disability: in bringing women up to the level of men as citizens, maternity has proved the biggest stumbling block. Yet in West Africa, it is said that mothers have proved by bearing children their capability for public office (Hoffer, 1974). Where maternity disqualifies, it does so by proving women's weakness; where it qualifies, this rule is inverted and mothers are strong. (We can see how this contention surfaces, faintly, in Margaret Thatcher's pragmatic justification for female prime ministerhood (p.302).)

Throughout this book I have tried to relate the position of women in contemporary Euro-American culture to their positions in quite different societies and periods of history. This, it seems to me, is essential in order to avoid the trap of being blinkered by the answers — and the questions — that are prompted by the study of the position of women here-and-now. This approach suggests that the two questions '*how* are women oppressed?' and '*are* women oppressed?' have different and ambiguous answers depending on where you are looking at that particular moment. Both men, in the guise of husbands, fathers and breadwinners, and capitalism, in the sense of a mode of production that gives rise to a certain division of class interests, can be held responsible for the habit of according women a second-class status. Because men can be individualized whereas capitalism can't be, men are the more immediately blameable of the two enemies. Yet in communist countries, for example, it is neither the simple failure to realize the full flowering of the classless society, nor an abundance of unadulterated male sexism that can be held solely responsible for the emergence of subversive feminist movements (*Guardian*, 29 February, 1980). The two are linked.

I have also argued (see pp.331−4) that we are in unfathomable water in deducing from sociological data a patriarchal model of society and then further presuming that this model bears a true correspondence to the cultural maps possessed and operated by women. It may be true that certain socio-economic groups have conspired to oppress women, and that a key conspiracy has been a contraction of the feminist vision to the formula of equal rights in a masculine world; but it is also true to say that women have conspired among themselves to deny men the rights of full citizenship in a female world, and this exclusion has sometimes been a powerfully conscious activity. At any given time and place patriarchy and the mental maps of women may correspond: or they may not.

This is where the second major difficulty with the search for the true origins of women's oppression is to be found. Burying one's head in theory is a way for academic women to profit from a movement that is against profiteers.[4] Teaching and research in women's studies provide a field of expertise for academic women: 'you can do yourself quite a lot of good by publishing respectable scholarly work on feminism . . . Unhappily you can probably do yourself *most* good by publishing material criticizing radical work by other women . . .' (Leonard, 1979, pp.32 – 3). Moreover, theory can be dangerously close to religion in its creed-like qualities. There is the self-righteous smugness of the believer and the ostracism of the agnostic; the missionary zeal to epistolic conversion and the disenfranchisement and isolation of the sceptic.

In the end it is difficult to see how any one alignment can overcome these difficulties. The rise of the second sex demands a new language and new structures of thought to gestate a *completely* different society. Not one in which women equal men or one in which men equal women or even one in which women have supplanted men in self-assertiveness and self-centred social engineering. Such a world exists at the margins of our imagination. To describe it is an act of fiction.

Feminist science fiction writers can redraw the limits of 'science'. That is, they have a licence to play around with the interface between 'nature' and 'culture' in a rather more imaginative way than researchers into sex differences have done. Anything becomes possible in the best of all possible worlds. Thus, we have 'Whileway', the one-sexed future world of Joanna Russ's *The Female Man* (1977), from which comes Janet Evason to challenge the thought processes of three other women from different time-continua — a present-day American, a woman from another contemporary society in which Hitler never took power and everyone is still in the grip of the 1930s economic recession, and a woman from a more immediate future in which the sex war has become a real shooting match. The four women finally participate in the revelation that they are all genetically identical and only have different personalities, physical appearances, mannerisms, thoughts, feelings, languages and life-chances because

---

[4] I fully admit that I could also be said to be a profiteer of the feminist movement in writing this book.

their different worlds have acted differently upon them. We have the glacial country of 'Winter', imagined by Ursula LeGuin in *The Left Hand of Darkness* (1973), in which there are no men or women but hermaphroditic individuals who experience a cyclical sexual potency. This makes them temporarily male or female from a reproductive point of view, but does not affect the fact that gender as we know it does not exist, a truly disconcerting experience for the human visitor to Winter. We have Connie in Marge Piercy's *Woman on the Edge of Time* (1976), who, impoverished in every earthly sense, is richly in touch with a world in which women have yielded childbearing to humanly kept machines in order to humanize men, and men through social motherhood (and breastfeeding), have learnt a generous human kindness.

Science fiction is an expanding territory for feminist writers, and I have chosen to end this book here for three reasons: firstly, as an apology for describing the looking-glass world of women's studies almost entirely with images invented this side of the glass; secondly, to stress the necessity of imagination in all feminist endeavours, and thirdly, to make the point that such stories as Russ's *The Female Man* or Piercy's *Woman on the Edge of Time* convey future possibility in a way that political arguments beginning in this culture never can. It may be difficult to tell from the science fiction accounts how we ought to negotiate, demand or institute change in those structures that particularly oppress us. But perhaps it is more a matter of imagining and deciding what we want, and then working out how to get it, than it is of deciphering what it is we have been given and who made us a present of this unsolicited gift in the first place?

Bibliography

ACTON, W.A. (1871) *The Functions and Disorders of the Reproductive Organs in Childhood, Youth, Adult Age and Advanced Life Considered in Their Physiological, Social and Moral Relations* (5th edition) London, Churchill.

ADAMS, C.T. and WINSTON, K.T. (1980) *Mothers At Work* New York, Longman.

ADDINGTON, D.W. (1968) 'The relationship of selected vocal characteristics to personality perception' *Speech Monographs*, 35, pp.492 – 503.

ADVISORY CONCILIATION AND ARBITRATION SERVICE (1978) *The Toy Manufacturing Wages Council Report no. 13* ACAS, Cleland House, Page Street, London SW1.

AINSWORTH, M.D., ANDRY, R.G., HARLOW, R.G., LEBOVICI, S., MEAD, M., PRUGH, D.G. and WOOTTON, B. (1966) *Deprivation of Maternal Care: A Reassessment of Its Effects*, in one volume with J. Bowlby *Maternal Care and Mental Health* New York, Schocken Books.

AITKEN-SWAN, J. (1977) *Fertility Control and the Medical Profession* London, Croom Helm.

ALCOHOLICS ANONYMOUS (1980) *Survey of Alcoholics Anonymous in Great Britain 1978* A.A., 11 Redcliffe Gardens, London, SW10.

ALEXANDER, S. (1976) 'Women's work in nineteenth century London: a study of the years 1820 – 1850' in Mitchell and Oakley (eds.).

ALMQUIST, E.M. (1977) 'Women in the labor force' *Signs: Journal of Women in Culture and Society*, 2, no.4 (Summer), pp.843 – 55.

ALTHUSSER, L. (1971) 'Ideology and ideological state apparatuses' in L. Althusser (ed.). *Lenin and Philosophy and Other Essays* London, New Left Books.

ANDRY, R.G. (1966) 'Paternal and maternal roles and delinquency' in Ainsworth *et al*.

ARCHER, J. (1976) 'Biological explanations of psychological sex differences' in Lloyd and Archer (eds.).

ARCHER, J. (1978) 'Biological explanations and sex-role stereotypes' in Chetwynd and Hartnett (eds.).

ARDENER, E. (1971) *Social Anthropology and Language* London, Tavistock.

ARDENER, E. (1972) 'Belief and the problem of women' in J. La Fontaine (ed.) *The Interpretation of Ritual: Essays in Honour of A.I. Richards* London, Tavistock.

ARDENER, E. (1977) 'The anthropologist as translator of culture'. Paper delivered to the Wenner Gren Symposium on *Focus on Linguistics* Burg Wartenstein, Austria.

ARDENER, S. (1975) 'Sexual insult and female militancy' in Ardener (ed.).

ARDENER, S. (ed.) (1975) *Perceiving Women* London, Malaby Press.

ARDENER, S. (1978) 'Introduction: the nature of women in society' in Ardener (ed.).

ARDENER, S. (ed.) (1978) *Defining Females* London, Croom Helm.

ARIES, P. (1962) *Centuries of Childhood* London, Jonathan Cape.

ARMS, S. (1977) *Immaculate Deception* New York, Bantam Books.

ARON, A. (1974) 'Relationships with opposite-sexed parents and mate choice' *Human Relations* 27, no.1, pp.17–24.

ATKINSON, D., DALLIN, A. and LAPIDUS, G.W. (eds.) (1978) *Women in Russia* Sussex, Harvester Press.

BACDAYAN, A.S. (1977) 'Mechanistic co-operation and sexual equality among the Western Bontoc' in A. Schlegel (ed.) *Sexual Stratification: A Cross-Cultural View* New York, Columbia University Press.

BAHR, S.J. (1974) 'Effects on power and division of labour in the family' in Hoffman and Nye (eds.).

BALBO, L. (1979) 'The British welfare state and the organization of the family' in L. Balbo and R. Zahar (eds.) *Interferenze: Io Stato, la Vita Familiare, la Vita Privata* Milan, Feltrinelli.

BALINT, M., HUNT, J., JOYCE, D., MARINKER, M. and WOODCOCK, J. (1970) *Treatment or Diagnosis: A Study of Repeat Prescriptions in General Practice* London, Tavistock.

BAMBERGER, J. (1974) 'The myth of matriarchy: why men rule in primitive society' in Rosaldo and Lamphere (eds.)

BANDURA, A. (1973) *Aggression: A Social Learning Analysis* Englewood Cliffs, New Jersey, Prentice-Hall.

BANDURA, A. and HUSTON, A.C. (1961) 'Identification as a process of incidental learning' *Journal of Abnormal and Social Psychology*, 63, pp.311 – 18.

BANKS, J.A. and BANKS, O. (1965) *Feminism and Family Planning in Victorian England* Liverpool, University Press.

BARDWICK, J.M. (1970) 'Psychological conflict and the reproductive system' in Bardwick *et al.*

BARDWICK, J.M., DOUVAN, E., HORNER, M.S. and GUTMAN, D. (1970) *Feminine Personality and Conflict* Belmont, California, Wadsworth.

BARFIELD, A. (1976) 'Biologic influences on sex differences in behaviour' in Teitelbaum (ed.)

BARKER, D.L. and ALLEN, S. (1976a) *Dependence and Exploitation in Work and Marriage* London, Longman.

BARKER, D.L. and ALLEN, S. (1976b) *Sexual Divisions and Society* London, Tavistock.

BARRETT, M. (ed.) (1979) *Virginia Woolf: Women and Writing* London, The Women's Press.

BARRETT, M. and ROBERTS, H. (1978) 'Doctors and their patients: the social control of women in general practice' in Smart and Smart (eds.)

BARRIE, H. (1976) 'Congenital malformation associated with intrauterine device *British Medical Journal* 28, no.2, pp.488 – 90.

BARRY, H., CHILD, I.L. and BACON, M.K. (1959) 'Relation of child training to subsistence economy' *American Anthropologist*, 61, pp.51 – 63.

BARTELL, G.D. (1971) *Group Sex: A Scientist's Eyewitness Report on the American Way of Swinging* New York, Peter H. Wyden.

BASS, B.M., KRUSELL, J. and ALEXANDER, R.A. (1971) 'Male managers' attitudes toward working women' in L.S. Fidell and J. Delamater (eds.) *Women in the Professions: What's All the Fuss About?* Beverly Hills, Sage Publications.

BAXANDALL, R. (1976) 'Women in American trade unions: an historical analysis' in Mitchell and Oakley (eds.).

BEECHEY, V. (1978) 'Women and production: a critical analysis of some sociological theories of women's work' in Kuhn and Wolpe (eds.).

BELL, C. and NEWBY, H. (1976) 'Husbands and wives: the dynamics of the deferential dialectic' in Barker and Allen (eds.) (1976a).

BELL, N.W. and VOGEL, E.F. (eds.) (1968) *A Modern Introduction to the Family* Glencoe, The Free Press.

BELOTTI, E.G. (1975) *Little Girls* London, Writers and Readers Publishing Co-operative.

BEM, D. and BEM, S. (1970) 'We're all non-conscious sexists' *Psychology Today*, 4, no.6, November.

BENET, M.K. (1972) *Secretary* London, Sidgwick and Jackson.

BENN, C. and SIMON, B. (1970) *Halfway There* New York, McGraw-Hill.

BENSON, R.C. (1964) *Handbook of Obstetrics and Gynaecology* Los Altos, California, Lange Medical Publications.

BENSTON, M. (1969) 'The political economy of women's liberation'. Reprinted from the September issue of *Monthly Review* by New England Free Press, 791 Tremont Street, Boston, Mass. 02118, USA.

BERAL, V. (1974) 'Oral contraception and health' (letter) *Lancet*, 1, p.1280.

BERAL, V. (1979) 'Reproductive mortality' *British Medical Journal*, 15 September, pp.632 – 4.

BERGER, J. (1972) *Ways of Seeing* Harmondsworth, Penguin.

BERNARD, J. (1971) *Women and the Public Interest* Chicago, Aldine-Atherton.

BERNARD, J. (1973) *The Future of Marriage* New York, Souvenir Press.

BERNARD, J. (1974) *The Future of Motherhood* New York, Penguin Books Inc.

BERNARD, J. (1975) *Women, Wives, Mothers* Chicago, Aldine.

BERNSTEIN, H. (1978) *For Their Triumph and For Their Tears: Women and Apartheid in South Africa* London, International Defence and Aid Fund.

BERRY, J. (1966) 'Temne and Eskimo perceptual skills' *International Journal of Psychology*, I, pp.207 – 29.

BIRNBAUM, J.A. (1971) 'Life patterns, personality style and self-esteem in gifted family-oriented and career-committed women'. Unpublished doctoral dissertation, University of Michigan.

BLACKSTONE, T. (1976) 'The education of girls today' in Mitchell and Oakley (eds.).

BLACKSTONE, T. and FULTON, O. (1978) 'Sex discrimination among university teachers: a British – American comparison' *British Journal of Sociology*, 26, no.3, pp.261 – 75.

BLOOD, R.O. and WOLFE, O.M. (1960) *Husbands and Wives* Glencoe, Free Press.

BOARD OF EDUCATION (1927) *The Education of the Adolescent: Report of the Consultative Committee* (the Hadow Report) London, HMSO.

BOCK, D.R. and KOLAKOWSKI, D. (1973) 'Further evidence of sex-linked major gene influence on human spatial visualizing ability' *American Journal of Human Genetics*, 25, pp.1 – 14.

BONE, M. (1977) *Preschool Children and Their Need for Day Care* Office of Population Censuses and Surveys, London, HMSO.

BOSERUP, E. (1970) *Woman's Role in Economic Development* London, Allen and Unwin.

BOULDING, E. (1977) *Women in the Twentieth Century World* New York, Sage Publications.

BOURNE, G. (1972) *Pregnancy* London, Pan.

BOWKER, L.H. (1978) *Women, Crime and the Criminal Justice System* Lexington, Mass., D.C. Heath and Co., Lexington Books.

BOWLBY, J. (1951) 'Maternal care and mental health' *Bulletin of the World Health Organization*, 3, pp.355 – 534.

BOWLBY, J. (1953) *Child Care and the Growth of Love* Harmondsworth, Penguin.

BOWLBY, J. (1979) *The Making and Breaking of Affectional Bonds* London, Tavistock.

BRAMAN, O. (1977) 'Comics' in King and Stott (eds.).

BRANCA, P. (1975) *Silent Sisterhood* London, Croom Helm.

BREEN, D. (1975) *The Birth of a First Child* London, Tavistock.

BREEN, D. (1978) 'The mother and the hospital' in S. Lipshitz (ed.) *Tearing the Veil: Essays on Femininity* London, Routledge and Kegan Paul.

BRENT, L. (1973) *Incidents in the Life of a Slave Girl* New York, Harcourt Brace Jovanich.

BRIMBLECOMBE, F.S.W., RICHARDS, M.P.M. and ROBERTSON, N.R.C. (1978) *Separation and Special-Care Baby Units* London, Spastic International Medical Publications.

BRISTOL WOMEN'S STUDIES GROUP (1979) *Half the Sky: An Introduction to Women's Studies* London, Virago.

BROVERMAN, I., BROVERMAN, D., CLARKSON, F., ROSENKRANTZ, P. and VOGEL, S. (1970) 'Sex-role stereotypes and clinical judgements of mental health' *Journal of Consulting and Clinical Psychology*, 34, pp.1 – 7.

BROWN, G.W. and DAVIDSON, S. (1978) 'Social class, psychiatric disorder of the mother and accidents to children' *Lancet* 18 February, p.378.

BROWN, G.W. and HARRIS, T. (1978) *Social Origins of Depression* London, Tavistock.

BROWNMILLER, S. (1975) *Against Our Will: Men, Women and Rape* New York, Simon and Schuster.

BUFFERY, A.W.H. and GRAY, J.A. (1972) 'Sex differences in the development of spatial and linguistic skills' in Ounsted and Taylor (eds.).

BUJRA, J. (1973) 'Women and fieldwork'. Unpublished paper presented to London Women's Anthropology Group Workshop, 3 March.

BULLARD, L.C. (1969) 'The slave-women of America' in O'Neill (ed.). First published 1870.

BULLOUGH, V. and BULLOUGH, B. (1977) *Sin, Sickness and Sanity: A History of Sexual Attitudes* New York, Meridian Books.

BURMAN, S. (ed.) (1979) *Fit Work for Women* London, Croom Helm.

BURNS, J. (1906) 'Inaugural address' *Report of the Proceedings of the National Conference on Infantile Mortality* Westminster, London, P.S. King and Co.

BURTON, E. (1944) *Domestic Work: Britain's Largest Industry* London, Frederick Muller.

BUTLER, N. and ALBERMAN, E. (eds.) (1969) *Perinatal Problems* Edinburgh, E. and S. Livingstone.

BUTSCHER, E. (1977) *Sylvia Plath: Method and Madness* New York, Pocket Books.

BYRNE, E. (1975) 'Inequality in education — discriminal resource-allocation in schools?' *Educational Review* 27, University of Birmingham.

BYRNE, E. (1978) *Women and Education* London, Tavistock.

CADOGAN, N. and CRAIG, P. (1978) *Women and Children First: the Fiction of Two World Wars* London, Gollancz.

CALHOUN, A. (1919) *Social History of the American Family* vol. 3, Cleveland, The Arthur H. Clark Co.

CALHOUN, L., SELBY, J.W., CANN, A. and KELLER, G.T. (1978) 'The effects of victim physical attractiveness and sex of respondent on social reactions to victims of rape' *British Journal of Social and Clinical Psychology*, 17, no.2, pp.191 – 2.

CALLEN, A. (1979) *Women Artists of the Arts and Crafts Movement* New York, Pantheon.

CALLOWAY, H. (1978) ' "The most essentially female function of all": giving birth' in Ardener (ed.).

CAPLAN, P. and BUJRA, J. (eds.) (1978) *Women United, Women Divided* London, Tavistock.

CARDEN, M.L. (1974) *The New Feminist Movement* New York, Russell Sage.

CARROLL, B.A. (ed.) (1976) *Liberating Women's History* Chicago, University of Illinois Press.

CARROLL, L.. (1950) *Alice Through the Looking Glass* Harmondsworth, Penguin.

CARTWRIGHT, A. (1970) *Parents and Family Planning Services* London, Routledge and Kegan Paul.

CARTWRIGHT, A. (1976) *How Many Children?* London, Routledge and Kegan Paul.

CARTWRIGHT, A. (1979) *The Dignity of Labour? A Study of Childbearing and Induction* London, Tavistock.

CARTWRIGHT, A. and MOFFETT, J. (1974) 'A comparison of results obtained by men and women interviewers in a fertility survey' *Journal of Biosocial Science*, 6, pp.315 – 22.

CASSELL, J. (1977) *A Group Called Women: Sisterhood and Symbolism in the Feminist Movement* New York, David McKay.

CENTRAL POLICY REVIEW STAFF (1978) *Services for Young Children with Working Mothers* London, HMSO.

CHALMERS, I. (1979) 'The epidemiology of perinatal practice' *Journal of Maternal and Child Health*, pp.435 – 6.

CHALMERS, I., CAMPBELL, H. and TURNBULL, A.C. (1975) 'Use of oxytocin and incidence of neonatal jaundice' *British Medical Journal* 19 April, pp.116 – 8.

CHALMERS, I. and MACFARLANE, A. (1980) 'Interpretation of perinatal statistics' in B.A. Wharton (ed.) *Topics in Perinatal Medicine* Tunbridge Wells, Kent, Pitman Medical Ltd..

CHALMERS, I., OAKLEY, A. and MACFARLANE, A. (1980) 'Perinatal health services: an immodest proposal' *British Medical Journal*, 22 March, pp.842 – 9.

CHALMERS, I. and RICHARDS, M. (1977) 'Intervention and causal inference in obstetric practice' in Chard and Richards (eds.).

CHALMERS, I., ZLOSNIK, J.E., JOHNS, K.A. and CAMPBELL, H. (1976) 'Obstetric practice and outcome of pregnancy in Cardiff residents 1965 – 73' *British Medical Journal*, 27 March, pp.735 – 8.

CHAMBERLAIN, H. (1973) *A Minority of Members: Women in the U.S. Congress* New York, Praeger Publishing Co.

CHAMBERLAIN, M. (in press) *Old Wives' Tales* London, Virago.

CHAPMAN, D. (1955) *The Home and Social Status* London, Routledge and Kegan Paul.

CHAPMAN, S. (1979) 'Advertising and psychotropic drugs: the place of myth in ideological reproduction' *Social Science and Medicine*, 13a, pp.751 – 64.

CHARD, T. and RICHARDS, M. (eds.) (1977) *Benefits and Hazards of the New Obstetrics* London, Spastic International Medical Publications.

CHESLER, P. (1972) *Women and Madness* London, Allen Lane.

CHETWYND, J. and HARTNETT, O. (eds.) (1978) *The Sex Role System: Psychological and Sociological Perspectives* London, Routledge and Kegan Paul.

CHILDREN'S RIGHTS WORKSHOP (1976) *Sexism in Children's Books: Facts, Figures and Guidelines* London, Writers and Readers Publishing Co-operative.

CHODOROW, N. (1978) *The Reproduction of Mothering* Berkeley, California, University of California Press.

CISLER, L. (1970) 'Unfinished business: birth control and women's liberation' in Morgan (ed.).

CLARK, A. (1968) *The Working Life of Women in the Seventeenth Century* London, Frank Cass. (First published in 1919 by G. Routledge and Sons.)

CLARKE, A.M. and CLARKE, A.D.B. (1976) *Early Experience: Myth and Evidence* London, Open Books.

CLARKE, E.H. (1873) *Sex and Education or a Fair Chance for the Girls* Boston, James R. Osgood.

CLIFT, P. and SEXTON, B. (1979) '. . . And all things nice' *Educational Research*, 21, no.23, June.

COHEN, G. (1978) 'Women's solidarity and the preservation of privilege' in Caplan and Bujra (eds.).

COHEN, G. (1979) 'Symbolic relations: male decision-makers — female support groups in Britain and the United States' *Women's Studies International Quarterly* 2, no.4, pp.391 – 406.

COLEMAN, J.S. (1961) *The Adolescent Society: The Social Life of the Teenager and its Impact on Education* Glencoe, The Free Press.

COLEMAN, R.R. (1889) 'Women's relations to the higher education and professions as viewed from physiological and other standpoints' *Transactions*, Medical Association of Alabama 238.

COLLIER, J.F. (1974) 'Women in politics' in Rosaldo and Lamphere (eds.).

CONSTANTINIDES, P. (1978) 'Women's spirit possession and urban adaptation' in Caplan and Bujra (eds.).

COOKE, W.R.I. (1945) 'The differential psychology of the American woman' *American Journal of Obstetrics and Gynaecology*, 49, pp.457 – 72.

COOPER, D. (1972) *The Death of the Family* Harmondsworth, Penguin.

COOPER, J. (1970) 'The Leyton obsessional inventory' *Psychological Medicine*, 1, pp.48 – 64.

COOPERSTOCK, R. and LENNARD, H.L. (1979) 'Some social meanings of tranquilizer use' *Sociology of Health and Illness*, I, no.3, pp.331 – 47.

COOTE, A. and GILL, T. (1975) *Rape: the Controversy* London, National Council for Civil Liberties.

CORNILLON, S.K. (ed.) (1972) *Images of Women in Fiction: Feminist Perspectives* Bowling Green, Ohio, Bowling Green University Popular Press.

COSER, R.L. (1960) 'Laughter among colleagues' *Psychiatry*, 23, pp.81 – 95.

COTTEN, S.S. (1897) 'A national training school for women' in *The Work and Words of the National Congress of Mothers* New York, D. Appleton.

COUSSINS, J. (1977) *The Equality Report* National Council for Civil Liberties Rights for Women Unit.

COWAN, R.S. (1974) 'A case study of technological and social change: the washing machine and the working wife' in M. Hartman and L.W. Banner (eds.) *Clio's Consciousness Raised: New Perspectives on the History of Women* New York, Harper Colophon.

CRICK, F.H.C. and WATSON, J.D. (1954) 'The complementary structure of deoxyribonucleic acid' *Proceedings of the Royal Society* A, 223, pp.80 – 96.

CRITES, L. (1976) 'Women offenders: myth v. reality' in L. Crites (ed.). *The Female Offender* Lexington, Mass.

CROOK, J.H. (1970) 'Introduction — social behaviour and ethology' in J.H. Crook (ed.). *Social Behaviour in Birds and Mammals* London, Academic Press.

CROWTHER REPORT (1959) *15 to 18 Report of the Central Advisory Council for Education, England* London, HMSO.

CZAPLINSKI, S.M. (1976) 'Sexism in award winning picture books' in Children's Rights Workshop.

DAHLSTROM, E. (ed.) (1967) *The Changing Roles of Men and Women* London, Duckworth.

DALLA COSTA, M. and JAMES, S. (1972) *The Power of Women and the Subversion of the Community* Bristol, Falling Wall Press.

DALTON, K. (1959) 'Menstruation and acute psychiatric illness' *British Medical Journal*, 1, pp.148 – 9.

DALTON, K. (1960a) 'Menstruation and accidents' *British Medical Journal*, 2, pp.1752 – 3.

DALTON, K. (1960b) 'Effect of menstruation on schoolgirls' weekly work' *British Medical Journal*, 1, pp.326 – 8.

DALTON, K. (1961) 'Menstruation and crime' *British Medical Journal*, 2, pp.1425 – 6.

DALTON, K. (1964) *The Premenstrual Syndrome* Springfield, Illinois, C.C. Thomas.

DALTON, K. (1966) 'The influence of the mother's menstruation on her child' *Proceedings of the Royal Society of Medicine*, 59, p.1014.

DALTON, K. (1968) 'Antenatal progesterone and intelligence' *British Journal of Psychiatry*, 114, p.1377.

DALY, M. (1979) *Gyn/Ecology: The Metaethics of Radical Feminism* London, The Women's Press.

D'ASCIA, U. (1971) 'Onorevolmente Cattive' *Noi Donne* no.50, 19 December: cited in Belotti (1975).

DAVIDOFF, L. (1976) 'The rationalization of housework' in Barker and Allen (eds.) (1976b).

DAVIDOFF, L. and HAWTHORN, R. (1976) *A Day in the Life of a Victorian Domestic Servant* London, Allen and Unwin.

DAVIDOFF, L., L'ESPERANCE, J. and NEWBY, H. (1976) 'Landscape with figures: home and community in English society' in Mitchell and Oakley (eds.).

DAVIES, M.L. (ed.) (1977) *Life as We Have Known It* London, Virago. (First published in 1931 by Hogarth Press.)

DAVIES, M.L. (ed.) (1978) *Maternity: Letters from Working Women* London, Virago. (First published in 1915 by G. Bell and Sons.)

DAVIS, A.G. and STRONG, P.M. (1976) 'Aren't children wonderful? a study of the allocation of identity in developmental assessment' in Stacey (ed.).

DAVIS, D. (1966) *A History of Shopping* London, Routledge and Kegan Paul.

DAVIS, T. and GOODALL, P. (1979) 'Personally and politically: feminist art practice' *Feminist Review*, I, pp.21 – 34.

DE BEAUVOIR, S. (1960) *The Second Sex* London, Four Square Books.

DE BEAUVOIR, S. (1963) *Memoirs of a Dutiful Daughter* Harmondsworth, Penguin.

DECKARD, B. (1979) *The Women's Movement: Political, Socioeconomic and Psychological Issues* New York, Harper and Row.

DEEM, R. (1978) *Women and Schooling* London, Routledge and Kegan Paul.

DELAMONT, S. (1978a) 'The contradictions in ladies' education' in Delamont and Duffin (eds.).

DELAMONT, S. (1978b) 'The domestic ideology and women's education' in Delamont and Duffin (eds.).

DELAMONT, S. and DUFFIN, L. (1978) *The Nineteenth Century Woman: Her Cultural and Physical World* London, Croom Helm.

DELANEY, J., LUPTON, M.J. and TOTH, E. (1977) *The Curse: A Cultural History of Menstruation* New York, Mentor Books.

DELPHY, C. (1976) 'Continuities and discontinuities in marriage and divorce' in Barker and Allen (eds.) (1976b).

DELPHY, C. (1980) 'A materialist feminism is possible' *Feminist Review* 4, pp.79 – 105.

DE MAUSE, L. (ed.). (1974) *The History of Childhood* New York, Harper and Row.

DEMOS, J. (1970) 'Underlying themes in the witchcraft of seventeenth century New England' *American Historical Review*, 75, pp.1311 – 26.

DENNIS, N., HENRIQUES, F. and SLAUGHTER, C. (1956) *Coal is Our Life* London, Eyre and Spottiswoode.

DEPARTMENT OF EDUCATION AND SCIENCE (1974) *Statistics of Education* London, HMSO.

DEPARTMENT OF EDUCATION AND SCIENCE (1975) *Curricular Differences for Boys and Girls* Education Survey 21, London, HMSO.

DEPARTMENT OF EMPLOYMENT (1977) *New Earnings Survey* London, HMSO.

DEPARTMENT OF HEALTH AND SOCIAL SECURITY (1976a) *Priorities for Health and Personal Social Services in England* London, HMSO.

DEPARTMENT OF HEALTH AND SOCIAL SECURITY (1976b) *Prevention and Health: Everybody's Business* London, HMSO.

DEPARTMENT OF HEALTH AND SOCIAL SECURITY (1977a) *Consultative Document on Equal Status for Men and Women in Occupation Pension Schemes* London, HMSO.

DEPARTMENT OF HEALTH AND SOCIAL SECURITY (1977b) *Health and Personal Social Service Statistics for England and Wales* London, HMSO.

DEPARTMENT OF HEALTH AND SOCIAL SECURITY (1977c) *Prevention and Health: Reducing the Risk: Safer Pregnancy and Childbirth* London, HMSO.

DEPARTMENT OF HEALTH AND SOCIAL SECURITY (1979) *Report on Confidential Enquiries Into Maternal Deaths 1973 – 5* no.14, London, HMSO.

DIGGORY, P., and McEWAN, J. (1976) *Planning or Prevention: The New Face of 'Family Planning'* London, Marion Boyars.

DIXON, B. (1977) *Catching Them Young: Sex, Race and Class in Children's Fiction* London, Pluto Press.

DOLL, R., WAYNE, P. and WATERHOUSE, J. (eds.) (1966) *Cancer Incidence in Five Continents* Berlin, Springer Verlag.

DOLLARD, J. (1937) *Caste and Class in a Southern Town* New Haven, Conn., Yale University Press.

DONEGAN, J.B. (1978) *Women and Men Midwives* Westport, Conn., Greenwood Press.

DOUGLAS, J.W.B. (1964) *The Home and the School* London, MacGibbon and Kee.

DOUGLAS, J.W.B., ROSS, J.M. and SIMPSON, H.R. (1968) *All Our Future* London, Panther.

DOUGLAS, M. (1970) *Purity and Danger: An Analysis of Concepts of Pollution and Taboo* Baltimore, Penguin.

DOUTY, H.I., MOORE, J.B. and HARTFORD, D. (1974) 'Body characteristics in relation to life adjustment, body-image and attitudes of college females' *Perceptual and Motor Skills*, 39, pp.499–521.

DRAPER, P. (1975) '!Kung women: contrasts in sexual egalitarianism in foraging and sedentary contexts' in Reiter (ed.).

DUNNELL, K. (1979) *Family Formation* Office of Population Censuses and Surveys, London, HMSO.

DUVERGER, M. (1955) *The Political Role of Women* UNESCO.

EAKINS, B.W. and EAKINS, R.G. (1978) *Sex Differences in Human Communication* Boston, Houghton Mifflin.

EHRENREICH, B. and ENGLISH, D. (1973) *Witches, Midwives and Nurses: A History of Women Healers* London, Writers and Readers Publishing Co-operative.

EHRENREICH, B. and ENGLISH, D. (1979) *For Her Own Good: 150 Years of the Experts' Advice to Women* London, Pluto Press.

EHRHARDT, A.A. and BAKER, S.W. (1973) 'Hormonal aberrations and their implications for the understanding of normal sex differentiation'. Paper presented at the meeting of the Society for Research on Child Development, Philadelphia.

EICHLER, M. (1980) *The Double Standard: A Feminist Critique of Feminist Social Science* London, Croom Helm.

ELLMANN, M. (1968) *Thinking About Women* London, Macmillan.

ENSOR, R.C.K. (1936) *England 1870–1914* London, Oxford University Press.

EPSTEIN, C.F. (1971) 'Law partners and marital partners' *Human Relations*, 24, no.6, pp.549–64.

EQUAL OPPORTUNITIES COMMISSION (1978 – 9) *Research Bulletin*, 1, no.1 (Winter).

EQUAL OPPORTUNITIES COMMISSION (1979) *Health and Safety Legislation: Should We Distinguish Between Men and Women?* Manchester, Equal Opportunities Commission.

EVANS-PRITCHARD, E.E. (1951) *Kinship and Marriage Among the Nuer* London, Oxford University Press.

FAIRBAIRNS, Z. (1979) 'The cohabitation rule: why it makes sense' *Women's Studies International Quarterly*, 2, no.3, pp.319 – 28.

FARMER, H.S. and BOHN, M.J. (1970) 'Home career conflict reduction and the level of career interest in women' *Journal of Counselling Psychology*, 17, pp.228 – 32.

FARR, W. (1885) *Vital Statistics* London, Edward Stanford.

FARRELL, C. (1978) *My Mother Said . . . . .* London, Routledge and Kegan Paul.

FEANDEL, K. (1975) cited in U. Kroll, *Flesh of My Flesh* London, Dartman, Longman and Tod.

FEDRICK, J. and BUTLER, N.R. (1978) 'Intended place of delivery and perinatal outcome' *British Medical Journal*, 1, pp.737 – 802.

FEE, E. (1976) 'Science and the woman problem: historical perspectives' in Teitelbaum (ed.).

FEIN, R.A. (1974) 'Male roles and men's lives: a current view of manliness in the United States'. Unpublished paper, Cambridge, Mass.

FERIN, M., HALBERG, F., RICHART, R.M. and VANDE WIELE, R.L. (eds.) *Biorhythms and Human Reproduction* New York, John Wiley.

FESHBACK, N.D. (1969) 'Student teacher preferences for elementary school pupils varying in personality characteristics' *Journal of Educational Psychology*, 60, no.2, pp.126 – 32.

FIEGEHEN, G.C., LANSLEY, P.S. and SMITH, A.D. (1977) *Poverty and Progress in Britain 1953 – 73* Cambridge, Cambridge University Press.

FINER REPORT (1974) *Report of the Committee on One-Parent Families* Department of Health and Social Security, London, HMSO.

FIRTH, R. (1965) *Primitive Polynesian Economy* London, Routledge and Kegan Paul.

FIRTH, R. (1966) *Housekeeping Among Malay Peasants* London, Athlone Press.

FISHMAN, P. (1977) 'Interactional shitwork' *Heresies: A Feminist Publication on Art and Politics* 2 May.

FLETCHER, R. (1966) *The Family and Marriage in Britain* Harmondsworth, Penguin.

FLEURY, P. (1967) *Maternity Care: Mothers' Experiences of Childbirth* London, Allen and Unwin.

FLING, S. and MANOSEVITZ, M. (1972) 'Sex typing in nursery school children's play interests' *Developmental Psychology*, 7, pp.146 – 52.

FORD, C.S. and BEACH, F.A. (1965) *Patterns of Sexual Behaviour* London, Methuen.

FORDE, C.D. (1957) *Habitat, Economy and Society* London, Methuen.

FOWKES, F.G.R., CATFORD, J.C. and LOGAN, R.F.L. (1979) 'Abortion and the N.H.S.: the first decades' *British Medical Journal* 27 January, pp.217 – 19.

FOX, A.J. and ADELSTEIN, A.M. (1978) 'Occupational mortality: work or way of life?' *Journal of Epidemiology and Community Health*, 32, pp.73 – 8.

FOX, R. (1967) *Kinship and Marriage* Harmondsworth, Penguin.

FRANK, R.T. (1931) 'The hormonal cause of premenstrual tension' *Archives of Neurology and Psychiatry*, 26, pp.1053 – 7.

FRANSELLA, F. and CRISP, A. (1974) 'Comparison of weight concepts in a group of (1) neurotic (2) "normal" and (3) anorexic females'. Paper read at tenth European Conference on Psychosomatic Research, Edinburgh.

FRANSELLA, F. and FROST, K. (1977) *How Women See Themselves* London, Tavistock.

FRASER, R. (ed.) (1968) *Work: Twenty Personal Accounts* Harmondsworth, Penguin.

FREEMAN, M.O.A. (1979) *Violence in the Home* London, Saxon House.

FREUD, S. (1938) 'Three contributions to the theory of sex' in *Basic Writings of Sigmund Freud* ed. A.A. Brill, New York, Random House. (First published 1908.)

FREUD, S. (1962) *Three Essays on the Theory of Sexuality* trans. J. Strachey, London, Hogarth Press. (First published 1905.)

FREUD, S. (1964) 'Femininity' in *New Introductory Lectures on Psychoanalysis* trans. J. Strachey, New York, Norton. (First published 1933.)

FRIDAY, N. (1976) *My Secret Garden: Women's Sexual Fantasies* London, Quartet Books.

FRIDAY, N. (1979) *My Mother, My Self* London, Fontana.

FRIED, B. (1979) 'Boys will be boys: the language of sex and gender' in Hubbard *et al.*

FRIEDAN, B. (1963) *The Feminine Mystique* London, Gollancz.

FRIEDAN, B. (1977) *It Changed My Life* New York, Dell.

FRIEDMAN, R.C., RICHART, R.M. and VANDE WIELE, R.L. (eds.) (1978) *Sex Differences in Behaviour* New York, John Wiley.

GAGNON, J.H. and SIMON, W. (1974) *Sexual Conduct* London, Hutchinson.

GAIL, S. (1968) 'The housewife' in Fraser (ed.).

GALBRAITH, J.K. (1974) *Economics and the Public Purpose* London, Andre Deutsch.

GAMARNIKOW, E. (1978) 'Sexual division of labour: the case of nursing' in Kuhn and Wolpe (eds.).

GARAI, J.E. and SCHEINFELD, A. (1968) 'Sex differences in mental and behavioural traits' *Genetic Psychology Monographs* 77, pp.169 – 299.

GARCIA, J. (1979) 'Women, health and reproduction' *Links* 10, December, pp.7 – 9.

GARRETT, C. (1977) 'Women and witches: patterns of analysis' *Signs: Journal of Women in Culture and Society*, 3, no.2, (Winter) pp.461 – 70.

GAVRON, H. (1966) *The Captive Wife* Harmondsworth, Penguin.

GENERAL HOUSEHOLD SURVEY 1976 (1978) Office of Population Censuses and Surveys, Social Survey Division, London, HMSO.

GIDDENS, A. (1973) *The Class Structure of the Advanced Societies* London, Hutchinson.

GIL, D. (1970) *Violence Against Children* Cambridge, Mass., Harvard University Press.

GILMAN, C.P. (1903) *The Home: Its Work and Influence* New York, McClure, Phillips and Co.

GILMAN, C.P. (1911) *The Man-Made World of Our Androcentric Culture* London, T. Fisher Unwin.

GLAZER-MALBIN, N. (1976) 'Housework' *Signs: Journal of Women in Culture and Society* 1, no.4 (Summer) pp.905 – 22.

GOFFMAN, E. (1961) *Asylums* New York, Doubleday.

GOFFMAN, E. (1979) *Gender Advertisements* London, Macmillan.

GOLDBERG, P. (1968) 'Are women prejudiced against women?' *Transaction*, 5, no.5, pp.28 – 30.

GOLDBERG, S. (1977) *The Inevitability of Patriarchy* London, Maurice Temple Smith.

GOLDBLATT, P.B., MOORE, M.E. and STUNKARD, A.J. (1965) 'Social factors in obesity' *Journal of the American Medical Association* 192, pp.1039 – 44.

GOLDTHORP, W.O. (1977) 'Ten minute abortions' *British Medical Journal*, 27 August.

GOLDTHORPE, J.H., LOCKWOOD, D., BECHHOFER, F. and PLATT, J. (1968) *The Affluent Worker: Industrial Attitudes and Behaviour* Cambridge, Cambridge University Press.

GOOD, T.L., SIKES, N.J. and BROPHY, J.E. (1973) 'Effects of teacher sex and pupil sex on classroom interaction' *Journal of Educational Psychology*, 65, no.1, pp.74 – 87.

GOODALE, J.C. (1971) *Tiwi Wives* Washington, University Press.

GOOT, M. and REID, E. (1975) *Women and Voting Studies: Mindless Matrons or Sexist Scientism?* Beverly Hills, Sage Publications.

GORER, G. (1971) *Sex and Marriage in England Today* London, Nelson.

GOSNELL, H.F. (1948) *Democracy, the Threshhold of Freedom* New York, Ronald Press.

GOSS, D.A. (1975) 'Current status of artificial insemination with donor semen' *American Journal of Obstetrics and Gynaecology*, 122, pp.246 – 52.

GOUGH, E.K. (1968) 'Is the family universal? The Nayar case' in Bell and Vogel (eds.).

GOULD, R.E. (1974) 'Measuring masculinity by the size of a paycheck' in J.H. Pleck and J. Sawyer (eds.) *Man and Masculinity* Englewood Cliffs, New Jersey, Prentice-Hall.

GOVE, W.R. (1972) 'The relationship between sex roles, mental illness and marital status' *Social Forces*, 51, no.1, pp.34 – 44.

GOVE, W.R. and TUDOR, J.F. (1973) 'Adult sex roles and mental illness' *American Journal of Sociology*, 78, January, pp.812 – 35.

GRAHAM, H. (1976) 'The social image of pregnancy: pregnancy as spirit possession' *Sociological Review*, 24, no.2, pp.291 – 308.

GRAHAM, H. (1978) 'Problems in antenatal care'. Paper given to Department of Health and Social Security/Child Poverty Action Group Conference on Reaching the Consumer in the Antenatal and Child Health Services, London, April.

GRAHAM, H. and MCKEE, L. (1978) 'The first months of motherhood'. Unpublished Report of Health Education Council Project on Women's Experiences of Pregnancy, Childbirth and the First Six Months After Birth.

GRAHAM, H. and OAKLEY, A. (in press) 'Competing ideologies of reproduction: medical and maternal perspectives on pregnancy and childbirth' in H. Roberts (ed.) *Women, Health and Reproduction* London, Routledge and Kegan Paul.

GRAY, J.A. and BUFFERY, A.W.H. (1971) 'Sex differences in emotional and cognitive behaviour in mammals including man: adaptive and neural bases' *Acta Psychologica*, 35, pp.89 – 111.

GREEN, R. (1974) *Sexual Identity Conflict in Children and Adults* London, Duckworth.

GREENSTEIN, F.I. (1973) 'Sex-related political differences in childhood' in J. Dennis (ed.) *Socialization to Politics: A Reader* New York, John Wiley.

GRIFFITHS, D. and SARAGA, E. (1979) 'Sex differences and cognitive abilities: a sterile field of enquiry?' in Hartnett *et al.* (eds.).

GRIFFITHS, M. (1976) 'Can we still afford occupational segregation? Some remarks' *Signs: Journal of Women in Culture and Society*, 1, no.3, (Spring) pp.7 – 14.

GROSS, E. (1968) ' "Plus ça change . . . . . ?" The sexual structure of occupations over time' *Social Problems*, 16, (Fall) pp.198 – 208.

GUILLEBAUD, J., BONNAR, J., MOREHEAD, J. and MATTHEWS, A. (1976) 'Menstrual blood-loss with intrauterine devices' *Lancet*, 21, no.2, pp.387 – 90.

HACKER, H. (1969) 'Women as a minority group' in Roszak and Roszak (eds.).

HAKIM, C. (1979) *Occupational Segregation* Research Paper no.9, Department of Employment, London, HMSO.

HAMILL, L. (1978) *Wives as Sole and Joint Breadwinners* Government Economic Service Working Papers no.13, London, HMSO.

HAMILTON, R. (1978) *The Liberation of Women* London, Allen and Unwin.

HAMMER, S. (1976) *Daughters and Mothers: Mothers and Daughters* London, Hutchinson.

HAMMOND, D. and JABLOW, A. (1976) *Women in Cultures of the World* Meno Park, California, Cummings Publishing Co.

HANMER, J. (1978) 'Violence and the social control of women' in Littlejohn *et al.* (eds.).

HANSSON, R.E., CHERNOVETZ, M.E. and JONES, H. (1977) 'Maternal employment and androgyny' *Psychology of Women Quarterly*, 2, pp.76 – 8.

HARKNESS, R.A. (1974) 'Variations in testosterone excretion by man' in Ferin *et al.* (eds.).

HARRIS, C.C. (1969) *The Family* London, Allen and Unwin.

HARRIS, M. (1977) *Cows, Pigs, Wars and Witches: The Riddles of Culture* London, Fontana.

HARRISON, B. (1978) *Separate Spheres: The Opposition to Women's Suffrage in Britain* London, Croom Helm.

HARTNETT, O., BODEN, G. and FULLER, M. (eds.) (1979) *Sex Role Stereotyping* London, Tavistock.

HASTRUP, K. (1978) 'The semantics of biology: virginity' in Ardener (ed.).

HEALTH AND SAFETY EXECUTIVE (1973) *Hours of Employment of Women and Young Persons* London, HMSO.

HEITLINGER, A. (1979) *Women and State Socialism: Sex Inequality in the Soviet Union and Czechoslovakia* London, Macmillan.

HENDERSON, A. (1964) *The Family House in England* Los Angeles, Phoenix House.

HENLEY, N.M. (1977) *Body Politics* Chicago, Prentice-Hall.

HENNIG, M. and JARDIM, A. (1978) *The Managerial Woman* New York, Pocket Books.

HERLIHY, D. (1976) 'Land, family and women in continental Europe, 701 – 1200' in Stuard (ed.).

HERSEY, R.B. (1931) 'Emotional cycles in man' *Journal of Mental Science*, 77, pp.151 – 69.

HETHERINGTON, E.M. (1965) 'A developmental study of the effects of sex of the dominant parent on sex-role preference, identification and imitation in children' *Journal of Personality and Social Psychology*, 2, pp.188 – 94.

HETHERINGTON, E.M. and FRANKIE, G. (1967) 'Effects of parental dominance, warmth and conflict on imitation in children' *Journal of Personality and Social Psychology*, 6, pp.119 – 25.

HEWITT, P. (1980) 'Sex equality' in N. Bosanquet and P. Townsend (eds.) *Labour and Equality* London, Heinemann.

HIATT, M. (1977) *The Way Women Write* New York, Teachers' College Press.

HILLS, J. (1978) 'Women in the Labour and Conservative Parties'. Paper presented to P.S.A. Conference, Spring.

HIMES, N.E. (1963) *Medical History of Contraception* New York, Gamut Press.

HINKLE, L.E. and WOLFF, H.G. (1957) 'Health and the social environment' in Leighton *et al.* (eds.).

HIRSCHMAN, L., GROSS, J., SAVITT, J. and SANDERS, K. (1975). Paper abstracted in Thorne and Henley (eds.).

HITE, S. (1977) *The Hite Report: A Nationwide Study of Female Sexuality* New York, Summit Books.

HOBSON, D. (1978) 'Housewives: isolation as oppression' in Women's Studies Group, Centre for Contemporary Cultural Studies, University of Birmingham (ed.) *Women Take Issue: Aspects of Women's Subordination* London, Hutchinson.

HOCHSCHILD, A.R. (1975) 'The sociology of feeling and emotion: selected possibilities' in Millman and Kanter (eds.).

HOFFMAN, L.W. and NYE, F.I. (eds.) (1974) *Working Mothers: An Evaluative Review of the Consequences for Wife, Husband and Child* San Francisco, Jossey-Bass.

HOFFMAN, M.M. (1975) 'Assumptions in sex education books' *Educational Review*, 27, University of Birmingham.

HOLCOMBE, L. (1973) *Victorian Ladies at Work* London, David and Charles.

HOLE, C. (1977) *Witchcraft in England* London, Batsford.

HOLLIS, P. (1979) *Women in Public: the Women's Movement 1850 – 1900* London, Allen and Unwin.

HOLTER, H. (1970) *Sex Roles and Social Structure* Oslo, Universitetsforlaget.

HOME OFFICE (1974) *Equality for Women* London, HMSO.

HOME OFFICE (1979) *Marriage Matters. A Consultative Document by the Working Party on Marriage Guidance* London, HMSO.

HOPE, E., KENNEDY, M. and DE WINTER, A. (1976) 'Homeworkers in North London' in Barker and Allen (eds.) (1976a).

HORNER, M.S. (1970) 'Femininity and successful achievement: a basic inconsistency' in Bardwick *et al.* (eds.).

HORNER, M.S. (1972) 'Toward an understanding of achievement-related conflicts in women' *Journal of Social Issues*, 28, p.157.

HORNEY, K. (1937) *The Neurotic Personality of Our Time* New York, W.W. Norton.

HORNEY, K. (1939) *New Ways in Psychoanalysis* New York, W.W. Norton.

HOUGH, J.F. (1978) 'Women and women's issues in Soviet policy debates' in Atkinson *et al.* (eds.).

HUANG, L. (1971) 'Sex role stereotypes and self concepts among American and Chinese students' *Journal of Comparative Family Studies*, 2, pp.215 – 34.

HUBBARD, R. (1976) Review of *Rosalind Franklin and DNA* by A. Sayre *Signs: Journal of Women in Culture and Society*, 2, no.1 (Autumn) pp.229 – 37.

HUBBARD, R. (1979) 'Reflections on the story of the double helix' *Women's Studies International Quarterly* 2, no.3, pp.261 – 74.

HUBBARD, R., HENIFIN, M.S. and FRIED, B. (1979) *Women Looking at Biology Looking at Women* Boston, Mass., G.K. Hall and Co.

HUGHES, M., MAYALL, B., MOSS, P., PERRY, J., PETRIE, P. and PINKERTON, G. (1980) *Nurseries Now* Harmondsworth, Penguin.

HULIN, C.L. (1966) 'Job satisfaction and turnover in a female clerical population' *Journal of Applied Psychology*, 50, no.4, pp.280 – 5.

HUNT, A. (1968) *A Survey of Women's Employment* London, HMSO.

HUNT, A. (1970) *The Home Help Service in England and Wales: A Survey Carried Out in 1967* London, HMSO.

HUNT, A. (1973) *Families and Their Needs* London, HMSO.

HUNT, A. (1975) *Management Attitudes and Practices Towards Women at Work* London, HMSO.

HURSTFIELD, J. (1978) *The Part-Time Trap* Low Pay Unit, 9 Poland Street, London, W1.

HUTT, C. (1972) *Males and Females* Harmondsworth, Penguin.

ILLICH, I. (1975) *Medical Nemesis* London, Calder and Boyars.

IN THEORY PRESS (1979) *Feminist Practice: Notes from the Tenth Year* London, In Theory Press.

IRVINE, J., MILES, I. and EVANS, J. (eds.) (1979) *Demystifying Social Statistics* London, Pluto Press.

JACOBY, R.M. (1976) 'Feminism and class consciousness in the British and American women's trade union leagues, 1890 – 1925' in Carroll (ed.).

JACKSON, E. (1979) *Childminder* London, Routledge and Kegan Paul.

JACQUETTE, J.S. (1974) 'Introduction: women in American politics' in Jacquette (ed.).

JACQUETTE, J.S. (ed.) (1974) *Women in Politics* New York, Wiley Interscience.

JANCAR, B.W. (1974) 'Women under communism' in Jacquette (ed.).

JANOWSKY, D.S., GORNEY, R., CASTELNUOVO-TEDESCO, P. and STONE, C.B. (1969) 'Premenstrual – menstrual increase in psychiatric hospital admission rates' *American Journal of Obstetrics and Gynaecology*, 103, pp.189 – 91.

JEPHCOTT, P. (1962) *Married Women Working* London, Allen and Unwin.

JOHNSON, J. (1978) *Bad Connections* London, Virago.

JOLLY, H. (1975) *Book of Child Care* London, Allen and Unwin.

JONES, B. and BROWN, J. (1970) 'Toward a female liberation movement' in L.B. Tanner (ed.) *Voices From Women's Liberation* New York, Signet Books.

JOSEPH, J. (1961) 'A research note on attitudes to work and marriage of 600 adolescent girls' *British Journal of Sociology*, 12, pp.176 – 183.

JOST, A. (1972) 'A new look at the mechanisms controlling sex differentiation in mammals' *Johns Hopkins Medical Journal*, 130, pp.38 – 53.

KAGAN, J. (1978) *The Growth of the Child* New York, W.W. Norton.

KAGAN, J. and KAGAN, N. (1970) 'Individuality and cognitive performance' in Mussen (ed.).

KAMERMAN, S.B. (1977) 'Public policy and the family: a new strategy for women as wives and mothers' in J.R. Chapman and M. Gates (eds.) *Women into Wives: the Legal and Economic Impact of Marriage* Beverly Hills, Sage.

KAMERMAN, S.B. (1979) 'Work and family in industrialized societies' *Signs: Journal of Women in Culture and Society*, 4, no.4 (Summer) pp.632 – 50.

KARDINER, A. (1955) *Sex and Morality* London, Routledge and Kegan Paul.

KARET, T. (1977) 'Popular fiction' in King and Stott (eds.).

KEELEY, L.H. (1977) 'The functions of paleolithic flint tools' *Scientific American*, 237, pp.108 – 26.

KEMENER, B.J. (1965) 'A study of the relationship between the sex of the student and the assignment of marks by secondary school teachers'. PhD Thesis, East Lansing, Michigan, Michigan State University.

KENDALL, I. (1979) *Mothers and Babies First?* Published by the National Maternity Grant Campaign (National Council for One Parent Families and Child Poverty Action Group) 255 Kentish Town Road, London, NW5 2LX.

KERR, M. (1958) *The People of Ship Street* London, Routledge and Kegan Paul.

KERR, M. (1978) 'Problems and perspectives in reproductive medicine'. University of Edinburgh Inaugural Lecture, 25 November.

KIMURA, D. (1963a) 'Functional asymmetry of the brain in dichotic listening' *Cortex*, 3, pp.163 – 78.

KIMURA, D. (1963b) 'Speech lateralization in young children as determined by an auditory test' *Journal of Comparative and Physiological Psychology*, 56, pp.899 – 902.

KING, J. and STOTT, M. (eds.) (1977) *Is This Your Life? Images of Women in the Media* London, Virago.

KING, R. (1978) *All Things Bright and Beautiful? A Sociological Study of Infant Classrooms* Chichester, John Wiley.

KING, W.H. (1965) 'Experimental evidence on comparative attainment in mathematics in single sex and co-educational secondary schools' *Educational Research*, 8, pp.155 – 60.

KINSEY, A.C., POMEROY, W.B., MARTIN, C.E. and GEBHARD, P.H. (1953) *Sexual Behavior in the Human Female* Philadelphia, W.H. Saunders.

KITZINGER, S. (1962) *The Experience of Childbirth* London, Gollancz.

KITZINGER, S. and DAVIS, J.A. (eds.) (1978) *The Place of Birth* Oxford, University Press.

KLAUS, M.H. and KENNELL, J.H. (1976) *Maternal – Infant Bonding* Saint Louis, C.V. Mosby.

KLEIN, J. (1965) *Samples From English Cultures* vol.1, London, Routledge and Kegan Paul.

KLEIN, V. (1949) 'The emancipation of women: its motives and achievements' in H. Grisewood (ed.) *Ideas and Beliefs of the Victorians* London, Sylvan Press.

KLEIN, V. (1965) *Britain's Married Women Workers* London, Routledge and Kegan Paul.

KOBRIN, F.E. (1966) 'The American midwife controversy: a crisis of professionalization' *Bulletin of the History of Medicine* July – August, pp.350 – 63.

KOERBER, C. (1977) 'Television' in King and Stott (eds.).

KOESKE, R.K. and KOESKE, G.F. (1975) 'An attributional approach to moods and the menstrual cycle' *Journal of Personality and Social Psychology*, 31, no.3, pp.473 – 8.

KOHLBERG, L. (1967) 'A cognitive – developmental analysis of children's sex-role concepts and attitudes' in Maccoby (ed.).

KOHLBERG, L. and ULLIAN, D.Z. (1974) 'Stages in the development of psychosexual concepts and attitudes' in Friedman *et al*. (eds.).

KOMAROVSKY, M. (1946) 'Cultural contradictions and sex roles' *American Journal of Sociology*, 52, pp.182 – 9.

KOMAROVSKY, M. (1967) *Blue Collar Marriage* New York, Vintage Books.

KRAMER, H. and SPRENGER, J. (1971) *The Malleus Maleficarum* trans. M. Summers, New York, Dover Publications. (First published 1486.)

KUHL, J.F.W., LEE, J.K., HALBERG, F., HARRIS, E., GUNTHER, R. and KNAPP, E. (1974) 'Circadian and lower frequency rhythms in male grip strength and baby weight' in Ferin *et al.* (eds.).

KUHN, A. and WOLPE, A. (eds.) (1978) *Feminism and Materialism: Women and Modes of Production* London, Routledge and Kegan Paul.

KUHN, T. (1962) *The Structure of Scientific Revolutions* Chicago, University Press.

KURTZ, R.M. (1969) 'Sex differences and variations in body attitudes' *Journal of Consulting and Clinical Psychology* 33, pp.625 – 9.

LACEY, C. (1970) *Hightown Grammar* Manchester, University Press.

LAING, R.D. (1969) *The Politics of the Family and Other Essays* New York, Pantheon.

LAKE, A. (1975) 'Are we born into our sex roles or programmed into them?' *Woman's Day* January, pp.24 – 5.

LAKOFF, R. (1975) *Language and Woman's Place* New York, Harper Colophon.

LAND, H. (1977) 'Inequalities in large families: more of the same or different?' in R. Chester and J. Peel (eds.) *Equalities and Inequalities in Family Life* London, Academic Press.

LAND, H. (1978) 'Who cares for the family?' *Journal of Social Policy*, 7, no.3, pp.257 – 84.

LAND, H. (1979) 'The boundaries between the state and the family' in C.C. Harris (ed.) *The Sociology of the Family: New Directions for Britain* University of Keele, Sociological Review Monograph 28.

LANGTON, K. (1969) *Political Socialization* New York, Oxford University Press.

LANSING, M. (1974) 'The American woman: voter and activist' in Jacquette (ed.).

LAPIDUS, G.W. (1978) 'Sexual equality in Soviet policy: a developmental perspective' in Atkinson *et al.* (eds.).

LASCH, C. (1978) *Haven in a Heartless World: the Family Beseiged* New York, Basic Books.

LAWS, J.L. (1979) *The Second X* New York, Elsevier.

LAZOWICK, L.M. (1955) 'On the nature of identification' *Journal of Abnormal and Social Psychology*, 51, pp.175 – 83.

LEACH, P. (1979) *Who cares? A New Deal for Mothers and Their Small Children* Harmondsworth, Penguin.

LEAVITT, R.R., SYKES, B. and WEATHERFORD, E. (1975) 'Aboriginal women: male and female anthropological perspectives' in Reiter (ed.).

LEESON, J. and GRAY, J. (1978) *Women and Medicine* London, Tavistock.

LEETE, R. (1979) 'New directions in family life' *Population Trends*, 15 (Spring), Office of Population Censuses and Surveys, London, HMSO.

LEGUIN, U. (1973) *The Left Hand of Darkness* London, Panther.

LEHRKE, R.G. (1973) 'Sex linkage: a biological basis for greater male variability in intelligence' in Osborne *et al.* (eds.).

LEIGHTON, A.H., CLAUSEN, J.A. and WILSON, R.N. (eds.) (1957) *Explorations in Social Psychiatry* London, Tavistock.

LENNOX, I. (1969) 'Problems of the Abortion Act in general practice' in The Medical Protection Society *The Abortion Act 1967*. Proceedings of a symposium held by the Medical Protection Society in collaboration with the Royal College of General Practitioners, London, 7 February 1969, London, Pitman Medical.

LEONARD, D. (1979) 'Is feminism more complex than the women's liberation movement realises?' in In Theory Press.

LEPPER, M.M. (1974) 'A study of career structures of federal executives' in Jacquette (ed.).

LEVER, J. and SCHWARTZ, P. (1971) *Women at Yale: Liberating A College Campus* London, Allen Lane.

LEVI-STRAUSS, C. (1960) 'The family' in H.L. Shapiro (ed.) *Man, Culture and Society* New York, Oxford University Press.

LEVY, J. (1972) 'Lateral specialization of the human brain: behavioural manifestations and possible evolutionary basis' in J.A. Kiger (ed.) *The Biology of Behaviour* Corvallis, Oregon State University Press.

LEWIN, K. (1941) 'Self hatred among Jews' *Contemporary Jewish Record*, 4, pp.219 – 32.

LEWIS, E.E. (1968) *Developing Women's Potential* Ames, Iowa State University Press.

LEWIS, I.M. (1966) 'Spirit possession and deprivation cults' Malinowski Memorial Lecture, *Man* (Journal of the Royal Anthropological Institute) 1, no.3, September.

LIDDINGTON, J. and NORRIS, J. (1978) *One Hand Tied Behind Us* London, Virago.

LISTER, R. (n.d.) *Man and Wife: A Study of the Cohabitation Rule* Poverty Research Series 2, Child Poverty Action Group.

LITTLE, K. (1954) 'The Mende in Sierra Leone' in D. Forde (ed.) *African Worlds* London, Oxford University Press.

LLEWELYN-DAVIES, M. (1978) 'Two contexts of solidarity' in Kaplan and Bujra (eds.).

LLOYD, B. (1976) 'Social responsibility and research on sex differences' in Lloyd and Archer (eds.).

LLOYD, B. and ARCHER, J. (eds.) (1976) *Exploring Sex Differences* London, Academic Press.

LLOYD, C.W. (1970) 'The ovaries' in R.H. Williams (ed.) *Textbook of Endocrinology* (3rd edition) Philadelphia, W.B. Saunders.

LOBBAN, G. (1976) 'Sex roles in reading schemes' in Children's Rights Workshop.

LOBBAN, G. (1978) 'The influence of the school on sex-role stereotyping' in Chetwynd and Hartnett (eds.).

LOPATA, H.Z. (1971) *Occupation Housewife* New York, Oxford University Press.

LUCE, G.G. (1970) *Biological Rhythms in Psychiatry and Medicine* U.S.P.H.S. Publication no.2088, Washington, DC, United States Department of Health, Education and Welfare.

LYNCH, A. and MYCHALKIND, W. (1978) 'Prenatal progesterone II: its role in the treatment of pre-eclamptic toxaemia and its effect on the offspring's intelligence: a reappraisal' *Early Human Development*, 2, no.4, pp.323–39.

LYNCH, A., MYCHALKIND, W. and HUTT, S.J. (1978) 'Prenatal progesterone I: its effect on development and on intellectual and academic achievement' *Early Human Development*, 2, no.4, pp.305–22.

LYNCH, M.A. and ROBERTS, J. (1977) 'Predicting child abuse: signs of bonding failure in the maternity hospital' *British Medical Journal* 5 March, pp.624–6.

LYNN, R. (1978) 'Ethnic and racial differences in intelligence: international comparisons' in Osborne *et al.* (eds.).

MACARTHUR, R. (1967) 'Sex differences in field dependence for the Eskimo' *International Journal of Psychology*, 2, pp.139 – 40.

MCBRIDE, T.M. (1976) *The Domestic Revolution* London, Croom Helm.

MCCARTHY, M. (1977) 'Women in trade unions' in Middleton (ed.).

MCCARTHY, P., DEWIT, J. and HARTUP, W. (eds.) (1974) *Determinants and Origins of Aggressive Behaviour* The Hague, DeMouton.

MCCLEARY, G.F. (1933) *The Early History of the Infant Welfare Movement* London, H.K. Lewis and Co.

MCCLEARY, G.F. (1945) *Race Suicide* London, Allen and Unwin.

MCCLELLAND, D.C. (1961) *The Achieving Society* Glencoe, Free Press.

MCCLINTOCK, F. (1963) *Crimes of Violence* London, Macmillan.

MACCOBY, E.E. (ed.) (1967) *The Development of Sex Differences* London, Tavistock.

MACCOBY, E.E. and JACKLIN, C.N. (1974) *The Psychology of Sex Differences* Stanford, University Press.

MCCRINDLE, J. and ROWBOTHAM, S. (1977) *Dutiful Daughters* London, Allen Lane.

MACFARLANE, A. (1977) *The Psychology of Childbirth* London, Fontana.

MACFARLANE, A. (1979a) 'Child deaths from accidents: place of accident' *Population Trends*, 15 (Spring).

MACFARLANE, A. (1979b) 'Social class variations in perinatal mortality' *Journal of Maternal and Child Health* September, pp.337 – 40.

MACFARLANE, A. (1980) 'Women and health: official statistics on women and aspects of health and illness'. Paper presented to the SSRC/EOC Seminar on 'Women and Government Statistics', 5 June.

MACFARLANE, A.D.J. (1970) *Witchcraft in Tudor and Stuart England* London, Routledge and Kegan Paul.

MCGUINESS, D. (1975) 'The impact of innate perceptual differences between the sexes on the socializing process' *Educational Review*, 27, University of Birmingham.

MACINTYRE, S. (1973) 'The medical profession and the 1967 Abortion Act in Britain' *Social Science and Medicine*, 7, pp.121 – 34.

MACINTYRE, S. (1976a) 'Who wants babies? The social construction of "instincts" ' in Barker and Allen (eds.) (1976b).

MACINTYRE, S. (1976b) 'To have or have not: promotion and prevention in gynaecological work' in Stacey (ed.).

MACKIE, L. and PATULLO, P. (1977) *Women At Work* London, Tavistock.

MACKINNON, P.C.B. and MACKINNON, I.L. (1956) 'Hazards of the menstrual cycle' *British Medical Journal*, 1, p.555.

MACMILLAN, M. (1979) 'Beyond jam making' *New Society* 28 June.

MCNALLY, F. (1979) *Women For Hire* London, Macmillan.

MCNAY, M. and POND, C. (1980) *Low Pay and Family Poverty* London, Study Commission on the Family.

MCROBBIE, A. and GARBER, J. (1975) 'Girls and subcultures: an exploration' in S. Hall and T. Jefferson (eds.) *Resistance through Rituals: Youth Subcultures in Postwar Britain* London, Hutchinson.

MCWILLIAMS, N. (1974) 'Contemporary feminism, consciousness-raising, and changing views of the political' in Jacquette (ed.).

MADIGAN, F.C. (1957) 'Are sex mortality differentials biologically caused?' *The Milbank Memorial Fund Quarterly*, 35, no.2, April, pp.202 – 23.

MAHL, M.R. and KOON, H. (1979) *The Female Spectator: English Women Writers Before 1800* Bloomington, Indiana University Press.

MAIR, L. (1977) *Marriage* London, The Scholar Press.

MAKHLOUF, C. (1979) *Changing Veils: Women and Modernisation in North Yemen* London, Croom Helm.

MALINOWSKI, B. (1932) *The Sexual Life of Savages* London, Routledge and Kegan Paul.

MALINOWSKI, B. (1963) *The Family Among the Australian Aborigines* New York, Schocken Books.

MALOS, E. (1977) 'Housework and the politics of women's liberation'. Reprinted from January – February *Socialist Review* by RSM publications, 11 Waverly Road, Redland, Bristol BS6 6ES.

MANDELL, A. and MANDELL, M. (1967) 'Suicide and the menstrual cycle' *Journal of the American Medical Association*, 200, pp.792 – 3.

MANLEY, P. and SAWBRIDGE, D. (1980) 'Women at work' *Lloyds Bank Review*, no.135, pp.29 – 40.

MARCUS, S. (1966) *The Other Victorians: A Study of Sexuality and Pornography in Mid-Nineteenth Century England* London, Weidenfeld and Nicolson.

MARKS, P. (1976) 'Femininity in the classroom: an account of changing attitudes' in Mitchell and Oakley (eds.).

MARTIN, M.K. and VOORHIES, B. (1975) *Female of the Species* New York, Columbia University Press.

MARTIN, R. (1972) 'Student sex behaviour as determinants of the type and frequency of teacher – student contacts' *School Psychology*, 10, no.4, pp.339 – 47.

MARWICK, A. (1977) *Women at War 1914 – 18* London, Fontana.

MARWICK, M. (ed.) (1970) *Witchcraft and Sorcery* Harmondsworth, Penguin.

MASTERS, W.H. and JOHNSON, V.E. (1966) *Human Sexual Response* Boston, Little, Brown and Co.

MAURICE, F. (1903) 'National health: a soldier's study' *Contemporary Review*, 83, January.

MEAD, M. (1935) *Sex and Temperament in Three Primitive Societies* New York, William Morrow.

MEAD, M. (1940) 'Toward a new role for women' *The Woman's Press*, 34, pp.466 – 7.

MEAD, M. (1954) 'Some theoretical considerations on the problem of mother – child separation' *American Journal of Orthopsychiatry*, 24, no.3, pp.471 – 83.

MEAD, M. (1962) *Male and Female* Harmondsworth, Penguin.

MEAD, M. (1966) 'A cultural anthropologist's approach to maternal deprivation' in Ainsworth *et al*.

MEIGHAN, R. (1979) 'The pupils' point of view' in Meighan *et al*. (eds.).

MEIGHAN, R., SKELTON, I. and MARKS, T. (eds.) (1979) *Perspectives on Society: An Introductory Reader in Sociology* London, Thomas Nelson.

MEISSNER, M., HUMPHREYS, E., MEIS, S. and SCHERR, J. (n.d.) 'No exit for wives: sexual division of labour and the cumulation of household demands'. Unpublished paper.

MEYER-BAHLBURG, H.F.L. (1974) 'Aggression, androgens and the XYY syndrome' in Friedmann *et al.* (eds.).

MGM MARKETING RESEARCH AND SURVEYS (1978) *Husbands and Wives Shopping For Food* MGM Marketing Research and Surveys, Athene House, 67 Shoe Lane, London, EC4.

MICHAEL, R.P. and GLASCOCK, R.F. (1963) 'The distribution of C^{14}- and H^3-labelled oestrogens in the brain' *Proceedings of the Fifth (1961) International Congress of Biochemistry* 9, p.1137.

MIDDLETON, L. (ed.) (1977) *Women in the Labour Movement* London, Croom Helm.

MILL, J.S. (1929) *On the Subjection of Women* London, Everyman. (First published 1869.)

MILLER, C. and SWIFT, K. (1979) *Words and Women* Harmondsworth, Penguin.

MILLER, J.B. (1976) *Toward A New Psychology of Women* Boston, Beacon Press.

MILLER, R. (1978) *Equal Opportunities* Harmondsworth, Penguin.

MILLETT, K. (1971) *Sexual Politics* London, Rupert Hart-Davis.

MILLETT, K. (1976) *The Prostitution Papers* New York, Ballantine Books.

MILLMAN, M. and KANTER, R.M. (eds.) (1975) *Another Voice: Feminist Perspectives on Social Life and Social Science* New York, Anchor Books.

MILLS, C.W. (1959) *The Sociological Imagination* New York, Oxford University Press.

MILLUM, T. (1975) *Images of Women: Advertising in Women's Magazines* London, Chatto and Windus.

MINISTRY OF HEALTH (1937) *Report on An Investigation into Maternal Mortality* London, HMSO.

MISCHEL, W. (1967) 'A social-learning view of sex differences in behaviour' in Maccoby (ed.).

MISCHEL, W. (1970) 'Sex-typing and socialization' in Mussen (ed.).

MITCHELL, H. (1977) *The Hard Way Up* London, Virago.

MITCHELL, J. (1966) 'Women: the longest revolution' *New Left Review*, no.40.

MITCHELL, J. (1971) *Woman's Estate* Harmondsworth, Penguin.

MITCHELL, J. and OAKLEY, A. (eds.) (1976) *The Rights and Wrongs of Women* Harmondsworth, Penguin.

MONEY, J. (1970) 'Impulse, aggression and sexuality in the XYY syndrome' *St John's Law Review*, 44, pp.220–35.

MONEY, J. and EHRHARDT, A.E. (1972) *Man and Woman, Boy and Girl* Baltimore, Johns Hopkins Press.

MONEY, J. and TUCKER, P. (1977) *Sexual Signatures* London, Sphere Books.

MONTAGU, A. (1968) *The Natural Superiority of Women* London, Macmillan.

MORANTZ, S. and MANSFIELD, A. (1977) 'Maternal employment and the development of sex role stereotyping in five to eleven year olds' *Child Development*, 48, pp.668–73.

MORGAN, D.H.J. (1975) *Social Theory and the Family* London, Routledge and Kegan Paul.

MORGAN, E. (1972) *The Descent of Woman* London, Souvenir Press.

MORGAN, L.H. (1877) *Ancient Society* New York.

MORGAN, P. (1975) *Child Care: Sense and Fable* London, Maurice Temple Smith.

MORGAN, R. (1970) 'Introduction: the women's revolution' in R. Morgan (ed.).

MORGAN, R. (ed.) (1970) *Sisterhood is Powerful* New York, Vintage Books.

MORRIS, J.N. (1979) 'Social inequalities undiminished' *Lancet*, 13, pp.87–90.

MORTON, J.H., ADDITON, H., ADDISON, R.G., HUNT, L., and SULLIVAN, J.J. (1953) 'A clinical study of premenstrual tension' *American Journal of Obstetrics and Gynecology*, 65, pp.1182–91.

MOSS, H.A. (1967) 'Sex, age and state as determinants of mother–infant interaction' *Merrill-Palmer Quarterly*, 13, pp.19–36.

MOSS, H.A. (1974) 'Early sex differences and mother–infant interaction' in Friedmann *et al.* (eds.).

MOSS, P. (1976) 'The current situation' in N. Fonda and P. Moss (eds.) *Mothers in Employment* Uxbridge, Middlesex, Brunel University Management Programme.

MURDOCK, G. (1949) *Social Structure* New York, Macmillan.

MURDOCK, G. (1968) 'The universality of the nuclear family' in Bell and Vogel (eds.).

MURGATROYD, L. (1979) 'Notes on the development of women's studies'. Discussion paper for colloquium on the History of Academic Disciplines, London, November.

MURPHY, J.M. (1962) 'Cross-cultural studies of the prevalence of psychiatric disorder' *World Mental Health*, 14, no.2, pp.53 – 65.

MURPHY, R.F. (1959) 'Social structure and sex antagonism' *Southwestern Journal of Anthropology*, 15, no.1, (Spring).

MURPHY, Y. and MURPHY, R.F. (1974) *Women of the Forest* New York, Columbia University Press.

MUSSEN, P.H. (ed.) (1970) *Carmichael's Manual of Child Psychology* New York, John Wiley.

MUSSEN, P.H. and RUTHERFORD, E. (1963) 'Parent – child relations and parental personality in relation to young children's sex role preferences' *Child Development*, 34, pp.589 – 607.

MYRDAL, A. and KLEIN, V. (1956) *Women's Two Roles: Home and Work* London, Routledge and Kegan Paul.

MYRDAL, G. (1944) Appendix 5 'A parallel to the negro problem' in *An American Dilemma* New York, Harper and Row.

NANDY, L. and NANDY, D. (1975) 'Towards true equality for women' *New Society* 30 January.

NATIONAL CENTER FOR HEALTH STATISTICS (1978) *Contraceptive Utilization United States* United States Department of Health, Education and Welfare, Publication no.(PHS)79 – 1978.

NATIONAL COMMISSION ON WORKING WOMEN (1979) *Study of Working Women* reported in *Businessweek*, 5 February.

NATIONAL COUNCIL OF WOMEN (1976) 'Alcohol problems of women and young people'. Obtainable from NCW, 36 Lower Sloane Street, London SW1W 8BP.

NEFF, W.F. (1966) *Victorian Working Women* London, Frank Cass. (First published in 1929 by Allen and Unwin.)

NELSON, C. (1973) 'Women and power in nomadic societies of the Middle East' in C. Nelson (ed.) *The Desert and the Sown: Nomads in the Wider Society*. Research series no.21, Institute of International Studies, University of California, Berkeley.

NELSON, N., ENKIN, M.W., SAIGON, S., BENNETT, K.J., MILNER, R. and SACKETT, D.L. (1980) 'A randomized clinical trial of the Leboyer approach to childbirth' *New England Journal of Medicine* 20 March.

NEWCOMBE, R. and CHALMERS, I. (1977) 'Changes in distribution of gestational age and birth weight among firstborn infants of Cardiff residents' *British Medical Journal* 8 October, pp.925 – 6.

NEWLAND, K. (1979) *The Sisterhood of Man* New York, W.W. Norton.

NEWSOM REPORT (1963) *Half Our Future. Report of the Central Advisory Council on Education England* London, HMSO.

NEWSON, J. and NEWSON, E. (1970) *Four Years Old in an Urban Community* Harmondsworth, Penguin.

NEWSON, J. and NEWSON, E. (1976) *Seven Years Old in the Home Environment* London, Allen and Unwin.

NEWSON, J., NEWSON, E., RICHARDSON, D. and SCAIFE, J. (1978) 'Perspectives in sex role stereotyping' in Chetwynd and Hartnett (eds.).

NICHOLS, T. (1979) 'Social class: official, sociological and Marxist' in Irvine *et al.* (eds.).

NORLAND, S. and SHOVER, N. (1977) 'Gender roles and female criminality' *Criminology*, 15, no.1, pp.87 – 104.

NORTHERN WOMEN'S EDUCATION STUDY GROUP (1973) 'Sex role learning: a study of infant readers' in Wandor (ed.).

OAKLEY, A. (1972) *Sex, Gender and Society* London, Temple Smith.

OAKLEY, A. (1974a) *Housewife* London, Allen Lane.

OAKLEY, A. (1974b) *The Sociology of Housework* London, Martin Robertson.

OAKLEY, A. (1975) 'Sex discrimination legislation' *British Journal of Law and Society*, 2, no.2 (Winter) pp.211 – 17.

OAKLEY, A. (1976) 'Wisewoman and medicine man: changes in the management of childbirth' in Mitchell and Oakley (eds.).

OAKLEY, A. (1979) *Becoming a Mother* Oxford, Martin Robertson.

OAKLEY, A. (1980) *Women Confined: Towards a Sociology of Childbirth* Oxford, Martin Robertson.

OAKLEY, A. and OAKLEY, R. (1979) 'Sexism in official statistics' in Irvine *et al.* (eds.).

O'DONOVAN, K. (1979) 'The male appendage — legal definitions of women' in Burman (ed.).

O'DRISCOLL, K. (1975) 'An obstetrician's view of pain' *British Journal of Anaesthetics*, 47. p.1053 – 59.

O'FAOLAIN, J. and MARTINES, L. (eds.) (1973) *Not in God's Image* London, Temple Smith.

OFFICE OF HEALTH ECONOMICS (1978) *Accidental Deaths* OHE, Briefing pamphlet no.8, London.

OFFICE OF HEALTH ECONOMICS (1979) *Perinatal Mortality in Britain: A Question of Class* OHE, Briefing pamphlet no.10, London.

OFFICE OF POPULATION CENSUSES AND SURVEYS (1977) *Mortality Statistics: Accidents and Violence* London, HMSO.

OFFICE OF POPULATION CENSUSES AND SURVEYS (1979) *Monitor* 7 August, General Household Survey 1978, London, HMSO.

OHMANN, C. (1971) 'Emily Bronte in the hands of male critics' *College English*, 32, May, pp.906 – 13.

OKELY, J. (1978) 'Privileged, schooled and finished: boarding education for girls' in Ardener (ed.).

O'LAUGHLIN, B. (1974) 'Mediation of contradiction: why Mbum women do not eat chicken' in Rosaldo and Lamphere (eds.).

OLIVER, M.F. (1974) 'Ischaemic heart disease in young women' *British Medical Journal* 2 November, pp.253 – 9.

OLSEN, T. (1972) 'When writers don't write' in Cornillon (ed.).

O'NEILL, N. and O'NEILL, G. (1975) *Open Marriage* London, Sphere Books.

O'NEILL, W.L. (ed.) (1969) *The Woman Movement: Feminism in the United States and England* London, Allen and Unwin.

ORBACH, S. (1978) *Fat is a Feminist Issue* London, Paddington Press.

ORMEROD, M.B. (1975) 'Subject preference and choice in co-educational and single sex secondary schools' *British Journal of Educational Psychology*, 45, no.3, pp.257 – 67.

ORTNER, S.B. (1974) 'Is female to male as nature is to culture?' in Rosaldo and Lamphere (eds.).

OSBORN, A.F. and MORRIS, T.C. (1979) 'The rationale for a composite index of social class and its evaluation' *British Journal of Sociology*, 30, no.1, March, pp.39 – 60.

OSBORNE, R.T., NOBLE, C.E. and WEHL, N. (eds.) (1973) *Human Variation: The Biopsychology of Age, Race and Sex* London, Academic Press.

OUNSTED, C. and TAYLOR, D.C. (1972) 'The Y chromosome message: a point of view' in Ounsted and Taylor (eds.).

OUNSTED, C. and TAYLOR, D.C. (eds.) (1972) *Gender Differences: Their Ontogeny and Significance* Baltimore, Williams and Wilkins.

OVERZIER, C. (1963) *Intersexuality* London, Academic Press.

PAGELS, E.H. (1976) 'What became of God the Mother? Conflicting images of God in early Christianity' *Signs: Journal of Women in Culture and Society* 2, no.2 (Winter) pp.293 – 303.

PAHL, J.M. and PAHL, R.E. (1971) *Managers and Their Wives* London, Allen Lane.

PAIGE, K.E. (1971) 'Effects of oral contraceptives on affective fluctuations associated with the menstrual cycle' *Psychosomatic Medicine* 33, no.6, pp.515 – 37.

PANKHURST, C. (1924) *Pressing Problems of the Closing Age* London, Morgan and Scott.

PARLEE, M.B. (1976) 'The premenstrual syndrome' in S. Cox (ed.) *Female Psychology: The Emerging Self* Chicago, Science Research Associates.

PARINDER, G. (1958) *Witchcraft: European and African* London, Faber and Faber.

PARSONS, T. and BALES, R.F. (1956) *Family: Socialization and Interaction Process* London, Routledge and Kegan Paul.

PASTINE, M. (1979) 'Library instruction in women's studies research' *Women's Studies International Quarterly*, 2, no.2, pp.219 – 38.

PATTERSON, G.R., LITTMAN, R.A. and BRICKER, W. (1967) 'Assertive behaviour in children: a step toward a theory of aggression' *Monographs of the Society for Research in Child Development*, 32, serial no.113.

PAYNE, J. (1978) 'Talking about children: an examination of accounts about reproduction and family life' *Journal of Biosocial Science*, 10, no.4, October, pp.367–74.

PECKHAM RYE WOMEN'S LIBERATION GROUP (1970) 'A woman's work is never done'. Paper presented at Women's Liberation Conference, Oxford, March. Reprinted by Agitprop, 160 North Gower Street, London, NW1.

PEEL, J. and CARR, G. (1975) *Contraception and Family Design* Edinburgh, Churchill Livingstone.

PERSKY, H. (1974) 'Reproductive hormones, moods and the menstrual cycle' in Friedman *et al* (eds.).

PERSON, E. (1974) 'Some new observations on the origins of femininity' in J. Strouse (ed.) *Women and Analysis* New York, Grossman.

PETERSEN, K. and WILSON, J.J. (1976) *Women Artists: Recognition and Reappraisal from the Early Middle Ages to the Twentieth Century* London, The Women's Press.

PETERSEN, M.J. (1972) 'The Victorian governess: status incongruence in family and society' in M. Vicinus (ed.) *Suffer and Be Still: Women in the Victorian Age* Bloomington, Indiana University Press.

PHILLIPP, E.E. (1973) in Ciba Foundation Symposium 17 (new series) p.66, Amsterdam, Elsevier.

PHILLIPS, A. and RAKUSEN, J. (1978) *Our Bodies Ourselves* Harmondsworth, Penguin.

PIAGET, J. (1952) *The Origins of Intelligence in Children* New York, International Universities Press.

PIERCY, M. (1973) *Small Changes* New York, Doubleday.

PIERCY, M. (1976) *Woman on the Edge of Time* London, The Women's Press.

PINCHBECK, I. (1969) *Women Workers and the Industrial Revolution 1750–1850* London, Frank Cass. (First published in 1930 by Routledge and Kegan Paul.)

PIZZEY, E. (1974) *Scream Quietly or the Neighbours Will Hear* Harmondsworth, Penguin.

PLANT, M. (1952) *The Domestic Life of Scotland in the Eighteenth Century* Edinburgh University Press.

PLATH, S. (1963) *The Bell Jar* London, Faber and Faber.

PLATH, S. (1977) *Letters Home* ed. A.S. Plath, New York, Bantam Books.

PLOWDEN REPORT (1967) *Children and Their Primary Schools* London, HMSO.

POLITICS OF HEALTH GROUP (1979) *Food and Profit* London, Politics of Health Group.

POMEROY, S.B. (1976) 'A classical scholar's perspective on matriarchy' in Carroll (ed.).

PORTER, A.M.W. (1970) 'Depressive illness in a general practice. A demographic study and a controlled trial of imipramine' *British Medical Journal* 28 March, pp.773 – 8.

POTTS, M., DIGGORY, P. and PEEL, J. (1977) *Abortion* Cambridge, Cambridge University Press.

PRESTON, B. (1974) 'The surplus of women' *New Society* 28 March.

PUNER, H.W. (1947) *Freud: His Life and Mind* New York, Dell.

PURCELL, K. (1979) 'Militancy and acquiescence amongst women workers' in Burman (ed.).

PURCELL, S.F. (1974) 'Ideology and the law: sexism and supreme court decisions' in Jacquette (ed.).

PUREFOY, E. (1931) *Purefoy Letters* ed. G. Eland, London, Sidgwick and Jackson.

REDDAWAY, W.B. (n.d.) 'Economic and social aspects of family life' in J. Marchant (ed.) *Rebuilding Family Life in the Postwar World* London, Odhams Press.

REED, E. (1969) *Problems of Women's Liberation* New York, Merit Publishers.

REES, A.D. (1950) *Life in a Welsh Countryside* Cardiff, University of Wales Press.

REITER, R.R. (ed.) (1975) *Toward an Anthropology of Women* New York, Monthly Review Press.

RENDEL, M. (1978) 'Legislation for equal pay and opportunity for women in Britain' *Signs: Journal of Women in Culture and Society*, 3, no.4 (Summer) pp.897 – 908.

RHEINGOLD, H.L. and COOK, K.V. (1975) 'The content of boys' and girls' rooms as an index of parents' behaviour' *Child Development*, 46, no.2, pp.459 – 63.

RIBEIRO, A.L. (1962) 'Menstruation and crime' *British Medical Journal*, 1, p.640.

RICH, A. (1975) 'Toward a woman-centred university' in F. Howe (ed.) *Women and the Power to Change* New York, McGraw-Hill.

RICH, A. (1977) *Of Woman Born* London, Virago.

RICH A. (1979) *On Lies, Secrets and Silence. Selected Prose 1966 – 78* New York, W.W. Norton.

RICHARDS, L. (1978) *Having Families: Marriage, Parenthood and Social Pressure in Australia* Ringwood, Victoria, Australia, Penguin Books.

RICHARDS, M. (1975a) 'Innovation in medical practice: obstetricians and the induction of labour in Britain' *Social Science and Medicine*, 9, pp.595 – 602.

RICHARDS, M. (1975b) 'Non-accidental injury in an ecological perspective' in Department of Health and Social Security *Non-Accidental Injury to Children*. Proceedings of a Conference held at the DHSS, 19 June, London, HMSO.

RICHARDS, M. (1978) 'A place of safety? An examination of the risks of hospital delivery' in Kitzinger and Davis (eds.).

RICHARDS, M.P.M., BERNAL, J.F. and BRACKBILL, Y. (1976) 'Early behavioural differences: gender or circumcision?' *Developmental Psychobiology*, 9, no.1, pp.89 – 95.

RICHTER, C.P. (1968) 'Periodic phenomena in man and animals and their relation to neuroendocrinic mechanisms (in monthly or near monthly cycles)' in R.P. Michael (ed.) *Endocrinology and Human Behaviour* London, Oxford University Press.

RILEY, E.M.O. (1977) ' "What do women want?" — The question of choice in the conduct of labour' in Chard and Richards (eds.).

ROBBINS REPORT (1963) *Report of the Committee on Higher. Education* London, HMSO.

ROBERTS, H.E. (1977) 'The exquisite slave: the role of clothes in the making of the Victorian woman' *Signs: Journal of Women in Culture and Society*, 2, no.3 (Spring) pp.554 – 69.

ROBY, P. (1975) 'Sociology of women in working class jobs' in Millman and Kanter (eds.).

ROFF, M. (1950) 'Intra-family resemblances in personality characteristics' *Journal of Psychology*, 30, pp.199 – 227.

ROGERS, S.C. (1978) 'Woman's place: a critical review of anthropological theory' *Comparative Studies in Society and History*, 20, no.1, January, pp.123 – 62.

ROSALDO, M.Z. (1974) 'Woman, culture and society: a theoretical overview' in Rosaldo and Lamphere (eds.).

ROSALDO, M.Z. and LAMPHERE, L. (eds.) (1974) *Woman, Culture and Society* Stanford, California, Stanford University Press.

ROSE, R.M., GORDON, T.P. and BERNSTEIN, I.S. (1972) 'Plasma testosterone levels in the male rhesus: influences of sexual and social stimuli' *Science*, 178, pp.643 – 5.

ROSEN, A. (1974) *Rise Up, Women! The Militant Campaign of the Women's Social and Political Union 1903 – 1914* London, Routledge and Kegan Paul.

ROSENBERG, B.G. and SUTTON-SMITH, B. (1968) 'Family interaction effects on masculinity – femininity' *Journal of Personality and Social Psychology*, 8, p.117.

ROSENKRANTZ, P., VOGEL, S., BEE, H., BROVERMAN, I. and BROVERMAN, D. (1968) 'Sex role stereotypes and self-concepts in college students' *Journal of Consulting and Clinical Psychology*, 32, pp.287 – 95.

ROSS, H.L. (1976) *Women and Children Last* in J.R. Chapman (ed.) *Economic Independence for Women* Beverly Hills, Sage.

ROSSI, A. (1964) 'Equality between the sexes' in R.F. Lifton (ed.) *The Woman in America* Boston, Houghton Mifflin.

ROSSI, A. (1972) 'Family development in a changing world' *American Journal of Psychiatry*, 128, March, pp.1957 – 65.

ROSZAK, B. and ROSZAK, T. (eds.) (1969) *Masculinity/Femininity: Readings in Sexual Mythology and the Liberation of Women* New York, Harper and Row.

ROVER, C. (1967) *Women's Suffrage and Party Politics in Britain 1866 – 1914* London, Routledge and Kegan Paul.

ROWBOTHAM, S. (1972) *Women, Resistance and Revolution* London, Allen Lane.

ROWBOTHAM, S. (1973a) 'The beginning of women's liberation in Britain' in Wandor (ed.).

ROWBOTHAM, S. (1973b) *Woman's Consciousness, Man's World* Harmondsworth, Penguin.

ROWBOTHAM, S. (1973c) 'Women's liberation and the new politics' in Wandor (ed.).

ROWBOTHAM, S. (1979) 'The women's movement and organizing for socialism' in S. Rowbotham, L. Segal and H. Wainwright *Beyond the Fragments: Feminism and the Making of Socialism* London, Merlin Press.

ROYAL COLLEGE OF GENERAL PRACTITIONERS (1974) *Oral Contraceptives and Health* London, Pitman Medical.

ROYAL COLLEGE OF GENERAL PRACTITIONERS (1977) 'Recommendations from the findings by the RCGP oral contraception study on the mortality risks of oral contraceptive users' *British Medical Journal* 8 October, p.947.

ROYAL COLLEGE OF PHYSICIANS (1949) *Family Limitation and its Influence on Human Fertility During the Past Fifty Years.* Papers of the Royal Commission on Population, vol.1, London, HMSO.

RUBIN, L.B. (1976) *Worlds of Pain: Life in the Working Class Family* New York, Basic Books.

RUBINS, J.L. (1978) *Karen Horney: Gentle Rebel of Psychoanalysis* London, Weidenfeld and Nicolson.

RUSS, J. (1972) 'The image of women in science fiction' in Cornillon (ed.).

RUSS, J. (1977) *The Female Man* London, Star Books.

RUTTER, M. (1972) *Maternal Deprivation Reassessed* Harmondsworth, Penguin.

RYDER, J. and SILVER, H. (1970) *Modern English Society: History and Structure 1850–1970* London, Methuen.

SACHS, A. (1978) 'The myth of male protectiveness and the legal subordination of women' in Smart and Smart (eds.).

SACHS, A. and WILSON, J.H. (1978) *Sexism and the Law: A Study of Male Beliefs and Judicial Bias* London, Martin Robertson.

SACHS, J., LIEBERMAN, P. and ERICKSON, D. (1973) 'Anatomical and cultural determinants of male and female speech' in R.W. Shuy and R.W. Fasold (eds.) *Language Attitudes: Current Trends and Prospects* Washington, DC, Georgetown University Press.

SACHS, M.P. (1977) 'Unchanging times: a comparison of the everyday life of Soviet working men and women between 1923 and 1966' *Journal of Marriage and the Family* November, pp.793–805.

SALPER, R. (ed.) (1972) *Female Liberation: History and Current Politics* New York, Knopf.

SAN FRANCISCO REDSTOCKINGS (1969) 'Our politics begin with our feelings' in Roszak and Roszak (eds.).

SARSBY, J. (1972) 'Love and marriage' *New Society* 28 September.

SCHAFFER, H.R. and EMERSON, P. (1964) 'The development of social attachments in infancy' *Monographs of Social Research in Child Development*, 29, no.94.

SCHAFFER, R. (1977) *Mothering* London, Fontana/Open Books.

SCHERER, R.A., ABELES, R.P. and FISCHER, C.S. (1975) *Human Aggression and Conflict* Englewood Cliffs, New Jersey, Prentice-Hall.

SCHOFIELD, M. (1968) *The Sexual Behaviour of Young People* Harmondsworth, Penguin.

SCHÖPP-SCHILLING, H.B. (1979) 'Women's studies, women's research and women's research centres: recent developments in the U.S.A. and in the F.R.G.' *Women's Studies International Quarterly*, 2, no.1, pp.103 – 16.

SCHREINER, O. (1978) *Woman and Labour* London, Virago. (First published in 1911 by T. Fisher Unwin.)

SEAMAN, B. and SEAMAN, G. (1978) *Women and the Crisis in Sex Hormones* New York, Bantam Books.

SEARS, R.R., RAU, L. and ALPERT, R. (1965) *Identification and Childrearing* Stanford, California, Stanford University Press.

SEBASTYEN, A. (1979) 'Tendencies in the movement: then and now' in In Theory Press.

SECOMBE, W. (1974) 'The housewife and her labour under capitalism' *New Left Review*, 83, January – February.

SECONDARY SCHOOLS EXAMINATION COUNCIL (1943) *Curriculum and Examinations in Secondary Schools* (the Norwood Report) London, HMSO.

SELECT COMMITTEE ON TAX-CREDIT (1973) *Evidence* vol.2, London, HMSO.

SHARPE, S. (1976) *'Just Like a Girl': How Girls Learn to be Women* Harmondsworth, Penguin Books.

SHAW, J. (1976) 'Finishing school: some implications of sex-segregated education' in Barker and Allen (eds.) (1976b).

SHAW, N.S. (1974) *Forced Labor: Maternity Care in the United States* New York, Pergamon Press.

SHELLEY, M. (1970) 'Notes of a radical lesbian' in R. Morgan (ed.).

SHEPHERD, M., COOPER, B., BROWN, A.C. and KALTON, G.W. (1966) *Psychiatric Illness in General Practice* London, Oxford University Press.

SHERMAN, J.A. and BECK, E.T. (eds.) (1979) *The Prism of Sex: Essays in the Sociology of Knowledge* Madison, University of Wisconsin Press.

SHIELDS, S.A. (1975) 'Functionalism, Darwinism and the psychology of women: a study in social myth' *American Psychologist*, July, pp.739–54.

SHORTER, E. (1977) *The Making of the Modern Family* London, Fontana/Collins.

SILVERMAN, C. (1968) *The Epidemiology of Depression* Baltimore, The Johns Hopkins Press.

SIMON, W. and GAGNON, J.H. (1969) 'On psychosexual development' in D. Goslin (ed.) *Handbook of Socialization Theory and Research* Chicago, Rand McNally.

SINCLAIR, A. (1966) *The Better Half: The Emancipation of the American Woman* London, Jonathan Cape.

SKAR, S.L. (1979) 'The use of the public/private framework in the analysis of egalitarian societies: the case of a Quechua community in Highland Peru' *Women's Studies International Quarterly*, 2, no.4, pp.449–60.

SKEGG, D.C.G., DOLL, R. and PERRY, J. (1977) 'Use of medicines in general practice' *British Medical Journal* 18 June, pp.1561–3.

SLATER, E. and WOODSIDE, M. (1951) *Patterns of Marriage* London, Cassell.

SLATER, P. (1975) *The Pursuit of Loneliness: American Culture At Breaking Point* Harmondsworth, Penguin.

SLOCUM, S. (1975) 'Woman the gatherer: male bias in anthropology' in Reiter (ed.).

SLUNG, M.B. (1976) *Crime on Her Mind* London, Michael Joseph.

SMART, C. (1979) 'The new female criminal: reality or myth?' *British Journal of Criminology*, 19, no.1, pp.50–9.

SMART, C. and SMART, B. (eds.) (1978) *Women, Sexuality and Social Control* London, Routledge and Kegan Paul.

SMART, E. (1978) *The Assumption of the Rogues and Rascals* London, Jonathan Cape and Polyantric Press.

SMITH, C.F. (1979) 'Jane Lead: mysticism and the woman cloathed with the sun' in S.M. Gilbert and S. Gubar (eds.) *Shakespeare's Sisters: Feminist Essays on Women Poets* Bloomington, Indiana University Press.

SMITH, D.E. (1979) 'A sociology for women' in Sherman and Beck (eds.).

SMITH, M.G. (1960) *Government of Zazzau 1800 – 1950* Oxford, Oxford University Press.

SMITH, P.K. (1979) 'How many people can a young child feel secure with?' *New Society* 31 May.

SMITH-ROSENBERG, C. (1975) 'The female world of love and ritual: relations between women in nineteenth century America' *Signs: Journal of Women in Culture and Society*, 1, no.1, (Autumn), pp.1 – 30.

SMOLENSKY, M.H., REINBERG, A., ELEE, R. and MCGOVERN, J.P. (1974) 'Secondary rhythms related to hormonal changes in the menstrual cycle: special reference to allergology' in Ferin *et al.* (eds.).

SNYDER, E.C. (1979a) 'The selective eye of sociology' in Snyder (ed.).

SNYDER, E.C. (1979b) 'That half of "mankind" called women: an introduction to women's studies' in Snyder (ed.).

SNYDER, E.C. (ed.) (1979) *The Study of Women: Enlarging Perspectives of Social Reality* New York, Harper and Row.

SOOTHILL, K. and JACK, A. (1975) 'How rape is reported' *New Society* 19 June.

SPEERT, H. (1958) *Obstetric and Gynaecologic Milestones: Essays in Eponymy* New York, Macmillan.

SPENDER, S. (1966) 'Warnings from the grave' *New Republic* 18 June.

SPERRY, R.W. (1974) 'Lateral specialization in the surgically separated hemispheres' in F.O. Schmitt and R.T. Wardon (eds.) *The Neurosciences: Third Study Program* Cambridge, Mass., MIT Press.

SPIRO, M.E. (1968) 'Is the family universal? The Israeli case' in Bell and Vogel (eds.).

SPOCK, B. (1957) *Baby and Child Care* New York, Pocket Books.

SPOCK, B. (1979) *Baby and Child Care* London, Star Books.

SPRING, A. (1978) 'Epidemiology of spirit possession among the Luvale of Zambia' in J. Hoch-Smith and A. Spring (eds.) *Women in Ritual and Symbolic Roles* New York, Plenum Press.

SPRING RICE, M. (1939) *Working Class Wives* Harmondsworth, Penguin.

SPRUILL, J.C. (1972) *Women's Life and Work in the Southern Colonies* New York, W.W. Norton. (First published 1938.)

STACEY, M. (1960) *Tradition and Change* London, Oxford University Press.

STACEY, M. (ed.) (1976) *The Sociology of the N.H.S.* Sociological Review Monograph 22, University of Keele, Staffordshire.

STACEY, M., BATSTONE, E., BELL, C. and MURCOTT, A. (1975) *Power, Persistence and Change* London, Routledge and Kegan Paul.

STACEY, M. and PRICE, M. (1980) 'Women and power' *Feminist Review*, pp.33 – 52.

STAR, S.L. (1979) 'The politics of right and left: sex differences in hemispheric brain asymmetry' in Hubbard *et al.* (eds.).

STEFFENSMEIER, D.J., STEFFENSMEIER, R.H. and ROSENTHAL, A.S. (1980) 'Trends in female violence, 1960 – 1977' *Sociological Focus*, 12, no.3, pp.217 – 27.

STEINER, N.H. (1974) *A Closer Look at Ariel: A Memory of Sylvia Plath* London, Faber and Faber.

STEINMETZ, S.K. and STRAUS, M.A. (eds.) (1974) *Violence in The American Family* New York, Harper and Row.

STEVENSON, J. (1974) 'Food riots in England, 1792 – 1818' in R. Quinault and J. Stevenson (eds.) *Popular Protest and Public Order: Six Studies in British History 1790 – 1920* London, Allen and Unwin.

STEVENSON, T.H.C. (1928) 'The vital statistics of wealth and poverty' *Journal of the Royal Statistical Society*, 91, Part I, pp.207 – 20.

STEWART, D. and STEWART, L. (eds.) (1976) *Safe Alternatives in Childbirth* Chapel Hill, North Carolina, Napsac, Inc.

STEWART, F.H., STEWART, G.K., GUEST, F.J. and HATCHER, R.A. (1979) *My Body, My Health: The Concerned Woman's Guide to Gynecology* New York, John Wiley.

STIMSON, G.V. (1976) 'G.P.'s, "trouble" and types of patient' in Stacey (ed.).

STOLLER, R. (1968) *Sex and Gender* New York, Science House.
STONE, L. (1977) *The Family, Sex and Marriage in England 1500 – 1800* London, Weidenfeld and Nicolson.
STONE, M. (1976) *The Paradise Papers* London, Virago.
STRACHEY, R. (1928) *The Cause: A Short History of the Women's Movement in Great Britain* London, G. Bell and Sons.
STRATHERN, M. (1976) 'An anthropological perspective' in Lloyd and Archer (eds.).
STUARD, S.M. (ed.) (1976) *Women in Medieval Society* Philadelphia, University of Pennsylvania Press.
SZALAI, A. (1972) *The Use of Time* The Hague, Mouton.

TANNER, N. and ZIHLMAN, A. (1976) 'Women in evolution: Part I: Innovation and selction in human origins' *Signs: Journal of Women in Culture and Society*, 1, no.3, Part I, pp.585 – 608.
TAWNEY, R. (1930) 'Foreword' to M. Weber *The Protestant Ethic and the Spirit of Capitalism* London, Allen and Unwin.
TAYLOR, S. (1978) 'Parkin's theory of working class conservatism: two hypotheses investigated' *The Sociological Review*, 26, no.4, pp.827 – 42.
TEITELBAUM, M. (ed.) (1976) *Sex Differences* New York, Anchor Books.
TERMAN, L.M. and ODEN, M.H. (1947) *The Gifted Child Grows Up* Stanford, California, Stanford University Press.
TEW, M. (1978) 'The case against hospital deliveries' in Kitzinger and Davis (eds.).
THOMAS, M.C. (1969) 'Present tendencies in women's college and university education' in O'Neill (ed.). (First published 1908.)
THOMPSON, C. (1974) 'Penis envy in women' in J.B. Miller (ed.) *Psychoanalysis and Women* Harmondsworth, Penguin. (First published 1943.)
THOMPSON, D. (1976) 'Women and nineteenth century radical politics: a lost dimension' in Mitchell and Oakley (eds.).
THOMPSON, E.P. (1963) *The Making of the English Working Class* London, Gollancz.
THOMPSON, E.P. (1971) 'The moral economy of the English crowd in the eighteenth century' *Past and Present*, 50, pp.76 – 136.

THORNE, B. and HENLEY, N. (eds.) (1975) *Language and Sex: Difference and Dominance* Rowley, Mass., Newbury House Publishers.

THORSELL, S. (1967) 'Employer attitudes to female employees' in Dahlstrom (ed.).

TIETZE, C., BOUGAARTS, J. and SCHEARER, B. (1976) 'Mortality associated with the control of fertility' *Family Planning Perspectives*, 8, no.1, pp.6 – 14.

TIFFANY, S.W. (1978) 'Models and the social anthropology of women: a preliminary assessment' *Man*, 13, pp.34 – 51.

TILGHER, A. (1931) *Work: What It Has Meant to Men Through the Ages* (translated from the Italian) London, Harrap.

TILLER, P.O. (1967) 'Parental role division and the child's personality development' in Dahlstrom (ed.).

TILLY, L.A. and SCOTT, J.W. (1978) *Women, Work and Family* New York, Holt, Rinehart and Winston.

TINGSTEN, H. (1975) *Political Behaviour Studies in Election Statistics* New York, Arno Press.

TITMUSS, R.M. (1950) *Problems of Social Policy* London, HMSO.

TITMUSS, R.M. (1958) 'War and social policy' in *Essays on the Welfare State* London, Allen and Unwin.

TIZARD, J., MOSS, P. and PERRY, J. (1976) *All Our Children* London, Temple Smith.

TJIO, J.H. and LEVAN, A. (1956) 'The chromosome number of man' *Hereditas*, 42, pp.1 – 6.

TOLSON, A. (1977) *The Limits of Masculinity* London, Tavistock.

TOWNSEND, P. (1979) *The Poverty Report* Harmondsworth, Penguin.

TRESEMER, D. (1975) 'Assumptions made about gender roles' in Millman and Kanter (eds.).

TREVELYAN, G.M. (1942) *History of England* (2nd edition revised) London, Longman, Green and Co.

TUNSTALL, J. (1962) *The Fishermen: The Sociology of an Extreme Occupation* London, McGibbon and Kee.

TURNBULL, C. (1965) *Wayward Servants* New York, Natural History Press.

TURNER, B. and TURNER, C. (1974) 'Evaluations of women and men among black and white college students' *Sociological Quarterly*, 15, pp.442 – 56.

TURNER, M. (1964) *Women and Work* University of California, Institute of Industrial Relations.

TYLOR, E.B. (1865) *Researches Into the Early History of Mankind and the Development of Civilisation* London, J. Murray.

VAN ALLEN, J. (1974) 'Memsahib, militante, femme libre: political and apolitical styles of modern African women' in Jacquette (ed.).

VANEK, J. (1974) 'Time spent in housework' *Scientific American* November, p.116.

VESSEY, M.P., DOLL, R., JOHNSON, B. and PETO, R. (1974) 'Outcome of pregnancy in women using an intrauterine device' *Lancet* 23 March, pp.495 – 8.

VOSPER, J. (1974) *The Good Housekeeping Baby Book* London, Ebury Press.

WACHTEL, S.S. (1979) 'The genetics of intersexuality: clinical and theoretic perspectives' *Obstetrics and Gynecology*, 54, no.6, December, pp.671 – 85.

WALKER, J. (1972) 'The changing role of the midwife' *International Journal of Nursing Studies*, 9, pp.85 – 94.

WALKER, J. (1976) 'Midwife or obstetric nurse? Some perceptions of midwives and obstetricians of the role of the midwife' *Journal of Advanced Nursing*, 1, pp.129 – 38.

WALKER, B. and SMITH, M. (1979) 'Women's studies courses in Australian universities' *Women's Studies International Quarterly*, 2, no.3, pp.375 – 84.

WALLEY, D. (n.d.) *What Boys Can Be* and *What Girls Can Be* Kansas City, Hallmark.

WALTERS, M. (1976) 'The rights and wrongs of women: Mary Wollstonecraft, Harriet Martineau, Simone de Beauvoir' in Mitchell and Oakley (eds.).

WALTERS, M. (1979) *The Nude Male: A New Perspective* Harmondsworth, Penguin Books.

WALUM, C.R. (1977) *The Dynamics of Sex and Gender: A Sociological Perspective* Chicago, Rand McNally.

WANDOR, M. (ed.) (1973) *The Body Politic: Writings from the Women's Liberation Movement in Britain 1969 – 72* London, Stage I.

WARNER, M. (1976) *Alone of All Her Sex: The Myth and Cult of the Virgin Mary* London, Weidenfeld and Nicolson.

WATSON, J.D. (1968) *The Double Helix* New York, Atheneum Publishers, Mentor Paperback.

WATSON, J.D. and CRICK, F.H.C. (1953) 'A structure for deoxyribose nucleic acid' *Nature*, 171, pp.737 – 8.

WEBSTER, P. (1975) 'Matriarchy: a vision of power' in Reiter (ed.).

WEIDEGER, P. (1978) *Female Cycles* London, The Women's Press.

WEISSMAN, M.M. and KLERMAN, G.L. (1977) 'Symptom patterns in primary and secondary depression: A comparison of primary depressives with depressed opiate addicts, alcoholics and schizophrenics' *Archives of General Psychiatry*, 34, pp.854 – 62.

WEITZ, S. (1977) *Sex Roles: Biological, Psychological and Social Foundations* Oxford, Oxford University Press.

WEITZMAN, L.J., EIFLER, D., HOKADA, E. and ROSS, C. (1976) 'Sex-role socialization in picture books for pre-school children' in Children's Rights Workshop.

WELDON, F. (1978) *Praxis* London, Hodder and Stoughton.

WELLS, H.G. (1943) *Ann Veronica* London, Everyman. (First published 1909.)

WERTZ, R.W. and WERTZ, D.C. (1977) *Lying-In: A History of Childbirth in America* Glencoe, The Free Press.

WEST, D.J., ROY, C. and NICHOLS, F.L. (1978) *Understanding Sexual Attacks* London, Heinemann.

WESTOFF, C.F. and RINDFUSS, R.R. (1974) 'Sex pre-selection in the United States: some implications' *Science*, 184, 10 May, pp.633 – 6.

WHITE, C. (1970) *Women's Magazines 1693 – 1968* London, Michael Joseph.

WHITEHEAD, A. (1976) 'Sexual antagonism in Herefordshire' in Barker and Allen (eds.) (1976a).

WHITEHEAD, R.E. (1934) 'Women pilots' *Journal of Aviation Medicine*, 5, pp.47 – 9.

WHITING, B.B. (ed.) (1963) *Six Cultures* New York, John Wiley.

WHITTICK, A. (1979) *Woman Into Citizen* London, Athenaeum with Frederick Muller.

WICKHAM, M. and YOUNG, B. (1973) *Home Management and Family Living*. Report of the questionnaire of the Home Economics Sectional Committee. National Council of Women, 36 Lower Sloane Street, London, SWIW 8BP.

WILD, R. and HILL, A.B. (1970) *Women in the Factory: A Study of Job Satisfaction and Labour Turnover* London, Institute of Personnel Management.

WILLIAMS, D. (1975) 'Brides of Christ' in Ardener (ed.).

WILLIAMS, N. (1972) 'The new sweat shops' *New Society* 29 June.

WILLIAMS, P., JOHNSON, B. and VESSEY, M. (1975) 'Septic abortion in women using intrauterine devices' *British Medical Journal* 1 November, pp.263 – 4.

WILLMOTT, P. (1963) *The Evolution of a Community* London, Routledge and Kegan Paul.

WILLMOTT, P. (1971) 'Family, work and leisure conflicts among male employees' *Human Relations*, 24, no.6, December, pp.575 – 84.

WILLMOTT, P. and YOUNG, M. (1960) *Family and Class in a London Suburb* London, Routledge and Kegan Paul.

WILSON, E. (1977) *Women and the Welfare State* London, Tavistock.

WINNICOTT, D. (1964) *The Child, the Family and the Outside World* Harmondsworth, Penguin.

WITELSON, S.F. (1976) 'Sex and the single hemisphere: specialization of the right hemisphere for spatial processing' *Science*, 193, pp.425 – 7.

WOHL, A.S. (ed.) (1978) *The Victorian Family* London, Croom Helm.

WOLFF, C. (1971) *Love Between Women* London, Duckworth.

WOLFGANG, M.E. (1969) 'Who kills whom?' *Psychology Today*, 3, no.5, pp.54 – 6 and pp.72 – 5.

WOLLSTONECRAFT, M. (1796) *Letters Written During a Short Residence in Sweden, Norway and Denmark* London. (Reprinted in 1889 by Cassell.)

WOLLSTONECRAFT, M. (1929) *Vindication of the Rights of Women* London, Everyman. (First published 1792.)

WOLPE, A. (1977) *Some Processes in Sexist Education* London, Women's Research and Resources Centre, Explorations in Feminism no.1

WOOD, C. and RENON, P. (1976) 'Fetal heart rate monitoring' in R.W. Beard and P.W. Nathanielsz (eds.) *Fetal Pathology and Medicine* Philadelphia, W.B. Saunders.

WOODHAM-SMITH, C. (1952) *Florence Nightingale 1820 – 1910* London, The Reprint Society.

WOOLEY, O.W., WOOLEY, S.C. and DYRENFORTH, S.R. (1979) 'Obesity and women II: a neglected feminist topic' *Women's Studies International Quarterly*, 2, pp.81 – 92.

WOOLF, V. (1942) 'Professions for women' in *The Death of the Moth and Other Essays* New York, Harcourt Brace.

WOOTTON, B. (1966) 'A social scientist's approach to maternal deprivation' in Ainsworth *et al*.

WORLD HEALTH ORGANIZATION (1978) *Social and Biological Effects on Perinatal Mortality Volume I* Budapest, Hungary, Statistical Publishing House.

WYNN, A. and WYNN, M. (1979) *Prevention of Handicap and the Health of Women* London, Routledge and Kegan Paul.

YOUNG, M. (1975) *The Poverty Report* London, Temple Smith.

YOUNG, M. and SYSON, L. (1974) 'Women: the new poor' *Observer* 20 January.

YOUNG, M. and WILLMOTT, P. (1957) *Family and Kinship in East London* London, Routledge and Kegan Paul.

YOUNG, M. and WILLMOTT, P. (1973) *The Symmetrical Family* London, Routledge and Kegan Paul.

ZARETSKY, E. (1976) *Capitalism, the Family and Personal Life* New York, Harper and Row.

ZELDITCH, M. (1956) 'Role differentiation in the nuclear family: a comparative study' in Parsons and Bales.

ZIHLMAN, A.L. (1978) 'Women and evolution: Part II: subsistence and social organization among early hominids' *Signs: Journal of Women in Culture and Society*, 4, no.1 (Autumn) pp.4 – 20.

ZIMMERMAN, D.H. and WEST, C. (1975) 'Sex roles, interruption and silences in conversation' in Thorne and Henley (eds.).

ZIMMERMAN, E. and PARLEE, M.B. (1973) 'Behaviour changes associated with the menstrual cycle: an experimental investigation' *Journal of Applied Social Psychology*, 3, no.4, pp.335 – 44.

INDEX